Ghosts
of the
Northeast

Also by David J. Pitkin

Saratoga County Ghosts

Spiritual Numerology: Caring for Number One

**Aurora Publications e-mail address:
pitkinaurora@aol.com**

Ghosts
of the
Northeast

David J. Pitkin

Illustrated by
Linda C. Setchfield

Aurora Publications
Salem, NY

Copyright 2002 By David J. Pitkin

Illustrated by Linda C. Setchfield © 2002

1st printing June 2002
Salem, NY

Printed in the U.S.A.

Aurora Publications
18 East Broadway
Salem, NY 12865

Library of Congress Cataloging-in-Publication Data
Pitkin, David J. 1939-
Ghosts of the Northeast
ISBN 0-9663925-2-3

Library of Congress Catalog Card Number:
2002090804

Cover design and illustrations: Linda C. Setchfield

Table of Contents

Preface

GHOSTS OF THE NORTHEAST by David J. Pitkin is a painstakingly accurate collection of true ghost stories in which Mr. Pitkin, a teacher by profession and a resident of the area he writes about so knowingly, reports the true experiences people have had with the denizens of the Other Side who somehow have not yet found their way to that world.

Both David and his wife, Linda, who did a splendid and eerily atmospheric cover for the book, are themselves psychic and sometimes share in the experiences they report here.

Following up these cases with a deep trance medium and speaking through her to the restless ones directly, might have led to more information about the reason for their continuing residence on this side of the curtain, but even so, the book is genuinely fascinating and lovely.

Prof. Dr. Hans Holzer

INTRODUCTION

After the funeral of a relative, my cousin Teresa reminisced about her husband's death a few years earlier. "I believe in Heaven," she said, "but I know I'll never see him again." With all the ardor of one who'd had his first experiences with ghosts and the afterlife, I wanted to dispute her statement with the truths of our shared religion. Surely we get to meet our loved ones again; doesn't First Corinthians, Chapter 13, promise that? I was frustrated at my inability to change her mind with convincing proof.

In 1971 I went to Trinity Temple of the Holy Spirit, a Spiritualist church in Albany, NY, seeking to test the possibility of contact with the dead. Near the end of the service, Rev. Penny Thorne asked if I'd received a spirit message yet. I said no. Pausing, she said, "I see a father figure here." Lots of luck, I thought cynically, my father is still alive. I sensed she was fishing for facts, and when she said, "I get the name George, does that mean anything to you?" I said "No."

I knew many Georges, one being my Uncle George, Cousin Teresa's father, who was then in a Vermont nursing home. "I get the image of two box cars backing together and coupling, but that's all," Penny said as she ended the message.

My Uncle George had been Chief Dispatcher for the D & H Railroad for years. As I drove home, I wondered if he was near death and had tried to communicate with me. Maybe Rev. Thorne really was tuned into another world. But days passed with no funeral notice for my uncle. I surmised that Rev. Thorne had just been lucky in what she'd perceived.

Uncle George died a year later. At the wake, thinking my uncle might have been in a coma during his last year, and thus able to travel in spirit, I asked Carol, Teresa's sister and an R.N., who had attended her father daily. She dashed my theory, saying Uncle George had slipped into a coma only in the half-hour before death. But what, she wondered, was behind my question? I told her of my experience at Trinity Temple in 1971. Her jaw dropped and she asked me to tell the story to Teresa.

Crossing the room in the funeral home I gave Tee, as everyone calls her, the whole tale. She smiled strangely for a moment, then broke into a broad grin. She began, "When George and I were first married...." I was stunned. I'd always known her husband by his nickname, Nern. Tee and her two sisters had each married men named George, and they also had a father and brother named George—five Georges in one family! She continued, "...he was a student at Siena College, and worked for the railroad too—in the Menands freight yards, during the summer. One day he came home and said, 'Honey I almost got killed today. I was sitting on the train rail eating my lunch and thought I saw something move in the boxcar on another track. When I got up to investigate, the two boxcars behind me slammed together. If I hadn't moved just then, I'd have been dead!'"

There it all was—the two boxcars and a man named George, whose given name I was unaware of! A George whose narrow escape from death I'd never known. Only the members of Teresa's family knew that story. Nevertheless, the imagery was given to me through a psychic minister when I most needed confirmation that love transcends death, as I, myself, was about to be diagnosed with cancer. These images, which were over three years coming to me, finally allowed me to offer Teresa the evidence that I'd once been unable to provide. This personal experience was incorporated into my growing understanding of life and death. In the process, I received further proof that when one does seek, one usually *does* find.

Thirty years have passed, and I've been drawn more deeply into a search for how to live the good life and die the good death. In researching *Saratoga County Ghosts* in 1998 I discovered over 120 ghost stories in a single county. Up to that time I believed, as so many others do, that haunted houses are rare, but now I know that it's a rare house that *hasn't* been visited by spirits at least once.

Many, if not most, spirits seem to return home briefly after their funeral, to "tidy up" before moving into The Great Beyond. Letting go of the old realities can be difficult, even for the living, and souls seem to go about the task in different rhythms. Some even return to their workplace or visit loved ones far away in distance, though apparently not in thought. Some simply want their loved ones to know they still exist. My friend Mary, grieving over her husband Bill's death following his long and painful illness, was sobbing in her kitchen one dreary day. The room was suddenly illuminated from above by a bright light. "It's me, Babe," Bill's voice said. "I just wanted to let you know I made it!" The voice and light ended abruptly, but accomplished their mission. Bill's voice had been friendly and open—it was the way he would have talked to her on the phone during life. Much of Mary's grief ended there and then.

Other souls apparently hang around for much longer periods, attempting to complete a task, fulfill a vow or bring a hidden issue to light. On the edge of Paradise, the individuals we know as ghosts may struggle *harder than they did in life*. Stories of these struggling ones' interruptions of others' lives get the most media attention, as the entities are powerfully motivated, narrowly focused and quite active. Very little is recorded about such souls harming the living. Many times they are so immersed in their dilemmas that they are unaware of the living. Many investigators also report such obsessed spirits are also unaware of other ghosts at the location.

The troubled ones may not know, or care, that The Bright Light, available to all who have died, can be their point of release into Peace. They cannot see The Light in death because they didn't seek true light in life. They need the assistance of light-bearers and other light-seekers if they are to find freedom. The type of paradise found at death depends on the treasures sought while still having the gift of physical life.

But there are others—those who are not peacefully departed spirits. They usually require professional help to exit gracefully, and some only depart kicking and screaming. A Catholic priest, when leaving a friend's haunted home (on the site of a colonial massacre) after a successful exorcism, muttered, "This was no ghost!" It turned out that the poltergeist activities in the house emanated from a spirit entity attached to the man himself, not the house or environs. In many such cases, the host individual is not aware of the darkness he has invited into his life. There are beings and energies in this world that laymen shouldn't trifle with, and which ignorant thrill-seekers deal with at their own peril. A discerning person will know them by their fruits—do they generate terror or seek to resolve something? Light always can conquer darkness in the end, and even these vile malefic energies can be overcome in time and banished by knowledgeable practitioners.

This book chronicles the experiences of over two hundred ordinary people throughout northeastern North America, highly-educated professional people and unlettered laborers, men, women and children, young and old, rich and poor. None of them deliberately sought ghost experiences, but found them anyway. Ghosts of long or short duration are everywhere, all the time, and all cultures throughout history have experienced and pondered their mystery. It is my wish that the reader will consider the issues that tethered these spirits to the earth plane when, through love, forgiveness, generosity or hard work during life, they might have found Beauty, Peace and Rest, instead of post-mortem confinement.

Over and over, as my wife and I and many seeker friends have investigated hauntings, we have noted the vital importance of prayer in aiding departed souls to see and reach out for The Light Which Casts No Shadows. In this time of cataclysms and disasters, it behooves all people who espouse brotherhood, and who claim to walk the spiritual path, to do everything possible to assist those beings who find the passage from life to Light difficult. We are not freed from Golden Rule obligations by death.

David J. Pitkin
Salem, NY
June 2002

"Seven years dead," mused Scrooge. "And traveling all the time?"

"The whole time," said the Ghost. "No rest, no peace. Incessant torture of remorse."

"You travel fast?" said Scrooge.

"On the wings of the wind," replied the Ghost.

"You might have got over a great quantity of ground in seven years," said Scrooge.

The Ghost, on hearing this, set up another cry, and clanked its chain so hideously in the dead silence of the night, that the Ward would have been justified in indicting it for a nuisance.

"Oh! Captive, bound, and double-ironed," cried the phantom, "not to know, that ages of incessant labour by immortal creatures, for this earth must pass into eternity before the good of which it is susceptible is all developed. Not to know that any Christian spirit working kindly in its little sphere, whatever it may be, will find its mortal life too short for its vast means of usefulness. Not to know that no space of regret can make amends for one life's opportunities misused! Yet such was I! Oh! Such was I!"

"But you were always a good man of business, Jacob," faultered Scrooge, who now began to apply this to himself.

"Business!" cried the Ghost, wringing its hands again. "Mankind was my business. The common welfare was my business; charity, mercy, forbearance, and benevolence, were, all, my business. The dealings of my trade were but a drop of water in the comprehensive ocean of my business!"

A Christmas Carol by Charles Dickens

1
Haunted Houses

The Prichard House

Walter Prichard was born on an ocean steamer when his parents emigrated from Wales to Bolton Landing, NY, in 1802. First a farmer, he later turned to blacksmithing and built a shop on the east side of Maple Street. When he gave up the business in the 1870s he converted the shop to a small house and moved it to the west side of the street. His pretty daughter, Mary, stood only 4'10" tall, but had black piercing eyes and rosy cheeks. She wore her beautiful black hair pulled back so that its natural curl (which she thought "sinful") didn't show. Strong and energetic, and inclined to get her own way, she expected a lot from her suitors, a tendency that grew stronger as she grew older, her great-granddaughter Mary Martha recalls.

Mary found that tractable mate in Allen G. Goodman, local storeowner, and later, boardinghouse keeper. Unfortunately, through ineptness, a dishonest partner and bad luck they lost "The Goodman House," all their property and much of their self-esteem. Then Allen became ill. Finally, the only home they could afford was the old "tenant house" that had been the blacksmith shop, a small, rude domicile which mortified Mary. She hid her shame under an outer courtesy, but otherwise became "absolutely inflexible and bossy" according to Mary Martha, known simply as Martha to her friends.

As age overtook her body, widowed Mary lived with her daughter Clara, a schoolteacher, who soon married Charles Maxim. The three lived together in the small cottage for over twenty-five years, and Mary dominated them throughout the period. After Mary died at eighty-two, Clara became uneasy and assailed by vague fears. Her controlling mother was gone but something was still watching them. Continually nervous, Clara slept only fitfully, and Charles began to fear for her stability.

"One night when Charles was out, and Clara Maxim was reading in the kitchen," Martha told me, "a bitter chill swept over her. There, in the pantry doorway, Clara saw a filmy, semi-transparent figure, too vague to be recognizable, but to Grandmother it was clearly there. Though shaking uncontrollably, she walked the ten feet to that doorway, and stood nose-to-nose with the figure until it dissipated. Then, collapsing into a chair, she noticed her tension and fear had also vanished.

For a moment, Clara reflected on her father Allen's words, "I'm coming back someday," a remark which, as a Spiritualist, might have referred to reincarnation or haunting. But Clara concluded the figure had been her mother, and not Allen Goodman.

She never experienced that spirit again, and thought it likely that her boldness had finally broken her mother's hold on her.

Martha believes the central figure of this story should be the house, and not Mary Prichard. "It was very small," she said, "with a small parlor, small living room, two small bedrooms and a kitchen/pantry downstairs. Up a steep stairway were two bedrooms. In time, the old woodshed became the new kitchen. Then, over the next eighty years the building underwent change after change, though the original plaster and lath lasted until 1955."

Then, Clara's daughter Nellie (Martha's mother) had the walls and ceilings of the living rooms stripped to the old blacksmith era timbers. Walking alone through the building before the new sheetrock was installed, she felt every ancestor that had ever worked or lived in the structure was watching, though she saw no one. Nellie's sense of humor caused her to take up the family Bible and open it at random, and read from St.Paul, "Do thyself no harm for we are all here." She smiled. All the significant Prichard family events had taken place in the room with that Bible: marriages, funerals, and births.

Nellie, a teacher in Rensselaer, NY, continued to use the restored home in the summer and closed it up for the rest of the year. In the winter of 1963, however, she rented it, withholding the house's history from her tenant. Even so, the tenant later told Nellie:

"One night before going to bed I put out the lights and stood beside the stove in the old sitting room. As I stood there, in my mind's eye, I saw the old rooms—sitting room and connecting parlor, with the wide board floors with cracks, the old wall paper; the cookstove and wooden washtubs. I saw an armchair, a lamp and an open book, and a table set for supper. Then, in the parlor, I saw a casket, and I believe it related to the death of an old man."

She showed Nellie where she had spied a door into the pantry, which Nellie knew had been boarded up and covered with wallpaper prior to 1903.

On another occasion the tenant viewed four men dressed in heavy outdoor clothing, carrying an injured young man on a stretcher, probably hurt in a logging accident in the nearby mountains.

Nellie, who was often alone there at night, correcting papers, knitting or reading, had many visions of the house's history. "And the noises got so bad," Nellie recounted, "that I finally stopped getting up and just said aloud, 'I hear you!'" Her grandmother's portrait crashed on the table one winter's night when there was no breeze. Nellie also experienced knockings as frequently as twice a week. It was a "live house" that she willed to her daughter.

When Martha inherited the property, relatives informed her of its unusual events. Although not sure she really believed these happenings, she was open. Then, she began having her own strange experiences.

In March 1986, two months after her mother's death, Martha was upstairs in the bedroom removing blankets from a chest. "I heard three very distinct knocks on the dining room door. When I got halfway down the stairs, there were three more loud knocks. I called out that I was coming. There was nobody at the door or on the sidewalk, but there hadn't been time enough for anyone to go far. I walked out to the end of the sidewalk, and there was nobody in sight, and not even a car on the street.

"Almost exactly eight years later I was cleaning house between tenants, and was in the doorway between the parlor and living room, facing the window onto the front porch, when someone knocked on the dining room door. Since I was looking right out the porch window I could plainly see nobody was there. I just stood there, staring. Then I heard the door open and from the deliberate, heavy footsteps, I'd say a man walked across the dining room and through the kitchen, opened the back door and went out, shutting the door distinctly," she said.

Martha was startled by these events, but not scared. She thought that someone was trying to tell her something, though she didn't know what. She concluded that the spirits of ancestors who once called the Prichard House home might still consider it their home, and feel secure enough to visit occasionally. And why not? Bolton Landing, NY is one of the prettiest towns along the length of Lake George in the summertime.

The Wooley House

Edgar Montillion Wooley, better known as Monty Wooley, Hollywood character actor, lived at 718 North Broadway, Saratoga Springs, NY, sporadically from 1918 to 1943. The house was a fashionable Italian villa built in 1854 by James Westcott. North Broadway by then had become "the place to live" for America's rich and famous, when they attended thoroughbred races in the Spa City. Of the many owners between the Westcotts and the Wooleys, James Wooley, hotelkeeper and Monty's father, was probably the most notable. Of the many owners who rented the house during the Saratoga Racing Season, few knew of its ghosts. Their housekeepers and caretakers, however, did.

Jean, a former housekeeper, lived in a poorly ventilated third floor room in the back. At the end of a long summer day in the early 1980s, with temperatures hovering in the upper 80s, she went to bed. Suddenly an icy breeze swept over her. She found herself uttering the words, "Oh now, Charlie. That's enough of that!" Then she caught herself. Who's Charlie? At that time she didn't know anyone by that name to whom she'd say such a thing. Eventually, she discovered that the Wooleys had named the spirit "Charlie." But how had she known what name to use?

Eventually, "Mrs. H.," another former housekeeper, told Jean that one year when she and her husband were readying the house for the owners, they took all the sheets off the furniture and piled them at the foot of the stairs. A few minutes later, Mrs. H. came back and found what looked like fresh drops of blood on the white sheets—not hers or her husband's, and they had been the only ones there. Later, someone told Mrs. H. a murder had once taken place in the house.

Mrs. H. told Jean that she had arrived at the house early another summer when it was still closed up for the winter. She saw the living room's sheer curtains blowing out, as if from a breeze, with all the windows and doors still closed. She also told of a Scottish cook named Lily, who could feel the ghosts. When Lily went to bed at night, she would down a shot of the owner's brandy, then lock herself in the bedroom until morning, unaware that doors and walls are usually permeable to ghosts. One night, she poured her shot, then heard a knock at the front door. Setting the glass down, she went to answer it, and when she returned, the glass was empty.

Jean and her husband worked for a recent owner as housekeeper and chauffeur. Another woman was hired to help this new owner's disabled wife with her wheelchair. The woman helper was quite sensitive and, moving the family's luggage upstairs on her first day, turned to Jean and asked if there were ghosts in the house. Jean nodded in assent.

One summer, Jean reported, one of the three switches inside the front door, that controlled the outside lights, reversed its function—being off when turned on and on when switched off. An electrician inspected the system, but found no explanation.

Glenn and June served as wintertime caretakers for several years, a role that June's parents had performed for years before them. During June's mother's employment in the Wooley House, she documented the long-ago murder and gave the details, which may no longer exist, to the owner. When I requested a police department search of homicide files, the officer found no records of a murder in the Wooley House since the 1930s, but couldn't substantiate a crime there before that because, he explained, city homicide records are spotty before the 1930s.

Once, Glenn and June found all the interior doors they'd closed in the autumn open, and all the doors they'd opened now closed. Soon after, they heard voices upstairs when they entered the front door. Fearing a break-in, they went up, but nobody was there. Then, as they searched upstairs, they heard the same indistinct voices downstairs. Likewise, no one was there.

A few years ago, a new family bought the old house, and became year-round residents. They removed the century-old white paint from the original brick exterior. The house now appears much as it looked over a century and a half ago. Apparently, the vibrations have changed. The new owners have heard and seen nothing.

The Presence

"Moon Over Maine B&B (Maxwell's)"

Behind the Key Bank building in Ogunquit, ME, stands an old house built by Barak Maxwell in 1876. A plain duplex, it was constructed as two units with a common entrance hallway, each consisting of three bedrooms, a sitting room, and a small kitchen in the above-ground cellar. The latter room was illuminated by two windows, one larger and one smaller, in the cellar wall. Civil War veteran Daniel Tucker, a dry goods salesman, and his wife Annie lived in one part of the house, and Albert Littlefield, a salesman at Wilbur Cousens' Dry Goods Store, his wife Susie and their two small children lived in the other. There was room for some chickens and a pig in the small back yard. Susie took in laundry from the town's summer residents, carefully ironing and preening the starched lace of that era's garments.

Susie made new white curtains for the apartment's windows, but on their first day there in 1892 she was filled with foreboding. "I don't think I'll even hang the curtains—we won't be staying long," she told Albert. He scoffed at this, then encouraged her to invite her sister, Olive, to live with them, so she would have a companion and help with the laundry. That first night, putting the children to sleep upstairs, Susie heard a strange sound in the dimly-lit room. Seeing nothing, she dismissed any concern.

On the second evening, she heard the sound again and was startled to see a shadow moving back and forth on the wall, as if an invisible woman were rocking in an invisible chair. She quickly summoned Olive, a strictly religious woman, who saw the same sight. "Right there," she pointed at the moving shadow, and asked "what makes that?" They summoned Albert, but he dismissed it as wind blowing the curtains past the lamp.

Susie remained troubled for months to come. Upon putting the girls into bed and lighting the small night lamp, she continued to hear the rocker sound and see the woman's shadow. Concerned for her children's safety, she touched and moved objects in the room, to see if the shadow might disappear, all to no avail. Fearing the advent of some disaster, she wondered why the shadow always appeared next to the children's' crib.

Then came another distraction. Susie and Olive arose early on a sultry summer morning to iron clothing they had sprinkled with water the previous night. The kitchen, already heated by a coal stove, was unbearably hot, so they opened the door for ventilation. They propped the heavy door open by angling an axe, head down, against the door's face. Slipping wooden handles into their hot irons, they found them stuck to the stove, impossible to move. Again and again they tried, but the flatirons seemed welded down. So, the women distracted themselves with housework, washing and drying the dishes, which Olive stacked on the sink's metal drainboard. At the far end of this surface stood a small water pail, beneath the small cellar window. Suddenly the neatly piled dishes slid across the drainboard and into the sink with a resounding crash—all without breaking a single dish!

As the stunned women stared at one another, they heard a hideous laugh either outside the small window, or behind the water pail—they weren't sure. Then, a powerful gust of wind swept through the kitchen, knocked down the axe and slammed the heavy oak door. Each woman swept up a child and scurried to the upstairs bedroom, where they huddled in fear.

"Stream bank behind Maxwell's"

When Albert returned from his work at the store that noon, they told him of their frightening experience. With no dinner ready, Albert cooked it himself, while hearing the women describe their morning trials. He lifted the irons from the stove easily. One can imagine the looks that must have passed among the three. Over the next few days the women avoided the kitchen as much as possible, but gradually slipped back into their usual routines.

When gathering eggs in the hen yard, Susie often found broken and empty eggshells. One day, she noticed a lanky, grey-haired old man sipping water from the stream below their hill.

None of her neighbors recognized him. She wondered if he was eating her eggs. Several times she spotted him by the brook, hat in hand, always turned away. One day, while in the hen yard, she saw him with hat pulled down over his eyes, standing next to the gate! Summoning all her courage, she walked deliberately through the gateway, past the stranger, without looking at him or speaking. She never saw him again.

On a cold and rainy day in autumn Albert lit a fire in the sitting room stove while Olive and Susie sat sewing and darning. Soon they heard music, as if from a band parading on Berwick Road. Then, the music seemed to come from inside the coal stove! More puzzled than scared, they sat in awe of the beautiful sounds until they faded in the spectral distance. After that, Albert grudgingly accepted the women's' stories, and identified with their fears. He borrowed a shotgun and many times sat up at night waiting for something to appear. Nobody, ghostly or otherwise, ever appeared, and he fired no shots.

The ghosts of Berwick Road, not content with disrupting the Littlefields, now began to tantalize the Tuckers, also. One dark and rainy winter night the families were awakened by a woman's wailing outside the building's front door, "Please mister, won't you let me in? Won't you let me in?" Albert dressed quickly and went downstairs, encountering Dan and Annie Tucker coming from the other apartment. Dan Tucker, remembering the nurses who'd assisted his fallen comrades on Civil War battlegrounds, said, "I'm not afraid to open the door to a woman in the night, as many nights as I have laid on the battlefield." Opening the door wide, they saw only pelting rain and the fog of a seacoast night—not another person in sight.

Still, the spirits had not finished their ghostly work. One night, Albert sprang out of bed at the crash of toppled furniture. In the hall he again collided with Tucker, each believing the noise had come from the other's apartment. No toppled furniture was ever found. Soon after, the Littlefield family moved out.

None of these events were ever explained. Perhaps they originated from prior events on Berwick Road, before Maxwell built his apartments. They might also have originated elsewhere, as it is known that haunts can attach themselves to structures where the spirits never lived. And when their origins are unknown, the events can be truly scary.

I'm indebted to Martin Damren, Vivian Moore and Donna Howe, descendants of these two families, who graciously shared this marvelous tale from their family history.

The Girl in White

Pat, plumber and handyman, was fixing my sink when he discovered my ghost book nearby. It didn't take him long to offer a tale from his own experience. He once rented an old farmhouse, off Junction Road in Central Bridge, NY, in the mid-1980s. It looked as if it had been built in Colonial times. Exploring the old barn, he found dates from the 1700s carved into its timbers. An elderly neighbor told him the building had a ghost. "Maybe. I'll see," was his jocular response. But he didn't have long to wait.

On his first morning, having coffee at the kitchen table, looking out toward the barn and enjoying the orchard's apple blossoms, he rose to answer the phone. When he returned, his coffee cup was moved. "I knew where I'd set it down when I got up. Cups do not usually move themselves." He remembered his neighbor's warning.

Later that afternoon, while searching for something in the cold cellar, he saw movement from the corner of his eye—a young woman in a white nightgown, standing with her hand outstretched. "It didn't feel strange, even though I knew I was alone in the house. It was as if she wanted to give or receive something. Then she just wasn't there. I didn't see her fade away; she just vanished."

On another occasion, going up the front stairs, he saw her standing with a book in her hand, ready to enter a bedroom near the stair top. "By then, I understood what she was—seventeen to twenty-one years of age, a pretty ghost with long hair, and it was okay with me if she wanted to live there with me. I'd hear her moving from floor to floor, too. The stairs have a creak as you step on them, and I'd often hear her going upstairs while I watched television at night. Her favorite place, though, seemed to be the kitchen—almost as if she enjoyed waiting on me. Every day she moved my coffee cup as if to teach me the etiquette of some earlier time in history.

"On one occasion I invited friends from New Jersey to spend a weekend with me—there were plenty of bedrooms. These were city people, so I warned them about the nice ghost girl. They all laughed and went to bed. About 2 to 3 a.m. I heard screams. Rushing to their bedroom, I found the woman jabbering about people talking and laughing in her room. Well, it's not as if I hadn't warned them."

At least several times each week Pat had to turn the front stairway light off in the morning, though he always turned it off when going to bed at night. "Before I moved away I saw her one last time, entering that room on the right at the top of the stairs. Today it is a bathroom, but it is clear that it was once a bedroom. I miss her. She was a quiet presence that sometimes made me think I was living with people from somewhere back in history." Now Pat lives in a small nearby city, but he often thinks of his "girl in white," and wonders if she is now tending to the new owners.

The Dunn House

"I didn't come to town to buy a haunted house, I just stopped to get groceries," Janet said. "However, leaving the Johnsburg, NY, supermarket in 1983, I saw a side street that I'd never noticed before. Driving slowly downhill, I spotted the town's quaint old church and, as I drove past, a cloudy or wispy woman dashed from the graveyard into the bordering trees. It was fully daylight—I had to follow that apparition! Past the trees I saw a remarkable house. It was a magical old place set back in an overgrowth of trees; a two and one-half story white Federal Style home with wrap-around balconies on both floors, suggesting the leisure and fortunes once enjoyed by the upper class in the Adirondacks. I knew from that moment on I'd one day buy that house. Although the house was in terrible shape, Tom and I felt we could restore its former beauty. It took a while, but we purchased The Dunn House in 1998 and began to learn its history."

Old timers in the community told of two sisters, Catharine and Margaret, the last Dunns to live in the 1840 house. The two women were always keeping up the house and entertaining visitors, as their parents John and Catharine had done. After John's death the family fortunes declined. Through the second half of the 1800s, the sisters tried to maintain the graceful treed estate, with its extensive lawns, greenhouse, carriage and horse barns, outbuildings for servants and guests, and flower gardens.

Catharine died in 1878 and Margaret in 1893, and were buried in the cemetery between their home and the Methodist Church. One of them may have been the apparition that first guided Janet to the house. She and Tom suspect that at least one of the sisters frequently comes "home."

The property was then sold to Judge George R. Smith, a local entrepreneur, who dubbed it "The Adirondack Inn" and opened it to summer tourists. City vacationers came and went, often via the train, but the venture did not bring enough tourists to make it very profitable to Smith. Once, he leased it to Arvin Hutchins for a vacation lodge—more strangers vacationing and leaving, but yielding little profit to the owners. For a brief period after World War II it served as a girls' camp, then was sold to a family from downstate New York.

For a few years this family operated the Dunn House as Mt. Crane Lodge, but there were tensions and frustrations between the husband and wife, which were exacerbated by skimpy profits. In 1953 the wife was found shot dead by her own hand in Glen, a hamlet a few miles down the road. Following her death, the husband made sporadic efforts to improve the building's interior, but, in the end, gave up. Not much about the family is remembered by local folks, except that they had a son, Robert.

Janet and Tom responded to the obscured beauty of another time in purchasing the Dunn House. At first they didn't perceive the aura of unfulfilled dreams and the feelings of failure that had been generated by so many who'd lived there; not until they began uncovering the house's history.

Moving in and unpacking, they experienced vague presences. Janet couldn't find a treasured perfume bottle she had packed in its own box. Moving to other chores, she cleaned the small wood stove, but couldn't budge the ash drawer. Every few days she tugged on it, until one day, when she opened the stove door, the ash drawer popped open by itself. Inside—her perfume bottle! Amazing!

Tom fared no better. Relaxed on the living room couch at night, he often heard subdued conversations. At other times he heard soft music when no radio or television was on. They never found the source of these sounds. Several times they awakened from sleep hearing a child jumping on bedsprings above the ceiling of their second floor bedroom. Several times Janet noted a ball of light crossing the living and dining room floors. These are all common forms of expression for ghosts, but it wasn't apparent which former resident was creating them.

"Visitors often tell us of seeing a woman in old-fashioned dress in the upstairs window, watching as they approach," Janet said. "Sometimes she waves. But, of course, there is no live person there." Tom added, "The house was vacant so long and scavenged by pickers looking for treasures and memorabilia. The attic, where some people also say they've seen this woman in a window, is still as it was when we bought the house—sparsely littered with old furniture needing repair. That will probably be the last part of the house we renovate."

Hearing of the old house with many ghostly phenomena, I asked the owners for permission to assemble a group of intuitives I sometimes consult to help me investigate more than the physical phenomena. Seekers all, we wanted to understand the underlying spiritual issues that keep so many ghosts attached to property and material objects. Each team member uses a slightly different clairvoyant "tuning" to receive impressions of the present or past entities. In addition to Susan's and Grace's abilities to visualize past events and people, Paul has the ability to connect with a channeled information source that can elaborate on the spiritual implications of observed phenomena. We chose to hear none of the house's history until we had completed our tour of the house. Janet and Tom agreed to let us first explore and seek impressions, then later sit with them over tea to share our insights and hear of their experiences and the history they'd documented.

We commenced our journey through the house, passing through large pocket doors in the formal dining room, which led to the front parlor. There, Paul clair-voyantly spied an older man entertaining "a surveyor who was visiting Johnsburg" in some other time. A brass telescope stood beside them in their reality, visible only to Paul.

When we moved up a restored stairway to the second floor, then into the dimly-lit attic, we entered the space over the sprawling perimeter porches and the house proper. As Tom said, very little had yet been done to sort the debris there. Susan immediately noticed a ghost girl scampering behind a projecting chimney. She said the child (about age five or six) had been playing alone, but hid when we approached. In an austere bedroom at the top of the attic stairs, she spied a labor-er from some other time working away, unmindful of our group. Paul sensed a woman in black Victorian dress pacing the room, and felt her anxiety. Having sold the house, she resented the fact that her use of this former servant's bedroom came only through the new owners' charity. She was waiting for death and feared she would be taken away or forced out. Grace crossed the attic to a dark space beneath the eaves, where she noted a small boy, "frenzied from his experiences of unjust punishment of some type, cuddled up and sobbing in the darkness."

Descending to the second floor, into a bright bedroom overlooking the front veranda and road to the house, Susan noticed a woman with her back to us, look-ing out the window—maybe the same woman that visitors have seen waving. Susan may have been the first to see this "greeting woman" from behind. Paul clairvoyantly perceived an old man projecting his death scene on a bed located a short distance from the room's present bed. As we examined the upstairs rooms, Grace cooed with affection for the gracious old house and felt none of the appre-hension and fear that Susan and Paul commented on.

None of us liked the feelings in Janet and Tom's dark bedroom, except Grace, who reveled in what she sensed as its long ago gracious state. Susan felt a strong male presence there, though we saw no one. Through nurseries and bathrooms, we at last descended to the first floor and traversed the Victorian kitchen, exiting into an attached shed, behind which Paul noted, "someone used to kill chickens for the inn's guests." Then up a steep stairway into a deteriorated attic space over the shed. Paul saw the word "crying" in mid-air as we ascended. In the upstairs, Susan felt uneasy and wanted to cry. She felt someone had hanged himself there.

We then descended into the cellar. With her physical eyes, Susan saw a dark figure furtively moving behind an old coal or wood bin. Tom later told us he and Janet believed the cellar was used to hide fugitive slaves during the days of the Underground Railroad. This ghost may have been one such individual.

Most of us felt uneasy at the foot of the cellar stairs, but we couldn't immedi-ately identify the cause. Moving through the cellar we pried open a wooden slat door that led into a cold cellar. Paul saw a tearful, red-eyed man seated on a bench with a bottle of alcohol. "It was his place to come and grieve over his life," he noted. He is morose because he hasn't been able to achieve what was expected of him. Very sad."

Returning to the bottom of the cellar stairs, Susan perceived a young boy being shoved down the stairs and slammed against the stone cellar wall. Paul saw a small boy being beaten by his father, who appeared in a businessman's clothing: suit pants, white shirt, necktie and gold watch chain on the vest. "The boy could never do things right, or so his father thought. The father worked 'in the city' (and either worked for a railroad, or used the train for transportation) and punished the boy severely on his return to Johnsburg," he explained. When asked for the child's name, Paul answered, "Bobby." At that time we knew nothing of the former residents or their names.

By the appointed teatime sharing, our party was brimming with topics for show and tell with Janet and Tom. Some of their historical documentation revealed probable identities for the figures we had just experienced on our walking tour.

Tom said he thought the front parlor might have served as an office, perhaps during Judge Smith's ownership. It is logical to assume a judge's work might have included land transactions, deeds and a surveyor. Janet showed us photographs that she'd come upon, including some of little girls. She speculated that one of them may have been a young Catharine or Margaret. Thus, the ghost girl in the attic may have been one of the two sisters during childhood. The woman at the upstairs window had probably been either Catharine or Margaret Dunn. The drinking man in the cellar may have been the father whose wife killed herself, and the strong, often violent images of the boy in the attic and basement suggested the man's son, who Tom and Janet said, indeed, was named Robert or Bobby.

Janet revealed that she always experienced anxiety when opening her bedroom closet, and they only chose that room for a bedroom because of its size.

Tom noted that neighbors informed him a woman once hanged herself from the rafters in the attic space over the back shed room where Paul had seen the word "crying" in the air. It was there that Susan had experienced overwhelming feelings of fear, and was near tears, thinking that a person had been hanged nearby.

The owners told of some puzzling phenomena that have become a normal, if not fully accepted, part of their life in the Dunn House. Tom said that one of the biggest problems presented by the ghosts involves the furnace. It is a big old cellar furnace, having a straight heat pipe through the floor to the formal dining room, just three feet overhead. "There is no way the furnace can operate and heat not rise into the room above it. Yet, for several years, on many Saturday mornings around 10:30, though the furnace is running red hot, only icy air flows through the massive four foot square floor register into the dining room. This cold blast makes the room very uncomfortable in the wintertime and we oftentimes schedule errands at such times, leaving the house until the phenomenon ends. When we return, the room is toasty warm, as if nothing ever happened," Tom said.

A week later, we reviewed the house's phenomena in a channeling session with Paul, where further pieces to this house's puzzles were connected.

We asked for an explanation of the mysterious cold-blasting furnace. Paul's source noted that Bobby was often beaten by his father on Saturday mornings and, though he's still alive, his spirit or unconscious energy returns to the scene of his suffering from time to time. There, his unconscious energy erupts in what might be called a "tantrum" at the violation and frustration he felt in growing up there. When he remembers Saturday morning suffering, his memory energy blocks the

rise of heat through that short pipe—surely contradicting every law of thermody-
namics. Tom noted that this cold phenomenon continues whether the couple is
alone or entertaining visitors.

Remembering Grace's vision of a cringing boy in the attic, we asked Paul how
and why Bobby's energy is so active in several parts of the house. Paul said, "His
memory travels through the house. He goes back to the attic where he was punished. He goes into the cellar where he was punished. He's trying to make it right.
He feels he was responsible."

Paul's source continued that people, living or dead, whenever they think back
on a place or experience, can manifest energy there for a brief time. These energized memories of traumatic experiences, lodged in Bobby's psyche, continue to
resonate in the house's physical structure. On most Saturday mornings, whether
or not Bobby consciously remembers his beatings, the energy is still reinforced,
creating the icy cold phenomenon.

Paul's source indicated that Bobby's father is not yet dead, but has pretty well
passed into spirit, though his body lies in a nursing home. He feels guilty, as his
son is "dead" to him, and his wife killed herself. He had very high expectations
of others, but also drank whiskey. His spirit energy projects itself into the upstairs
front room, showing the deterioration of his health. But he does, likewise, in the
cellar storeroom, too. "He seeks to be forgiven, and he shows people his errors,
helping them see his mistakes. His energy helps recreate the scenes. He thinks

of the scenes and the energy of thought helps them become visible. He puts his energy there, then that energy imagines and thinks, and helps re-create the scenes for some people who are sensitive. And thus, his spirit travels the house, too."

During this session, Grace asked Paul why the sisters, whom Paul identifies as Catharine and Margaret Dunn, remain in the house, and how they reacted to our group's presence. He responded that Catharine was the more social of the two sisters. Margaret nicknamed her "Lizzie" to differentiate her from Catharine, their mother. Catharine's spirit is the one most often seen at the front window, and is sometimes felt on the stairs. Her life was one of expectations, and she was attracted to beauty, luxury, and new, exciting people, and likely wanted Susan to see her in that role. Margaret lived longer, but more fearful by nature, was less happy. She was the last of John Dunn's family to own the house, and is most often encountered in the attic and upstairs bedroom. Margaret was unhappy after her sister's death because she had lost a good friend and now, had very little money. Few of her friends remained alive at that time.

"Margaret was very protective of the house and the family name during life. She's had the hardest time letting go. Her sister Catharine's not fully there anymore, but they're living in another time, so they use the house, completely unaware of the other spirits there. In their day the house was filled with guests

and Catharine's now become used to so many strange people coming from the boarding house days, and from the days when it was a vacation lodge. Even when she lived there, there were foreigners, visitors that stayed there, too. And so, she thinks that's what's going on. She doesn't really try to understand. She just accepts it, then denies it and goes to another room, and she just stays busy mentally. She goes about her favorite activities all the time.

"At the same time, Margaret relives her stressful final days there, when she could no longer care for herself and could remain in the house she loved only with the support of other owners. She continues to look out, expecting to see a black wagon or carriage arrive to take her away somewhere. That was her image of death coming to claim her," he added. And when death finally came from atherosclerosis in 1893, she didn't recognize her transition.

Paul's source said that Margaret had died at a time when the church next door didn't have a full-time minister available, "so she didn't have a very good funeral. It wasn't clear to her that she was dead. So she does her 'work' of keeping up the place as she sees it in her time, until she gains the consciousness of her passing, and the better world that awaits her."

He noted that this could all be accomplished with a "spiritual cleansing ceremony" in the house, permitting the willing spirits to move on into The Light, and offering prayers for the peaceful repose of Catharine's and Margaret's souls in The Light That Always Shines.

Research to understand the spirits of The Dunn House continues. Old timers continue to visit, sharing with Janet and Tom their memories of other times in the old house. Historical memorabilia taken from the deserted house long ago is gradually being returned, and often a new insight on The Dunn House comes with them. Janet and Tom are hoping to once more show the community the beauty envisioned by John and Catharine Dunn over 160 years ago. The owners are both lovers of art and harmony, and will infuse this house with their own vision of great beauty. With a cleansing ceremony for all the sorrowing souls who return there, they may be able to re-dedicate the house to a higher purpose of spirit made manifest on the physical plane as they, also, become a part of its history.

Perhaps Paul best explained the events in the house's history when he said, "almost everyone who has lived there has been seeking money, social status and wealth. And none ever achieved it—that is where the sorrow is—they didn't raise their sights high enough spiritually. Those who live there now and those who visit are also being given the opportunity to pray for the spirits and bring light to the house. That's the biggest opportunity there."

Eyes and Faces

Corliss Avenue is a residential section of Greenwich, an old factory town in upstate New York. "We've lived in the house there for nineteen years," Judy said, "and it certainly kept us on our toes. It was run down when we moved in. Then, seeing the house's possibilities, we began remodeling, thinking we might buy rather than rent. It was built by the father of Edna Ryan, our landlady, who died soon after we began renting. There was talk her son would have an office there, but he never moved in.

"When my husband and I were putting up gypsum board, he said he felt watched. I agreed. We used to leave a light on downstairs when we went to bed. One night, when our son and his girlfriend came to the door, he said he could see a man seated in the recliner, but nobody was there when he opened the door.

"One night my husband and I awoke at the same time. I could see three sets of red eyes in the air on his side of the bed. He saw two sets of eyes moving over him. He jumped up and demanded, 'In the name of God, what is this?' The eyes disappeared. We searched, but nobody was there.

"Over time, all kinds of things disappeared. Once, some checks we'd left in plain sight turned up in a dresser drawer months later, where we'd never have put them. A watch disappeared from my jewelry box, but returned a few days later. My husband's trousers disappeared, but were found on a hanger in the closet a few days afterward. At first we doubted ourselves, but there were so many unexplained events that we knew something or someone else was the culprit!"

Their son, who now works in law enforcement, remembers other strange events. "One year near Christmas, the light in the hallway began to turn itself on. Whenever it did that, the car horn would go off in the driveway. We all questioned one another, but nobody admitted causing the mischief. Dad finally checked the wiring but found nothing. Then the light activity became less frequent, but didn't stop entirely.

"When our family lived on Bleeker Street, before coming to Corliss Avenue, we used to close off a room during the winter, so my brother and I shared a bedroom. The bedroom light hung on a long cord, and sometimes we'd look up to see it swaying, but there was no breeze. Our dog, Damien, used to sleep in the kitchen, and often would whine and stare intently at something. He'd get out of his basket and go to the doorway between the kitchen and bedroom, lay down and pant, as if he was worn out. Lots of times, as I dropped off to sleep, I'd hear voices, like a radio, but nobody had one on. Once, I looked from my bed out into the hallway, at Grandmother's mirror, and could see the reflections of small white moving images beneath my bed. For a while I thought they were my socks, but they weren't."

Living today in another upstate town, he says paranormal events follow him. When he attended the State University at Plattsburgh, and stayed in MacDonough Hall, he awoke to see a uniformed soldier standing in the room. Then it disappeared. In all likelihood he has a strong sensitivity to "the other side."

Recently, in the Corliss Avenue house, Judy fell asleep quickly one night, but awoke suddenly to see two faces in the air over her. Her husband was just coming to bed, and as he entered the bedroom, he felt a cold breeze pass into the hall as the faces disappeared. Judy screamed.

"It's one thing to know you've got ghosts in your house," she said, "but it's entirely different when you have to look them in the face!" she grimaced.

Plymouth Street

In 1976 radio personality Don Weeks moved his family into a large house on Plymouth Street in Schenectady, NY. Newly hired at WGY, Don eventually became the Capital District's number one morning show host. In 1976, however, he had to rent a home and the big old house was what he could afford.

"Things were quiet for the first few months," he said. "Then I noticed that the attic door wouldn't stay shut. I installed a lock, but often found the door open anyway. When I'd go up to look out the dormer window, I felt an abnormal cold spot, even in the summer. Our dog, Murphy, always guarded the attic door, and wouldn't let the kids go up there, getting very agitated when they tried.

"My wife, Sue, and I often awoke to the loud ticking of a Big Ben alarm clock about 3-3:30 a.m. We didn't own one. One night she awoke to see a filmy woman beckoning her to the hallway, then disappearing. Then she heard our daughter calling out. When Sue checked, she found her running a high fever."

One night Don stayed up late watching the *The Tonight Show*, gathering inspiration from Johnny Carson. As usual, Murphy slept behind the couch. When Don went up to bed, he and Murphy started up the stairs. Suddenly the dog darted past him and growled. Looking up, Don saw an indistinct woman at the top of the stairs. "She was like a photographic negative—dark where she should be light, and light where normally dark. I could make out her features. Then, in a flash, she imploded into herself—whoosh! and nothing remained. I knew I'd been watching too much Carson," he grinned.

A few days after the vision, he noticed a light shining beneath the attic door, but when he opened it, everything was dark. Then his children began to hear noises in that stairway, and again he found the door open. When they told Don, he went into the attic and pleaded, "I don't know who you are, but please leave my family alone." For the rest of the time he lived there, there was no further disturbance.

Attempting to paint the dormer which, even today, looks different from the house, Don couldn't keep his ladder steady. When it touched the dormer it began to vibrate and slide, even on a still day when there was no wind.

Time passed, Don endeared himself to his radio audience, ratings grew and promotions followed. After a few years, they were able to move. With the house empty, Don said a silent goodbye and dropped the house keys onto a wooden table. Alone, he tended to one last detail, then reached for his keys. They were gone. "Sorry, but we've got to leave!" he shouted. Walking toward the stairs, he found the keys on the newel post.

Meantime, Sue was outside, saying goodbye to her friend across the street. Reminiscing about former residents of their house, the neighbor said, "That lady had problems. She was always so sad. Her husband was cheating on her and she couldn't stand it. She used to sit up in that attic window and watch the children playing down on the street. The husband usually dragged in around 3 or 3:30 in the morning. One night she slit her wrists in the attic, but it didn't kill her, so she went into her husband's shop in the cellar and hanged herself."

Today, Don Weeks is famous for his Halloween "stunts" and remote broadcasts from haunted houses in the Capital District. Few of his listeners know that for years he *lived* Halloween.

Ontario Haunts

Estelle Butler, a matter-of-fact woman, genuinely believes in ghosts and has done so since childhood in Sunderland, in the north of England. "I'm not afraid of them—more curious than anything. When I was little, I visited my grandmother's small cottage. One day a strange young man walked into her bedroom, and I knew he didn't belong there. So I followed him, but he vanished. Then, a few days later, looking through some old photos with my grandmother, there he was. She told me he was an uncle who had bled to death aboard ship during the war. I remember remarking how young he still looked, while my other uncles, his brothers, had aged. Later, I moved to Canada."

As builders were finishing her new residence, a large condominium on Green Road in Stoney Creek, ON, she heard that excavators had discovered several military burials as they excavated the site. Uniform remnants indicated that the bodies were Americans who fell during the War of 1812 battle there.

"One year later, after we had moved in, my mother visited from overseas. One day she told me 'You have a ghost here—a man. He's very unhappy. He's dressed like an old soldier.'

"I asked what that meant, and she described a scarlet uniform with brass buttons, and his white trousers were dirty—as if he'd been lying on the ground. I never saw him but my mother did; she was pretty psychic. After she returned to England, she phoned and said, 'Estelle, you remember that soldier? Well, you don't have to worry about him any more—he came home with me.'

"Later, we bought a small house in Winona. Soon after we moved in, I began to hear a baby crying—almost continually. It was very disturbing. It wasn't a neighbor's baby—there were no nearby houses. Then my dad came to Canada. One day, he said, 'You've got a whole family of ghosts here, Estelle.' He was more psychic than mom, so I believed him. He said there was a father there named Joseph and a mother named Doris. He felt them moving through the house from time to time. He wasn't sure if they even knew about us. There were two children: little Joseph and a young girl who hadn't been named. They appeared in pioneer clothing. After a while the crying decreased.

"Finally, we moved to this house at 21 Arden in Hamilton. It was brand new, built in 1998, but we knew a prior house here that burned had been demolished. I was usually alone here during days, and always felt watched. I wondered who it was, since I couldn't see anybody. One day, as I worked downstairs, I saw a movement from the corner of my eye. The next time it happened, I saw a flitting shadow. The third time, in the bathroom, I saw a figure entering a bedroom, but couldn't tell if it was a man or woman. I followed, but it disappeared near the bedroom's outside wall. In June of 2001, from the kitchen window, I saw a shadowy woman walking across the yard. She paused at the spot where the old house's doorway had been, then walked away. I still don't know who she was."

A few months later Estelle met John, who'd grown up across the street from her condo, and he related a story his mother used to tell about the old house that once stood there. She had said two former residents of the house, a woman named Aileen, and her daughter Arleen, once saw a filmy woman rise up through their living room floor, asking for help. John said, "Hearing that story as a child was terrifying to me, and it has stuck with me for thirty years."

When he tracked down the two women in 2001, Arleen remembered the fear she had felt from the apparition. Aileen said that these scary events began soon after she started playing with a Ouija board, and she learned to avoid such experiences after that.

It cannot be stated often enough, especially to young people who believe they are invincible, that such seemingly harmless game boards can open a vulnerability that is not easily sealed later. A firm spiritual grounding is necessary for those who wish to venture into deliberate contact with ghosts, spirits or whatever lies "beyond."

The Old Beecher Farm

"In 1967, neighbors told us it was haunted," said Marjory, "but the price was right, and it's a big old place, so my parents ignored them. It had sat vacant for over a year. From time to time folks told us of having seen someone in the window of the corner bedroom, even when the house was deserted. After a while I came to believe it was haunted, too. I never felt alone there. It was almost as if the *others* here were still going about their business—it's just that I couldn't see them."

She referred to the old Beecher Farm on Beecher Road, west of Poland, NY. The Dygert family had lived there early in the 1900s. Marjory knew little of the house's history, except that neighbors said it had burned and been rebuilt years ago. Since that time there had been stories of inexplicable knocks on the front door when no one was there.

One night her sister, Sue, heard pounding on their bedroom door, and woke Marjory. Marjory hadn't heard it, so Sue woke their father. He'd heard it, but thought it was his daughters. In the mid-1980s the father awoke to find a man in a three-cornered hat rummaging through his dresser. Not realizing it was a ghost, the father blurted, "Do you want my shoes too?" The specter vanished.

In 1986 her brother began to hear their guitar, which had been stored in the attic, playing itself. He went upstairs to seek the musician. He found nobody, left quickly, and begged his sisters to accompany him back to the attic, saying he'd seen a strange letter on the floor. In his panic he'd left it behind, but was afraid to retrieve it without help. However, when the trio went upstairs, the letter had vanished.

After marrying, Marjory's husband came to live there. She and her husband were early risers. She made breakfast and sent him off to work before 6 a.m. each day. Some mornings, after he'd left, she would go back to bed for a while. Often, just as she began to doze, she'd feel the weight of someone sitting on the other side of the bed. Startled, she'd look, but there never was anyone there. On another occasion, while she slept, she felt the mattress levitate and drop back onto the springs. No one was there that time either, however, she moved to another bedroom. In less than a week she awoke feeling someone's hand on her breast. Glancing sideways at her sleeping husband, she was terrified, realizing that the hand couldn't be his. Fortunately, it didn't happen again.

Today, her daughter Lisa lives in the house, with the ghosts still active. Lisa's three-year-old, Sara, crawled out of bed one night and came downstairs, talking about "the man in the air" in her bedroom. This was new to her mother, so she accompanied Sara back to the room and, seeing nobody, lay down with the child. She slept briefly and then awoke in fright, but couldn't explain what troubled her.

When she left the house to Lisa, Marjory thinks one ghost relocated, frequently joining her in her travels. One recent day, Marjory drove westward toward Herkimer on winding Route 5. Just outside Newport, she heard a loud voice announce from the empty rear seat, "Stop, car in your lane!" She hit the brakes as she rounded a turn and, sure enough, found herself face to face with a car stopped dead in her lane. Without the warning she would have had an accident. Uttering a silent thanks to her spectral companion, she drove on. "About then, I decided that whoever these spirits are, they have my best interests at heart. I take it all in stride now," she said.

21

Mike's House

As you drive down Route 6A through Barnstable, MA, you pass a beautiful old 1747 Cape Cod style house owned by Mike Welch. A student of history for many years, and the creator of *The Cape Cod Ghost Map*, Mike is fascinated with eerie reverberations in old houses, regardless of who owns them.

Take his own home, for example. In the late 1970s he was enjoying a cup of coffee while leaning against the stove at lunchtime. His eye caught a movement outside—a man wearing a wool jacket and scarf—in July! The stranger peered in the window, then began to walk away. Mike went after him but found no one there, and no evidence that someone had just stood outside the window.

In January the next year, while he was watching television around 8 p.m., he saw the same man peering in the same window. Rushing to the window he saw nobody there, and no footprints in the snow outside.

The next spring while cleaning behind the refrigerator, Mike and his wife found a photograph in the cooling mesh on its back. The refrigerator came with the house, and this was its first cleaning. When he looked at the photo, he was stunned to see the same man who'd peered in the window. In the photo he was sitting astride a 1930s model Harley Davidson. Mike went to the former owner and showed her the photo. "Beatrice, does this guy look familiar to you?"

"Lands sakes," she said, "that was my husband's brother. He slipped under the train wheels and died at the West Barnstable railroad station during an icy winter back in the 1930s."

Glancing out his window one day Mike spotted a woman in black passing the window alongside his driveway. He estimates her garb dated from the late 1800s. A search outside turned up nothing. Neither stranger has returned to Mike's house, but he is watchful. Former residents seem to like his windows, so he expects company any day soon, and before long he'll have to list his home on the Ghost Map.

Eunice

Sheila loved 75 Clinton Street in Saratoga Springs, NY, when she first saw it, and bought it immediately. It had once been the home of socialite Amy Lathrop, who later married "a Hampton" around 1880. It was elegant. But the cost of keeping it up became a strain after several years—something always needed fixing. In a "down" moment on September 29, 1997, as she walked through her parlor, she noted scuffed woodwork here, small ceiling cracks there, all requiring expense. Frustrated, she spoke aloud to the female presence that she'd often felt there, "The least you could do is give me some numbers in the Lottery, so I can fix up this place!" There was no answer. She expected none. Off she went to her long day's work and, returning at day's end, went to bed early.

That night she dreamed—or did she? It all seemed so real. A woman in mid-1800s clothing appeared at the foot of her bed, and the entity spoke. "I've been thinking about what you said in the parlor this morning."

"I know who you are," said Sheila excitedly, "you're Amy Lathrop!"

"Of course not!" said the apparition. "I've never lived in this house. My name is Eunice Barnum and I come from Ballston Spa. My daddy likes politics, my sister likes pretty things, and I like sweets. 5-14-29-53-61." Then she faded, and the dream ended.

In the morning Sheila snapped awake. A lady had been there, and had given her Lottery numbers—what *were* they? It was all so vague. Could she remember them? Was it a 5 or a 15? She wished she could remember. And the woman had said she was Eunice Barnum—a funny name. Who was that?

Over the next year she researched the name at the Saratoga Springs Library. For a long time, nothing. Then, finally, she spotted an announcement for the wedding of "Miss Eunice Barnum of Ballston Spa and Mr. James Savage of Saratoga Springs" on September 29, 1850.

Sheila introduced herself to me when I told ghost stories at the Cultural Arts Center on Broadway. "Did you ever hear of a James Savage?" she asked.

"Sure, he's mentioned in my story, 'The Savage House,' *(Saratoga County Ghosts)*. He was an upstanding hardware store owner in the 1800s, who built his large columned house at 108 Circular Street, but later fell on hard times and had to sell it all."

"Did you ever hear of the Barnum family in Ballston Spa?" she asked.

"No, but I will do some research." I lived in Ballston Spa then, and had friends versed in village history.

"Don't you think it's ironic?" she asked. "Don't you know what today is?"

"Thursday?" I ventured.

"No. It's September 29, the anniversary of the day Eunice Barnum got married! Now, she's in my house, and you and I are talking about her and her family more than a hundred years later."

My research disclosed that Eli Barnum owned a saddle-and-harness shop on Front Street in the 1800s. He was well-to-do, a director of the Ballston Spa National Bank, and a village tax collector. He held high positions in the Saratoga County Republican Party, and loved "politics" as the ghost insisted. Records also showed Eunice had a sister, though they made no mention of her love of "pretty things."

Sheila and I had several more conversations. "One year when my Mom came to stay with me, she heard footsteps climbing the stairs," she said. "No one else was in the house. That was on September 28, the day before Eunice's marriage. Was it premarital jitters? Here's a strange sidelight. Whenever we hear the ghost's footsteps on the stairs, we silently count them. There are always more footfalls than steps—we've never been able to figure that out."

In addition, one of Sheila's houseguests saw a transparent woman in the second floor hallway. One day her cleaning woman came to the house and related a strange dream. In it, a woman in old-fashioned dress had been standing at the end of the sidewalk, looking up at Sheila's house. The cleaning woman was impelled to sketch

23

her—the full skirt and bonnet were similar to Sheila's first vision of Eunice. And this dream had come on September 28th.

On another occasion, a friend who was housesitting for Sheila told of hearing a woman's voice calling out, "Carol. Carol." It was the friend's name, but there was no one else in the house to call it out. Another friend staying over, walked into the front hallway and approached the front door, with its panels of frosted glass. Either in the glass, or in the foyer outside, was the outline of a woman wearing a bonnet. When she opened the foyer door, nobody was there.

A tantalizing mystery for me is why Eunice Barnum Savage would appear to Sheila and others in a house where she never lived. And almost always on September 28th or 29th. She may have befriended the Hamptons, but that would be hard to establish today. Evidently, she likes the house and its new owner. She told Sheila that she liked "sweets," but has never left any for the present owner, or snitched any.

Sheila, however, if she had her choice, would like just one more shot at the Lottery. She now has a pad and pencil right beside her bed—just in case.

Mary Lou's House

Hartford is an old farming community in Washington County, NY, that was settled in the 1700s. Old stores, taverns, mills and houses keep their stories and ghosts. Mary Lou Gibson knows many of Hartford's stories. One of her favorites concerned the Pattons, who renovated the old gristmill, once powered by a water wheel, and though the wheel is gone today, they still hear it sloshing in the creek. A strict Baptist woman told her everything was peaceful when she entertained Baptist friends. But when Methodist friends came to call, the rocking chair would begin to rock with no one in it. The rustle of skirts could often be heard when nobody was visible. The Baptist woman often felt a weight, like a heavy skirt, when she walked up the stairs. And while digging her garden, she often felt soft hands placed upon hers. Also, long ago there was a house, which Mary Lou described as "filled with nastiness" on Swamp Road, but fortunately it was abandoned and has since fallen down. That's quite a bit of spirited activity for a small town, but when Mary Lou moved into her house, she found more.

She told me, "There was nothing in my old house when we moved in in 1961. No ghost would have lived here—it was so run down. It took us years to make it nice. When I had my babies, we always used the keeping room as a nursery. Once I heard a baby's cry and rushed in, but Peter was sound asleep. Ten minutes later, another cry. This time, I knew it wasn't his voice—it had a different pitch. I left the door open to hear more clearly, but there were no more cries that day. The *other* baby used to cry between 4 and 10 p.m. Once I had my Girl Scout troop over here to work on a project. They all knew little Peter was sleeping upstairs, away from the girls' noise, and when the cry came from the keeping room, I got some really funny looks. After a while, all the girls knew there was a ghost baby in the house, but it ceased to bother them.

"Babysitters often heard the cry too. One waited downstairs as I put Peter to sleep upstairs. Suddenly the *other* cry came from downstairs. The girl called upstairs to tell me, but I said, 'No, Peter's up here with me.' Silence from downstairs! The poor girl had to try to figure out how a house with one baby could produce two distinct cries.

"That other baby cried for nine more months, until my little girl was born. We put her in the keeping room too, and there never was any sound from the ghost baby while she was there. My third baby was given another room, and the crying started again downstairs in the keeping room. We finally moved to our new house in 1971.

"We pieced together what we knew of the place. My in-laws had originally bought it around 1932, and lived there until they moved to their farm in 1941. After that, a family with no babies lived there, and had no experiences. We lived there for ten years before moving out, though we came back a few years ago. We've heard no more crying, though when I walk into the keeping room, I still talk softly to whatever baby might still be listening. I wonder sometimes if it was a specific baby, or more of a 'house memory' of all the babies that came into the world and lived their first years there. It's a nice old house today."

Chef Sarah

Referring to the old house on Roast Meat Hill Road in Killingworth, CT, Jane said, "It's out in the middle of nowhere. A 1740 salt box —a real 'colonial home.' That's why we liked it when we bought it. Bill and I hired a local contractor and he ripped the place apart, a total restoration. But, in the process, we uncovered a ghost."

After the contractor left at 5 p.m. each day, Jane augmented their restoration by scraping and sanding. "One day, working alone on the stairs, tired, frustrated, and exasperated, I yelled, 'I don't like being here alone!' The work light blinked, which I thought validated my upset, so I knocked off work, and went to the kitchen. It had been a day when not many things had gone right, and when I got to the kitchen, I felt impelled to yell there, too, 'Nobody'd better cross me!' A wrought iron kitchen lamp rose up in the air eighteen inches. I went into the dining room. Someone or something was playing games with me and I didn't like it. I yelled, 'Cut it out!' A standing lamp beside me shook back and forth several times. I was more irritated than scared. There's usually some reaction to my speech, but it varies," Jane said.

"I smell perfume at times, like roses or spring flowers. It feels as if someone has just walked past. I smell it in bed at night, as if someone is bending over me. Our stairway goes up to a narrow hallway, and sometimes our guests notice the scent, too. Once five people here smelled it. It's obviously a woman, but who? I took to calling her 'Sarah.'

"One day I had gone out to pick up my grandchildren, and when I came back, I smelled old-fashioned talc. It reminded me of my grandmother. The four year-old said, 'Yuk! What's that Grandma?' When my daughter came to pick up the kids, she smelled it, too, and associated it with her great-grandmother. We had to wash our clothes and hair to make the scent go away. We have much old family furniture in the house, and I wonder if ghostly vibrations and smells are trapped in them."

In the morning, Jane regularly identifies bacon, coffee and corn bread smells when nobody has been cooking. She also encounters the strong smell of lye when passing the cellar door, and wonders if long-ago residents made soap down there. In the attic she has heard voices. Once, a man's voice whispered "Andersonville." Another time, the word "lice." And once she heard a woman sobbing.

They have lived in Killingworth long enough to get to know its history, especially the derivation of their road's name, Roast Meat Hill. "In Colonial times," Jane said, "crops weren't always plentiful and many folks were malnourished or died of hunger. According to legend, horses were once butchered for food up here. But it's interesting about the words I heard."

At the time of the Civil War (1861-1865) many men from Roast Meat Hill Road joined the Army. Many were in a regiment captured by the Confederates, and were sent to the infamous Andersonville Prison in Georgia, where over one-fourth of them died of malnutrition, disease and filth. She has not been able to uncover stories of any former resident having died in the house, but perhaps memories of sickness and starvation are still in the wind. It's possible that the presences telepathically communicate these memories to the present generation, to remind them that the "good old days" weren't always good.

Counteracting the memories of starvation, the wind also carries the smells of home cooking, thanks to the presence we can only know as "Chef Sarah."

Ken and Mary's House

Ken and Mary built their house in a small village south of Rochester, NY, in 1970. They liked the small town atmosphere and enjoyed the pond they installed in the back yard. As far as they knew there had never been any other structure on the property, and no Indian graveyards either.

"We lived here for eighteen years before the strange events began," Mary said. "I awoke one night at 2:30 a.m., hearing the shower running. I wondered if it was one of our kids. When I got to the bathroom the water was off, but the shower stall was wet. Another night I heard the cellar door open, and wondered if my son had become a sleepwalker, but found him asleep. The next year, when all our kids were in college, and Ken and I settled in for a quiet night of TV, I heard the crash of glass from the cellar, directly beneath my chair. I knew it had to be my canning jars. But, as I hurried to the cellar door, I realized my jars were in another corner. Below my chair was Ken's gun reloading table. I got down there and turned on the light. Nothing was out of place. There were no broken jars anywhere. Nothing was disturbed on his table either.

"I wondered if we had a ghost. I didn't want to say it at first, but I had had experiences with them when I was young. When I was twelve I used to clean house for people on Merrill Street every Saturday morning. One day, I went upstairs to clean their bathroom, and saw a shadow move. Then, I saw somebody walking in the bedroom across the hall. I finished my cleaning, then went downstairs to quiz the woman who lived there. She said the movement was her son, who'd died in a car accident some years ago. She accompanied me back upstairs, but no one was there.

"A few years after the canning jar incident, when Ken and I were watching TV again, I saw the fireplace tongs and poker swaying in their rack. I said to Ken, 'Honey, please tell me those tools aren't moving!' He glanced over and said, 'Sorry, Mary, they are.' It was winter, so no windows were open. But, anyway, how strong a breeze would you need to nudge iron fireplace tools?"

At other times she felt icy spots in an otherwise warm room. She never found any doors open. One summer, while in the shower, she heard the kitchen door bang and footsteps, as if someone had just entered. Expecting Ken, she called out that she'd be ready soon. She dried off, put on her housecoat and went to the kitchen. Nobody was there, and Ken's truck wasn't in the driveway.

One night, while she was in the bedroom, dressing to go out, Mickey, their Labrador was dozing beside the bed. Suddenly his head shot up, he stared, raised his ears, growled, stood and bared his teeth. "What do you see, Mickey?" Mary coaxed. A tour of the house disclosed nobody. When Mickey and Mary returned to the bedroom, she felt no cold spots or other evidence of a ghost.

Other nights, when she was watching TV, Mickey would suddenly stare at the corner of the room or out through the family room door. He'd cock his head and listen for several minutes, then go back to sleep.

When Ken retired, his mother bought them an artificial table-size tree with two electric birds to sing in its branches. When you touched them they'd warble for several minutes. But the bird would often chirp several times a night without human touch, and when there was no vibration from passing trucks or airplanes to explain it. Finally, Ken took the batteries out of the birds. *Still*, from time to time, they'd hear them singing during the night.

"We never could understand what was going on there," Mary told me. "My dad died in the house in 1993, but the phenomena had been going on for years before that. One new event was our motion-detecting outside lights suddenly switching on. All we could think of was rabbits. Often I'd stand outside in the dark, waiting for the lights to snap on and reveal a rabbit. But I never saw one."

Mary had a relative, Diane, who lost her husband in a plane crash. After the funeral, Mary was helping Diane pack and move. Mary went upstairs to fetch two flowerpots from the bedroom. As she turned toward the bedroom door, she saw a blurred, luminous human image in the corner. She left the room quickly and went downstairs. Diane asked, "You okay?" Mary assured her she was, but whispered to Ken, "I gotta get out of here!"

Soon, the couple left. Mary pondered that event for a while afterward. Diane's house was out in the country, and there were no streetlights. If the figure she had seen was the reflection of car lights it would have moved. This one just stood there. Afterward, she wondered if it had been Diane's husband, and if he was trying to manifest in the house to assure his wife of his survival of death.

"Guess I'm just weird!" Mary smiled.

I reminded her of the hundreds of thousands of such stories from people in every walk of life, all ages, cultural and religious backgrounds. Being willing to share our experiences shows others how un-supernatural ghosts are.

Chauffeur John

When John Widders came to North Adams, MA, in the 1870s he thought he'd died and gone to Heaven. He had quickly found work tending stables and chauffeuring for Albert Houghton, the biggest industrialist in town.

Houghton had gone from Vermont farm boy to owner of Arnold Print Works and several cotton mills. He served on boards of directors for many organizations and nearby Williams College. In 1896 he was elected North Adams' first mayor, and when he stepped down he built a mansion on Church Street.

On A.C. Houghton's advice, Widders invested his wages in stocks and bonds, and acquired a tidy sum for retirement. He loved the Houghtons and doted on their three girls, especially Mary, the youngest, whom he knew from birth to womanhood.

On August 1, 1911, a hot day, A.C. invited the family to motor up to Bennington, VT, enjoy a fine meal, then a leisurely return to North Adams. They invited Sybil Hutton, a local girl who'd married a New York City doctor, to accompany them. Only one thing worried Mrs. Houghton—they'd have to traverse an area she'd always feared—Pownal Center Hill.

She put that concern aside because of the nice breeze. They could afford to take the day off, and left North Adams about 9 a.m. John Widders, as usual, enjoyed driving the big Pierce-Arrow, which he kept at 25 m.p.h., as they climbed Pownal Center Hill. Near the crest, he still managed 13 m.p.h., but slowed to pass a work crew just south of the rock cut, and had to swing wide around a team of horses pulling a stone sled. In an instant, the shoulder of the road gave way, the fill dirt avalanched into the valley, and the Houghton auto tumbled after it.

Sybil Hutton died when the car roof crushed her. Mary was rendered unconscious and in critical condition. All the other passengers suffered lesser injuries. An ambulance brought Mary home, but she died within hours. All North Adams was shocked at the tragedy. A.C. went into a prolonged grief, which led to a stroke and his death within three years. But John Widders was inconsolable.

He sat up all night in the stable behind the Houghton home with two friends who were concerned for his safety. When dawn came, one friend went home. John Widders told the other that he was going to check on the horses, but a few minutes later the friend heard a shot. He found Widders in the cellar of the horse barn, with blood oozing from a bullet hole in his right temple.

The Houghton tragedy was compounded by Widders' suicide. John had loved "little Mary," who was thirty-eight when she was laid to rest in Southview Cemetery. John was also buried in the family plot there. But his spirit refused to find rest.

In 1920 the Houghton mansion was sold and became the Masonic Hall. Despite some interior renovations, it is essentially the same today as it was in 1911. Ornate parlors flank a broad center staircase. The old family ballroom has become the ritual room for the Masons and Eastern Star, which hold meetings and ceremonies there. From the second floor, two smaller stairways ascend to the third floor, where small servant bedrooms are used for storage today.

John Widders climbed those stairs to his room every night for years. Doing maintenance work in 1993, Bill, a carpenter, and two other workers took a lunch break in the second floor office at the top of the stairs. They heard the plodding of heavy feet ascending the stairs, and Bill went to investigate. With the last footfall still echoing, he peered down the staircase. Nobody was there. He looked downstairs, but no one was there either. In 1994, at midnight, following a Masonic carnival fund-raiser, Robin, an accountant, finished his accounting work in the same office. He heard no noise on the stair, but was hit by a sudden blast of icy wind. The hair on his arms and head stood up. He felt that someone had just passed him from the stairway. Many others have reported heavy footsteps during the last eighty years— but no one can be seen on the stairs. John Widders continues upward night after night, but hasn't found Heaven yet.

"Who Dat?"

When Nina, her husband and their baby, Martha, entered their new home on Pines Bridge Road near the Taconic Parkway, Ossining, NY, she was immediately "undone" by its size. The huge 1830s frame house would require lots of upkeep. With an energetic daughter to tend, it seemed daunting.

"My first experience came almost immediately after we moved in. The baby was in bed, so I was amazed to see a little girl scampering down the hall. I took time to study her because I couldn't comprehend what I was seeing. She was dressed in a long white muslin frock with a check pattern, and a ruffle along the yoke. Her brownish, curly hair stood out against the lightness of her dress. When I searched the room she'd run into, nobody was there. I realized I'd seen a ghost, but I wasn't frightened.

"We had trouble with the attic light. When my husband or I turned it on, it wouldn't stay on, and when we turned it off, it wouldn't stay off. It was as if someone were playing tricks on us. I tried to dismiss it—how could there be someone in the house besides my other two family members? One day I was feeding Martha in her highchair in the kitchen. She looked past me, through the dining room, into the library, and said, 'Who dat?' pointing at someone I couldn't see. I went into the room and asked 'Who was just here?' and saw a woman in Victorian dress, about thirty, with her hair in a bun. She floated about three inches off the floor. Unsure what to do, I left. When I came back, she was gone."

Well-educated, Nina's intellect wanted more information about the old house and she began to query her neighbors. Few knew much. A year later, Martha pointed at another invisible someone, and said the lady wanted to hug her. Martha, responding to the invitation, sat with spread arms, as if waiting to be picked up. Nothing happened. Nina gathered her up and they went to the market.

Later, a friend and her children, ages three to five, visited. When the children returned home they told their grandmother of seeing another woman in the house besides Nina.

Eventually, her husband changed jobs and they put the house up for sale. One prospective buyer who brought her children to view the house commented that the children, who had clambered onto the window seat, looked snug and cuddly, as if sitting in someone's lap.

"One early summer day, after the house sold, I sat on the dining room floor packing. I saw a shape on the wall that became clearer—a face that 'bubbled and sparkled.' I wondered if it was the lady we all had seen. That was enough for me. I had work to do. I just chose not to see any more. It was a nice old house and we always felt happy and comfortable there, despite the little annoyances and excitement. Whoever lives there now, surely must feel well cared for by the lady and child that go with the house."

Joanna

"Ghosts do play favorites, you know. I lived in a haunted house, and I'm the only one who never saw the ghost!" said Linda. She bought the house on 5th Street in Scotia, NY, in 1978, and set about adjusting the décor with her personal touch. "My friend from work and I were having coffee at the kitchen table when she got a funny look on her face. 'Linda, who is the little girl sitting on your stairs,' she asked. The kids weren't home, I knew that, but I looked anyway, and saw nobody. 'There's nobody,' I told her."

"Sure there is, I see her clear as day. She has blonde curly hair and is wearing an old-fashioned white ruffle dress. She says her name is Joanna, and that she's eight years old. She wants you to know she likes your new hat!"

"I really didn't know what to make of it," said Linda. "I'd never seen or heard a little girl. After pondering for a while, I remembered Gerry, a noted local psychic and asked her to drop in. A few days later she came, looked at the stairs, smiled, and said, 'Oh, you've got a ghost here!' Her description of the child and her name were identical. She told me the girl liked my cat and was calling her. My kitty, sleeping on the floor then, suddenly woke up, walked over to the stairs, went up to the third step and lay down, purring.

"One day my mother-in-law visited. She noted an old photograph I had framed and hung of a little girl in Victorian dress—an old picture I'd found in an antique shop and liked. My mother-in-law looked at it, and said, 'Oh, where did you get that picture of the little ghost girl?' Until then I hadn't realized that she had seen the child, too.

"I worked at Sunnyview Hospital then, and asked a co-worker from my neighborhood if she'd ever heard any strange stories about my house. She asked my address, then smiled and said, 'Oh, you live in the house with the ghost girl!' So, it seems the child had been there for some years before we moved in. However, nobody seemed to know who she was.

"We lived there for four years, but when it came time to go, I decided someone had to take action to release the little ghost, and asked Gerry how to do it. She advised talking quietly to her near the stairs. 'Tell her she died, and everyone she loves is waiting for her; if she'll just turn around, she can join them. Tell her to look for the bright light and she'll see them.' I did, and after that, I wasn't aware of her presence, and nobody else was either. But, one day, while raking leaves, I saw a small girl watching from the window. I went into the house to check, but found nobody. Shortly after that, we moved. I hope the little girl did so, too."

Weymouth

In the 1700s Dougal Campbell and his brothers came to America from Scotland. They lived in New England for a while, but soon were drawn to the endless forests and shores of Nova Scotia. The offshore waters teemed with fish to be exported to Europe for a tidy sum. Lumber for ships, houses, and masts was plentiful and promised riches to those bold enough to harvest them. The Campbell clan engaged in all these businesses, and coastal shipping too. They built a house, sawmills and wharves near the village of Weymouth.

A huge tree fell on Dougal Campbell as he supervised his work crews in the forest one day. It crushed and severed his hand. For the remainder of his life he ran the family businesses with his brothers, always worried about the safety of his ships in the treacherous waters of the Bay of Fundy. He installed a large bell on his beach, to be rung whenever fog was thickest, fearing a fog-bound ship might crash onto the rocks near his harbor. Indeed, one did, and Campbell rushed to the beach and furiously bawled out the captain. Returning to his home fuming, he suffered a heart attack and died. He was buried under a willow tree in the family cemetery. After his death, however, the bell is said to have mysteriously rung whenever there was a storm or fog.

Campbells lived there for over one-hundred years more before World War I. During that conflict more tragedy struck the family as a new generation of Campbell brothers went into military service, and none ever returned. In 1945, a descendant of the Campbells, Josephine Aimee Campbell Leslie, fictionalized the house as Gull Cottage, incorporating its mystique in her famous novel, *The Ghost and Mrs. Muir.* Twentieth Century Fox turned it into a romantic film that remains popular today, even having its own Internet website. Most Canadians and Americans today know that *Mrs. Muir* is fiction, but the old Campbell house for many years had at least one genuine ghost.

Cayllan was three years old when she spent her first summer in the enchanting old house in Weymouth, Nova Scotia. Her parents were friends of the owner. She loved to play on a swing under the old cherry tree. By that time the seaside house had been in the Campbell family for over two hundred years. Only when she was nine did she realize the house had a real story

That year, she summered in a room once occupied by one of the World War I brothers who died in action. One morning, she knelt, tying her shoe on the bedroom floor. Looking sideways, she saw another foot—a man's shoe. Looking up, she saw a man in uniform looking out the bedroom window. Her brother, Spencer, later told of awakening at night to see a man looking in his window.

Soon after, a woman guest in the house told of awakening around midnight to see a man standing over her bed. In the morning she told the others she felt he wanted her to leave. "That was strange to me," said Cayllan, "The old house was always pleasant in the summer. Once, while reading on the living room couch, Mom saw a woman looking out over the harbor. She and I felt only benevolence from these spirits who came and went."

Around 1980 her cousin, exploring the attic, said she found an old trunk. Inside were old ship's logs, journals and a large brass bell. Having heard of the Campbell legends, she wondered if this had been Dougal's bell. Then, in the bottom of the trunk, she found an old pickle jar. And in the pickle jar—Dougal's hand, severed almost two hundred years before!

The youngsters thought it over, and eventually agreed that Dougal's hand belonged in the cemetery with his body. In procession, they marched to his grave, excavated a small hole, and buried the jar.

The next night the densest fog in years settled over the Weymouth coast. Strangely, no one now heard the ghost bell. Not then, and never since. Perhaps Dougal Campbell—all of him—is finally at rest.

2
Military Ghosts

Oswego Ghosts

Icy winds blew the snow horizontally and created high drifts along the path they had trod three mornings ago in January 1752. The eight British soldiers knew they might never reach the Indian village to beg food. The garrison at Fort Ontario was dangerously low on provisions, and the winter was only half over. They knew they might not even survive the storm, much less regain the Fort. Snow had already drifted to four feet in spots, and their snowshoes were almost useless. It required the utmost effort just to stay on their feet. Bit by bit men began to lag behind as the storm worsened.

The lieutenant ordered a halt for the night in the shelter of dense woods and a great boulder. They could only scavenge enough fallen branches for a small fire. Private Wyeth had no feeling in his feet, then Edwards complained of frostbitten hands. There was nothing to do. In the bitter winds that swirled over their camp that night, the two men died. Those remaining knew their survival depended on food, and soon. Then they agreed to the unthinkable—consuming their dead comrades' bodies. Within days, cold, wind and exhaustion felled two others. The stronger ones pushed on, and the corpses vanished into the snowdrifts. Only four bedraggled snowmen straggled out of the storm to re-enter the sally port gate of Fort Ontario.

The British recognized its importance when they fortified the lakeshore at the confluence of the Oswego River and Lake Ontario in the middle 1750s. The lake offered passage westward into the wilderness and a link to the Atlantic Ocean to the east; Fort Ontario controlled the center of the lake. Whenever the autumn supply ship was late, conditions were perilous until springtime at the Fort. England disputed control of the lake with France before 1763, and after the French and Indian War, used it as a base from which to attack the Mohawk Valley during the Revolution. After 1796 the United States occupied the fort and held it against powerful British forces during the War of 1812. Later it became a border fort looking into Canada, and those stationed there for the next 140 years learned a new definition of "tedium."

Garrison duty was occasionally broken by the appearance of the ghosts. Arrayed in his red jacket, white breeches, white cross belt and musket, one frequently appeared on the fort ramparts for more than a century. The name "George Fykes" was assigned to him, perhaps inspired by a gravestone in the cemetery. "Pvt. George Fykes, late of His Majesty's Second Battalion, Kings Royal Regiment, died in 1782." As American military units were posted there, George dutifully appeared to each one until sometime in the 1930s. Deep, bone-chilling cold was the signal of George's presence, even on the sultriest summer nights. Rampart sentries were more startled than fearful when he appeared. He seemed to be mumbling to himself, lost in thought, unmindful that a new army had taken over.

There's also a tombstone for one Lt. Basil Dunbar, of His Majesty's 60th Regiment of Foot. A duel with a fellow lieutenant ended his life. Mortally wounded, Dunbar told the fort's chaplain he was at peace with His Lord, so historians believe he did not stay long after he died.

Another specter is said to have appeared in a post-Civil War blue uniform. He was spotted walking on the parade ground. He is only mentioned in the fort's history after 1901, when regular army troops left it to a "skeleton staff." Wally Workmaster, former director of the Fort Ontario Historic Site, thinks Sgt. Fawdry, who was charged with "housekeeping" the fort for the government, and who often complained of loneliness, was the only one to see the "soldier in blue."

"Re-enactors bring history alive at Ft. Ontario."

Another presence from "the inter-in-between" was seen around World War I. Frederick, in the 28th Infantry, reported a "playful ghost" while standing guard at Post 3 one night. Looking upward, he saw a small luminous sphere about a foot over his head. Thinking it was a buddy trying to spook him, he kept it to himself when he retired from guard duty. The next night, however, a friend returned from guard duty at that post and muttered, "Fred, I saw some kind of a ghost light over my head just now," Both men concluded that pranksters in their unit were trying to scare them. They feared ridicule if they told their stories. "Let's fix those guys," Fred said.

The next evening, when Fred took his turn at the guard position, his friend hid nearby, hoping to catch someone shining a light on Post 3. When the light appeared at midnight and followed the pacing Fred, his friend could spot no jokesters. Eventually the two revealed their sighting during a mess hall conversation, and discovered that others had had the same experience. They were not ridiculed; "the light" became a permanent fixture of fort lore.

The 28th Infantry was rotated out of garrison duty at Fort Ontario at the start of World War II, and new troops moved in. The Quartermaster Corps and three different MP battalions continued to see the ghost light on their nightly rounds. It appeared in all kinds of weather, even in the sleet and snowstorms. Soon, the men balked at guarding Post 3. The commander held a fact-finding hearing, but no cause for the light could ever be discovered. Privately, the enlisted men decided that the light was the disembodied soul of a British or American guard, who had returned to work off demerits, or to atone for some long-forgotten dereliction of duty.

When the war ended and the soldiers were "promoted to civilian," the old fort was decommissioned. New York State designated it an historic site. Apparently ghosts weren't in the state budget, because they disappeared when the stronghold was placed under state jurisdiction. But not the lights!

In April, 1968, Laura and her boyfriend John were strolling the fort grounds. They sat by the "rose and crown cannon" and kissed. Then, opening her eyes, Laura looked at the "grenadier bastion" and saw a "reddish-colored ball hovering over it. It stayed for about five minutes, then moved into Officer's Quarters Number 2. It did not return," she declared. John was oblivious to the light, but Laura was so certain of her vision that she carefully noted the time—9:15 p.m.— and air temperature—fifty degrees, and wrote a memo for the fort archives.

Thirty years later a fort employee joined with friends in an "after hours search," looking for evidence to report to the American Ghost Society. She assembled a team of six investigators, with cameras, video cameras, thermal scanners, electro-magnetic force meters and a tape recorder. The group spent an hour and a half exploring the four main buildings and the inner and outer grounds. They began at Officer's Quarters Number 1, a duplex for the fort's two highest ranking officers, where passersby often heard footsteps inside when the building was unoccupied, and where doors unaccountably slammed and one door would not stay locked.

Sometimes tourists suddenly depart from a tour when they hear a baby giggle or cry and there is no child in the party. Several years ago a visitor became so dis-traught in the third floor servant's quarters that she fled, swearing never to return. She would not talk about her experience. One of the investigators' photographs showed a woman's face (with a distinctive 1800s hairstyle) in a mirror. The inves-tigators noted discomforting feelings—dizziness, tightness in the head, nausea, high EMF readings and sudden temperature drops. When they returned to the building later they heard a loud banging, but couldn't locate the cause. The furnace was not running that night. When they went to the third floor to retrieve the video camera, which had been left set up and running, the banging suddenly stopped.

In the almost dark Enlisted Men's Barracks, "something metallic bounced off the floor in front of us," as if "something was tossed in our direction," the investigator wrote. But nothing was found there. Her compatriot heard a floorboard squeak, as if someone had stepped next to her. When all photographs were developed, light orbs were found in many pictures. Inveterate ghost seekers will recognize light orbs as common in haunted sites, even when no human form is sighted. And why *should* ghosts always have to use a body form? They've been reduced to conscious energy, and probably a ball is much more comfortable.

Perhaps the old guard ghosts have served their terms, and have mustered out with the World War II GIs, accepting promotion to The Great Beyond. But what about the British who suffered dismemberment along Ontario's shores? Even in peace-time, other murders were alleged within the fort's walls. Perhaps those spirits have also taken up residence.

Today, Fort Ontario is a delightful museum. Uniformed re-enactors add color to its educational functions. Perhaps other souls close ranks with these volunteers at day's end, when the performance is done. If you visit Fort Ontario on a raw, windy and gray day (as I did) you are likely to absorb the atmosphere of gray stone, gray skies and vacant ramparts which once hosted ghosts. As World War II vets make their Transition in greater numbers, who can say one of *them* will not also return? Some old soldier may discover he hasn't really died, just "faded away."

Oyster Bay Plantation

Durham Point, just outside the University of New Hampshire, is one of the earli-est centers of British settlement in the United States. English settlers arrived around 1630 and built a fortified village of timber dwellings. The strong point of the ham-let was The Matthes Garrison, fortified with muskets and a small brass cannon, ready to ward off surprise attacks from unfriendly Indians. After local tribes were pacified, the settlers put their energies into farming and fishing The Piscatauqua River and Atlantic Ocean. The settlement enjoyed a relative peace until Britain and France became locked in a struggle for dominance in North America. Expecting attacks from French Canada, England ordered the strengthening of the post in the 1750s. "And the raids did come, but the garrison was well defended and never sur-rendered," said Kenneth Matthes, descendant of those early settlers, "As a child I spent many summers in the old family homestead that had been built in the 1650s. I remember seeing an arrowhead stuck in the timbers of an old house—a relic of those attacks.

"One remnant of the old days, which I could never understand, though I witnessed it many times, was the little girl that lived within our house walls. We would see her emerge from the wooden panels, walk over to the table, steal one of our apples, and then disappear back into the walls. She seemed to be part of the house's history. We learned not to be surprised, though as an adult, I find it hard to believe that nobody ever cried out or asked for an explanation." Was the child an illusion to so many people? Or a ghostly survivor from one of the "hungry times" that plagued many frontier settlements?

Many of the strict New England Protestants feared The Devil's snares as much as the savages outside their stockade. Like their southern neighbors in Salem, Massachusetts, Oyster Bay settlers feared witches. Ken's grandmother, Zella Stevens Matthes, told him about "Witch Miriam, " a village outcast. "When she passed through the village or rural areas, the farmers' oxen were unable to pull together as a team. Grandmother Matthes told how her ancestors decided they had to find the old woman's footsteps and make a cross in each of them. Then the local oxen would work together once again. "Our ancestors really believed such tales," Ken said.

Old Coot

In the late 1850s William Saunders, his young wife Belle and their two children moved into the Berkshires near North Adams, MA, and established a large farm quite near the present day Bernard farm on the lower slopes of Mt. Greylock. When the Civil War began in 1861, Saunders enlisted in the army in North Adams and was shipped to the battlefront, leaving Belle to care for the children and farm. Bill just wasn't much of a writer, and she received only one letter, and this was to inform her that he had been severely wounded. After that—silence. She believed he had perished in an army hospital and was buried in some distant cemetery. She hired Milt Cliffords to help out, and he eventually became a good friend. The children loved him. When he offered to become her husband she agreed. The farm prospered.

Then, one day in 1865, with the war over, a strange man with his face hidden in a scraggly beard, and sporting a tattered Union Army jacket, stepped off the train in North Adams. He had been gone for four years. Slowly he walked up the hill. As he approached the split-rail fence of his property he saw his children playing in the field. He heard Belle's voice calling them to dinner and saw her embrace Milt on the porch. He recoiled at his children's words addressed to Milt— "Father," and "Daddy." Stunned, Saunders sagged against the fence post, realizing that they considered him dead, and that his wife had remarried. From their porch, the family saw the stranger lurch past the house and disappear up the old Stage Road.

Bill Saunders camped out in the brush at Bob's Hill, as he had done on battlefields in Virginia and North Carolina. The woods were quiet—no more artillery explosions or screams of dying men. The glade was peaceful and he had no place else to go. Neighbors watched the scruffy, bearded stranger walking down the road to town from time to time, investing his pension and wages in lumber and nails. He carried these into the forest and built a crude cabin that would become his shelter for the remainder of his life. From time to time he hired himself out as a day laborer to local farmers, perhaps even to Belle and Milt. One legend tells of him eating lunch at his own former dinner table while he worked for the couple. But he spoke little, and nobody recognized him. That was the way he preferred it. The disheveled stranger did good work and became a fixture in the Greylock area, a vagabond who roamed The Bellows Pipe Trail. Area residents began to call him "The Old Coot."

During one long, cold winter the stranger disappeared. Hunters found his body in his cabin one late January day. They knew who it was, though they never discovered his given name. As they peered into the cabin's frosted window, they were horrified to see a shadow shoot forth from the corpse, through the cabin wall, and into the forest. They ran from the snowy woods and reported the incident to the constable. Eventually Old Coot was given a pauper's burial.

In 1975 ten-year-old Gordon and his dog Lady were playing at the foot of the Bellows Pipe, near the old Thunderbolt Ski Trail where his grandmother lived. Gordon was sitting astride his new bike, talking to Lady, when a stranger in an old blue coat stumbled up the road in his direction. He, also, had a black dog. Lady watched the other dog and stranger pass but uttered no sound. The stranger shuffled up the trail and out of sight. "Nothing was up there," said Gordon, "and I knew that sooner or later he'd have to come back down. I'd never seen anyone dressed like that, so I decided to wait. Lady and I watched from Grandmother's porch until dusk. Nobody came down. I asked Grandmother if she knew about the man and dog. She gave me a strange smile and said, 'Honey, you saw Old Coot. People have seen him for years, but he's just a ghost, nothing to be scared of.'"

Old Coot has been startling hikers and hunters in the Mt. Greylock area for over a century. Reporters and photographers at the North Adams *Transcript* have tried to photograph him for fifty years. In 1939 reporter Randy Trebold, tongue in cheek, claimed to have taken the definitive photo of Saunders stumbling uphill in the snow. Trebold, known for his pixilated humor, kept the legend of Old Coot alive every few years with a staged photograph, just when the newspaper needed a Halloween feature story. Recent reporters at the paper also claim to have seen Old Coot, but say he disappears into the woods before they can point their cameras.

William Saunders' ghost still seems to roam the rugged terrain of the old Thunderbolt Ski Trail. Recent sightings have been fewer, but he is kept alive in legend. Modern readers are still fascinated by "The Ghost of Greylock" and the real-life tragedies that marked his earthly life.

Inverawe

Robert Louis Stevenson, vacationing at Saranac Lake, NY, in the 1880s, heard many tales of the Adirondacks, which inspired his novels. He heard of Fort Ticonderoga's history and something clicked in his memory. Gathering information from his native Scotland, he published a story in *Scribner's Magazine* in December 1887. It became one of America's most famous ghost stories.

Maj. Duncan Campbell, of His Majesty's 42nd Regiment of Foot, also known as "The Black Watch," was mortally wounded in the British attack on the French fort at Carillon (Ticonderoga) in July 1758. His bleeding body was carried overland to Fort Edward, where he succumbed and was buried nine days later. How he came to those mountains and how he came to know he would die there is quite a story.

Campbell was *laird* (lord) of his clan's castle, Inverawe, on the River Awe in the western Scottish Highlands. One night he was awakened by frantic pounding on his door. When he opened it, a bruised and bloody stranger cried out, "Help me! I've been in the fight of my life and killed my opponent. Now his friends are trying to take my life!"

Campbell bade the man enter, fed him, and escorted him to the strongest room in his house.

"Swear you'll protect me!" the stranger begged.

"I swear on my *dirk* (dagger, symbol of manhood and honor)." He sheltered the man, then heard another pounding on the castle door.

When he opened it, he faced angry relatives, who cried, "Duncan, a stranger has just murdered your cousin Donald! We're on his trail. Has the scoundrel come here?"

This placed Campbell in a great moral quandary: he was honor bound to aid his family *and* the stranger. He chose to deny his kin. "I have not seen the man, ride on!" Campbell told them. And they did so. However, Campbell was conscience stricken, and went to bed deeply troubled.

He awoke in the middle of the night. At the foot of his bed stood his murdered cousin, who cried out, "Duncan, Duncan, shield not the murderer. Inverawe! Inverawe!"

Donald had been a favorite cousin. How could he now betray that love? He struggled for a compromise. Calling the stranger, Campbell gave the man one-day's food supply and secreted him in a mountain cave. But the next night, Donald appeared again. "Inverawe! Inverawe! Blood has been shed; you cannot shield the murderer."

Still sleepless, Campbell sought out the murderer the next morning, but the cave was empty. Had the man been captured or escaped? He retired to his bedchamber again but slept fitfully. Once more Donald's voice came, "Farewell, Inverawe, we meet again at Ticonderoga!" Campbell bolted upright. Ti-con-der-oga, what was this strange name?

Over the next few months his cattle and crops failed. Friends shunned him—or did he just imagine it? Fellow clansmen whispered furtively behind his back. He sought to escape it all by joining a regiment of fellow Highlanders in His Majesty's Army.

France and England were contending for North America at that time. Campbell's Black Watch Regiment moved up the Hudson River to the old Indian Portage between Lake Champlain and Lake of the Holy Sacrament (Lake George). French General Montcalm had built a fort called Carillon there, which the Black Watch had to conquer.

The French had strewn the Fort's narrow peninsula approach with *abatis* (felled trees). The British would have to break their assault formation and speed to struggle over, under and through the labyrinth as they advanced. In the process they'd be easy targets to French sharpshooters.

Even before he ordered his pipers to begin their slow march into that maze, he knew that he would die there. Campbell's blood ran cold when a scout had spoken the Indian name for this place, *Ti-con-de-roga*. Also, on the night before battle, Donald's ghost had appeared in Campbell's tent, reminding him that his debt was about to be paid. Fixing bayonets, raising the regimental flags, and with the pipes skirling "Scotland The Brave," The Black Watch marched into bloody history. Two-thirds of the Regiment, including Campbell, lay dead or wounded at that day's end. Campbell's body was taken to his eventual grave near Ft. Edward. It would be another year before the British could mount a second attack.

The tale of the ghostly voice that foretold Duncan Campbell's fate is one of the best-documented ghost stories in American history. Stevenson later wove elements of this tale into his work, *The Master of Ballantrae.*

Carillon

They headed back to their cars on the moonlit September night. Sally and her daughter, in Colonial dresses, were ending a re-enactment weekend at Fort Ticonderoga, NY. Her husband was conversing on the old fort's North Bastion for a moment, intending to follow them shortly. Suddenly a tall man with a rifle and fixed bayonet blocked the women's path. He demanded the watchword. Sally smiled and said, "Good job! I thought we were done for the weekend, but you did that real well." The man disappeared.

Later, on the drive home, she told her husband about the incident. "But all the uniformed re-enactors were still in the Place d'Arms inside the fort!" he said.

"A ghostly sentinel from the Revolution, still on guard after over two hundred years? It's entirely possible," said Drum Major Mike Edson, a staff member who leads the fort's crack fife and drum corps. He's worked at the fort for over twenty-six years and notes that in recent years he has heard stories of apparitions in that north parking lot.

James Fenimore Cooper's author son, James, wrote of a ghost experience there in 1910. He saw a ghostly pair in the ruined fort: a British officer and an Indian maiden, who threw herself to her death below the walls. The fort, just a ruin at that time, was not the reconstructed tourist attraction of today. "I've never heard that one," Mike said. "The most common experience among our staff is hearing footsteps on the third floor in the mornings. When our security people enter the second floor of the Southwest Barracks, they hear heavy walking that makes the floorboards creak."

Begun as a French fortification in 1755 (and named "Carillon," or "place of the bells") the star-shaped fortress guarded the strategic passage between Lake George and Lake Champlain. A British attack came in 1758 and was repulsed by Gen. Montcalm's army, killing almost two-thirds of the invading British 42nd Regiment of Foot (The Black Watch). The next year the British captured the fort, gave it an Indian name *Ti-con-de-ro-ga*, and held it through the French and Indian War.

Then, in a midnight raid by Ethan Allen and his Green Mountain Boys on May 10, 1775, before hostilities were formally declared at the outset of the American Revolution, it changed hands once more. "Come out you old rat!" yelled Allen at the British commandant. He took the fort "in the name of Jehovah and The Continental Congress."

It was "Fort Ti's" large cannon, dragged several hundred miles through winter snows to Cambridge, MA, by American Gen. Knox, that forced the British to evacuate Boston without a fight. Gen. John Burgoyne invaded the Champlain Valley in 1777, moved his artillery onto neighboring Mt. Defiance, and ousted the Americans.

After the Revolution the unused Fort slowly disintegrated. In 1908 Stephen Pell dedicated his fortune to restoring it to its former glory as a historical site that all Americans could visit. Apparently, the ghosts had never left. The staff and re-enactors who annually encamp on the Fort's outlying grounds often have heard the ghostly wail of distant bagpipes, though the piper is never found. In the 1980s Roger worked in the fort's bakery. His fluency in French made him valuable to French-speaking visitors. At his post one evening, he heard a voice behind him, "Well! I have burned the rolls once more, I hope the *capitain* will not be angry." It was a dialect that hadn't been used in over two hundred years! When he whirled to confront the speaker, he saw nobody. About a month later, in the same room, he heard a Scot sergeant declaring that the rum ration had been watered down again, a remark sure to rankle the troops in the lonely mountain outpost.

In one barracks there is a weapons display and tables for visitors. A doorway leads to a video room, where tourists can see a short presentation on the fort's history. John, a summer guide, escorted visitors into the room and delivered his regular spiel for tourists. A man dressed in the gray-and-blue of the French army was standing in the doorway. John ignored him—re-enactors sometimes lurked around the Fort on weekdays. Later he remembered that no re-enactors were present that week. Sharon, another of the guides, said, "I saw that guy too! Boy am I glad *you* saw him." A fort historian told them that archaeologists had found the remains of a French soldier buried in that barracks wall when reconstruction started almost a century before. Was this *soldat Francais* still seeking to inform of his ignoble burial?

In 1997 a *demi-lune*, the rounded outer fortification, collapsed. As they cleared the rubble, the historians were able to examine the construction materials of 250 years ago. Soil samples assessed the environmental conditions before the walls were erected. It was all very professional work done by historians and archaeologists. But no professional training could explain the "glowing balls." "It's as if the collapse released some ancient energy," Mike Edson told me. "These two-inch luminous balls now move through the second floor barracks and museum from time to time." Maintenance men most often notice these energies. What they are, and what propels them, we don't know. No one has ever seen anything like them in the hundred years since the fort has been rebuilt."

Fort Ticonderoga, built to guard the passage between the lakes, may today serve as a passageway between the worlds of those who live and those who used to.

Brits Go Home!

In 1777, Walloomsac, NY, then called Bennington, NY, on the western slopes of the Berkshires and Green Mountains, was the battleground for American and British armies on August 16. Hessian Col. Baum, deployed from Gen. Burgoyne's main force in the Hudson Valley, attempted to raid Bennington with a force of 800, to capture Patriot artillery and military equipment. General John Stark and his Green Mountain Boys, supported by militia from New Hampshire and Massachusetts, ambushed the British. But Hessian Lt. Col. Breymann arrived with over 600 reinforcements and pushed the colonials back, until Seth Warner saved the day, arriving with American reinforcements to win the Battle of Bennington. British losses were 200 killed and 700 taken prisoner.

Col. Baum was killed. It is said the famous "76 Flag" was unfurled in that battle. The Americans lost but 30 dead and 40 wounded. Burgoyne received no help from Baum's contingent, lost the battles at Saratoga, and was himself taken prisoner two months later. The tide of battle then swung southward and the hillsides and forests of eastern New York were quiet once more.

Soon, the land to the east of Walloomsac became the State of Vermont, and the Walloomsac hills attracted hardy farmers and mill owners. Over the next two centuries, memories of the battle faded, except at the New York State Bennington Battlefield State Park, and at Vermont's spectacular Bennington monument. Among the many houses built near the battlefield was one constructed for mill workers in 1875 on Route 67, just outside Walloomsac.

Researching the house's history, Ally discovered it stood on the edge of the battle area. Apparently, one of the battle's casualties never left the battlefield, and stayed on during the years it had been a button factory, and then a brick kiln in the early 1800s. A barn had been built behind the house in the 1920s, but had burned.

Ally had a party in the house in 1988. When photographs of the guests were developed, many showed a hovering mist, like smoke, which obliterated their features. She attributed it to a camera malfunction.

Then, a friend from Great Britain visited her in 1993. "We had a raucous celebration party that first night of his visit, and when we tried to make coffee in the morning, none of the appliances worked. So, we had a cold breakfast, then cleaned up. A small salt cellar on the stove suddenly flew twelve feet across the kitchen and hit our British friend William in the back. Salt went all over the floor. Then we began to hear strange noises, whose source we couldn't locate; I'd never heard them before. Most of the phenomena took place between the dining room and the kitchen, however, when I placed small candies on our guests' bedside table, in the morning, the Brits found them in their shoes.

"A few years later another British friend brought small pieces of Staffordshire china as a present. We placed them on a desk and stood chatting nearby, admiring them. Suddenly, the desk turned over and the china was smashed. We were sad, but still hadn't figured it out. Later, we had German guests and the house was peaceful. However, after they left,our chimney flue began to open and close by itself. Keys, glasses and important papers disappeared. Then, a year later, other British friends came to stay in October. We introduced their four-year-old to pumpkin carving. Georgia, her mother, sat nearby, writing a story about American Halloween traditions. She took photos of the girl amid lighted jack-o'-lanterns. During this activity Georgia's mother called from England, to relay some family problems. When the pictures were developed, they showed a mist swirling all around the child, and the little girl staring into the mist." She and her husband have seen ghosts in other places too, and some of their photos taken while in Great Britain show swirling mist patterns.

Ally recalled that she has lived near battle sites throughout her life, whether in California or the east, and loves antiques of all periods. Today, no longer in Walloomsac, she speculates that an American who fell in the Battle of Bennington may still be clinging to his death site. Committed to the cause of American independence, he may continue to make life difficult for all English and German visitors until he learns their nations have declared peace, and can do so in his own soul.

AWOL

A car door slammed outside on Olive Street in Brooklyn, NY, and the young sailor looked quickly out the window. They were coming for him. Two Sea Police with billy clubs entered the downstairs door. "Oh God!" he groaned. "I didn't want it to come to *this*!" He was still hungover from two weeks of steady drinking. Now, they'd found him and he was going to the brig. He couldn't *stand* confined spaces—he'd told them that! That's why he hadn't left for minesweeping duty in the North Atlantic with his shipmates. World War I was almost over, and he knew he'd die of claustrophobia if he had to go back below decks! He grabbed the belt from his bathrobe, drew it into a loop, and slipped it around his neck.

Rap! Rap! Rap! sounded on his door. "Come on out, swabbie, we know you're in there," called the SPs. He stood on the bathtub, fastened the belt to a hook on the door, snubbed it tight and jumped—into eternity. When the landlord got there with a key, the SPs found only a corpse, still swinging in the doorway. His death was chalked up as another World War I casualty, and a dishonorable one at that. But the landlord soon forgot it, when he found new, permanent tenants.

Thomas Marone and his family came to the U.S. from Italy in 1922 and believed they found the house of their dreams on Olive Street, not far from Metropolitan Avenue. They hoped to buy it, but as one by one, family members met the spirit of the sailor who had unwittingly imprisoned himself there, they didn't stay long. They were relatives of radio personality and entertainer Chris Rush. "That house *looked* haunted," he told me. "I remember it from my childhood. It was the smell that always got us. Uncle Tony found it almost impossible to go into that bathroom. He'd bring rose petals in little containers to overcome the stench. We joked about it, but the humor wore thin. The bathtub dripped continually; nothing we did stopped it. My grandmother saw the sailor hanging on the door in his skivvies and sailor's hat one night. She said he looked transparent and artificial, then just faded away."

The youngest daughter in the family went to the bathroom one night, and found the sailor hanging on the door when she turned on the light. She screamed and the family came running. They found no sailor ghost, but the girl was shaking and her eyes were crossed. "Doctors couldn't help her," said Rush, "her eyes were crossed for almost two more years. No matter how we cleaned that bathroom and closet we couldn't get rid of that stench. Finally, the family moved out to Long Island.

"I revisited the place a few years ago," said Rush. "The building is still there. The City has given it a facelift and some organization occupies it now. I'll never forget the house—you could walk to the Navy Yard from there. It was a nice neighborhood. I wonder if that poor guy is still 'hanging out' there," Chris Rush said, making a face and a smile. He has an irrepressible sense of humor that audiences enjoy. Perhaps the ironies he encountered in his grandfather's house helped him fine-tune a sense of the ridiculous in the face of inevitability. And perhaps we can pardon him if his repertoire occasionally slips into "bathroom jokes."

Doughboys

Most who served America during the First World War have now passed over into the Summerland. Some "doughboys," as they were called, are reappearing as spirits, seeking to complete their spiritual and material agendas before moving into The Light. Here are reports of two:

The first cold morning of late summer settled on Lake George, NY, pulling mist from the still warm soil along Lake Road. Early morning was a favorite time for two women named Shirley to stroll through the village, taking the dog, Chief, for a walk. The beach and the steamboat dock were deserted that brisk morning in the 1980s. They had the street to themselves—except for a solitary figure walking toward them from the old train station. A hush settled over the area and the women no longer heard the squawking seagulls on the shore. The air grew unaccountably warm. As the man drew closer, they saw he was dressed in a World War I army uniform, and carried a duffel bag on his shoulder. Apparently he had just alighted from the morning train, though no train had visited the station since the 1950s; in fact the tracks were gone and the depot had been converted into a souvenir store.

Eyes fixed on some far-off place, the man strode silently past them. The dog stopped dead, watching intently as the soldier passed within feet. Chief didn't growl but pricked up his ears. The man finally walked out of sight into the Ft. Gage area south of the village. Suddenly, they heard the gulls again and noticed other morning strollers over on Canada Street.

Throughout the rest of the day Shirley McFerson pondered her experience. As librarian in Caldwell Library, she had access to local history records. She found that no Lake George citizen had perished in "the war to end all wars." So, who could he have been? She could only speculate. One of the tenants whose families farmed the land around Ft. Gage at one time? Or someone's friend returning to say goodbye, stepping down from a celestial express that's always punctual, but which most of us hope won't stop at our station—at least today.

* * *

It looked like a quiet, comfortable house where her family could recuperate from hectic jobs in Albany, NY. State Route 7 wound eastward from the Capital District through Pittstown and east into the Green Mountains. In Pittstown they rented an old farmhouse called "Gordon's House" in 1978. It had been in the Hall family for years.

"I just knew we were in for an experience the first night we moved in," said Joan. "As soon as we got into bed we heard 'tee-hee's' and snickering. Then quiet laughter from somewhere upstairs. I went to the children's bedroom to encourage them to sleep—we'd all had a very hard day, but the kids were asleep, or were they pretending—I wondered. When I got back to my bedroom the giggling began again. It was hard to tell if it was a child or adult. So I went back to the kids' room, but they were asleep in the same positions, so it couldn't have been them. So, who was it? I wondered.

"Within a few days a member of the landlord's family came by. 'How do you like the house?' she asked.

"'We really like it,' I told her, 'won't you come in and sit for a while?' I gestured to the living room.

"The woman got a funny look on her face and said, 'No. Thanks. I just wanted to know how things were going.' She backed toward the door and left quickly."

Joan devoted all her non-work time to moving furniture and hanging pictures—making it a real home. There were four large bedrooms to arrange upstairs, but one still contained the owners' furniture. Expecting a houseguest, she asked the landlord if she could move that furniture to the barn. When he said okay, she did it, then re-papered the walls and spruced up the floor. After setting up a bed, she decided she and her husband would use it as their bedroom.

Her husband woke her about 2 a.m., saying she'd been restless, talking, and seemed about to scream. She'd been dreaming of a short, dark figure sitting next to her bed. She didn't feel menaced, but was terrified at not knowing who the person was. Her husband invited her downstairs for tea, but when they reached the top of the stairs, he felt blocked by an icy wall.

On another night when Joan's husband was making his way to the downstairs bathroom, he encountered a spectral woman with "bent legs" in the middle of the stairs. Downstairs he found none of their furnishings, but old-fashioned rugs and furniture, as if he had stepped back in time. Then, in a split second the old décor vanished and their new furnishings reappeared.

One night their daughter fell asleep on the sofa in the downstairs living room. When she awoke she saw the lights on in the dining room, and an old man in a World War I uniform in a wheelchair. Then he vanished and the dining room went dark again.

At her government job in Albany, Joan mentioned these events to a co-worker, who told her of a priest who did spiritual cleansings.

"When the priest came, he said prayers and sprinkled holy water. He held a crucifix on the upstairs hallway wall, but it wouldn't lay flat." Later, she wasn't sure that the exorcism, if that is what it was, was effective. Noises continued for a time, but then Joan got her old job back in Massachusetts, so they moved.

Investigating, I learned that Gordon Hall's brother, Henry, was the only family member to serve in the army during World War I. Henry received an honorable discharge in 1919 and returned home. Later, he moved to Vermont and married, though the records beyond that are sketchy. The Pittstown historian stated that Henry was convicted of assault with intent to murder his wife, and had died at Windsor Prison in Vermont in 1943. But further investigation in NY State and Vermont archives indicates that Henry didn't die in prison, but had been paroled a year before he died.

At any rate, I think Henry's spirit returned to the old farm in Pittstown, and that the injured or deformed woman who blocked the stairs was his aggrieved wife, who followed him. Her failure to forgive him may hold her there too.

I contacted the present owner, whose family purchased the house in the early 1970s, and had been Joan's landlords. "I was about sixteen then," said Peter, "and brought some friends over to play Rummy. As typical teenagers, we speculated about whether Gordon's spirit was still there. I didn't believe in ghosts, and said so; I still don't believe in ghosts, but we had a very strange experience that night. At midnight the power suddenly went off in the house. We'd had the TV on in the background and, of course, it went off too. But a Seth Thomas electric clock, plugged into the same outlet as the TV, was still running. It chimed twelve times. We got out of there! Was that Gordon? The next day we questioned the neighbors. None of them had had a blackout. So, how do you explain that?"

Though Gordon had lived a peaceful life, the old homestead became a magnet for his brother Henry's angry spirit after 1943. Thirty years have passed since these events, so we hope all family members have finally sorted through their joys and failings, and have passed on from life's battlegrounds to a more peaceful place.

Let There Be Light

Chet Boice left his home in South Colton, NY in 1917 to fight in World War I. He was a changed man when he returned. "Shell-shocked," he had become a loner, preferring the company of children to adults. Most serious, he consumed almost a gallon of wine per day, according to Bill Smith, Chet's next door neighbor. Bill is renowned as an Adirondack musician and raconteur, and has a vivid memory of the old days.

He remembered, "Chet had been a mechanic before entering the service, but wasn't worth a darn with mechanical things when he got back. He'd become pretty good with electrical things in the Army, however, and wired his two Tiffany floor lamps, hoping one day we'd get electric service in our Gulf Road neighborhood. A few months later, the power company said they would install the poles and wires if any three houses on the road would sign up for electricity." Chet joined in with Bill's father and his uncle, and the project began. Bill's dad had a team of horses for hire, and profited by hauling away the brush and timber from the right of way. The three men and horses went to work each day, with young Bill watching from the sidelines. Chet would return home exulting at night. He'd turn on his flashlight and move it around inside the kaleidoscopic Tiffany glass lampshades for his wife. "See! This is what electricity will look like! Won't it be wonderful?" he exclaimed. He then began wiring his house.

A power company inspector arrived to view the crew's progress and announced that if the remaining stand of brush was cleared by the end of the workday on Friday, the neighborhood could have electricity Monday noon. The crew redoubled their efforts on that last Friday, but by noontime Chet was pale and told Bill's father that he felt sick and needed to go home. "Sure," Bill's father thought, "I'll bet he just wants to get at that bottle early today," but, as they were almost done, he gave Boice permission to knock off early. Finishing up, Bill and his dad returned home, did the chores, had supper and went to bed.

During the night Bill awoke to hear his mother and father talking excitedly. He slipped out of bed and went to their bedroom door just in time to hear his mother declare that Chet was in trouble. She had just seen his pale form looming over the bed. The entire family went downstairs to go next door. Before they could leave the house, however, a knock came at the door—it was Chet's wife, with tears in her eyes. She wailed, "Come quick. Something's happened to Chet. He's on the floor and I can't get him up!" In Chet's living room they found him dead. They placed him in bed and called the undertaker. The Boices were neither well to do nor overly religious, and opted for a house funeral after the two-day mourning period was fulfilled.

On Monday morning the preacher arrived and stood before the Army veteran's open casket. Friends and neighbors gathered in Boice's living room to say their good-byes. The undertaker, knowing the family couldn't afford large candles at the head and foot of the casket, had moved Chet's two lamps into those positions. With family, neighbors and friends assembled at 10 a.m., the reverend began his prayers and eulogy.

A certain "opener," he was sure, was the 23rd Psalm, calculated to restore hope and the certainty that God would not forget the man who labored in such difficulty throughout life. *"The Lord is my shepherd, I shall not want,"* he intoned. Few were looking at him, seeming to gaze elsewhere in the room. *"He maketh me to lie down in green pastures,"* he assured them. Now, not one of the assemblage seemed to see or hear the minister. In apparent rudeness, the group was looking wide-eyed at the area behind him. *"He leadeth me beside the still waters, he restoreth my soul. He leadeth me in the paths of righteousness for his name's sake,"* the minister continued more insistently. Shifting his gaze slowly to the side, so he could scan the casket, he continued, *"Yea, though I walk through the valley of the shadow of death..."*

His prayer and eulogy stopped abruptly as he took in the scene behind him. Illuminating Chet's body, both Tiffany lamps were brightly aglow. It was still almost two hours before the Power Company would send electricity!

It seemed that Chet, released from his mortal confinement, had found the secret of sharing a heavenly light with his mourners. The soldier who returned from war as a childlike man may indeed have found the peace denied to him in life, but instead of keeping it to himself, had engineered a way to share it with them all.

The Old Soldier

"You girls all claim to be psychic," Jamie, a former National Park Service ranger at Saratoga Battlefield, teased his New Hampshire employees. "I know a place where you might see ghosts." He'd never seen them himself, but was sure he'd felt them there. Now, as director of a New Hampshire historic site, he suggested they drive all the way to Saratoga National Historic Park. At Stop #6 on the battlefield tour road—The Balcarres Redoubt—he said, he was sure they'd find ghosts.

American troops were never able to conquer the log-reinforced stronghold and lost many men there in the second battle. Today the neatly trimmed grass and silent historic markers belie the ferocity that accompanied the end of so many soldiers' lives. On a sunny October afternoon, two hundred and twenty years after the conflict, Jamie and his friends visited the site.

"I always felt something near this big tree and also near that historic marker over there," he told his group. So they spread out, each one seeking her own perceptions. "I first went to the tree, then the monument, then back to the big old tree," Pam remembers. "Someone was walking in my periphery, but I assumed it was a woman from our group, so I didn't look. When I reached the tree I turned to speak to her, but found a black man in Colonial uniform!"

"I died on this site and I want to tell you my story," he told her.

I asked Pam if the soldier had been wispy, like many ghosts. "No, he looked as solid as you do. He wore a dark grey or navy jacket without gold braid or lace; no ruffles on his shirt. His leggings were wide and dark. He was hatless and had close-cropped black hair. He held no rifle or other weapon.

"He said he came from Connecticut with a militia company, though he was not an enrolled member of the group. He had worked on a large farm there. The farmer or master had sent him in his place, enabling the owner to stay home and direct the harvest." (N.B. It was the custom in some militia companies that if a member could not march to battle with the others, he could send a substitute—paid or unpaid—in his stead. Apparently this is what happened here.) The black man had found just one friend in the unit, and knew his place. He marched at the rear of the column.

"When the battle began I did my best," he said. "I fired my rifle, then saw my friend fall wounded. I dashed to his side and bent over his body. I felt a bullet hit my back. I saw my body fall upon his. Saddest of all," opined the soldier, "I think my own men shot me."

"Then, as I watched," Pam said, "the old soldier simply came apart. Finally there was nothing left. I felt a great emotional release as I stood there."

Stunned, she said little to the others on the way home. When they returned to New Hampshire Jamie quizzed her. She told him her story and they recalled the significance of the great tree there, its two limbs rising upward, just as two comrades stood together in friendship before the last violent experience of their lives. From his National Park Service work, Jamie remembered that, indeed, two Connecticut regiments of militia (Poor's and Lattimore's) had suffered many casualties there.

Whenever any of my psychically gifted friends are headed to Saratoga Battlefield, perhaps for a picnic, some biking or a stroll, I ask them to "tune in" around Stop #6. Is anyone still there? All of them return with negative results. Apparently the old black soldier waited at that spot trying to communicate his felt betrayal to a compassionate stranger. Finally, after 220 years a sensitive woman arrived, one who would listen and understand, and he gained release from an imprisoning suspicion. Friends tell me many other spirits still roam the now quiet fields at the National Historic Park, soil which absorbed without prejudice or favoritism, the red blood of Americans (black and white), Canadians, Englishmen and their German mercenaries.

The Commander's House

When World War II burst upon America in 1941, the government bought many sites for military bases, such as "The Mattydale Bomber Base," on the old Bill Muench farm outside Syracuse, NY. Soon, survey stakes appeared, then were replaced by concrete runways, a control tower, barracks, large hangars and massive fuel tanks. The sturdy old farmhouse out beyond the runways was designated as a billet for the base commander. While planes came and went for the next forty years, as the Air Corps became the U.S. Air Force, it was renamed "Hancock Field," and became a North American Radar Defense base. Then, as air defense shifted toward satellites, the old base was converted into the Syracuse Municipal Airport.

"You can't get there from here," my escort told me with a smile, as we left the air terminal. I'd wanted to visit the old Commander's House and had received permission. The house lay on a tortuous trail in the midst of old runways, and could only be found by one who knew the way. The whitewashed building with its green shutters reminded me of cottages in Ireland. All it needed was a thatched roof.

Curiously, an Irish immigrant had built it. James Lynch came to Onondaga County from Ireland in 1839 during the potato famine. He found the land fertile and surprisingly cheap. He purchased 100 acres. Soon after he arrived his wife died. He hired two Irish girls as house servants and remarried a few years later. This puzzled his neighbors, who saw him as a harsh, quick-to-threaten "the back o'me hand to ya!" to his opponents. He died in 1868 at age fifty-seven, leaving the farm to his widow, who tried to keep it up. She gave up after seven years, selling to the Bausinger family, who owned it until World War II.

A man named Rodney, in Rome, NY, worked on a petrol truck crew in "gasoline alley" at Mattydale base in 1943-44, and often drove near "that house." He'd seen women in dresses peering out through a side window, when he knew the only inhabitants at that time wore uniforms. He knew several who stayed there overnight, who had heard a woman weeping. Rodney and his comrades used to speculate about all this while transporting the aviation fuel. Twenty-five years later he urged me to investigate its history.

Marilyn Chambers, wife of the last base commander, reported strange events right from the start. "When my husband had been appointed, but not yet installed as C.O., I got to our house early and was surprised to find a telephone company technician installing phones. I asked him why he was doing this. Only the COs wife could sign an order to arrange phone service. The man said to me, 'I don't know, lady, some woman called in and placed the work order.' That would have been my task, and I know I didn't do it! Try as we might, we never found who did it," she concluded.

The house's cellar had a dirt floor. Snakes loved to wriggle in there and nest. For that reason she and her husband always kept the cellar door closed and locked. They hired workmen to do house repairs, but one morning, returning from shopping, she was surprised to find them already at work in the cellar. She'd expected to let them in, but they'd found the cellar door open, and assumed she did it because they heard footsteps upstairs. However, neither she nor her husband had been home.

To add to her wonder, radios and stereos often turned on in the middle of the night. Clothing that had been dry-cleaned and hung in a closet sometimes disappeared by morning. Bed linens they'd placed in the linen closet were missing a few days later. Most of it was returned to them. "We laughed a lot, and called it 'funny stuff'. We didn't let it bother us. There was a real mystery there, but we didn't care to be frightened by it."

In the early 1970s Col. Donald Ewing and Gerry, his wife, had similar experiences while living there. "We never felt entirely alone there," said Gerry. "Though we turned out the stairway lights on our way to bed each night, we often found them on in the morning. This really bothered our family cats; they never knew whether it was daytime or night. Sitting in the living room in the evening, sometimes we'd look up and see dark shadows flitting from the den. But there was never anything definite that we could identify, just a rush of darkness which vanished before our eyes."

One night the colonel sat exhausted in the living room. He turned off the end table lamp, prepared to stand, but sank back down into the cushion. For a few minutes he stared at the lights from the base about a half-mile away. "Then I looked at the doorway and saw a tall man dressed in an Inverness coat. He had long, flowing salt and pepper hair. Around him was a faint glow. We stared at one another. When he walked, the floorboards creaked under his boots. He vanished around the corner. *That* got me up fast! But when I searched the hallway and adjacent rooms there was nobody."

One wonders if James Lynch still believes himself lord of the estate he created in the lush hills of central New York. Maybe he realizes that crops no longer grow there, for the old house has changed. "I wonder if the present inhabitants still experience ghosts?" I said aloud.

My escort smiled. "David, they assigned me to you because *I* live here now. I assure you that we have no ghosts." So that was that. James Lynch appears to have voyaged to yet another New World, on which shores he might seek a fortune that endures.

Powder

The Hudson River was once the major gateway between Europe and the settlement of the American west. When the War of 1812 loomed, the Army constructed Fort Hamilton on the Brooklyn side of the river, to guard the Narrows from naval attack. Much gunpowder for artillery was brought to the fortress in anticipation of an invasion of New York City, the young nation's transportation and commercial center. A small island just one-hundred yards offshore became the Fort's powder magazine and it mounted eighty artillery pieces in defense. It was originally known as Fort Diamond, later renamed Fort Lafayette. Having explosives at a distance from the main fort decreased the threat of explosion at Fort Hamilton. The island had barracks and stables for the horses that pulled gunpowder wagons and caissons. The War of 1812 came and went, but there was no attack on the city. Military duty at Fort Hamilton settled into torpor.

In 1861 the island became a prison for Confederate prisoners of war, including Fitzhugh Lee, Robert E. Lee's brother. The prisoners had been repatriated when, on December 1, 1868, shortly after noon, a workmen's fire spread to roof shingles, then to the gunpowder magazine which held over ten tons of gunpowder. The resulting explosion rattled New York City and New Jersey. Stables and barracks burned to the ground, though no loss of human life was reported. Spectators lined the Brooklyn shores, aghast at the terrible beauty and horror of the firestorm.

THE CONFLAGRATION—VIEW FROM FORT HAMILTON.

With little threat of war, Congress chose not to rebuild the powder storage facility, and Fort Hamilton continued with other military missions. The charred ruins stood silently on Powder Island until the Verazanno Narrows Bridge was built in the 1950s.

However, a block from Shore Road, "Louie," operated a candy store in the 1940s and '50s before the bridge was built. On quiet nights when the wind was blowing right, he used to claim, he'd hear the screams of terrified soldiers and frenzied horses, still wafting from the river.

Bridge engineers placed a major foundation pier on the island, essentially encasing it and the demolished fort in stone and concrete. Completed in 1964, the double-deck Verrazano Narrows Bridge today allows passage of thousands of vehicles between Staten Island and Brooklyn each day.

Though there seems to have been no human casualties in the explosion at Powder Island, the tumult and screams, if they still exist, are masked by traffic sounds from the bridge. Travelers of today pass over an ancient scene of conflagration and carnage, hearing only the dull roar of traffic.

Room 4714

Cadet Captain Keith Bakken thought he'd heard it all in his four years at the U.S. Military Academy at West Point, NY. Now, two perspiring plebes with ashen faces stood trembling in front of him in a brace position. It was October 22, 1972 and the two described what they had seen—an unbelievable story. " A ghost just walked through the wall of our room in the 47th Division Barracks," one said. "This is serious, sir. It was a soldier in an old cavalryman's uniform. He came through the wall, looked at us, did an about-face and sauntered back out!"

Bakken held his tongue at this report. He was about to graduate as an engineer officer, and was sure the students had mistaken some natural phenomenon for a ghost. "All right, gentlemen, I'm going to sleep in room 4714 tonight, and let's see about your ghost." He did, but no ghost appeared. Still, something bothered him. The Cadet Honor Code forbids lying, and he could see from the plebes' demeanor that they'd been frightened. He needed another opinion.

Bakken arranged for a trusted first-classman to bunk with the plebes. At the morning report the first-classman was wide-eyed. "About 0230 the room got very cold. All three of us were awake. And all three of us saw that guy walk right out of the wall, look at us, then turn and amble back into it. I ran up to the wall and felt what seemed like frost where he vanished!"

Before noontime the story was out. Cadets took positions pro and con. Some were scornful and some believed an old cavalryman might have revisited The Point. Another upperclassman slept in the room, and reportedly witnessed a mustached face and arm appearing out of a wall locker. One after another, cadets requested permission to visit or sleep in 4714 to see the specter for themselves.

One of these, Cadet Victor, showered in the first floor bathroom before taking up his vigil. Drying off outside the shower, he noted his bathrobe swinging on the door hook. No window was open and there was no breeze. Grabbing the robe he sped to Room 4714, where he spent a quiet night. The next night, Victor entered the bathroom and spotted a roll of toilet paper slowly unwinding. He used the urinal and prepared to flush it, when the handle moved and the urinal flushed itself. He rushed back to 4714 and returned with his roommate, Cadet O'Connor. They found the toilet paper roll now half unwound.

A few nights later O'Connor entered the bathroom again and spied a soldier in full dress gray seated on the toilet seat. "He was about 5 feet and 6 inches tall and seemed old. In his hand he held a musket with fixed bayonet. As we stared at one another, he stood and then vanished! His eyes were strangely white, and seemed focused on some far-off place." O'Connor reported the incident to the Charge of Quarters cadet. The Academy launched a quiet inquiry.

Another evening, in an incident that lasted perhaps forty seconds, two cadets saw a soldier's torso about five feet off the floor in 4714. The legless entity was accompanied by a room temperature that they estimated suddenly plunged to 0 degrees Fahrenheit, then rose to about 45 degrees Fahrenheit after the apparition vanished.

A formal investigation was never conducted, only an "in-house" inquiry. To the consternation of West Point authorities, *Time* Magazine and *The New York Times* treated the story with humor during November and December. Army's football team took some ribbing from U.S. Naval cadets at the annual Army-Navy football game. Time to make an assessment of facts and get on with cadet education, the Commandant's Office decided.

A number of factors seemed certain. Rapidly declining room temperatures accompanied the ghost's appearances. In one incident, cadets felt so cold they couldn't detect heat when they placed hands directly on the room's hot radiator. When the apparition vanished, the radiator again felt hot. It also seemed certain that most witnesses saw the same thing: a soldier in military dress of the mid-1800s, sometimes in a cavalry uniform, at other times in full-dress cadet gray. The style of the shako, or uniform hat, varied but slightly in witnesses' sketches.

Investigators determined that the 47th Division Barracks (Old North Barracks) was built in 1938, on a site where a West Point cavalry instructor had burned to death in his house in the 1850s. The continuing phenomena created such a distraction on campus that authorities finally closed the room and reassigned its residents to new quarters. At intervals since the 1970s the room has been briefly reopened, only to find the phenomena remain—still disruptive. So, the two-cadet room is now used for storage.

"Don't forget the other place," a Regular Army soldier at West Point reminded me. He referred to the old Morrison House, a fixture on Professors' Row. The Academy's Archives Office offered some relevant information. The century-old house is now a multi-unit residence. After graduation, a cadet from the Class of 1960 lived there for some years with his wife and eight year-old daughter.

The girl often told her parents about conversations with "the lady." The parents didn't take her seriously until they heard of Captain J.B. Bellinger who had lodged there in the 1920s. At that time, Bellinger provided sleeping space for two servant girls in a supposedly "haunted" room. One night the two young women were witnessed running sparsely clothed into the night, and screaming about a hovering ghost woman. Bellinger had then asked Father O'Keefe from Highland Falls to exorcise the spirit. The priest later reported he'd "sent her across the Hudson River to stay under a railroad bridge."

The young couple discovered that the house had earlier been the residence of a young West Point professor in the late 1800s. The man's wife contracted a terminal illness and the wife's mother nursed her through it. During the long hours of care, it seems the professor and his mother-in-law fell in love. The dying young wife became aware of it and made her husband swear he'd never marry the mother. After the wife's funeral he changed his mind and did marry the older woman. This triggered the "lady ghost's" appearances into the late 1980s.

Although the Post Engineer sealed the haunted bedroom some years ago, phenomena still continue throughout the house. In the 1980s former residents told of having things moved or turned upside down by an invisible force. A broken clock suddenly resumed operation and chimed during the night. Residents often heard heavy wheels moving across floor of the sealed room when there was no one there.

This year the U.S. Military Academy celebrates its two hundredth birthday. During those centuries, many powerful emotions and memories have been generated along the highlands and shores at West Point. The gray stone buildings seem to have retained memories and energies of these. Perhaps one day America's newly-trained army officers can go forth to duty, strengthened by knowledge and understanding from The Academy that "another world" lies just beyond this one.

3

Ghosts
On Stage

Arthur?

In 1968 Arthur Dibden was very excited. As president of Johnson State College in Johnson, VT, he was going to have a new campus! The old buildings down below the hill had served for almost a hundred years, but now here he was looking over blueprints for a state-of-the-art theater. It would be on the bluff overlooking the village of Johnson, facing south toward the mountains. He never got to see it. In November, 1969, Arthur had a seizure and died. In recognition of his foresight and planning skills, the college named the new theater Dibden Center for the Arts. Then the entertainment began, but not for the security officers for whom the new theater has been nothing but headaches.

"Come on over here and I'll show you something," said security officer Mike. "Each night we make a sweep of every nook and cranny in Dibden Hall, then we set the security alarm and exit. But we don't go far," he noted. "Ten seconds after we lock the doors they pop open and the alarm goes off. We have to do another sweep, making sure nobody is inside. Some nights we have to do this three times before the doors will stay locked."

Marielle, a student, overheard my conversation with Mike. "Yes, I was looking out my dorm window one evening and I saw those doors fly open all by themselves. At the same time the alarm sounded and the security men started running."

According to Jan Herder, Theater Director, Arthur wanted the theater to face south. Authorities decided at the last minute to put the front doors on the north. Arthur may still be petulantly expressing his preference.

Herder, himself, has had his troubles. "I've felt presences all over this place. There are energies in the costume storage room and the cellar tunnel, but I think they were here before the college. I wonder if they are caused by the four springs that geologists say are under this building. Others say that they built on an American Indian sacred site. Doors often open and close by themselves. Running water is heard, though the source of the sound is never located."

Herder has had experiences with ghosts in other places, where they tantalized his philosophical nature, but in Dibden Center the spirits cause delays and frustration.

Preparing a drama a few years ago, he and his crew were hoisting heavy spotlights up into the arch over the stage. "I had a big two and a half foot long spot standing on its end just a few feet from me. I yelled instructions to one of the guys, then went to hoist that spot. It disappeared! I'm sure nobody got close enough to steal it, so how could it have disappeared?" The missing light was found a few days later in the Green Room downstairs.

In 1995 a visiting student from Middlebury College entered the theater. He decided that the catwalk, twenty-five feet over the seats, would be the ideal place to practice chin-ups. He lost his grip and fell. Security officers who rushed to him were amazed he hadn't broken his back. "At the last minute, in mid-air, he twisted into a sitting position and landed hard in a seat, perfectly upright. He only dislocated his collarbone," a security man said.

Next to the Green Room in the basement is a small bathroom. The toilet sometimes flushes itself. Security officer Joe was patrolling the lower hall a few years ago, while his partner searched the floor overhead. The partner laughingly called out, "OK, Arthur. Show us your stuff!" The toilet flushed. "It's Arthur," Joe yelled up the stairs, "this was the toilet he used during construction. Maybe he still does!"

Sam, another security man became unnerved when the mischievous ghost flushed that toilet on his shift. It was his duty to patrol the lower hallway each night. "I just *knew* that toilet was going to flush as soon as I turned the corner. So I tried to counteract it with mind over matter. As I came up the side hallway, approaching the Green Room, I'd repeat to myself, 'Don't flush. Don't flush!' Then I'd turn the corner. You know, it really worked for a couple of weeks. I was able to stop the flushing. We've had plumber after plumber in this building. Nobody can find anything wrong. But Arthur just keeps flushing that toilet. It's bad enough that I feel an icy chill whenever I enter this building!" he sighed.

People are so focused on Arthur Dibden that they usually overlook another possibility as the culprit. In the Dibden foyer is a large display case with memorabilia for Julian Scott, town hero. Scott was born in Johnson in 1846 and enlisted as a musician in the Third Vermont Volunteer Infantry Regiment during the Civil War. He received the Congressional Medal of Honor for heroism at the battle of Lee's Mill, Virginia. After the war he studied painting in New York City under Emanuel Leutze (famous for his painting of *Washington Crossing the Delaware*). Later, after falling into a dissolute life, he went west and painted many scenes of the Great Plains and American Indians. When he died in 1901, memorabilia of his life were collected. When Dibden Center opened, the display honored his memory. Scott's army hat, eyeglasses, Bible and other effects are on display there for visitors. If the mischief in the Arts Center has an "artistry" to it, why not Julian?

Experts believe our personal effects absorb our vibrations while we are alive, and that sensitive people can "read" and receive impressions from these when we depart. Arthur, Julian or a long-ago Indian are the best candidates for these mysterious events. Dibden Center was built for drama. The spirits provide that, whether or not a play is in production.

One in the Balcony

In 1912 Dr. Simon Baruch designed a European style health spa within the newly created Spa State Reservation in Saratoga Springs, NY. Architectural plans were drawn for The Simon Baruch Research Institute, a center that would attract world-wide interest in Saratoga's healing mineral waters. He designed a 574-seat theater in the Administration Building, where he hoped doctors would convene to discuss hydrotherapy treatments. Baruch died, however, before his ambitious plans were realized. His son Bernard Baruch's close friendship with President Franklin Roosevelt permitted the Spa's completion under the Reconstruction Finance Corporation in 1935. Over six million federal and state dollars were invested in the spacious facility, but by then America had fallen in love with pills and surgery as the answer to illness. Homeopathic medicine and hydrotherapy were coming more and more to be looked upon as "quackery." The doctors never came in any great numbers, and the symposia were never held. Then, as today, except during the summer season, the grounds are quiet, though not yet a ghost town.

After the end of World War II the theater finally came alive as "The Spa Summer Theater" on the Straw Hat Circuit. In the 1960s, when the theater was included in the Saratoga Performing Arts Center's (SPAC) summer season, it became the venue for many local and national performing groups. John Houseman, crusty star of television's long-running *The Paper Chase,* came to Saratoga Springs to film Peter Straub's novel, *Ghost Story* in 1971. He spent leisure time exploring the State Park grounds, admiring the buildings' Georgian architecture. In 1979 he reached an agreement with SPAC to bring his drama group, The Acting Company, to a summer residency in the old theater.

SPAC honored him by naming the facility "The Houseman Theater." Houseman had a four-year alliance with SPAC in the early 1980s. Then, following a dispute with management in 1984, he took his acting company back to New York City and his name was promptly removed from the marquee. He died on Halloween in 1988.

Today the "Spa Little Theater," as it is known, is a summer showplace for SPAC's popular chamber music concerts. In the fall and winter, however, it is the site of Home Made Theater's locally produced dramas. But whoever launches a program there must contend with the year-round resident ghosts. Stage crews often hear muted conversations taking place elsewhere in the theater, though the talkers are never found. Especially late at night, during tech rehearsals, a cast or crewmember often catches sight of a shadow flitting through the balcony's left doorway. Sometimes the shadow is accompanied by movement of the doorway curtain, though nobody is ever there. Most of them think the balcony ghost is a man.

Speculation about that ghost's identity centers on either Monty Wooley or John Houseman. Character actor Monty Wooley, famed for his portrayal of Sheridan Whiteside in *The Man Who Came to Dinner,* grew up in Saratoga Springs. Following his Hollywood career he often performed the role in the Spa Summer Theater during the late 1940s. Perhaps Monty stayed on after death to savor the certain applause of a hometown crowd. If it's Houseman, perhaps the prankster in this acerbic man surfaced, and he decided to return to his namesake theater as an invisible critic.

When she became theater manager a few years ago, Susan was told by crewmembers that the theater had at least one female ghost. They believed it was a woman, and dubbed her "Nancy." There is scant evidence who Nancy might be, but Susan thinks she may have been a former theater manager or an influential woman who lined up acts for the theater at one time. "I have seen her several times myself," Susan said. "She seems to be in her late forties or early fifties and wears a loose-fitting dress from the 1920s or early 1930s. Many times I can hear her high heels clicking through the halls before I see her. As originally designed, our floors are terrazzo, though they've been carpeted for the last ten years. I also hear piano music when I work late at night. We have three pianos in the theater, but only the one in the Green Room is kept tuned. No matter where I am in the building when I hear music it's always drifting from the Green Room.

"One night I sat at my desk, putting my hair up before the audience began to arrive. I sat for a minute with a hair clip held in my hand, deciding where to put it. Suddenly it was grabbed from my fingers and flew away. I spent precious time looking for it, but it was nowhere around my desk. I got another, did my hair, and went out to greet people. Three days later I found the clip right underneath the desk—an area that I'd thoroughly searched. I'm not the only one to lose things, though. One night we had a very famous musician readying himself in the Green Room before a concert. He knocked on my door, very agitated that his watch had disappeared from on top of the piano. I'm so used to the ghost,now,that I often talk to him or her. So, I left the musician's presence, went to a quiet corner and asked the ghost to please return the man's watch. Thirty minutes later he came to the office beaming. He had just found it in the pocket of a starched shirt he was to wear at the next night's concert.

"The ghost sure has a sense of humor," she smiled. "One night we had a seamstress finishing a costume in the work room. She found six matching buttons to sew on, and lined them up on her table. She walked across the room to get a spool of thread, and when she returned there were six buttons, to be sure, but they were all different! She picked them up and took them across the room, got six more matching buttons and returned. But when she got to her worktable, the original six matching buttons were there, all in a row."

Meantime, props continue to disappear though they usually reappear. Unseen hands move equipment, much to the consternation of the stage crew. The hollow voices continue to echo when the theater is empty. In the fall of 1998 a curious event took place during the staging of *Lettice and Lovage*. Prior to one performance two actors in The Green Room reminisced about roles they had played in various productions. There is a taboo in American theater against mentioning Shakespeare's *Macbeth* by name, so one of them used the euphemism "The Scottish Play." As he did so there was a power outage that plunged the theater into darkness. Coincidence? Then it was also discovered that the lead actress had, at that moment, lost her voice, so that night's production had to be cancelled. Was there a spectral belly laugh from the balcony as technicians tried unsuccessfully to explain the power failure? Was one of two great American thespians to blame? Or was this an example of Nancy's "management?"

Curtain Call

Cohoes Music Hall
Cohoes, New York

Constructed in 1874
Major Restoration in 1974

In 1874 the bank decided to become both the financial and entertainment center of the river city of Cohoes, NY. Famous for the mastodon skeleton found in the riverbank, Cohoes was a town of textile mills and foundries. The working men and women of the community needed classy entertainment, said the bank directors, and they shelled out $60,000 for the conversion of the building's top floor to a music hall. Before the century ended the building was known for its Music Hall more than its banking. "Build it and they will come," to paraphrase a recent film, and come they did…comedians, bands, singers, jugglers, magicians, trained animal acts, opera stars and dancers. Many neophyte entertainers "died" on that stage. Known as "The Hook" on the vaudeville circuit, the Cohoes Music Hall brought performers into contact, it is said, with one of the coldest audiences in the business. Either you made it in Cohoes, or you never saw Broadway's lights.

In 1882 a twelve year-old girl, a Canadian immigrant to Cohoes, Eva Tanguay, stepped before the gaslights and won the audience's grudging approval. Appearing at first with her partner George Graham, Eva's earthy singing style swayed the hearts of laborers and immigrants, and took her from Cohoes to the Ziegfield Follies on New York's Broadway, the "Great White Way." Then, as a risqué, bold and brassy solo act, she crisscrossed America, winning more hearts than heads with her rendition of *I Don't Care*. She became one of the most successful and wealthy performers in Vaudeville.

In the 1920s "talking pictures" slowly pushed vaudeville out of the public's affections, and most vaudevillians didn't survive the transition to movies or, later, television. In the 1930s Eva began losing her sight, and retired to California, where she died arthritic and blind in 1947. However there was no audience at the Music Hall to grieve her passing. The hall had closed its doors in 1901. When the spirit of Eva Tanguay returned to Cohoes, the old theater sat well-preserved—filled with dust, cobwebs and a thousand memories.

In the 1960s lovers of Cohoes history began to mobilize for the restoration and reopening of the old theater, which was accomplished in 1974, following the Cohoes Savings Bank's donation of the building to the city. Now, in addition to the theater, the structure houses offices and a terrific local museum. And Eva's picture is there…big as life. Perhaps her ghost is there too. Walter Lipka, city historian, doesn't believe the ghost in the building is Eva Tanguay, but his voice is almost lost amid the sentimental chorus of those who want to believe she has returned to the Music Hall. One thing nobody argues about is the spectral phenomena that continue to be reported.

The Opera Excelsior, a local performing group, offered music and plays following the reopening. Its director remembers that there developed a running joke about a feathered boa used by some long ago performer. Nightly it would appear on the backstage ready rack, as if a performer would use it that evening, but it was not needed as a prop. It was taken back downstairs for storage, but the next night there it was in the wings again. Then there was the incident concerning a mysterious raincoat that *was* needed as a prop in a later play, and which kept disappearing from the rack. There were two other props: a suitcase and a pair of pajamas, to be used in another play. The two items often disappeared and later reappeared with the pajamas *folded* inside the suitcase.

Martie Hamilton, Publicity Director for Heritage Artists, worked in the Hall during the 1980s, typing out lists of ticket holders and contributors. One night, on a special "rush job" she began printing out a computer list of major contributors. With the task about one-third done, the computer died. Her husband (a GE Company engineer) came in about ten o'clock that evening to assist her. As the two discussed the computer dilemma they overheard a man and woman conversing loudly out in the hallway. She went out to see who could have come into the building through the locked street doors. Nobody was there. She returned to the computer, only to have the discussion outside her door resume, this time rapidly and angrily. She and her husband went into the hall but, again, nobody was there. On the third repetition of the argument, both stayed put. Knowing the building's reputation, they knew they'd find no disputants outside. Then, as if by magic, without the engineer's intervention, the computer glitch simply vanished.

Bill Schwarting, retired teacher and expert dowser, heard mention of the Music Hall's ghosts on the radio and offered his services in dowsing where the ghost might be located. After careful perusal of the theater he found a woman (Eva?) sitting in seats 106-108 in the balcony. Some folks claim to have seen a filmy presence at that spot when no one is performing on stage. Linda Tremblay, the good-natured director of the Music Hall and Museum today, also had her difficulties. One evening she finished work, locked the door, and left the building for dinner with her husband. Later that night they drove back past the building and were surprised to see the theater ceiling lights on. To her husband, she said, "Didn't you *see* me turn those lights off?" He nodded yes. So, up she went to turn them off again. While not necessarily believing in ghosts, Linda did speak out quite forcefully to the empty theater (as she was leaving) "Go to sleep! Leave the lights off!" And they stayed off.

Throughout the 1990s the Clifton Park Players used the Music Hall as their performance center. Their final performance in the hall came in the late summer of 2000, when they staged *Grease*. On opening night, as the orchestra struck up the overture, the elevator arrived from downstairs, beeped and opened its doors. Nobody exited. A minor disturbance, to be sure, but it should not have happened. Each performance night, when the overture begins, a switch is thrown downstairs to turn off the elevator, and late arrivals deservedly must climb a flight of stairs to the theater. Finally, the elevator door closed and the audience turned its attention to the music once again.

The curtains opened and the play began. The empty elevator appeared once more, and opened its doors with a beep and a swoosh, this time at the balcony level. When the door opened, no passenger exited. The door closed again, while on stage the school principal spoke a line that would launch the play's first spirited song. Her words, about her school's alumni, concluded: "we remember them just the way they used to be!" Then came the rousing (and quite bawdy) song. At that moment, the elevator beeped on the balcony level, opened its doors, and then began a noisy and rapid opening and closing that continued throughout the first act. One staff member who saw it remarked that it was if the elevator doors were "applauding" the song. In the audience were a former city planner and an engineer. Rushing quickly to the balcony they were unable to figure a remedy for this distraction. The elevator company's emergency technician was called and he arrived near the end of the first act. "I'll be darned," was his comment. "The problem is with the electric eye in the system. It's not easy to get at, but *somebody* has moved it so that it can't make a contact, so it doesn't know whether to open or close!" Though he fixed the problem and the rest of the performance was uneventful, the entire idea of "knowing when to open or close" brings an echo of the old vaudeville days, doesn't it? One wonders if the spirit of the performance was just too much for Eva, so she joined in the activity in the best way she could.

Radio station WGY's "morning man" Don Weeks loves to do a Halloween spectacular each year, offering a contest in which lucky listeners can spend the night before Halloween in a haunted building. In October 2000 Don chose the Music Hall, and on Halloween morning he interviewed that year's winners after they had passed the previous night in sleeping bags on the theater floor. The couple told of thumps, bangings, ice cold drafts (in October?) and a window overlooking Remsen Street that just would not stay shut. Three times during the night they found it open to the weather. Weeks delights his listeners with his credulous interviews and has had personal experiences with a ghost in his former home in Schenectady.

If Eva did relatively few performances in Cohoes Music Hall, and if her fame came in New York City and other big cities, why would her spirit return to the city? The answer may lie in the unresolved issues of her heart. As a youngster she was enamored of Danny Cosgro, an Irish immigrant lad who became a respected and very ethical lawyer in Cohoes. Just as Eva left the city for Broadway fame, she and Danny had a powerful quarrel that cooled the ardor of their romance. He eventually was elected the city's mayor and she went on to become a show business legend. Whenever she had a performance scheduled in or near Cohoes in later years, Danny would always take her to dinner. Through the years Eva had three husbands but Danny never married. It's possible that her spirit has returned to Cohoes to recapture both the love of an old beau and the acclaim of the ghost audiences, which must still show up.

If her spirit came back in 1947, following her death, she would have found her old theater closed and filled with cobwebs. One can almost hear her outrage, and see her sweeping across the stage, yelling, "Let's get some *life* into this place!" And, sure enough, life did return to the old theater. So if she takes a hand in setting out what she thinks are the appropriate props, or rearranging a show's costumes, or even providing some impromptu sideshows, who can blame her? She knew what *style* was.

You Oughta Be in Pictures

In the 1920s Loew's Picture Corporation built a grand theater on South Salina Street in Syracuse, NY, just in time for the heyday of "talking pictures." Vaudeville was dying as entertainment, and movies came into vogue. For many years movies stayed in, but American lifestyles continually change, and with the coming of television, families found other diversions. Likewise, Syracuse's downtown lost its attractiveness in the face of multiplying suburban theaters. By 1976 business had declined enough for the owners to consider razing the old theater. Syracuse was about to lose a landmark.

That year, however, local history lovers and admirers of old theater décor combined their efforts to preserve the building, and renovate it to suit modern tastes. A combined task force purchased the building, and commissioned the theater's rejuvenation. As the work crews began their labors, however, they discovered a fact that had been whispered for years—the theater had a ghost. A deathly pale young woman dressed in white was seen moving through the middle balcony, and sometimes near the restrooms. Volunteers and employees alike testified to feeling icy drafts. When the building was relatively quiet, witnesses claimed to hear voices speaking somewhere else in the theater. The location of the speakers was never found, and the words were never distinct enough to understand, but it *was* human speech—of that they were sure.

The building was renamed The Landmark Theater, and its first manager, Richard Johnson was asked about the spectral trespassers that people encountered. "I don't believe in ghosts, and never saw one during my tenure there," he said. His stagehands, however, begged to differ—they had often heard a young woman's voice calling them by their first names. They never were able to find her. Theater volunteers Bonnie Beth Derby and Bill Knowlton were convinced The Landmark had a ghost. Derby was part of a group on stage rehearsing a Halloween program in 1983. A motion in the balcony caught her eye and she looked up. She described her experience as seeing "a walking mirage of a woman threading her way through the balcony seats. She opened an exit door up there, and went outside."

Several staff members sought the help of a local psychic, reputed to be sensitive and accurate in her information. She came to the theater and seated herself in the third row, relaxed, and then gave her impression. She sensed the name "Claire." The spirit is said to have spoken to the woman and told her she had once been married to a Loew's employee and always wanted to be an actress, but never went far in her tryouts. Apparently, she died before she could achieve fame, so as a spirit, came to the theater to be near her husband. Long after her death, and after Loew's went out of business, she found her permanent role—supervising all productions in The Landmark Theater from the balcony. It seems likely that she finds directing preferable to acting.

Dorset Playhouse

I walked up to the young construction man standing in the doorway of Vermont's Dorset Playhouse. He wore a hardhat and overalls, and was opening his morning coffee. He was in a good mood as he slipped off his work gloves. "Can I help you?" he asked.

"I hope so," I answered. "Let me give you a scenario. While you're working, you put a tool down, then turn to find it gone. Sometime later you find it, but other times it has vanished for good. When you lock up at night, you stow a piece of equipment carefully, only to find it moved when you return in the morning." His eyes widened and he stared. The coffee cup never got to his lips.

"How do you know that? Who told you?"

I laughed and explained to him that I already knew the theater had a reputation for being haunted. In fact, though not knowing specifically what the phenomena were, I was pretty sure the men remodeling the old theater building would have encountered the experiences I proffered. Construction men everywhere find such experiences common where there are ghosts and the structure is undergoing renovation. He relaxed and smiled, and we had a good conversation about the difficulties his construction crew had experienced since the fall of 2000, when the original summer theater was almost entirely demolished. "I never heard about ghosts here, but it sure explains a lot of things we've experienced. Lots of stuff has come up missing," he told me. "We're professionals here, and almost never mess with another guy's tools—they're our bread and butter. But it happens. Things disappear and sometimes they are never returned. I don't believe in ghosts, but I don't know who's taking our tools and moving the machines. There's no logical explanation for the things we've experienced." My research has turned up hundreds of such cases, and I was confident that the ghosts of Dorset Playhouse were making the transition to the new building. I found the proof I expected. In fact, such events *are* "logical."

In 1929 a group of theater lovers assembled three old barns into a rustic summer theater, which became an integral part of the summer theater "Straw Hat Circuit" throughout the northeastern United States. Famous stars of Broadway and Hollywood loved the opportunity to let down and vacation in Vermont's Green Mountains. There they could avoid urban heat and turmoil while acting in productions both dramatic and comical. By 1999 the old barn structure needed replacing and expansion, if growing numbers of patrons were to continue enjoying Dorset's summer season.

By the spring of 2000 architect's plans were completed for a state-of-the-art replacement that would retain the old theater's rustic facade. After that season everything except one barn was demolished. Concrete footings were poured, and throughout the winter of 2000-2001 work crews quickly built the frame, installed new electrical wiring and plumbing, and finished the interior of a new theater. The original barn was kept as the front entryway and ticket booths. Despite there not being much original structure for a ghost to cling to, there was apparently enough, as ghostly pranks continued in the theater workshop after construction was finished in the summer of 2001.

How does a theater acquire a ghost? In the 1960s a hard-working electrical technician, Barry, working late at night, readied the lighting system for an upcoming production. One spotlight near the low roof still needed adjusting during the dry tech rehearsal. Suddenly an electrical storm burst upon the village. The ground outside rapidly became soaked. Though his friends told him to wait, Barry sprang into the rafters and had just placed his hand on the light's metal supports, when a great flash of lightning struck outside. A great surge of electricity enveloped the building and Barry became part of the circuit through which it flowed into the earth. He died immediately. Family and friends missed him, and his funeral was well attended, but in theater "the show must go on." On opening night, some of Barry's tools were missing from the box where he'd always kept them. They were later found in spots where he used to sit and watch the show. One night an actor saw a semi-transparent man backstage and asked him for help, only to see the wraith walk through a closed door. A woman friend of Barry's swore she saw him backstage on another night. Those who acknowledged the theater's haunting just assumed the ghost was Barry, and drew comfort from the sightings because he was a trusted friend.

When I visited the theater during reconstruction, I spoke with a summer crewmember who also worked on the winter construction crew. PJ, as he is known, told me there are two ghosts that are often seen. Barry, the electrician, is one, and the second one appears to be a former longtime summer patron. Crew and staff members remember seeing her in the audience every summer for years, but time has obscured their memory of her name. She is instantly recognizable by her wide red straw hat and white gloves. Only about five feet tall, she sports an old-fashioned flower print dress and glasses. All who have seen her remember her unfailing quiet smile. "She never bothers anybody. She's just here. We're certain she died some years ago, but almost every summer somebody sees her, waiting in a ticket line or seated in the audience," he told me.

How nice that old traditions continue at the Playhouse. A summer visitor from yesteryear, who just can't soak up enough of Dorset's summer ambience, joins an electrician, dedicated to the precision of his craft. Hopefully they'll find adjoining seats, where they can talk over old times and productions between acts.

Smith's Opera House

For William Smith money grew on trees. Lots of them. He came to America from England in 1837 and, with his brothers, made a fortune in the nursery business in Geneva, NY. Ornamentals and fruit trees of good quality were in great demand in the Victorian Age. By the 1890s the kindly Smith was able to put up $12,000 for the construction of an opera house that bore his name. Many shabby houses were demolished to clear a space for the theater on Seneca Street. Built of the finest materials in 1894, it offered upholstered chairs for even the lowest price seats. An ingenious ceiling with illuminated stars and moving clouds gave patrons the impression of being outdoors once the theater's house lights were extinguished. America's most famous actors and actresses of that era came to Geneva. Their productions were interspersed with vaudeville shows until movies pushed both forms of theater aside. But other dramas took place; ones the public wasn't privileged to see.

William Smith was a dedicated Spiritualist, and his personal life was filled with spirit contacts during séances held in the theater's upstairs rooms. Perhaps some spirits stayed on. As so many investigators of spirit phenomena have testified, amateurs summoning discarnate entities non-selectively can cause trouble, as the beings may find their new surroundings more appealing and may enjoy raising havoc there. Once summoned, they may not want to return to the spirit kingdom after the séance conductor has dismissed them. The present theater staff cannot remember when the first stories of ghosts began to circulate, but they've been around for years.

In the early 1970s, when it was known as The Geneva Theater, stage crews often spotted a woman in turn-of-the-century clothing in the balcony. She would disappear by the time they could reach the balcony to confront her. "Up With People" played in the old Opera House in the early 1980s. They hired an overnight security guard to protect their equipment on stage. At 1:30 a.m. he heard loud footsteps crossing the stage. The work lights were on and nobody could be seen. He became nervous. About 3 a.m. he heard a person running across the stage, though he could clearly see that nobody was there. Then, in the projection booth at the rear of the theater he heard movement and a mechanical noise very like the loading of a film into the projector. There was no illumination in the rear of the house, and becoming increasingly ill at ease, he chose not to investigate further. When the group finally performed the next day, a mysterious light rain fell backstage, soaking performers readying to go on stage. No leak was ever found overhead. In later years Production Manager John Parker heard the same footsteps that the night watchman had heard, without any actor or crewmember being visible on stage.

In early 1994 an acoustical engineer ran tests inside the theater, making sure recent renovations hadn't changed the unique resonance there. He found a "dead spot" in the sixth row, just to the left of stage center, where for some reason, it is almost impossible to hear sounds from any other part of the theater. As the man brought his acoustic equipment to that spot, all other sounds in the theater vanished and he heard, "Help! Help!" He moved the microphones just a foot to either side and heard nothing through the headphones. Yet, at that single spot he heard an anguished voice calling out. Was it the timeless echo of James O'Neill long ago playing The Count of Monte Cristo? Or might the voice have resonated from the time of melodramas that appeared on the movie screen during the theater's incarnation as The Strand, and still playing in time?

Today the old theater has passed its centennial and has been wonderfully restored. When you visit Geneva, pop in and see "what's playing?" Maybe you'll find yourself perceiving a drama on which the final curtain has not yet dropped.

Olive

The fabulously gilded New Amsterdam Theater opened on Broadway in New York City on October 26, 1903, staging the best in European and American drama. In 1907 Franz Lehar's operetta, *The Merry Widow*, had its world premiere there. In 1913, however, in a departure from those lofty goals, it offered Ziegfield's "Follies" until 1927. During those years George M. Cohan produced his famous *Forty-five Minutes to Broadway* on its stage. With a final staging of Shakespeare's *Othello*, the theater closed in 1937. It was then recast as a movie house, showing less-than-memorable fare, and becoming scuffed and worn over time. Offerings dropped below B quality in the early 1980s, and historians and theater buffs contemplated The New Amsterdam's restoration.

Theo, a college student, worked at the Times Square Theater across the street in 1982, and liked to collect old playbills, posters and other ephemera. He often hung around The New Amsterdam when his shift finished. Sometimes a projectionist friend let Theo go up to the remains of the old Aerial Gardens, a smaller, abandoned theater built above the main theater. This small theater had once been the rage of café theater productions, but now was rented only occasionally for rehearsals. Several times it was used to stage the New York State Lottery drawings.

On his first trip "up into the rafters," looking for memorabilia, Theo took a flashlight, and upon going through an access door, found himself near the Ladies Powder Room. Only dim light penetrated the large old dirty windows. He heard a faint singing, but could not find its source, despite a thorough visual inspection. He recognized the music as a '20s show tune, distinct from the Kung Fu soundtrack wafting from the main theater downstairs. He feared a rehearsal was in progress and, as his friend had warned him about getting into trouble up there, he retreated.

On his next visit a few weeks later, he heard music again, but considering himself to be a logical, rational college science student, he didn't consider the possibility of ghosts. The curtain in the small theater was partially open, but nobody was visible—still the music continued. He ascended the ramp onto the stage. The melody was coming from a spot on stage left, near some old plywood sets and a door to the upstairs dressing rooms. Then the music shifted to stage right! He went to the door and now the music seemed to emanate from upstairs. It was all too spooky in the murky light, and despite his logic and reason, he left with only emotional memorabilia.

The next time, about 5:30 p.m., a movement on the stage caught his eye. "I saw the most fabulous, beautiful actress gliding from stage right to stage left. She wore a bright white gown with a crinoline or hoop skirt, and carried a small purse. Her jet-black hair hung in ringlets, and she was smiling. I was stunned by her beauty and wondered who she was. The music continued, and I approached the stage. Then she disappeared, and the music stopped. I walked upstage, behind the rear curtain, and searched the entire area. Nobody. Then the music came from the seats, and I peered out through the curtain. She was strolling in the balcony, and singing as she *drifted* among the seats! Before, she'd looked happy, but now was forlorn. Then she vanished again. I was covered with goose bumps and scrammed.

"I didn't want to be ridiculed by my projectionist friends, so I didn't tell them about my experiences at first. But, the next week, I felt compelled to return to the small theater. This time the music had such an emotional intensity that I simply couldn't stay. As I passed the projection booth, my friends asked why I'd returned so quickly. I told them of the strange rehearsal I'd witnessed upstairs, and asked what group had rented the space. They laughed at me and asked if I knew what was going on. Naively, I said I didn't. 'That's Olive's ghost, you fool. Don't you know this is the most haunted theater in New York City?' they joshed. Still, hard-headed, I rejected the idea, and didn't go back again. The cinema closed the following week, and the building was then boarded up.

"A friend, George, had a background in theater and was involved in dramatic groups, so I asked him what he knew about a ghost there. He offered to loan me his book about The New Amsterdam, and when I saw him a few months later, he gave it to me. Inside were pictures of old production scenes, of actors and actresses in costumes. And there *she* was—in the costume I'd seen. Olive!

"Olive Thomas was a Ziegfield girl, and had married Jack Pickford, actress Mary Pickford's brother. She died at age thirty-one on September 10, 1920, in a French hospital, after swallowing a large dose of mercury bichloride. But why she took the mixture, alone in her Ritz Hotel bathroom in Paris, while her husband allegedly lay drunk on the bed, was never satisfactorily explained. Some suspected murder; others thought suicide. I wondered why her spirit returned to the New Amsterdam, while her body was interred in the Pickford crypt in Woodlawn Cemetery. Having seen an apparently alive Olive on stage and then in a book, I was beginning to accept the possibility of ghosts.

"Then I remembered a man named Joe, that I knew at the Victory Theater. When I first asked him about Olive's ghost, he denied the ghost's existence. But two years later, after retiring, Joe admitted he knew the story. He'd worked at the New Amsterdam twenty years earlier, doing plumbing and maintenance work. He was told then (in the 1960s) not to go unaccompanied to the second floor, but nobody explained why."

Months later, after recovering from an injury, Joe returned to work and was told he had to fix a leak that had suddenly developed over center stage. Sure enough, water was dripping from up in the "grid," forty feet overhead. The only way to that spot was a rickety ladder on the stage wall. He climbed cautiously to the top, then inched his way out onto the catwalk. Directly over center stage, was a brass fire extinguisher turned upright, but with a wet nozzle. There was nothing to be fixed, so he descended, puzzled as to who could have upended the extinguisher, let it empty, then turned it upright for him to find. And, beside that, the only way such a prankster could have gotten down from the grid would have been to pass him on the ladder he'd just climbed. So, is there a maintenance man ghost in the old theater too?

In 1997 The Disney Corporation reopened a magnificently restored New Amsterdam Theater, and premiered *The Lion King* on November 13. But how many in today's audiences know that Olive, a former queen in that theater, is still rehearsing upstairs?

Public
Service
Ghosts

The Stations

"I've got a few minutes and a couple of questions," she thought, "so I'll just pop in the station and surprise my husband." Her spouse, Sean, is a veteran firefighter at Station 1 in Cohoes, NY. Moving into the truck bay, toward the rear of the ladder truck where old gear was stowed, she greeted her mate with a big smile. He was glad to see her, but they had hardly begun their conversation when she turned white as a sheet, started backing up, and excused herself. "I gotta go, Sean," she mumbled as she quickly made her way outside into the sunshine. "What's wrong honey?" he asked, following her, "you look like you've seen a ghost!" Shaking, she responded that indeed *that* was what just happened.

"Old Station Number One"

"Station Number Two"

Sean had heard rumors from the old timers but had never really given credence to their stories. Now, he listened as his wife described seeing a fireman in the old-style uniform walk through a doorway behind him in the firehouse. "He had the old-style suit on, but no airpack. He had the old-style helmet and a big handlebar mustache," she explained. "It was almost like one of the old photographs you have on the wall inside," she continued as they retraced their steps to the doorway where the apparition had vanished. There was just nobody answering that description on duty. He knew all the guys, and none of them would want to wear the old firefighter's gear. And he knew his wife took his job too seriously to invent such a tale.

After his wife left, Sean ran the story past his partner Shamus, also a veteran in the department. Shamus didn't believe in ghosts and gave no credence to any of the tales. However, he reminded Sean that there were many strange stories, especially at Station 2 on Pleasant Avenue. When he'd been assigned there, he admitted, he himself had had an unexplainable experience. Asleep at night in the bunk area upstairs, he'd heard and felt someone stride past his bed and enter the kitchenette. Opening his eyes Shamus saw clearly that nobody was in that room. In the year 2000, a fellow firefighter told him of bumping hard into some other body in that firehouse, though he could clearly see no one else was there. "Well, that's not the least of it," Shamus' friend had said. "We also have a coffee pot that turns itself on. Even the guys who know everything about electricity just can't figure how that can happen."

Sean was fascinated that these strange events were almost yearly adventures at Station 2. He began asking questions at both stations. Joe Holmes, a veteran at Station 1, said, "Over the years we've had difficulty with something turning the lights back on after we went to bed. It wasn't just the overhead lights, but also the bedside lamps. You might have to switch them off several times before they'd stay off. At other times, when we'd turn them on, they'd switch off. And the TV was the same. In the day room we'd be watching the news and the set would pop off; or vice-versa. In the day room, reclined in a chair one day, I felt a breeze, as if someone had just walked past. Then someone or something bumped my chair, but no one was there.

"One winter day my regular partner was off and a new man and I were on duty together. We worked on the truck all day, then he hung his gear on the side of the truck. As we did this, we heard someone walking down the stairs. We turned, because we knew no one was upstairs. Then we heard his gear hit the floor behind us. Walking back to the truck, we found his coat about three feet from where it should have fallen if it fell normally. We looked at each other and said nothing. He re-hung the gear and we went upstairs. Five minutes later we heard the coat hit the floor again—the metal clasps made a recognizable sound. We went down and found his coat apparently thrown about ten feet from the truck this time. We looked at one another and asked, 'Wilkie?' Wilkie had been a fireman's fireman, a big guy who had died a few years before. We had to blame this ghostly stuff on someone we knew from this station."

Another of the Station 2 firefighters told him about "Lowell." This man had been a firefighter at Station 2 but had been murdered by another fireman in a "lover's quarrel triangle" in the 1980s. Shortly thereafter, the woman dispatcher looked up from her console one day and saw Lowell peering in the window at her. Stunned, she had to be temporarily relieved from duty.

Sean learned that certain doors at Station 2 sometimes would open and close themselves, and that Lowell was sometimes seen seated on the rear seat of the hook and ladder truck, ready to answer the next alarm. On that particular truck, near that rear seat, are stowed old chains seldom used anymore. Firefighters walking past that vehicle in the station are sometimes startled by the sound of jingling chains, when nobody is visible on the truck.

Readers of ghost stories are likely knowledgeable that ghosts can haunt their former place of work as well as the house they lived in. Men and women dedicated to their jobs in life are likely to return to those familiar places, perhaps re-enacting their lifetime labors for some time before letting go of their assignment and "moving on." It is to the credit of the City of Cohoes Fire Department that they have inspired such loyalty in at least one "old hand," who likes to return to the station from time to time. The firefighters who work there wish their former comrades would stay "retired."

Rescue

"Rescue Ten, this is 307," came the radio call. Mark, already on duty, took up the mike and responded, "307, this is Rescue Ten." "Rescue Ten, we have an EMS call for you on Division Street," came the response, which then furnished the house number. "That's *my* old house!" Mark said out loud. He and his partner hurried to the site and found a roofer sitting on the ground, where a small crowd had gathered. The man had slipped unaccountably from the steep-pitched third floor roof. A bit feisty, he denied medical treatment, so Mark turned his attention to the man's story. He had fallen but hadn't slipped. He didn't know why he was on the ground. Greatly mystified, he resumed the roof work. Mark and Rescue Ten went on to other work in Amsterdam, NY.

"That's where I lived for thirty years," Mark said, "and it was one thing after another all the while we lived there. The house dates from 1889 and we learned that a roofer had once fallen to his death there before we moved in, but we didn't know the previous owners. Our extended family had its own tragedies during our years there. Cousin Rita, who lived with us, died of an illness. Shortly afterward her grieving father, my Uncle Leo, who also lived there, hanged himself in the garage.

"I later became a city fireman, then a fire investigator after our family moved out, and one of my earlier investigations was a fire that destroyed the house's old garage. By the time I got there the police had arrived and we tried to take evidence photos because arson was suspected. The police camera wouldn't work. Mine did, but take a look at the pictures I took," he said.

Mark and I looked over the evidence photos and most of them showed either a ball of light in mid-air or smoky clouds. I figured it was ambient smoke rising from the charred beams. "That's not so," Mark continued, "the fire was out! Look at these pictures taken from a different angle—there is no smoke in any of them. But right there, where that fog is, is where Uncle Leo hanged himself. Next day, the police used another camera and that second batch of photos did come out, but theirs' were as fogged as mine, even though the fire had been out for a day and a half! In a way, I wasn't surprised. When Sharon and I married, we lived upstairs, and had lots of strange experiences while we lived there.

"My father died shortly after we were married. Just a short time later she began to feel someone right behind her as she climbed the stairs, and wondered if it was Dad. Then, when I was taking a shower one day, I felt someone tap me on the shoulder. Of course nobody was there. I told Sharon about it, and two weeks later she had the same experience. Whoever the spirit was, it then frightened us in our bedroom. Sharon woke me several times in the middle of the night saying, 'Mark, look! He's right here at the side of the bed!' But each time, I didn't dare to look." In desperation, Sharon sought out Mark's grandmother (who lived downstairs), told her of the incidents and described the ghost. Grandmother got out some old photos and Sharon immediately picked out the visage of Uncle Leo.

On another night Sharon saw a girl in white walking through their bedroom, and wondered if it was Cousin Rita. The couple began to postulate that the physical similarities between Sharon and the deceased Rita were attracting the family ghosts. At Christmastime in 1984 Sharon, Mark, and Grandmother were admiring the Christmas tree, when suddenly a ghostly woman appeared, circled the tree and disappeared into the bedroom. No one was there when they pursued to look. After all this spectral activity, Sharon confessed she'd seen a ghost man in a rocking chair when she had first moved in. Grandmother also had her experiences there, but seldom talked about the strange noises she heard in the basement.

At her job in an area hospital, Sharon registered a new patient with tuberculosis. "He didn't make it, though," she said, "he died the next day. Then, a few days later, I developed a cough. Oh no, I've got TB, I thought, so I had myself tested. Worried, I went home to bed, where I slept fitfully. In the middle of the night I awoke to see a woman in white floating in the bedroom. She gestured toward me with hands outstretched, but I couldn't understand what she wanted. Two days later I got my test results and they were negative. Shortly thereafter, relatives told me the cause of Cousin Rita's death was TB. I had always thought it was cancer. The apparition could have been Rita watching over me, and telling me that everything would be okay."

At work Sharon chatted with a woman who had known Uncle Leo, and learned that he had given her a parrot just before he committed suicide. Two weeks after Leo's death she found the bird dead, hanged inside a bird toy, which would have been almost impossible to get into.

Eventually, after Grandmother died, Mark and Sharon built a new house elsewhere in Amsterdam, and in 1991 bid farewell to the old place on Division Street. The house sat vacant for almost three years waiting for a new owner. During that time a city Code Enforcement Officer came to inspect the place and noticed the downstairs side porch door open. As he approached the house he heard a dog barking and a woman screaming inside. Upon entering, he found nobody there. When Mark heard the story he remembered that Grandmother used to rest on a couch just inside the door and yell at her dogs. Two neighborhood girls told him that when the house was vacant, they had seen the side door open and went in, only to have objects fly off a shelf, right at them. Needless to say, they beat a hasty retreat.

In early July 2001 Mark saw a story on WTEN-TV about the house's new owner having been cheated by a window installer. He learned she worked at a local store and went to visit her. Gingerly approaching the subject of ghosts after he introduced himself, he asked her if anything strange ever took place there. "Yes, people talk to me out of nowhere," she responded. "Last year I passed by the house and fell in love with it. I got out of my car and stood by the porch and began crying. I said to God, 'Oh how I wish I could own this house, but I just don't have the money.' Then I heard an inner voice say, 'Buy the house, the money will come!' I investigated the financing and found I was *just* able to afford it. My husband and I began to fix it up and I noticed a problem in the front hallway. The door into the living room would continually open itself, even though I shut it several times a day."

Mark took me to meet the woman, and she spoke frankly to me also. "One day I asked out loud why this door keeps opening, and a voice said loudly, 'She's looking for something.' Having known Mark for a short time, I asked him about it. He told me his grandmother always had tried to keep the door closed, too, and he thinks it is his grandmother's ghost still prowling the house."

The old house still sits on Division Street, and is being restored to some of its former beauty. Its new owner loves it. And apparently it still has some of its former family members. Mark and Sharon and their children have a new home, but have special fond memories of the house on Division Street, where the term "extended family" took on a whole new meaning to them.

Engine Company 18

"The Old Engine 18 Firehouse"

Firefighter John Shirley, roused from his sleep in the second floor dormitory, muttered, "Which one of the guys is up walking tonight?" Looking at his watch, which read almost 2 a.m., he peered toward the doorway, forty feet away. The room was not that dark, as moonlight and the streetlights outside shone in the window. "I stood up and started toward the man I saw in the doorway," Shirley said. "Suddenly the guy just wasn't there—nothing. I yelled downstairs to Charlie Ward, 'Was that you at the top of the stairs?'" Ward yelled back, "No, John, I was asleep in the watch room down here!" Fire Captain John Larison told of hearing footsteps echoing on concrete floors when he knew he was the only firefighter in the station. "The ghost guy paced, almost as if he was on an inspection tour of the station. Who it was and how he got in, I never figured out," he said. These were not the first, nor were they the last eerie visitations at the old firehouse at 176 W. Seneca Turnpike in Syracuse, NY.

Other former crewmembers were puzzled by another incident, and are unsure if the ghostly activity in the building was prompted by it. Next to the fire station runs the Onondaga Creek. One of the firefighters found a tombstone in its waters, perhaps washed there by the high water of springtime. As he recalled, the stone memorialized a little girl with the surname of "Hogan." The man, unsure what to do with the relic, brought it up the bank and installed it as a doorstep for the fire station's side door. "It just disappeared in the 1980s and nobody ever discovered who took it or where it went. We often wondered if the spirit of the child was still walking the earth, upset over the disturbance of her grave, and whether she finally reclaimed the pretty white stone. No one will ever know."

Another mystery for fire crews to focus on, when not combating a fire, was the puzzle of the station house doors. They apparently would open and slam themselves shut without any visible person being near them. Some began to wonder if it was Shammy O'Brien or Tyler Green, deceased members of the department coming back to inspect them, but nothing could ever be proved. Charlie Ward was late to turn in one night on his overnight shift, though his partner had already gone to bed. Consequently, he was surprised to hear someone open the door behind him and come in. He looked. Nobody was there and there was nothing he could do, so he gave up and went to bed.

Captain Larison, veteran of forty-one years on the Syracuse Fire Department, remembers seeing a ghost near the Officer's Room as he filled out reports. When he heard footsteps climbing the metal stairway behind him, he turned and caught just a flash of something moving, something lacking the solidity of a human leg. Larison speculates that it may have been the spirit of a former firefighter who had died in the station. Regular crewmembers in those days called this entity "Clarence."

Still others caught glimpses of the spectral inhabitants of the station. Lieutenant John Whitney claimed to have seen a ghostly figure but couldn't describe it in detail. A deacon in his Catholic parish, Whitney gave the others his word, and they knew that this religious man would only attest to what he knew to be the truth. Jimmy Vossler, another retired member of the department, tells of having heard someone walking around the fire truck as he and Charlie Ward watched television one evening. They heard the knob on the door behind them rotating, and turned to see the door beginning to move. It stopped, then they both heard footsteps upstairs in the dormitory—feet walking the wood floors, just as Capt. Larison had reported. However, on investigation, they too found no one there. Whether or not this entity was Clarence is difficult to say. No one in the station ever got a good look at the man or men who keep returning to their work.

Some day in the future the old building, built in 1927, will be razed. And with that will go the last chance to establish who the ghosts are and what keeps them there. In the early 1990s the Fire Company moved to a new station on Midland Avenue. The old fire station today serves as a Senior Citizen's Center by day, but is emptied by nightfall. And the seniors only occupy the first floor, as insurance for a second floor is prohibitive. Almost all the crewmembers mentioned in this story are now retired, or soon will be. With them will go the last witnesses to an intriguing tale of firefighters who didn't take well to retirement, and who stay on the job until the Last Fire Alarm sounds.

I'm Still Here

Basil Debelack lives a few hours north of New York City. A deeply religious man, he's always believed that life is a continuum and has several times experienced visions of the dead. However, as with many psychically sensitive individuals, he carefully chooses who hears about his impressions.

On September 11, 2001, Basil sat in Fred's auto repair shop in his village, watching in awe as television showed the World Trade Center collapsing and fire consuming part of the Pentagon. This was the greatest disaster that those assembled could ever have imagined. Stunned, Basil left. A few days later, however, when he brought his car in for repairs, Fred told him that a cousin, Michael, a New York City firefighter, had died in the conflagration. Michael had been a military reservist, a nurse and a firefighter, and his family and friends grieved. Basil, no stranger to grief, gave his condolences, then walked toward home.

Passing out Fred's driveway, Basil sensed a strange figure on the lawn. A semi-transparent man in ordinary street clothes, with a mustache and just the beginnings of a beard, stood to the side and smiled. Basil scrutinized the figure, but didn't speak to it, though he felt sure it was Michael without his uniform. A day later, when he returned to pay his repair bill, he tested his insights with the owner. "Fred, did your cousin have a mustache and beard?"

"No, Basil, just a mustache," he responded.

Not seeking to intrude into the family's sorrow, and not sure how his insight would be received, Basil changed the subject, paid his bill and drove away.

In October, Basil heard through friends that Michael's remains had been retrieved and a funeral held in New York City. A few weeks later Basil was again at the auto shop, and Fred brought out a memorial book that NYFD provided to families of the deceased. Several nice photos of Mike were included, especially one in color that caught Basil's eye, showing Mike in a mustache, but also with the wispy beginnings of a beard. For Basil, this was proof of the identity of the apparition.

He sensed that Fred might welcome the details of his spectral experience and gently told Fred the details of the vision. He added that Fred could share the episode with Michael's family if he thought it would help their grief.

In December, Basil mentioned the incident to an old friend, a New York State Trooper, just returned from temporary duty at the World Trade Center site. Still overcome by his personal experiences there, the trooper offered to give a memento to Fred—a small Bible pin with stars and stripes, that might be affixed to the uniform of peace officers who had served in the disaster aftermath. Basil accepted it gratefully and returned home, driving to Fred's house and offering him the pin. Fred was greatly pleased. As Basil drove into the first turn on the road home, he was suddenly swept with a great warmth. Asking his intuition the source of the heat, he was told it was Michael's reassurance that his gift was welcomed.

In the years ahead we can expect to hear more stories such as this one. During and following wars, dead servicemen and women have communicated their survival to relatives and friends. Some of those who died on September 11, 2001 will also likely reappear in visions or dreams. As families share their unique stories of loved ones' communications, faith in survival beyond death of the body will be strengthened.

Capitol Hill

The Capitol, Albany, N. Y.

In March 1888 Cormack McWilliams decided to work late, plastering the new ceiling of the Assembly Chamber in the State Capitol in Albany, NY. For an Irish immigrant, having a plasterer's skill, and the willingness to work late on a Saturday night, he was certain he'd find success. High on a scaffold underneath the arched ceiling, he worked on alone, long after other laborers had quit for the weekend. The night watchman estimated that, around 3 a.m., McWilliams made one misstep and plunged to the stone floor forty feet below. He was carried home but his injuries were untreatable, and he died three days later. Dedication to his job, in the end, earned McWilliams only an early death. After the funeral his casket was interred in St. Agnes Cemetery. Later, his family erected a brownstone marker, which looks very much like the stone used in building the Capitol's "Million Dollar Staircase."

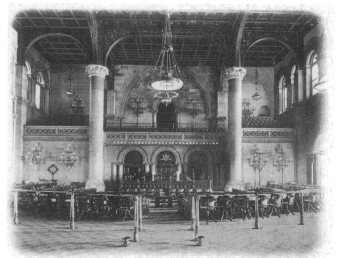

Assembly Chamber; State Capitol, Albany, N. Y.

In 1911, not far from the ceiling where McWilliams fell, Civil War veteran and night watchman Samuel Abbott prowled the third and fourth floors of The Capitol late at night. The faint smell of smoke alarmed him, but he could see no flame. He moved to the fifth floor and opened a door. For just a second, he saw a sheet of flame rolling across the ceiling, then the room exploded, he lost his vision, and was thrown back down the stairs. He knew there was a fire extinguisher in the library and staggered there. Opening the door, he fainted, never more to rise. He died of smoke inhalation, becoming the first employee to die in the new Capitol Building.

Whenever ghost stories are told about the Capitol, the spirits are said to be one man or the other, not yet finished working for the State, and moving throughout the building. In recent years, night cleaners who have never heard of McWilliams or Abbott, have told of feeling watched. In 1990 a night cleaner leaned his mop against a wall in order to attend to another task. Returning, he saw his mop suddenly stand upright and begin moving about the floor, as if a phantom cleaner had joined the work crew. After a minute or so, it simply fell to the floor. A down-to-earth guy, who believes everything has a rational explanation, he finally reached an epiphany and now believes in ghosts.

Of course, there are the usual cold spots along the corridors, usually felt only at night. Workers seldom think of these as ghostly phenomena because the building is old and large, and a draft might be expected from anywhere. But some daytime employees, such as Ellen, in the late 1990s, have felt the chill breezes blowing over them on the fifth floor.

In 1982 Lena, a cleaner, came to work at 5 a.m. Her task was to ensure that rest rooms were spick and span before the State workers arrived. By 6:30 she finished her last bathroom on the fifth floor and went into the hall. A man in old-fashioned clothing suddenly emerged from the dark Assembly Office into the hallway, and vanished. The lights were off inside and she knew the workers had not yet reported for work. Her supervisor saw her hurriedly stumbling downstairs, saying, "I just saw something on 5; you're not going to believe me. I gotta sit down!" The next day she requested, and was granted, a transfer.

Late one night a member of the Assembly staff worked alone in the office, awaiting the State Legislature's final action on the State Budget. He knew he was the last one on the fifth floor. Coming from the Assembly Office, he turned right and saw a man in a brown suit halfway down the hall, walking away from him. "Who could this be? I thought to myself. I followed him. He turned left at the end of the hall. I walked faster to see where he was going. When I got to the corner, there was nobody in that hall. I stopped and scratched my head—where had he gone? I turned back toward the office, only to see him back there, walking away from me. I followed him again, as fast as I could, but when I turned the corner near the Assembly Office, that hallway was empty. The man had simply vanished," he told me.

Which is it then? Samuel or Cormack? Could both men still be active spirits, trying to complete the tasks that were suddenly cut short by tragedy?

Buckingham's Palace

785   CAPITOL, HARTFORD CONN.   ILLUSTRATED POST CARD CO., N. Y.

Identifying a ghost is seldom easy, but Republican staff member Chet Dalzell believes The Connecticut State Capitol, opened in Hartford in 1879, is haunted by William Buckingham, the state's Civil War governor. In February 1984, Dalzell, working late at his computer in Room 324, the Republican Caucus Room, reported an encounter with a ghost he believes was Buckingham. Dalzell heard the door open behind him, and when he turned, the heavy door stood open, but nobody was there. He was suddenly engulfed in cold air. Thinking that someone had left a window or door open, Dalzell walked into the Senate Chamber to investigate. However, all its windows and the ones in his workroom were closed. The sudden cold was too eerie, Dalzell donned his coat and left.

When he shared the experience with other staffers, one old-timer remembered that a hard-working lieutenant governor in the 1920s, also working late, saw the apparition of William Buckingham standing in that room. Startled, the politician had fled. Buckingham was easy to recognize because a bronze statue of him stands inside the Capitol's west entrance. The lieutenant governor is said to have left work before dark during the remainder of his term.

"Gov. William Buckingham"

Known for his strong will, Buckingham retired in 1866, after prodding and guiding the Connecticut legislature through the momentous Civil War years. Returning to business, the ex-governor found it too tame, so he re-entered politics and was elected to the U.S. Senate in 1869. He died in office on February 5, 1875. At the time of his death the gold-domed Capitol was still under construction, so he never served there in life. Perhaps retiring from mortal life, Buckingham found Heaven too tame, and preferred the contentious political life of The Nutmeg State.

The Trooper

In July 1991 Jeanette worked as a medical transcriptionist for a doctor in Albany, NY. Listening to the physician's dictation through earphones, she typed comments onto patients' medical records. "My mind was in neutral and my fingers were moving automatically on the typewriter," she said. Suddenly, a male voice beside her said, "Jeannie, where *are* you?" His tone was urgent. The voice was that of a man she had loved dearly forty years before. He had been a New York State Trooper with Troop G in the Capital District when they had met, and he was the only person ever to call her Jeannie. And there was no mistaking his Brooklyn accent. All the old mixed feelings of anger, resentment and love returned.

She had not let herself think about him much during the forty years. He had abandoned her romantically when he suddenly transferred to a Troop on Long Island. Angry and confused, she had watched him depart, and neither had attempted further contact with the other. Now his voice had reawakened memories of their youthful romance. His presence seemed to hover nearby during the next few days, even while she was driving. She tried to find his address, but couldn't. Though the voice seemed warm and loving, he seemed to need something from her. Memories of him were both good and bad, so she pushed the feelings away, mentally asking him to leave.

Well aware that the transition from this world to the next is a process, and not a single event, Jeanette eventually concluded that he must have been ill, dying or dead when he made contact. She wondered why she hadn't seen the trooper, as she had both felt and seen her father's presence when he died in 1989.

In the years following the trooper's visitation she sought information and found that, indeed, her former lover had died—almost a month *after* she had heard his voice! Jeanette deeply pondered this event and, after sharing her experience with me, asked if a person could go out of his body, perhaps while in a coma, prior to death. I told her of such a case, involving a former student who, pronounced dead in a diabetic coma, had revived and related an out of body journey. Further inquiry revealed that her trooper had been comatose for some time before death.

Jeanette informed me that this spirit communication caused her to rethink his possible motivations for reconnecting with her as he prepared to die. Her quest for more information has caused her to reconsider her beliefs on life and death, and induced her to return to the church of her youth. She is grateful for this contact.

After she shared this story, we lost touch for several months. Then she called to relate a recent dream. "I was walking through a quaint town with brick streets, to a bridge over a wide river. He walked on his side of the river and I walked on mine. As I watched, he crossed the bridge. I, also, stepped onto the bridge. We met and he kissed me. He then turned and walked away, where he vanished in a mist. I knew I couldn't follow him—yet."

She now believes he had personal or family troubles, which he couldn't confide to her when they parted, and has forgiven him for that. She believes he left without a word rather than hurt her further. Deeply touched by his deathbed search for her, she believes he did love her and the dream promises a future reunion.

5

Health &
Medicinal
Spirits

Ghosts of the Asylum

"Tratelje"

Deep in the woods of the Town of Bolton, north of Diamond Point, NY, stands a ruin once known as *Tratelja*, Scandinavian for "the wood cutter." Much Adirondack timber was cleared on the three hundred acres there prior to 1907 on orders of Dr. Carl Nordstrom, the owner, who had emigrated from Scandinavia. The magnificent estate consisted of a thirty room, three story manor house, two farms, barns, a stable, a sawmill, ponds, a small power station, a caretaker's cottage and many outbuildings for smaller animals. *Tratelja* offered the Nordstroms luxury in the bosom of nature. They employed over thirty-five servants in and around their sumptuous summer home.

In 1922 Dr. and Mrs. Nordstrom opened *Tratelja* as a home for the elderly poor, but closed it within a year because of its inaccessibility. The doctor had no local practice and, with his wife Emily, a militant suffragette, wintered in Palm Beach, FL. She died in 1934 and is buried in Bolton. Carl, in his grief, simply abandoned the estate. *Tratelja* lay deserted in the forest between 1934-1938, when Nordstrom sold it. Glens Falls doctors Millet and Blair, new owners of *Tratelja*, converted it to a health center for indigents in Warren County.

The few old timers who remember the institution are divided as to what patients were treated there: the insane or alcoholics. This lack of certainty led, in later years, to scary ghost stories about the old hospital. It burned to the ground in 1941, leaving only the rock walls and massive chimney, sitting on a mountain bluff overlooking a distant Lake George. Locals later referred to it as "the castle," and teenage campers often embellished its history with ghoulish yarns.

The former hospital's medical staff residence is separated by a highway from the caretaker's house, barns and the forest that hides the mansion's remains. Lynn and her husband bought the estate and moved into the old staff residence, where she immediately felt a presence, though she saw no one. A guest remarked one morning at breakfast that he'd seen a blonde haired woman who had spoken to him during the night. "I'm eighteen," she had said. Shortly after that, Lynn began to catch movements in her peripheral vision. Hutch doors and cupboards would open themselves, as if by a housekeeper's hand. The blonde ghost seemed very disturbed whenever Lynn's husband was present. Her activity escalated whenever he was home. After he later left the house and ended the marriage, the blonde's disturbances lessened.

Lynn briefly used the caretaker's cottage and barns as a dude ranch. The main barn was a constant focal point for spectral events. As ranch owner, Lynn had to constantly check her brood mares during foaling. One evening, hearing the mares stomping, she rushed into the barn, only to see dozens of flying squirrels stunting raucously in the rafters, and scaring her mares. On a return trip a few hours later, to see if the squirrels had vacated or at least worn out from their energetic play, she found the horses' water pails filled with drowned squirrels! Not one was left alive. The mares were sleeping contentedly. Squirrels have not returned to the barn since.

"Horse barn"

On other occasions Lynn saw the blonde woman walking placidly between the horse stalls, as if bestowing peace on the animals. At other times Lynn or family members saw a light in the barn at night. Fearing a fire, they rushed to the barn, but never found any light source once they opened the door.

Many other strange events take place from time to time on the old *Tratelja* property. Objects move themselves or simply disappear in the Caretaker's House. Strange lights and sounds have been experienced in several places on the old estate.

From time to time young people discover the ruins of *Tratelje* hidden in the forest, but find themselves fleeing from noises that have no human origin. Whether the unseen guide for the old *Tratelja* estate is Dr. Nordstrom, his wife Emily, or one of the unnamed medical staff that lived or worked on the property, no one has determined. Though some visitors or residents become startled, the spirits seem determined only to bring healing and maintain harmony in this quiet section of the Adirondack forest.

The Wait House

In 1977 The Adirondack Planned Parenthood Association moved into new quarters at 135 Warren Street in Glens Falls, NY. Though changed into an office building, the grand old house once had been the snug home of prosperous citizens. Serving clients today permits scant time for the staff to speculate about former residents, but all office buildings fall silent at day's end. At such times the Planned Parenthood workers know they are not alone.

Somewhere beneath the Victorian exterior is the original 1851 brick Federal Style house. Also hidden today is the gracious bay window of a sitting room that was a domestic haven for William and Mary Eliza Wait late in that century. Called "Elsie" by her husband, Mary Eliza was sensitive to a ghost that had come with the house, perhaps a woman of the Cushing family from the early 1850s, or another spirit loitering in the neighborhood. Edith Goodman, a friend of the Wait children, recalled a ghost visit when William had gone into the city on business and the children were asleep. As Elsie sat alone sewing, a rocking chair in the room quietly creaked, then rocked slowly. This activity occurred whenever William was away, and lasted until he returned. As he lifted the front door latch, the rocking chair stilled, as if his wife's silent companion had retired to her quarters after the master of the house returned. This activity continued for years until the Waits rebuilt the brick exterior and did extensive inner renovations.

With William's increased prosperity the family decided to enlarge the house. They raised the roof from one and one-half to two stories and added a Victorian turret. While continuing to spend evenings in the "library," as the old sitting room was now called, they no longer encountered the ghost. It seemed the haunting had ceased, as there were no subsequent sightings during the years when the Gingras, Aronson and Geller families' owned the house.

Matters changed, however, when Planned Parenthood took over. Mary Ellen, the night cleaner, recalled very cold drafts in the upstairs hallway when there was no air conditioning. A friend, who believes she is somewhat psychic, visited Mary Ellen while she was cleaning. The friend had a thought that "the woman" (Eliza?) who quietly treads the upstairs hall hated her husband's cigar-smoking friends, and used to escape onto the upstairs front porch. From the outside a small porch is visible, but at the time of this friend's visit its interior doorway was blocked off, and the friend could not have known of the porch.

Michelle, another staffer, often feels a presence following her up the stairs. Several times, she has heard children's voices talking quietly in the second floor hallway. In the downstairs rear of the building she has sometimes turned lights off, only to walk a few steps and have them turn on again. On one occasion she saw an indistinct female form in the old kitchenette area at the end of the hall.

Evelyn, who worked there in the 1980s, often found lights going off and on when she worked alone on Saturday mornings. "When you came in the front door you felt *her* strong presence," Evelyn said. "I once saw a woman wearing a black skirt and a white blouse, fastened at the neck with a fancy broach, when I entered the kitchenette area that has now been converted to an office."

Women were a dominant presence there during the Wait ownership—live women, girls and a silent ghost or two. Now mainly women staff the facility dedicated to women's health services, and women from another time may still be keeping watch.

The Observer

What an opportunity! She needed a bigger house in which to expand her Reiki healing and teaching services, and a friend suddenly needed someone to house-sit an old farmhouse on Dunns Corner Road in Westerly, Rhode Island. What was called the Old Crandall Farm was a plain two-hundred-year-old building, and it had lots of space for Norine and her son, Jay. Moving in, she noted the building's quietness—not an unsettling feeling, just a calm. At the same time, her intuition told her she was not alone. Many times she expected to turn around and see a man, though when she did turn nobody was there. Norine Laferriere felt he was protective, and probably supportive of her healing therapies, so she felt little apprehension. She first saw the entity as an area of wavy lines in the middle of a doorway, an energy-field, or like heat rising from a hot road. But he was never an impediment to her passage, so she decided to happily co-exist with him.

Those who visited her had to pay attention, however. Several old friends came to visit soon after she took up residence there. The first one was happily conversing about her life and Norine motioned her to the sofa. When the woman sat down, almost instantly a strange look came to her face. "Norine, who is it that just sat down beside me?" she inquired. "So *that's* his game, taking part in our conversations," mused Norine. She laughingly put her visitor at ease, attributing the woman's experience to her imagination, though Norine knew differently.

On another occasion she hosted a healing meditation group in her home. The group's coordinator entered the house and almost instantly said, "Norine, you've got someone here!" and urged her to smudge (a Native American cleansing ceremony) the building. But the ghost man really didn't trouble her, and she began to affectionately call him "Charlie," though she isn't sure how the name came to her.

Charlie's pranks are usually confined to the second floor of the house, where he seems to enjoy pestering Norine's son. Jay, a college student, has his preferences in television programs and radio music, but hardly does he set the station and sit down to relax, than Charlie changes the stations or channels. It is a polite tug-of-war between the two. Charlie is also adept at meddling with Jay's computer, turning programs off and on at will. Perhaps this unseen resident, a holdover from a previous occupancy, is just trying to learn 21st Century technology.

Charlie seems to harbor no tolerance for birds, however. Norine has a pet cockatiel, which she has heard squawking loudly, as if threatened, in its first floor cage. When she investigates, she usually finds the bird with its head bent down inside the cage, as if some invisible hand is pressing on its neck. Charlie has never hurt anyone, but keeps up his active schedule. Like most ghosts he just wants to be acknowledged. "I'm here" or "I'm still here" seems to be his message.

Norine's healing center often hosts drumming classes, a therapy that has become popular in recent years. Sometimes she records the evening's music on tape as a way of improving her instructional skills. Charlie offers his impression of the music by leaving a loud "Brrrrh!" raspberry sound at the end of each tape. So, Charlie the observer is a critic and yet a guardian. Norine's next move is to involve him in some form of healing...*if* she can focus his attention!

Pineland

"Pineland Administration Building"

Pineland Center near New Gloucester, ME, looks from the road as if it might still function in a medical capacity, but today its cavernous buildings sit almost abandoned. From time to time a state agency makes temporary use of a structure, but the greater part of the facility sits boarded up—remembering. Until it closed in 1995, Pineland housed the state's feeble-minded and mentally ill. Once committed there in the early days, it was almost impossible to leave. Many of the patients didn't belong in such a warehouse of souls, and were inwardly angry at a "lifetime sentence" inflicted upon them. As hundreds lived out their lives in court-imposed concealment at Pineland, did they release a negative energy that still remains? During the Center's last days I spoke with employees whose experiences offered an answer.

Cliff told of sitting on a couch in the lounge, on break from his night shift duties in Cumberland Hall, when suddenly a hand grasped his shoulder from behind. "That's impossible," he thought, "there's a *wall* behind me!" Instantly he turned, still feeling the grasp of the phantom hand, but saw only the wall. Karen and Audrey, his co-workers, were not shocked. The night shift was the time such inexplicable events normally happened. A few nights later the women, hoping to find some answers, brought a Ouija board to occupy the trio during the long quiet periods. When inmates were settled for the night, they put the board into operation. Placing their hands on the pointer they inquired, "Why did you touch Cliff?"

"Like him," was the response.

"Who *are* you?" they asked.

"Pam" was the terse reply. Letter by letter she spelled out words that told the story of her commitment and eventual death there many years before. Sometimes she played games with the questioners, by not responding to their queries. "Give us a sign you're here," said Karen, "and we'll leave you alone."

Suddenly an adjacent door rattled, as if in response. Startled, Cliff jumped up and opened the door, behind which he found only an empty room with its window closed.

On another occasion, when Pam wouldn't "come through," they addressed her as "Pammy." Suddenly the Ouija pointer began to whirl and whirl, putting an end to that night's communication.

In a later Ouija session she told her inquisitors she'd been put in Pineland because she "was sick." Then came, "baby, baby." The communicators speculated that Pam had been mentally retarded and pregnant, and may have lost the child during childbirth. One woman went to the State Capitol in Augusta and found old records that gave Pam's family name. The issue of pregnancy was unclear, but she had been a Pineland patient, had died young, and was buried in Pineland's cemetery. A few weeks later, another night worker, Pat, compassionately used a technique known as "guided imagery" or "reverie," to communicate with Pam and led her to the spirit of her child. After that, Pam never appeared on the Ouija again.

Other caregivers became fearful at disquieting noises in the unoccupied sections of the building, though many of those areas were kept illuminated throughout the night. Cumberland's top floor was closed because the elevator and stairs

"Cumberland Hall"

had become unusable. When a Pineland engineer drove into the building's parking lot he saw a woman in the top-floor window. He entered and inquired who was upstairs. Amazed, they told him it was impossible to go up there. Who was it? Pam? Or does another specter still need release at Pineland?

When employed in nearby Doris Anderson Hall, Audrey often noticed objects missing or moved. She and a co-worker attempted another Ouija contact. They were shocked when a purported male ghost spewed vulgarity in response. When questioned if he had known anyone who died at Anderson, he spelled out "Yes," and gave a name. The group surmised it was his. "He choked to death. Burned," he ventured.

Knowing that Anderson had never had a fire death, the workers suspected a trick or lie. But when they mentioned the story to a longtime aide in the building, she confirmed that a former patient had choked, and was later cremated.

The hospital buildings of Pineland Center now have only a resident watchman to oversee the State of Maine's investment. The facility is otherwise a ghost town. Hearings at the State Capitol some years ago revealed many wrongs done to simple patients who had no knowledge of their rights. Often, the staff members were poorly paid and poorly trained. Hundreds committed against their will, sometimes only because they were an embarrassment to their families, may have died with "scores" to settle. Perhaps they still roam Pineland's vacant corridors and wards.

Locks

Lockport Memorial Hospital, in Lockport, NY, is bright, friendly and efficient by day. However at night, when most treatment rooms are closed, and the night nurses come on duty, those charged with the building's security are liable to find their jobs becoming more complicated. Windows are found open after they have been secured. Lights that have been turned off may be found glowing brightly hours later. It is as if some invisible night worker is trying to carry out tasks that are no longer assigned.

Mark, a former night security officer, often found himself making tedious re-checks of the doors at the hospital. He usually knew what awaited him. In addition to the windows and lights that seemed to have a mind of their own, he'd find doors that he had previously locked now standing open or unlocked. There would be locked doors in rooms that had no keys. A hub of healing activity during the day, the hospital seemed to replay its memories of yesteryear during the night shift. Security work wasn't normally the most exciting way to make a living, but it was at least supposed to be manageable!

The hospital no longer offers pediatric services and the fifth floor, always reserved for children's care, is closed. It's now entirely devoted to record storage. "Of course," Mark said, "they lock it at the end of each work day, because the records aren't needed at night. But I hated to go up there for door checks. When I unlocked the doors and turned on the lights—sometimes even before, I'd hear children crying. It was eerie—as if the sounds were echoing from the past.

It always made me nervous until I'd locked the door behind me and left, even though I knew it wouldn't stay locked."

The Kenan-James Building is adjacent to the hospital. Today it is used mainly for storage. It began as a nurses' residence in the late 1920s, though in later years it was used for staff meetings. One R.N. told me of a ghost nurse in that building. Attending a staff meeting in Kenan-James a few years ago, she saw a nurse in the old-fashioned nurse's cap and cape stride through the group and straight through the back wall. "I looked at the others' faces to see if they saw her, too. If they did, they played poker-face, but I know what I saw," she said.

Those who provide love and care in health facilities bear a great responsibility. At Lockport Memorial no door seems locked to those who continue caring, even after death.

The Angel

"You write about ghosts? You ought to come over to where I work!" It was only by chance that I met Brenda in Milbridge, ME.

"Where do you work?" I asked.

She gave me the name of a large, sixty-five-bed nursing home in a town northwest of Bar Harbor, where she was a Registered Nurse. The building had been a stagecoach stop in the early 1800s, and had become a health care facility around the time of World War II.

"We sure have something going on there, and it's been going on for years. In the late 1960s, when I came to work there, one of the old women patients was dying. Evelyn's family was keeping watch, so I was used to people traipsing in and out past my desk at all hours. About 9:45 p.m. I looked up and saw a man in a black suit and 'pointy hat,' maybe from the 1920s, carrying a black overcoat. He started down the hall. We have angled mirrors in the hall that allow me to see all the way down to the elevators from my desk. I watched, but he didn't show up in the mirror. I left my desk and went directly into the hall—there's no place else he could have gone, and nobody was in sight. The elevator didn't chime or open its doors, and no alarms went off.

"Bea was a nurse on staff at that time. As she came up the hall, I asked her if she'd seen anybody. She replied, 'No,' then, thoughtfully said, 'Wait—was he dressed in black?'

'Yes!'

"Bea got this big grin on her face and told me, 'Oh, you've seen our angel of death. We're going to lose Evelyn in Room 212, and he's come to help her out.' Sure enough, an hour later, Evelyn died peacefully."

Bea's first experience with the Angel had been years ago, on a night when she sat with a dying woman. She heard someone enter. The man in black stood there.

"Who *are* you?" she asked. "He turned and slowly exited. He wasn't bad looking, maybe thirty-five years old, clean-shaven with brown hair—fairly tall."

On another night, Sue and Stephanie, both Certified Nursing Assistants, chatted

in the hall. Sue saw the man in black emerge from Lloyd's room, and then turn and re-enter the patient's room. Lloyd had been moved for treatment elsewhere in the building. "When did Lloyd come back?" Sue asked Stephanie.

"He hasn't." Stephanie replied.

"Then we ought to check his room, because somebody just went in," said Sue. They looked inside, but found no trace of the phantom visitor. But, the next morning Lloyd died. A surprise to the nurses, perhaps, but not to the man in black who had just arrived early.

Sue learned that the stranger usually disappeared if confronted. Some of the healthier long-term patients have seen The Angel too. One has seen him three times without getting "carried away." Some residents have clearly seen him when the attending nurses could not. Other patients speak about a mysterious "Lady in White," though Brenda has never seen her, and hasn't heard other staff members speak of her.

I pondered all this one winter, occasionally telling the story at lectures. Eventually, I telephoned Brenda to check my notes. "Yes," she assured me, "I've been there since 1968. Every couple of years we hear of this stranger. What else could he be, except The Angel of Death?"

That puzzled me. I'd always considered The Angel of Death to be merely a Biblical metaphor. "Do you mean there are many others who have seen this guy?"

"Since we talked last time," she offered, "I wondered exactly how many of us had encountered him, and took a poll. Ninety-five percent of the night shift has seen him at least once through the years!" The night staff is composed of nurses and assistants, whose jobs depend on precise observation and definite action.

The Angel's clothing seems to be about eighty years old. If not overtly joyous in his work, he's at least diligent and effective, whether or not he is a true ghost. He travels from this world to the next, but doesn't seem to be an "angel" in the scriptural sense either, as no one has ever observed wings. In the end, I like to think of him as an employee of a distant "package delivery service" that has never missed a pickup. "Fragile—Handle With Care."

6
Haunted Things

Morrison Flats View Farm

Her grandparents' century old farmhouse stood a short distance outside Warrensburg, NY, on Horicon Avenue. It was a summertime haven for Cynthia's family, escaping the heat of Florida. It had no indoor plumbing, yet they hoped it would otherwise be a peaceful sanctuary. Long ago, the building had belonged to a recluse, Lidge Pratt, and all who visited the house came away with uncanny experiences.

One evening while looking in her mother's bedroom mirror, Cynthia saw the reflection of a bearded old man. Whirling, she found nobody behind her. "Later that night Grampa and I were alone in the living room and a thunderstorm was brewing. Sheets of rain drenched the Schroon River valley, then moved toward Chestertown. Grampa and I heard the sound of someone running across the porch. He jumped up and opened the door, thinking it was Mom returning home. No one was there. Then the lights flickered and the hair on the back of my neck stood up. We heard someone tramping across the kitchen floor and up the stairs. I scurried into the kitchen just in time to see the door to the upstairs shut."

When her mother did return home later, Grampa and Cynthia recounted their experience. Grampa attributed the strange events to wind and the horses in the barn. "But the horses are always stomping out there," Cynthia countered, "we've never heard those noises before!" Later, sharing her experience with her visiting cousins, she learned they had often experienced an old crystal set turning itself on in the house, and refused to stay there overnight.

"I tried to believe the skeptics, but eventually, came to know that the old farmhouse was haunted. Our cat, Buffy, was my chief witness. One summer Mom brought an old whiskey jug down from the attic. Grampa laughed when he saw it. He reckoned it had belonged to old Lidge Pratt. There was still a corncob stuck fast in the opening. When it was time to return to Florida, the jug was packed in the car trunk. My mother thought it would make a fine conversation piece in the doorway of our Florida home. The return trip was uneventful. The jug was unpacked and washed, though we weren't able to remove the corncob. The jug was then placed near the front doorway. As he prowled our house, Buffy made wide circles around the jug, refusing to get anywhere near it.

"That night we began to hear the same footsteps we'd heard in Warrensburg. Upon investigation, we found no one, and nothing was out of place. Buffy accompanied me and hissed at the jug. Though we tried to get him used to it, he always hissed. He wasn't skittish with anything else we'd brought from New York State. My Dad and I often heard footsteps and saw skulking shadows, never before experienced in our house. A cold spot developed in the front hall, despite the Florida heat. The hair on the back of our necks stood up whenever we went through there," Cynthia said.

"Dad finally told Mom to get that jug out of our house. Mom sold it to an antique dealer. She told him about its 'haunting' appeal. He seemed intrigued and paid her more than the jug was worth.

"After that the strange sightings and sounds in our Florida house ceased. Later, we found out the antique dealer had removed the corncob plug, and his dog growled at the jug. He said he never saw anything unusual, but his dog sure didn't like that jug," Cynthia laughed.

102

The Trailer

Harry Shannon was a gravedigger. He worked many years in the cemeteries surrounding Port Schuyler, the southern end of the city of Watervliet, NY. He loved his family and lived with his sister, Helen, and brother-in-law, John, in that city. Harry also loved the open road and the twenty-foot long camper/trailer that was his "getaway home" on vacations. Tragically, just a few months after his retirement, Harry died.

Harry's white trailer sat unused in John and Helen's back yard for some time, until Cousin Margaret, a resident of Colonie, purchased it. When she took it home, Margaret began to clean the trailer, readying it for eventual travel. Her detergent and pails, however, would not stay where she left them in the evening. Sometimes, items were missing or moved. Margaret's yard was secure, so who could be making this mischief? When she finished cleaning at night she shut the trailer door, but often found it open in the morning. Who could the culprit be?

The disruptions continued for weeks. Margaret, in frustration, decided to talk it over with John and Helen. In the end they agreed it must be Harry's restless ghost, but how could they mollify him and bring peace and quiet to Margaret's yard? Helen remembered that Harry had been a collector of sorts—little things that he picked up and believed to have special energies. One such favorite item was a plastic yellow duck, probably won at an area carnival. Helen gave the duck to Margaret, who placed it on a table in the trailer. In the vehicle's emptiness, as she departed, Margaret pleaded, "OK Harry, here's your rubber ducky. Now leave me alone—please?"

And Harry complied, perhaps satisfied that his survival was recognized. Now with his lucky duck, and his soul perhaps bathing in some celestial pool, Harry has never again caused Margaret any consternation. She has used the trailer several times and Harry has been her "silent, but no longer disruptive, traveling companion."

Clara's Dress

Abraham Lincoln sat just a few seats to Major Henry Rathbone's left in the box at Ford's Theater. From time to time Lincoln grinned and chuckled at the actors' dialogue as he warded off the weariness of a long and bitter war. Also smiling at Henry's left was his fiancée, Clara Harris, as she whispered into the ear of Mary Todd Lincoln, about a line in *Our American Cousin* that the four of them were enjoying that Good Friday evening. "Finally we'll have some peace," thought Henry, "with Lee surrendered at Appomattox, the President will be able to bind our nation together again." The President was visibly relaxing.

Then, what was this? Another military messenger entering their box? This would be the second one tonight! He stood to intercept the man moving from the shadows. "No, something is wrong here!" thought Rathbone. "This one has a pistol…" He never concluded that thought. A gunshot exploded. Rathbone lurched at the intruder. Grappling with the man, Henry felt the searing pain of a

knife slicing into his arm. He heard women screaming and saw the President crumpled. Henry felt life draining away. He glimpsed his beloved Clara's white satin dress spattered with red blood, and he couldn't fathom whose blood it was. Fighting to remain conscious, he heard only bits of sentences. And then a dark pall engulfed him.

When he awoke Lincoln was dead. Plans were underway for a state funeral and the President's burial later in Springfield, Illinois. Rathbone settled into a despondency of guilt that was broken only sporadically during the remainder of his life. Clara's wound was the haunting lifelong memory of Mrs. Lincoln screaming, "My husband's blood!" as she had looked at the blood-soaked dress.

In the early summer 1865 the betrothed couple managed to return to the Harris' summerhouse, "Loudon Cottage," in Loudonville, just north of Albany, NY. There, Clara unpacked her bloodstained dress and hung it in a bedroom closet. She then had the closet sealed and covered with wallpaper, as if to permanently obscure the tragedy.

When the Good Friday anniversary came in 1866, Clara Harris went to bed early, praying not to remember the previous year's trauma. Around midnight she awoke to the sound of her bedroom rocking chair moving rhythmically, accompanied a man's low chuckling. Then she saw Abraham Lincoln in the moonlight, seated in her chair, quietly enjoying a drama not visible to her. The President gazed in the direction of her now-concealed closet. At that moment her chime clock struck midnight and the entire scene vanished. Sobbing uncontrollably, she awoke the entire household to tell of the apparition.

Most family members felt it was just a nightmare until, on succeeding Good Friday evenings, others who stayed in the Loudon Cottage bedroom had similar experiences. One man told of awakening to see a bloodstained dress hanging inside the room's seemingly-transparent wall during *his* terrifying encounter with the dead president. Compounding the tragedy, in 1883, when the Rathbones were living in Germany, Henry, overcome with guilt at his inability to save Lincoln, murdered Clara and attempted suicide. He ended his days in a German asylum.

Eventually, the Harris house passed to other owners—one being Daisy Ransome, who operated it as a boarding house and knew nothing of its spectral past. On a Good Friday evening, Mrs. Ransome lost a tenant, who fearfully recounted his midnight experience in *that* room: "Suddenly, I could see the rocker move! The tall man sitting in it looked so sad. The dark girl in the white gown rested her hand on the rocker! I sat up—I could see so plainly now, but I could not speak—I was petrified! The girl's gown was white satin adorned with a long silken wreath of red roses and lilacs across the bodice and down the skirt. She sobbed loudly, holding herself by leaning on the mahogany rocker. Then I heard it—a shot rang out—I screamed as I saw the beautiful white satin dress splashed with spots of blood— red blood mingling with the red of the roses. The young girl fell to the floor. I screamed again and again," he said. No amount of persuasion could keep him from fleeing the house in anguish.

Some folks think the Major's son, Henry Rathbone, Jr., destroyed the dress before he put the home up for sale. Daisy Ransome is also said to have uncovered

the hidden closet and burned the dress, in order to lose no more income from fleeing tenants. In any case, Clara's dress has disappeared. One might think the dress's
destruction would have ended the haunting, but early in the 1900s the Governor of
Massachusetts visited his cousin, Hobart Thompson, who was then the cottage's
owner. The politician went to bed late, pondering the fate of a pending bill in the
Massachusetts Legislature. He, also, awoke just before midnight and saw Lincoln
rocking in the moonlight. Reaching for the light switch, he overturned a pile of
books with a crash, and Lincoln disappeared.

In 1927 Loudon Cottage was moved to the present location, about five hundred
feet from its original site on Cherry Tree Road. A succession of owners since that
time have reported no further Lincoln sightings, so perhaps the Harris and
Rathbone families have finally found peace.

The life and death of Abraham Lincoln continue to touch the hearts of millions.
Nowadays, in April, many people still report the wind and sounds of Lincoln's
passing funeral train on the old New York Central Railroad tracks between New
York City and his Illinois grave. Many others report seeing Lincoln's ghost in the
White House in Washington, DC.

Many thousands more, especially foreigners studying United States history, discover Lincoln's *living* spirit in his writings, which inspired and uplifted our nation
in its time of deepest trouble. Though he is one of the first American teachers to
thrill hearts of the world's people seeking to understand democracy and freedom,
his fellow countrymen are rapidly losing knowledge of, and respect for, the man.
His birthday is feebly honored or simply ignored by the young, who are no longer
certain just which presidents are honored on Presidents' Day or why. Lincoln's
birthday has degenerated into cynical consumerism and hucksterism. Better his
memory, principles and spirit, than his ghost, be re-awakened in the 21st
Century.

The Air Conditioner

Irene, making her annual visit to her dentist in Albia, a suburb of Troy, NY.,
awaited her turn in the office. In casual conversation with the receptionist, she mentioned that she had an air conditioner for sale. Another waiting patient remarked
that *she* was looking for a good used air conditioner. A day later she came to Irene's
house in Valley Falls, liked the machine, paid Irene and took her purchase home.

At her next annual checkup, Irene met the buyer again and they struck up a conversation. After brief pleasantries, the woman confided that the air conditioner was
now running well, but they'd had some difficulty at first, and wondered if something invisible might have come with the machine. Her husband had installed it in
the family's den window. It immediately began to cool the room, but their small
daughter heard a pounding sound that was at first inaudible to the parents. The
child complained that she couldn't sleep at nap time. Her father thought the sound
emanated from a neighbor's property, but when he removed the air conditioner
from the den window, the pounding stopped.

As the noise seemed to emanate from the air conditioner, the new owners wondered if the machine might have brought a ghost from Irene's house. The father thought that, if not, perhaps the air conditioner gave off some sub-sonic vibration that only the little girl could hear. But he still had to cool the house in the summer. The family was still pondering the situation at the time of this chance meeting in the dentist's office.

Irene, well read in parapsychology, had a strong feeling that the difficulty was not in the machine itself. She questioned the young wife about the house: how long had they lived there? Had they made any structural changes since moving in? What did the woman know of the house's history? Some things the woman could tell immediately; they had owned the house only a short time and had, as yet, made no major changes. She knew almost nothing, however, about the house's previous owners, but agreed to check on this.

A few months later the young woman called Irene. In questioning neighbors about the house's past owners and residents, she had learned that a handicapped older man had previously lived and died there. In his last years he sat in a wheelchair in the den all day, watching the world through his window. Events outside the house became his television screen. After his death the family cleared the interior, repainted some rooms, then put the house up for sale.

"Good heavens," exclaimed Irene, "now I understand. That air conditioner I sold you is pretty large. If you also have a high window sill, I'll bet the machine was blocking the old man's view, even though he's now in the spirit state."

"Exactly!" said the young wife, "that is what we figured too, so we just put the air conditioner in another window and the house is finally cool." She told Irene that they had no feelings of a ghost or other presences in the house, but she and her husband's conclusions about the matter seemed to have resolved the problem.

Now, ten years later, the episode has faded from the family's memory. It was just a brief encounter with an old man's spirit while he moved from this world into the next. The pounding may have been his attempt to draw attention to his plight. Let's hope he now has a more glorious vista in the other world and doesn't need a window any longer. And likely he has also been able to lay aside his wheelchair.

In this episode, I was fascinated that a young couple would early-on consider a ghost among the causes of the noise. Recent national polls indicate that over half of Americans accept the reality of ghosts. As readers will come to recognize, there is no truly *super*-natural world, only a vast natural continuum of consciousness, whose dimensions we have only begun to understand.

The Desk

Three young women, all students at Albany, NY, colleges, shared an apartment at 520 Madison Avenue. Their graduate degree programs were exhausting and they treasured their down time. Therese sat in the large living room playing with Lurch, roommate Lisa's cat. Suddenly, Lurch, startled, arched his back and hissed loudly. Following Lurch's stare, Therese saw a man standing in the hallway between the living room and kitchen. He wore a brown suit and a derby. Astounded by this stranger in her apartment, Therese demanded, "Can I help you?" The man did not answer, but turned and walked into the kitchen. She jumped up, pursuing him into the kitchen, but it was empty. A thorough search of the apartment turned up no intruder.

When Lisa and Gloria returned from their classes, the three roommates held a quick meeting. If some vagrant had been able to enter their apartment from the street, they wanted assurance that he would not return. They set up a meeting with Rich, their landlord, who checked all locks only to find them working properly. None of the four could imagine how the stranger could have entered the building.

Knowing my metaphysical interests, Lisa, my eldest daughter, called me, seeking my advice, suspecting the intruder may have been a ghost. I informed her that if the man had never been seen there before (as seemed likely) then something in the building must have changed recently. "Check again with your landlord to see if that's possible," I urged. When they queried Rich once more, he silenced our theory of renovations in the building. He did, however, mention that he was storing in the basement an antique roll-top desk that he'd acquired in Boston the previous weekend. The young women asked to see the desk, and he led them to the cellar. It was beautifully made of mahogany, and Gloria noted that it was stored directly under the hallway upstairs, where the intruder had first appeared. Rich offered to store the desk elsewhere and did so the next day.

From that time onward there were no further spectral incidents at 520 Madison Avenue. Who the spirit was, how he became associated with the desk, and why he attached himself to it may never be known. What is evident, however, is that ghostly appearances can occur when purchases such as antiques, or even garage sale items, are brought into homes or offices.

The Wheelchair

Robert's specialty was restoration carpentry. In 1978 he was hired to restore a three-hundred-year-old house on Route 5W in Scotia, NY. The interior had to be gutted to elicit and reclaim its former beauty. One of the first removals was a rotted section of the downstairs floor. At first, he didn't know where to get the wide pine planks to restore that section, but the woman owner informed him that the attic was also floored with it. He could pull up some planks and bring them downstairs. Grabbing his "wrecking bar," he went up the narrow attic stairs. It was murky and dusty, but otherwise bare. Then he saw the antique wheelchair that stood in the corner.

He later explained to a friend, "I wasn't interested in antiques. I had lots of work ahead of me. I ignored it, and began prying up the first plank. After some squawking, the old nails gave a bit and the board pulled up. Resting just a minute, I glanced up. There was someone in the wheelchair! A gray man sat there staring off into space. His lap was covered with a robe. He wasn't looking at me, but my heart was racing. Frankly, I was scared; I knew he wasn't living. I yanked and

pulled on that plank, and up it came. I hustled it downstairs. When I placed the board over the hole, my heart sank—almost two feet short. I had to go up to get another board!"

Once more, with great trepidation, he made his way up the narrow staircase. Timidly, he peeked over the attic floor, toward the chair in the corner. He was relieved. Nobody was in it. He scampered up onto the floor, got his wrecking bar under the next plank and levered it up. A second nervous glance drained the color from his face—the ghost was back! Like a neon sign that's malfunctioning, the specter was there, then not there, flickering in the attic's faint light. He got the second board up in record time and fled downstairs relieved, knowing he would not have to come back. He finished the repair with wood left over, and Robert went on to the next task.

The owner always came to inspect at the end of the workday. Robert muttered, "You've got some attic here. I never want to go back up there!"

When she asked why, he told her the story. She pursed her lips but said nothing, and left.

The next day he concentrated on further construction. At day's end, the owner drove up and got out of her car, with a packet of old photographs in her hand.

"She held one out to me and asked me to look. I recognized it instantly as the old house, long ago when it was new. A group of men in 1800s dress stood posed out front."

"Do you recognize anyone?" she asked.

"Yes, that guy in the middle—he's the one I saw in the attic!"

She smiled and said the picture was taken a hundred years ago. "The man in the center was the builder and owner then. He raised broom corn here and had a broom factory in the building. Out back he raised prize bulls. One day a bull gored him so badly he almost died. He recovered but was unable to walk for the rest of his life. He spent it pushing himself around in that wheelchair you saw in the attic. Apparently, owners since his time hadn't wanted to move it downstairs, so it just sits there."

The injured businessman and original owner may have transferred the trauma of injury and the frustrations of his physical limitation to the old chair. His memories may reside in the house until he finally releases them, and himself, in the process. The wheelchair remains in its dusty corner yet today.

The Clock

How nice, a present from Scotland! Edgar Shopmeyer and his wife, Mary, were as happy to have daughter, Susan, and her husband, Harold, back home from Navy duty, as they were to receive the unique gift. Harold had been assigned to a Navy Intelligence post near Aberdeen for years, and when his tour of duty ended, he and Susan spent a few days scouring Scotland's antique shops for presents. They found three beautiful antique grandfather clocks, and brought one to Edgar and Mary's home in Clifton Park, NY. The Shopmeyers placed the timepiece in their foyer.

When Edgar prepared to leave home the next morning, on his way to the General Electric Company in Schenectady, he noticed the front door on the clock cabinet stood open. Absentmindedly he pushed it shut. Next day, preparing to leave, he found the clock door open again. He took a moment to examine the latching mechanism and noticed that friction between the door and its casing was supposed to keep it closed. He secured the door again and left for work. By the third morning Edgar knew something strange was taking place. An expert machinist at GE for over thirty years, he had little tolerance for mechanisms that didn't operate properly. Nevertheless, he left the clock door ajar for a few months until he found time to examine it in greater detail in his cellar workshop.

He carefully removed the clock on top and checked its works. He hadn't started the device since it arrived at his Vischer Ferry Road home, though his initial examination suggested flawless operation. In the vertical section of the cabinet he inspected the weights and chains that turned the clock. The almost three-hundred-year-old mechanism was only slightly corroded. He pulled the chain and the clock began ticking. "OK, so it just needs a cleaning," he chuckled. Removing the clockworks, chains and weights from the cabinet, he dusted and oiled them. Standing the wooden case upright on the shop floor he noted the small keyhole in the door had no key. So he crafted one. Now, with the door locked, he retired to bed. In the middle of the night a crash resounded from the cellar. Seizing a flashlight he hurried down for a look. The cabinet had somehow toppled onto its face on the floor. He set the case up once more, with the key in the lock but leaving the door ajar. He never locked the case again.

The tall cabinet needed another repair—a broken or missing wooden decoration on top. Figuring the entire project would be time-consuming, he packed the works in cardboard boxes and moved them to his barn until he could invest the time in restoration. Then he hauled the cabinet to the barn and stood it facing a wall to prevent another crash. One thing after another interfered with the restoration, and it was almost two years before he could resume his tinkering. During that period he retired from GE and spent time researching grandfather clocks. His looked like European grandfather clocks from the 1690s. His son-in-law had told him the Scottish antique dealer had originally acquired it from an old castle.

After retiring, able to devote his full time to the clock, he brought it back to his workshop. He remembers that's when the strange events began again. Originally designed with three finials or ornamental tops, two were missing when it came into Edgar's possession. After re-gluing all loose surface decorations and attaching them with square nails, matching the original craftsmanship, he turned his attention to making finials on his wood lathe. Unable to find fine grain oak wood such as they had in Scotland, he substituted locust wood. Installing the new finials on their dowel receptacles, he went contentedly upstairs to bed. He slumbered only a short time when somebody shook him awake, and a voice warned, "Those finials are not right! They should be made in the shape of a flame." That was the end of the message, curt and to the point. Mary was still asleep and it wasn't her voice. "Then I had a thought," he said. "Not really a regular thought, but all I could think of is that it was a 'thought injection' that came from outside of myself." He returned to sleep, puzzling over the source of information as he drifted off.

The next day, recognizing that there was some intelligence attached to the antique, he began re-lathing the finials, this time making three in a design different from the remaining one, which he now considered an unoriginal substitute. Not completely satisfied with the result, as he wasn't sure how to interpret "flame shaped," he installed the new pieces and glued them into position. Carrying the clock upstairs, he set it in the corner of their living room. Making sure the cabinet was completely level, he pulled the chain inside, starting the clock. It ran for just two minutes and then stopped. He wound it some more and again it ran for just two minutes. Looking for some item jammed in the mechanism, he found nothing amiss. Turning off the light he went to bed.

In a repetition of the previous night's visitation, he was shaken awake by some unknown force or person. "The stirrup is bent," the voice observed tersely, then fell silent. As he'd never heard that term, he researched books on clockworks at the local library. In a clock encyclopedia he found a mechanism almost like his, and noted that there was a metal piece called a "stirrup" through which the pendulum swung. Examining that part of his clock mechanism he, indeed, found it slightly bent. When he straightened the imperfection the clock ran perfectly and continuously.

Edgar had made his successful career working with objects measured by a micrometer and milled to thousandths of an inch. Voices that came in the night, (however accurate) or clock cases that unlocked or overturned themselves, distressed him. Calling his daughter, Susan, he and Mary explained that the clock caused too much commotion and they wanted to put it up for sale. Susan agreed, and they took it to an antique dealer at a local shopping mall. The antique dealer was fascinated with the clock, accepted it and received many inquiries from potential buyers.

The dealer's assistant, however, was a disbeliever—ghosts were a lot of hooey in his estimation. As these things often go, the assistant had to work alone in the shop one night. He heard the store's front door bell jingle, indicating the entry of a customer. Looking up, he saw the door still closed and no customer. A few minutes later the scenario repeated, except this time the front door opened. As before, no one had entered the shop. A shiver ran up his spine, as he was unprepared to confront invisible customers.

The next day a man entered the shop to examine the grandfather clock. "As he stood in front of the cabinet," the shop owner related, "he looked as if he were about to have a seizure." The ashen man quickly fled. Later that day another customer entered, gave the clock a cursory examination, paid in cash and carried it away.

Nobody except the present owner knows what has become of the old castle clock. One thing we can be sure of, it isn't sitting quietly in its new home. In all likelihood it will continue to be rebellious until someone either soothes its restless spirit or returns it to the highland mists and moors from which it came.

.

7
Strangers

116-118

Strangers

In 1989, Howard Hayes had a thriving auto repair business on Burgoyne Road in Schuylerville, NY. One September evening, a man brought in a car with a leaking gas tank. Howard backed the car into his garage, positioned it over the repair pit, then descended to take a look underneath. The leak wasn't apparent at first, and Howard looked for it a long time as gas fumes filled the pit. Then the car owner, standing on the garage floor level, lit a cigarette, and instantly a flash fire engulfed the pit, temporarily blinding Howard. Unable to see which direction the stairs were, he suddenly felt two strong hands pushing him toward them. At first, Howard thought the car owner had jumped into the pit to rescue him. But no, the man had immediately fled for his own safety, and was now trembling and pale-faced on the driveway outside. Whose firm hands guided Howard and saved his life? Howard felt that it was a ghost of some departed friend. Or an angel.

*   *   *

Kathy, who lived in South Glens Falls, NY, in the early 1980s, was invited to stay overnight with a friend from Glens Falls, across the Hudson River. "It was late," Kathy told me, "as we walked down Route 9 and onto the bridge. Suddenly, behind us, we heard heavy footsteps. Strange, we thought—we hadn't seen anyone else on the street as we traveled down the hill. We turned to look behind us. The eeriest sight we'd ever seen greeted us. A man in a dark blue or black overcoat, with no legs, following us in mid-air," Kathy said.

They raced to the Glens Falls side and up the steep hill. Breathless when they neared the top, they glanced back. The figure was hovering at the foot of the hill. Why had he stopped? They never found out who he was, why had he appeared on the bridge just as they were crossing, and why only a part of him was visible.

Many times ghost sightings appear only as a torso, lacking feet or legs, or sometimes legs or feet with no body. Perhaps it is most important to their unfinished work that others see the physical elements of their individuality, as if to communicate some message. Or perhaps to show themselves at a certain time in their lives, involved in some mission. As this man had no crutches, and both girls heard only his heavy footsteps, his lower extremities apparently were superfluous. But what mission was he on, or what lifetime activity was he re-enacting? What message might his countenance have communicated if they'd delayed to see him close up? They never found out.

*   *   *

Jim was riding the elevator to the top floor of the Key Bank in downtown Albany, NY, a few years ago. "As I rode up, somewhere around the second or third floor," he told me, "I became aware of another man in a camel hair coat and cap standing there with me. We politely smiled at one another. I got off at the top floor and went to my appointment. Afterward, when I rang to descend, the man was still there as the doors opened. A bit nervous as to who he was, and why he hadn't gotten off, I remarked on the nice weather as the elevator went down. 'I don't know what I've done to deserve such a nice day,' I said idly. He looked me in the eye and very seriously said, 'Oh, you've lived a *very* good life, you deserve it!' That hit me—how did *he* know the kind of life I've lived?

"When we reached the ground floor, he quickly departed and exited through revolving doors onto the street. I paused only a second to ponder how he could know the kind of life I'd lived. I bolted after him, following through the doors; I was only a few steps behind him. Yet, out on Pearl Street, there was no one in sight—and no one on the side streets. Who was he, where did he come from, and where did he go? I think he was either a ghost or an angel," Jim told me.

* * *

In the 1970s I was driving to Bennington, VT, on Route 7 from Troy, NY. Somewhere east of Troy I spied a hitchhiker in the distance. As I drew nearer I noticed him weaving, as if drunk. The closer I got, his ragged clothing and unkempt hair became more and more apparent—"not a good passenger," I told myself, and sped by.

A few hours later, returning to Troy on the same road, I saw the hitchhiker in the distance. He had changed lanes and was hitching back toward Troy. I was to have a second chance. "No," I thought, "not this time either!" But, immediately the skies opened up in a torrential downpour. I had no choice; I stopped to give him a ride.

He reeked of body odor and alcohol. Almost incoherent, he couldn't express clearly whether he wanted to go to Troy or Albany. We traveled in silence until, entering Troy, I slowed for a red light at the top of Hoosick Street hill.

"This is good enough—here," he mumbled.

"Let me pull in to the curb," I said, "so you don't get hit in traffic." I let him out at curbside. He failed to close the door and lumbered onto the sidewalk. I reached over, pulled the door shut, straightened in the seat, looked in the rear view mirror and signaled left into traffic. Then, I couldn't see my hitchhiker—where had he gone? I scanned the full 360 degrees around my car, for at least a hundred yards in every direction. He was nowhere in sight.

Where could he have gone? There were no nearby doorways where he could hide. He had just vanished into thin air. I have wrestled with this experience for years. Was he a ghost? An alien, as some have suggested? My imagination? Or "an angel unaware?"

* * *

Several years ago a church in Elizabethtown, NY, held a centennial celebration. Those attending were asked to dress in one-hundred-year-old costumes. Joanie, a regional artist, put on her best Victorian outfit and set up a display of Victorian art.

Standing by her exhibit, she marveled at the ingenuity of others' marvelously accurate costumes. One man in particular caught her eye.

She figured his perfectly tailored suit had been made especially for the occasion. Several times that afternoon he passed near her display. Packing up around 6 p.m., she spied him walking toward the church and through its wall. Later, she couldn't find any other participants who remembered seeing the distinctive man. Who was he, and where and when did he come from?

* * *

In Ogdensburg, NY, in 1994, Carol walked down Washington Street near the famous Remington Art Museum. The bright, warm sun cast her shadow on the sidewalk. Then, ahead, a group of people alighted from a coach in front of a large old house. Other buggies and their teams of horses had already arrived. Women in long dresses and large hats milled around laughing and conversing with men in Edwardian outfits. Is there an historic celebration here today? she wondered. Is someone shooting a film? She glanced at her shadow again, then at the crowd across the street. But the street was empty. No horses, no buggies, no coach and no people in antique dress; everything had vanished. Where had they gone and who were they? What historical event was powerful enough to leave ripples in time? If they were an apparition from the past, why had they appeared to her? She never found an answer.

* * *

None of these people found logical answers, but for all, their thought deepened and their sense of the possible enlarged. Perhaps the unexplainable has purpose in that it deepens the mind and expands the heart.

8
Cemeteries

Oswego Bitter

The hamlet of "Oswego Bitter" lies on Bennett's Corners Road in Camillus, outside Syracuse, NY. It sits on what was once the land of the Onondagas, central to the Iroquois Nation. Revolutionary War veteran John Marshall originally donated the land for the cemetery in the early 1800s, when Oswego Bitter was a thriving farming community. It became "the place to go" when the hardy farm families came to the end of their lives.

First reports about its ghost were published around 1952. Newspapers referred to a "will-o-the-wisp" moving through the hilly countryside near Bennett's Corners Road. Robert Fletcher, who lived across the road from the cemetery, had used parts of Marshall's old homestead in the construction of his own house, built in the early 1950s. Fletcher began noticing phosphorescent balls of light which traveled down the hill and into the cemetery at night. Most folks at that time ascribed the phenomenon to Indian spirits seeking the Happy Hunting Ground, though no one ever explained why an Onondaga would visit a burial ground reserved for the race that had dispossessed his people. After watching the light phenomenon for thirty years, Fletcher began to think it was a natural phenomenon, though of unknown origin, and stated this theory when interviewed by the *Post-Standard* on October 30, 1987.

Many locals, when first witnessing the light, thought it was someone walking with a lantern. There seemed to be a consciousness to the light, which seemed to skip or bob across the land, but always extinguished itself in the cemetery. Those who came upon the marvel unaware were usually startled. Once, a tired farmer in a wagon some miles from home, flicked the reins, and fell asleep, knowing his horse would find the way home. After some time, he awoke to find his wagon stopped at the cemetery gate. The horse was mesmerized by a ball of light dancing in the road outside the gate. Until the light entered the cemetery the horse refused to move on.

On another occasion two farmers in a wagon spotted the light coming down the hill and stopped their rig to watch, unaware that their wagon was directly in its path. The light approached the wagon, moved between the men and through the center of the seat, then into the cemetery. Fortunately, each substantiated the other's story, so their neighbors withheld their ridicule.

The cemetery is in a poor state of preservation today. No one maintains it, though a service group cut brush there in 1985, so its outlines are clearer. Many old tombstones are cracked or broken.

Since 1987, neighbors have heard a never-before-heard sound, sometimes accompanying the light down the hill, across the valley, into the cemetery. Some have likened the sound to that of a wild creature, though unidentifiable to local outdoorsmen. One man suggested a Sasquatch or Bigfoot, but there have been no other Central New York State sightings of such creatures. So the mysteries at Oswego Bitter only deepen with the passage of time.

Number 5

David worked part-time as a gravedigger in Madison, CT. He enjoyed the work, as it led him to ponder profound issues of life and death.

"I was working at the Willard family plot one day," he told me. "It was hot and the soil was hard. I was really earning my money. I took a break and went topside to read epitaphs, especially the Willard tombstones, while I cooled down. I noticed that Joshua Willard, husband, had had four wives. Their stones stood in a row, along with the gravestones of deceased children who'd died in a single year. Four wives! I thought to myself—that's a lot."

He then returned to his digging. In an hour or so, during another break, he found a grave marker across the access road, inscribed "Mary Willard." "That's strange," he thought, "must be the Willards were a large family. I wonder if she's related to the other guys across the road."

"I'm a fifth wife! I'm supposed to be with my husband on the other side." The words poured into his consciousness. He chided himself, "I gotta give up this job; it's really getting to me. I'm tired and I don't want dead people talking to me!" But he suddenly found himself asking her questions. "What do you mean 'on the other side?'" No answer. He asked again and again. No response. "Must be she wants to be across the road," he concluded.

David's wife suggested that they plant flowers on Mary's grave, which they did—petunias. They didn't grow. Later they tried geraniums, which flourished briefly, then died. All the flowers planted on her grave withered and died.

David believes that Mary feels snubbed because she is separated from her husband. She died first, and was likely the first of his five wives. She expected Joshua to join her after his death. However, he remarried—several times! When his second wife died, along with their children, in an epidemic, Joshua Willard needed a larger plot to bury them all, and found one across the road. Joshua being buried alongside his later wives and children must have riled Mary's pride. Considering the temper that Mary still exhibits after more than a century, he likely wouldn't have wanted to be *too* close.

The Flyover

When Sal's father died in Ogdensburg, NY, the family returned from the hospital heavy-hearted. He'd been a good father and husband, and had served his country in World War II. To ease their sorrow, they dwelt on the good times with mirth and humor as they recalled the events of his life. It seemed strange then, that, as they sat at home reminiscing, awaiting the viewing hours at the funeral home, they heard women wailing. They checked outside the family home. No one was there. The sound vanished, but resumed the next day. They found no one weeping in their house or outside. The next day, while awaiting the evening wake, the family observed a blackbird that had landed on the back door screen. Blackbirds don't normally come close to a busy doorway, and they had never seen one that early in the season. For two days he clung to the screen of the door.

During the military funeral at the cemetery, while the family stood around the casket and the minister concluded the eulogy, the honor guard sergeant barked an order. The honor guard fired one volley in salute, then another. Before the final volley, a blackbird buzzed low in flight over the mourners, then alighted on a nearby tree branch. Boom! The third volley resounded. As the bugler began Taps the bird took wing again. He circled the crowd once and flew out of sight.

Afterward, an uncle remembered that Father had always said he'd come to his own funeral.

Fly Away

After a long illness, Arlene's mother died and was cremated in 1986. Her ashes were buried in the Greenfield Cemetery in Greenfield Center, NY. Arlene was happy that her mother no longer suffered, but missed their friendship. She went to the cemetery a week after the burial.

As she and her husband approached the grave, they could hardly believe what they saw. A Canada goose was lying on her mother's grave. Not standing or squatting, but sprawled out full-length. They stood and looked at the bird, and without lifting its head from the ground, the bird looked back at them. After about five minutes it lifted its head, pushed to a standing position, slowly walked away, sprang into the air and flew off. No other geese had ever been seen in the cemetery and to the best of Arlene's knowledge, none has appeared since.

Buried?

"Here's a story for you, David," said the young man at a book signing. "It happened in a cemetery near my home." Randy was a personable man with a passion for epitaphs. He and his wife often meander through cemeteries in Washington County, NY. One day Rebecca, a co-worker, told him of The Old Burying Ground, a cemetery in Salem, NY. which contains the graves of many Revolutionary War veterans. He put it on that weekend's agenda.

He and Ann, his wife, and Alyssa, two, went to the stonewall-enclosed cemetery on a sunny day. It was breezy—a wonderful day to peruse gravestones etched in no longer fashionable styles. Here was a hand motif, there a weeping willow design, and beyond, a grim skull. Some stones contained sacred scripture. Laid to rest there were teachers, soldiers, lawyers and families that had settled Salem before the 1800s. After about a half-hour of wandering, with Randy holding Alyssa in his arms the entire time, the child broke into a scream. "What's wrong, honey?" he asked. The little girl raised her hand, in which was embedded a one-inch long wooden sliver. The flesh around it was red and blood oozed from the wound. Randy and Ann both tried to extract it, but to no avail.

"Well, we'd better get her to an emergency room," he said. They hurried out the gateway to the family car. Randy handed the baby to Ann in the front seat, who said, "I've got some Wipes in the glove compartment. At least I can clean the outside of the wound." With Alyssa in her lap, Ann inspected the child's hand. "Maybe I've got the wrong hand." Ann tried the other. It had no sliver either!

"Salem's Old Burying Ground"

Neither hand had a blood spot on it, even a pink spot! The parents stared at one another. "Who's ever going to believe this?" mumbled Randy. They returned home satisfied with that day's adventure.

At work on Monday, Randy overcame his reluctance and shared Saturday's experience with Rebecca. "I know you're not going to believe this…." he began, as he spilled out the tale. She said to him, "That's not the first strange story I've heard about that place. Don't you realize how many *doctors* are buried where you were walking?"

Could some energy or the unseen hand of a long-dead physician have reached from the grave to heal his child? That thought was even more incredible than the experience that Randy's family had been through.

I have walked among those gravestones, as Randy and Ann did. In fact, I moved to Salem. To date I have turned up gravestones for Dr. Abram Allen, Dr. Asa Fitch, Dr. Joseph Tomb (I love that one!), Dr. Thomas Clark and Dr. Seth Brown. Local history lovers assure me that there are as many as nine physicians buried in that acre. Many of them served in the Revolution and were interred with honors. This allotment of doctors and surgeons seems unusual to me. Randy's story is what I call a "head scratcher." It has no rational explanation. Ghost story fans will easily want to believe Salem's buried doctors are still working on the spirit plane, if no longer in their offices.

9

Hotels, Inns & B&B's

The Lamplighter

An old 1850 ship captain's home, retaining many qualities of bygone seacoast life, sits on Bradford Street hill in Provincetown, MA. It later became The Lamplighter Guest House. Many visit in summer, but in winter, one of the recent owners, Mike, and friends such as Maggie, relaxed, attended to minor repairs, and prepared brochures for the next season. At such times, when the house is quiet, "another world" seems to intrude.

"I was house-sitting for the owners a few years ago in March," said Maggie, "and kneeling on the ground, taking fish out of the pond so it could be cleaned. Taking a break, by straightening my back, I glanced toward the house. My attention was captured by an upstairs window, in which I saw two men and a woman in late 1800s dress peering at me. They seemed to go with the house, but the house was unoccupied except for me! Later that night, while I was drifting off to sleep, someone tickled me! I was then pressed down by someone I couldn't see, so I yelled and it stopped. The next day, thinking this couldn't be real, I jokingly told the story to Mike."

"It's not funny, Maggie," Mike responded, "Something similar happened to me. I had just turned onto my stomach one night, when something pushed my face into the pillow. I struggled to rise and had an awful time escaping. When I turned on the lights I was the only one in the room." Mike weighs 280 pounds and stands over six feet tall. So something powerful *was* there.

Another time, while Maggie and friends were preparing supper in the kitchen, an iron skillet filled with hot oil flew off the stovetop and crashed against the opposite wall. Sharing stories in the living room after dinner, they saw a mirror suddenly detach from the wall, move across the room, and remain poised in mid-air. Several jumped up, grabbed the mirror, and eased it to the floor.

Setting up for the coming season several days later, another of Mike's friends leafed through a Provincetown magazine. "Oh look," he said, "here's an article about a former owner!" Taking the magazine, Mike, who is sensitive to the other world, recognized the transparent man he'd once seen talking to a cat in the kitchen. He hasn't seen him since.

Another entity seems to prowl upstairs. A previous owner before Mike, sensing such a spirit, tried to capture ghost sounds on audiotape by putting a recorder in his bedroom. It was configured to turn on automatically if there was any sound. Playing back the tape after a few days, he was surprised to hear a faint voice slowly calling his name "Allen." He believes he captured a ghost voice because he was alone in the house during that period. It wasn't clear, however, whether the voice was male or female.

The final straw that convinced Mike to sell the house was seeing a woman in a plaid dress move through his bedroom and vanish into a wall. "I loved that house and was sad to leave it, but I'm pretty sensitive to ghosts, and there was just too much activity there for me."

The new owner reports cold spots that come and go. "Too bad we can't get *them* to cooperate," he said. "We have a couple of really hot summer days each year in P-town. It would be nice to send a ghost up to a guest's room to cool things down for them. But, of course, we'd only send the friendly ones," he laughed.

The Lady of the Basin

When Drake Hewitt first saw the old hotel at Smith's Basin, NY, he felt an eerie fascination. Situated between the old Champlain Canal towpath and the railroad, it once offered hospitality to travelers. He knew he'd buy, restore and bring it to life again, naming it "The Lady of the Basin." As he fulfilled his dream in 1998 he interviewed old timers to unfold its history.

Most recently, in the 1930s and '40s, Frieda Stearns had operated a post office and general store there. He interviewed Frieda and Mrs. Shaver, a neighbor who had lived on the property during those years. They told him that in 1825 the building was assembled from units constructed in Canada and transported down the Champlain Canal. Named for farmer and businessman Ezekiel Smith, the hamlet of Smith's Basin figured to enjoy prosperity.

The structure was first used as a storehouse for locally grown apples. Other outbuildings stored potatoes, timber from the Adirondacks and limestone from nearby quarries—all brought for shipment on the canal. Before the Civil War the original structure was transformed into a 150-guest full-service hotel. A steady flow of visitors came via the canal and the railroad, which passed near the building. Its large second-floor ballroom was popular for celebrations. A lavish Victorian façade was added. Eventually, after the canal was rerouted, fewer people came. The activity and frivolity lessened until Smith's Basin was notable only for its small post office and store, its golden days almost forgotten by Washington County's people. Drake Hewitt later found the old structure sleeping, and determined to awaken her.

"That old hotel has ghosts!" a friend advised me. And the Hewitts, hoping that one of my psychic friends, Susan, and I would help them understand more of the building's emotional past, gave us a tour. Susan, a professional woman, has a fascination with old houses, and sometimes accompanies me to seek impressions of former dwellers. As we walked through "The Lady" we psychically heard a woman complaining in the dining room, "For heavens' sake, Morgan…" she began, apparently prodding her husband to hurry to the train. Names came to us as we walked: "Borden" on the upstairs porch, "Marella" at the top of the side stairway, "Roger," "Robert," and "Williamson" on the downstairs porch, and "Jack" in the back wing. At the top of the main stairway Susan heard a man saying, "I'm sorry Eva," as she sensed him tumbling down the steps. We wished we knew the real-life details behind these brief echoes from the past.

The Hewitts and their friends report many recent experiences in the bright and friendly rooms. Little Patrick, visiting with his parents, and returning from the upstairs bathroom, said he saw "people in the corner up there." A few weeks later he said he felt a ghost on his back. Lacking a logical adult sense of reality, he innocently told what he perceived and felt.

Standing in the back yard one day, Drake's daughter looked up to see a little girl in a white dress, with a small Scottie in the bathroom window. Her sister also has seen a dog in the front upstairs bedroom window. Curiously, in front of the house, near some shrubs, the children showed us a small tombstone inscribed with the name, "Chubby."

Family friend Lisa has spent many nights in the old building, and once was locking the doors for the night, accompanied by her dog, while a thunderstorm erupted outside. At one thunderclap, her dog disappeared. She asked Drake for help in finding him and he joined in the search. As they passed through "the library room," they spied the animal *outside* on the closed porch, frantically scratching to come in. They had to unlock the door to let him in. Who or what had locked the dog out was never determined.

Dogs do seem to enjoy the old hotel. Apparently many former owners or guests had dogs and treated them well. Once, when Drake was painting the library room and playing lively music on the radio, he looked up to see their dog dancing across the room on its hind legs, but the dog had never been taught that trick.

Lisa often hears "happy chatter" and clinking teacups in the dining room. On one or two occasions she has heard what she terms "desperate men talking" in hushed voices, leaving us to wonder what momentous events might have been discussed there.

The process of returning the hotel to its former appearance has been arduous. Hewitt prefers to do most of the work himself, aided by family members. "I often hear voices when I'm working alone at night," he said. "Sometimes I hear people arriving downstairs. Other times I hear vague conversations—almost always happy ones. But I can't make out the words. Many times I hear the chatter of children too. And I sense animals, usually dogs."

Though "The Lady of the Basin" is not yet fully renovated, it is rented for various functions, such as weddings and parties. Another specialty is the Hewitt's "Murder Mystery Weekend." Conducted for small groups, the dramas offer visitors a chance to take part in solving a "murder" enacted in their midst. In summertime, small private dinner parties with chamber music are offered for visitors who are charmed by the old building's unique atmosphere. But it's not as if the hotel ever really *stopped* entertaining. Presences from its glory days still linger, savoring their stay just a bit longer before moving on.

128

By Any Other Name...

Lombardi Farm is a favorite bed-and-breakfast in Saratoga Springs, NY. Kathy and Dr. Vince Lombardi restored the two 150 year-old buildings as a cozy retreat. In the off-season, Kathy hosts interesting metaphysical groups there, and the house once had a ghost child from the Underground Railroad days, as reported in *Saratoga County Ghosts*.

An hour before a scheduled metaphysical meeting, a stranger appeared at the door, saying she'd heard the Lombardi's son had died. Kathy acknowledged her adult son had recently died. The stranger said she was mourning her sixteen year-old daughter's death in a car accident. Her daughter had disobeyed a rigid family rule: "Don't ride in anyone else's car. If transportation is needed, your parents will provide it." In a hurry, however, the girl had accepted a ride with a young classmate and had been killed in a crash. "I'm so angry at her for doing that," the mother said, "I can't forgive her!"

She stayed for the meeting and then left. Kathy cleared the table and went to bed. During the night she heard a voice calling, "Kathy! Kathy!" She thought someone had entered the house, but an inspection turned up no one. She returned to bed, but not to sleep. She felt that someone was calling her from the spirit world, so she slipped into a meditative state and waited.

"My name is Janine. Tell my mother I send her yellow roses," said the girl's voice. That was all. Who was she, the deceased daughter that Kathy had learned of earlier? The mother hadn't told Kathy her daughter's name, only of her anger and bitterness. The next morning Kathy shared her experience with her husband and sought his advice. She was inclined not to tell the woman, feeling she might not welcome the message. Vince reminded her that if the situation were reversed, she would certainly want the other woman to convey the message. "So I telephoned her," Kathy said, "and she was furious."

"How dare you get a message from my daughter! You didn't even know her. If she wants to contact anyone, it should be me! And yes, her name is Janine," the woman blustered.

"Soon after this we had a B & B guest who was interested in the metaphysical, and I told her of my amazing experience," Kathy remembered. "The guest was Puerto Rican. 'Oh my,' she responded, 'I wonder if that family was Puerto Rican.'"

Kathy said, "I don't know. Why is that important?"

"Puerto Ricans only send yellow roses to people they hate," the woman responded.

When Kathy recounted the story to me, I mentioned that an Internet website listed yellow roses as an expression of "decreased love."

Why should a girl who tragically entered the spirit world turn to an angry mother, only to receive a reprimand? Perhaps the daughter, perceiving Kathy's sympathy for families who've lost a child, sought a compassionate channel through which she could accurately send a message of whatever meaning, that only her mother could interpret.

Lombardi Farm looks out on quiet green meadows to the east, the ideal setting for spirits to contact loved ones. And many have done just that there.

Rideau Inn

On a hill in Ottawa, Canada, sits a beautiful Edwardian era house dating from 1907. It was once the home of a doctor who served across the street at St. Luke's Hospital. After his death it became a seven-bedroom rooming house. In 1986 George Hartsgrove started a bed and breakfast at the doctor's old residence, aware that the woman from whom he purchased the house claimed to have seen a strange sight in the dining room—a bodiless, faceless, yellow turtleneck sweater floating in the doorway. Since then Rideau View Inn Bed & Breakfast manager, Richard Brouse, has seen many strange things. "The dapper man in the sweater" visited his room nightly, and often sat on the bed during the first several weeks after Richard came there. He dubbed the ghost "Oscar." On several occasions he awoke to find Oscar standing beside his bed staring.

Oscar was not the first apparition Richard encountered. When he started work in 1997, he noted a sewer stench in his bedroom. Simultaneously, he saw a shadow move across the wall and out his door. Descending into the basement, he expected to find the sewer overflowing, but nothing was amiss. Sometime later, he awoke to find two dark-complexioned men, perhaps Africans, standing at the foot of his bed. Startled, he grabbed his blanket, threw it at them, and fled the room. They never returned. Then a bald Caucasian man appeared, hovering stiffly in mid-air over the foot of his bed—staring at him. Richard began to feel as if he were a patient being observed by an international group of medical people.

Once he awoke to find his room bathed in a soft glow. He sleepily reached to turn his bedside light off, thinking it was already on. However, the light came *on* instead of banishing the glow. He realized the light didn't emanate from his lamp because the strange glow persisted even in an illuminated room. There were no ghosts or movements in the room, so finally he went back to sleep. Sometimes he also felt scrutinized in an upstairs bathroom, but no specter has yet shown itself there.

"A full house" now has more meaning for him, as guests tell him of ghosts in the dining room and several bedrooms. One recent guest reported a filmy ghost which seated itself on the bedroom settee before vanishing. Nobody seems frightened, and several guests have promised to return, hoping for the thrill of future sightings.

In the summer of 1999 all males—staff and guests, awoke at the same time. This was only discovered at breakfast, when one of them told of being startled awake and noticing the time. One by one the other men at the breakfast table, mystified, confessed they, too, had awakened at the same time. The wives seated at table were suspicious of the entire conversation, but weren't quite sure how to interpret the incident, this being an era of equal rights.

Ghost sightings occur at intervals and are now accepted as part of the normal routine. However, there are other strange phenomena such as the smoke episode. In early 2000 the living room suddenly filled with smoke—just the living room. The smoke didn't spread to nearby rooms and was quickly dissipated by opening the windows. No source for it was ever found.

Renamed The Rideau Inn in 2001, its guests still come and go, charmed by the old house's elegant interior. There are many bed & breakfasts in Canada's capital city, but guests return often to The Rideau Inn. With its genteel atmosphere and wonderful breakfasts, the conversation often centers on apparitions, delightful and intriguing, but never disturbing.

Spring House Hotel

By the mid-1800s America's upper middle class was expanding. Many families no longer had to labor in fields or factories every day of the year. Leisure time was now possible for thousands, and during the hot summer months many headed for vacations along the New England coast. Hotels and guesthouses sprang up along uninhabited shores. One of the more secluded sites was Block Island, twelve miles south of Rhode Island and east of Long Island. In 1852 entrepreneurs built the Spring House Hotel, Block Island's oldest resort, on a hilltop. Guests "took the air" on spacious verandas overlooking the ocean and fifteen acres of lawns, bathed along miles of sandy beaches and enjoyed fresh food from Block Island's farms in capacious dining rooms. Spring House Hotel was the place to go for genteel families who could afford to escape the grimy and smoky industrial cities of the northeast.

Spring House wanted visitors to return year after year, and went to great lengths to assure them pampering and luxury in every detail. Business was so good by 1870 that management installed large porches, an ornate cupola and a new wing. Construction of an annex building gave the hotel a total of forty-nine rooms. By the 1880s Spring House's elegant Saturday evening ball, with the upper crust donning jewels and fine clothing that rural folk could only dream of, became a tradition throughout the island. Hotel business was seasonal, causing owners and managers to focus on keeping customers happy and cash registers ringing.

Even if the local populace couldn't afford the elegance of Spring House's guest and dining rooms, they could vicariously experience the opulence by working there. The hotel also offered farmwives the opportunity to supplement meager incomes before the harvest. Girls and women took summer jobs as chambermaids, scullery maids and cooks. A few became executives of sorts in a hierarchy of servitude. One of these was remembered only as "Clossie," the chief housekeeper at Spring House before 1900. She fussed endlessly over her guestrooms and those who prepared them. Woe to the chambermaid who forgot to turn down the covers before a guest arrived; woe to the cleaner who missed a dust bunny under the bed! Today's managers think Clossie died around 1922, but insist that though she went "off payroll," she has not slackened her attention to detail.

Kate, a manager during the season, stays on to do repairs when the hotel closes. In the winter of 1999 she and co-worker Stephanie were cleaning Room M13 in the Annex. As she moved toward her vacuum cleaner, a large standing fan suddenly turned on. "In a way I wasn't surprised. That room has its stories. During the previous summer a woman came to the desk and complained the bed vibrated at night with 'a glassy rattling sound.' We offered her another room. Two weeks later parents in that room complained that 'someone else' in the room, an old woman, invisible to everyone else, troubled their little boy. Last winter we painted the radiators in M13. It was fun. I used masking tape to cover wall and floor areas around each radiator before painting. I set the roll down to tape a section. When I reached for it again, it was gone. I didn't find it until a few days later, underneath a dresser across the room!

" Clossie roams the main building too," she said. "I was doing all the cleaning on third floor during the off-season of 2000-2001. All the doors self-lock when they close. At the end of the day I closed all the doors, but a few minutes later found every door on that floor standing open. I was working alone. I think Clossie did her own inspection after I thought I was finished. But Clossie isn't our only year-round guest. A few weeks later I cleaned Room 315 and, after finishing the bedroom, moved into the bathroom. As I did, I glanced into the mirror and saw the reflection of a man in old-style clothing sitting on the bed. I dashed back, but no one was there. It doesn't upset me because I'm interested in ghosts, but they never stay around long enough to talk. I think Clossie has them all on a tight schedule," she grinned.

Wiawaka

"Fuller House"

The fall colors were still beautiful, but a cold wind now swept over Lake George. "So this is what the place looks like in autumn!" she said happily to herself. Twenty-three-year-old Rachel remembered the place from childhood. When she was seven, her mother cooked there in summers, and she had played joyously along the lake. Now, in 1958, she was hitchhiking "on the road," having cut loose from family, and desperately trying to find an inner peace that her mother had never found.

Wiawaka, a summer resort for working women on Lake George, NY, had closed for the winter and night was coming on. She knocked at the caretaker's house and asked for shelter, but he refused. Rachel walked over the hill to Waconda Lodge, Wiawaka's beachfront residence. It was a frosty night. She found a door open, and disappeared inside.

"Waconda Lodge"

In the early 1970s workmen found Rachel's mummified, skeletal corpse where she had frozen to death in Waconda's porch attic years before. Today, many visitors believe that Rachel continues to prowl Wiawaka's buildings.

Wiawaka was constructed in 1903 as a haven for "working women of modest income from the mills in Troy, NY." The property and buildings were a gift from Spencer Trask, Wall Street financier and stockbroker, and his wife Katrina. Summer visitors to the lower Adirondack region, the Trasks later provided Yaddo, their home in Saratoga Springs, as an artist's retreat after their deaths. They named Fuller House on Lake George, the resort's main house, after Mary Fuller, the first director, and Katrina Trask's friend. Built as a large cottage in the Second Empire style, Fuller House has been recently restored. Its façade conceals some whimsical ghosts.

Jackie, who cooked there during the 1990s, often had contact with unseen residents. During a brunch in 1995, she looked up just in time to see a woman's lower legs and feet disappearing up the back stairway. All the guests were accounted for and eating dinner. Then, one morning in 1996 she saw feet (nothing above the ankles!) walking up the front stairway. Tantalized, she sprinted up the rear kitchen stairs hoping to confront the intruder. She arrived on the second floor at the same time a workman reached the top of the front stairs. There was nobody between them. Both then heard footsteps in the attic, but nobody was there either when they searched.

"We had one electrical problem after another for a few years," Jackie reported. "In the spring of 1999, before we opened for the season, we had all the smoke detectors examined and repaired. Even though we weren't cooking, the detector in the kitchen went off twice. Also, Dan, our handyman, was troubled by downstairs lights that flicked off and on. He couldn't fix them because nothing was wrong. Eventually it just stopped. We wondered if someone was trying to get our attention.

"I like to get up early and swim in the lake before 6 a.m. I met Rose, my assistant, coming out to greet me as I returned one morning. She had heard dishes rattling in the kitchen, and thought I was already up, so she dressed and came down to help. She found the kitchen empty and me walking toward the house. We've decided that our ghost is just trying to help with the work," she smiled.

Helen, a parapsychologist living near Lake George, visited Wiawaka once and said she felt at least one presence at Fuller House, a confirmation for Jackie, Rose and others, who feared they might be "losing it."

Jackie remembered yet another incident in Fuller. "My boyfriend stayed over one night. I dropped off to sleep early and he stayed up reading. He's a big guy—six and a half feet tall, but he was white as a sheet when he woke me around midnight. He said he had heard footsteps on the stairs, and something like a cane hitting each step. He found an excuse to leave soon afterward."

Rose Cottage, a small residence, is decorated in turn-of-the century furnishings. One night Wiawaka's director invited her sister and boyfriend to stay there. He was a private detective and former bodyguard to the Governor. Just as he drifted off to sleep he awoke with a jolt—there was a man's face (nothing else!) floating at the foot of the bed. He went to the dresser, took his revolver, and placed it under his pillow. He hasn't returned, even for a visit.

Some of the older staffers recalled that the old Crosbyside Hotel once stood where Rose Cottage is now, but burned before the present buildings were built. They speculate that the bodiless man may be the old caretaker, who was blamed for the fire.

Dan, caretaker and handyman for Wiawaka, sat relaxing outside Fuller late one evening. Everyone inside had gone to bed. He saw shadows on the kitchen window shades, but when he went to look, he found all the kitchen doors locked and the room empty. He has had many incidents of keys disappearing from their hooks, and being mysteriously returned.

When I revisited Fuller in 2001 I found a new cook. "I've been here a few years and I second what Dan said. Last month I sat outside at the picnic tables around 11:30 p.m. I looked into the kitchen, which I'd just locked, the night light was on as usual, and there were moving shadows, but nobody was inside when I checked."

Some think the shadows are Rachel, or perhaps Rachel and her mother looking for one another. Others think the shadows may be the old Crosbyside caretaker, wanting to atone for his century-old carelessness. Despite it all, however, Wiawaka still offers peaceful and inexpensive summer vacations to workingwomen. Wiawaka's directors take it all in stride, and point with pride to the intellectual and spiritual, if also "spirit-filled," growth that guests experience each summer.

The Blue Door

Philip Knight II was born in the mid-1650s, later married Margaret Wilkins, and in 1673 bought land in Topsfield, MA. He and his descendants lived for over a hundred years in a large home in what is now Middleton. He was a cooper, a builder of wooden casks; also held many township offices, attended church in Salem, and gave evidence at the famed witch trials there. His son Philip married Rebecca Towne, the niece of two executed witches, and built a house on East Street in 1692, which today is known as the Blue Door Bed and Breakfast Inn.

"All we have in the historical records is that young Philip 'died an untimely death at twenty-seven,' leaving a wife and two daughters," owner Ethel Marino told me. "I bought the house in 1977, following a psychic's prediction that I'd leave my house in Lynn. A customer in my store told me about an 'old dark house' for sale in Middleton, old Topsfield's new name. It turned out to be the old Knight house, and everything occurred as predicted. The sale went quickly, and my husband and I held an open house here on Christmas Day. We restored the house for eighteen years before he died in 1995.

"We've worked with the historical society to determine the many owners and uses of the house. Originally built with four rooms, it has been expanded over the years to the current eleven. After the Knights, the home had many owners, and at one time was the local Masonic lodge. By the late 1800s Henry Quiner, a Marblehead sea captain, lived here. In the late 1930s and early 1940s, storekeeper Mr. Butler, who was known to take walks in a velvet cape, owned it. Charred timbers hidden in today's walls testify to a fire in the building at one time.

"Throughout our family's ownership several intuitives have perceived spirits here. Some were forewarned that there were ghosts, and others discovered them by chance. Often, the phenomena occur in the old Masonic meeting room. We think it's young Philip and the Captain too. A few years ago, a psychic took a photo, and came away with a picture of a mustachioed face in the curtains. Guests have heard ringing bells, smelled candle wax and roses, and many have felt cold spots. Some visitors have approached the house hearing riotous parties within, but when they entered—nothing but stillness. One guest awoke to see a booted green figure sitting in his room's rocking chair. When my son-in-law was repairing the roof a few years ago, he joked, 'I hope there are no bad ghosts around to knock me off.' Just then, he heard three loud knocks on the wall next to him.

"My grown granddaughter, Heather, lay down upstairs when she didn't feel well one day. When she got up, feeling better, she sensed a female spirit present. Having heard the spirit's name from the cleaning lady, she said, 'Hi, Rosemary!' and heard four notes played on the piano downstairs, though she was alone. My friend, Janice, figures it was Rosemary who tipped over some drinking glasses and made lights flicker at a dinner party in 1998."

On another occasion, Heather saw a woman wearing a brown cloak walk through the dining room, the original kitchen. Behind the woman coffee cans and other small objects flew off the shelves. Possibly Rosemary?

Ethel told of a Peabody man, Russell Harden, who used to rent an apartment in her house. His bed would shake without apparent cause. Fortunately he learned to yell, "Philip, knock it off!" and the movement would cease. Harden also experienced sudden cold spots, and sometimes found objects missing. He had no doubt that he'd tangled with the ghost of Philip, Jr., but never really let the wraith bother him.

Another guest told Ethel of seeing a man, face down, behind the house, but observed there was no blood. When they went to check, the lawn was empty. Ethel wondered if Philip's ghost was trying to show where and how he died.

Ethel has always felt a presence watching over the house, but seldom informs her visitors about *the other* guests until check out. Some are surprised—they've had a restful stay. Others raise an eyebrow, smile and wink at her, feeling they received an unexpected bonus during their stay.

Eagle Mountain House

"This area around Jackson, NH, and Mount Washington is a little bit of heaven," the tourist guide explained. "People have been coming up here for a 150 years to enjoy the forests and clean air. Ghosts too. You must talk with Ernie, because he's felt 'em." He referred to Ernie Menard, who retired after working at the Eagle Mountain House in Jackson for ten years.

Eagle Mountain House has been a summer resort since the Gale family converted a large farmhouse to a tourist boarding house in 1879. Over the years it was expanded to handle over a hundred guests at a time. Sadly, it burned in 1915. The owners quickly rebuilt the structure, this time with a grand 280-foot long veranda, 125 rooms and 100 baths. Over the years a pool and nine-hole golf course were added. And sometime during all the construction, the building acquired a ghost.

"She is seen dressed all in red," said Ernie, "and she only comes out when the building is quiet. We think she used to be one of the kitchen workers, and she may even have died on the job, but she doesn't frequent the kitchen anymore. Her activities seem confined to the attic, where she moves things around from time to time. Some hotel guests have described her as middle aged and blonde haired. Always shy, she roams the hallways, just as the head housekeeper would, but only when the house is quiet. When the upstairs is noisy, with parties, celebrations, and such, she retreats to the quieter space beneath the fifth floor roof.

"I have felt her presence upstairs, but she doesn't scare me," said Ernie. "She's like just another employee, going about her duties. A woman artist from New York City stayed at Eagle Mountain House a few years ago and presented us with a painting of our inn. It's unlikely that she knew about our ghost lady—we don't advertise her—but there in our front doorway she'd painted a woman in red. Isn't that nice, she captured our lady's appearance for all the hotel guests to see! No one needs to be frightened of her. She just wants them to be comfortable and enjoy the mountains." When at Eagle Mountain House, I strolled the long veranda and took photographs, hoping for an image of the "permanent guest." Others, besides "The Lady in Red," have appeared to guests.

Ten years ago a male guest left the front porch to tell Ernie about a rocking chair on the porch moving all by itself. The day was hot and very humid. Nothing moved outdoors, and only the whirring blades of ceiling fans inside. Ernie investigated, but by then the chair was motionless, which perplexed the guest. Inveterate ghost story lovers read dozens of "rocking chair" tales; they aren't uncommon, but the guest experienced the story first-hand. "That's what Eagle Mountain House is all about," the jocular desk clerk told me, "sitting back, rocking and relaxing."

The Dorset Inn

As Cindy hustled between a busy kitchen and a busier dining room in the old Dorset Inn, she mused, "Such a hot summer night! The dining room and taproom are overflowing. Something special must be going on tonight at the Dorset Playhouse."

In the dining room she had noticed a couple and child in costume—he in an old fashioned dark military uniform with gold braid, and she in an especially full, floor-length skirt, reminiscent of late 1800s finery. The child was costumed, too, with a lace collar and long dress. Cindy made a mental note to get to them as soon as she delivered the next order. However, when she approached their table on her return, it was vacant, the dinnerware undisturbed, as if no one had ever sat there.

The hotel staff has had other encounters with "The General" during the last half-century, according to people I interviewed. He and his lady have often been seen in the 1797 inn's taproom, waiting to enjoy drinks that would never be served.

Cindy had a second encounter when she heard loud deliberate footsteps pacing to and fro overhead on the third floor at the rear of the building. She had been working in a second floor storeroom below, and climbed the stairs to investigate, as no one was supposed to be up there. Each room was empty. Who had that been, and why?

As other workers told me about the all-too-common sightings of the military man, I wondered if both of Cindy's experiences were related. Why had so many visually or audibly experienced what seemed to be The General? I invited the intuitive, Paul, to lunch and questioned him as perceptions of the *other world* rose in his consciousness.

"His name is Richard Evans, and he's a state militia man. He visited here. It was a favorite place. They came to the inn to drink spring water because he had a digestive problem. There was a spring in Dorset. The woman and child the waitress saw were his wife and daughter. His wife had a strange name, like Argentine or maybe Angeline. The daughter, Mary."

When asked why their energy remains at the inn, and if they are true ghosts, Paul said, "These are more memories of the building, and yet, their consciousness in time returns to happy summers, returns to the happiness as they reflect on the happy times there. These were times away from the job that they could spend together, very happy memories. The clunking that waitresses hear upstairs over the kitchen area is when he is remembering his decision to resign. He gave up influence, the money. He had to make these decisions when he stayed in Dorset, with politics involved, and he didn't want to let go of his position."

"Why did he decide to?" I asked.

"It could be his health…it could be Mary's health…the little girl had a vision problem. They remember all this from where they are now. It's like remote viewing. The waitresses can see them when Evans is thinking these thoughts. That's why the waitresses are not frightened—these are happy memories."

A few years ago a New York City couple spent the weekend at the inn, enjoying Vermont's autumn leaves. After their first night they asked the waitress at breakfast about a ghost. "Yes, we have them," she said, "but they are usually friendly."

"Not this one!" responded the wife. "He hovered over our bed all night, and tried to push my husband out." The couple had spent the night in a front bedroom on the second floor. Management obligingly moved them to a more tranquil room for the second night.

When I asked Paul if other ghosts inhabited the inn, he laughed. "There is an old man who is bitter, and he is the one that bothered the couple. He is very confused;

he is angry. He does not want to admit he is dead. He is a writer of letters. He sat in his room and wrote letters. People owed him a pension and never paid him. He died without an answer. He has not released himself."

I asked if he was angry at someone being in his room and Paul responded, "Not really, he's just angry. He thought he deserved a pension, but the government never paid him one. He spent most of his life writing letters, and stayed there in 1880."

Over the centuries old hotels and taverns have sheltered thousands of transients, each with their own trauma, plots or misfortunes. The Dorset Inn has graced the Dorset Corners for over two hundred years, offering today, as in olden times, wonderful meals, comfortable rooms and gracious hospitality. Those who love history and mystery might well enjoy its room and board on a quiet visit. Perhaps they will meet new "old" friends.

What Price?

"The Inn at Duck Creek"

The Price family traveled from Philadelphia to visit Cape Cod in 1810, found the harbor at Wellfleet to their liking and settled there before 1813. Outfitting a merchant ship, they undertook an import/export business and made a tidy fortune, which they invested in a large frame house on the hill overlooking the village of Wellfleet. Their descendants lived there until 1918, then with the First World War having changed international trade, they became landlubbers, converting the house to The Inn at Duck Creek. Columns imported from a demolished building in Orleans were installed on the rear of the building. An old 1700s Salt Works building from Brewster was brought to the site two years later. A tavern and restaurant

"The Restaurant"

were built next door. An old carriage repair shop completed the settlement. The grouping assembled quite a number of historic buildings and building parts and, apparently, collected a few ghosts.

Bob Morrill and Judy Pihl lived in the Salt Works building for a few years after they bought the property in the 1980s. From the building's structure, they believed it was once a home. No spectral visitations accompanied the frequent sound of a bead dropping and rolling across a hard surface. Despite frequent searches, they never found the source of the sound.

In the early 1990s two southerners, vacationing from Dixie's summer heat, took rooms in the inn. In the second floor hallway they saw two little girls who suddenly vanished. While relaxing in Room 130 they experienced sudden icy blasts and had a "whirling" sensation. Virginia, the hostess, smiled politely when the guests shared their experiences. She'd heard such stories so many times before.

It is not uncommon for management to find radiators turned on during the summer in the older part of the house. Closed windows are unaccountably found open, and vice versa. Lights turn themselves on and off. Toilet seats are sometimes found raised in rooms that have no male guests. Voices are heard in the back stairway when no one is there. Guests and staff often report smelling perfume at the foot of the front stairway.

"I worked in the inn from 1945 until just a few years ago," said Virginia, "and I'm sure that it's Lalie's perfume. A descendant of the Price's who ran the inn, her name was really Eulalia, but few people knew her well. She died in 1971, but she liked it here, and she might still be around. We had comments from guests in Rooms 18 and 19, too. They're in the oldest part of the house. An airline agent staying with us one summer awoke to see a woman staring out her room's window. The ghost woman turned and looked directly at the visitor, then moved to the bed to calm her fright before disappearing. The spirit wasn't successful. The agent checked out early the next morning.

"Later that day," Virginia said, "she returned to ask the staff about the incident. 'What's going on here?' With lots of humor we put her at ease. 'It's only ghosts.'"

Bob and Judy, the current owners, take ghosts in stride. Judy noted, "A few years ago a little girl guest saw an old woman standing by the window each night of her stay. The old woman kept saying, 'Don't forget to take your medicine.' But the girl wasn't on any medication at the time. We wondered what child from the past she was speaking to."

Bob and Judy helped our investigators unravel the impressions that our trusted intuitive friend, Paul, had received there. "What do we need to know about this place?" we asked. Paul saw the image of a woman chasing a man down the tavern's back staircase. "That may have been the couple who ran the restaurant until the 1950's," said Judy. "They fought a lot and the husband was eventually placed in a mental hospital."

"Two men stand in the doorway of the old carriage shop," Paul said, "and they argue over 'the traces.' Work was apparently done on one man's carriage, and he wasn't happy with the costs or results. He is still very angry."

At the front of the tavern Paul saw a transparent overwrought woman. "She stands there and tells me how hard she works just to make ends meet. She lists all the things she's doing to pay the bills, then adds, 'I'm a widow,'" related Paul. "We definitely have several women ghosts here," Judy assured us. "People have seen one near the stage. She may be the same woman that appears in the lobby—short, with a bustle on her back. She may also be the woman often seen walking through the kitchen.

"Two musicians have died in the restaurant over the years, and the live performers during the summer notice electronic glitches in their equipment near the stage. They often spot ghostly figures on the stairway between the lobby and the restaurant."

Just past the tavern the hill rises. Paul perceived an ancient Indian sitting there. "He's a hunter and loves the shellfish from the harbor, especially snails. He used to squat on the hill and dig the meat out of shells. Now he just surveys the changes his hilltop has undergone over the years. He is interested in life here today."

"That rings a bell," said Judy. " A few years ago an amateur archaeologist stopped by and asked permission to dig on that hill. He found artifacts and many shells over there."

During our off-season visit my family found The Duck Creek Tavern taking a winter rest. Last season's menu was still posted, though the restaurant wouldn't reopen until late spring. A beef and shrimp plate is their *piece de resistance*—one that will bring us back again. Perhaps we'll sample our shrimp outdoors, and contemplate the hilltop where the old Indian returns our gaze. Perhaps my daughter will go to the Inn and see if the little girls in the second floor hallway will play. There are enough friendly and hard-working ghosts here to engage a whole family.

Spirits á la Mode

Robert Kerr

Visiting the Village of Cambridge, NY, today, you'll see a marvelous architectural gem dating from 1885, the Cambridge Hotel. Built in Second Empire Victorian style, it served railroad passengers in this bustling, small upstate village. Business was flourishing at local shops and mills, and the railroad daily brought many out-of-town buyers and salespeople. The magnificent three-story hotel and its dining room were thriving.

But times and lifestyles changed. American business was less and less centered in farms and villages and more in urban industry. Fewer passengers came to town on the railroad and larger industries left this Washington County village for the cities. In the 1930s a local man, hoping to innovate a fad and thus publicize Cambridge, ordered ice cream with his apple pie at the Cambridge Hotel. A few weeks later he entered Delmonico's Restaurant in New York City, ordered *apple pie á la mode*, much to the confusion of the waiters, to whom he then haughtily explained its composition and origin. Delmonico's, fearing to be left out of a new American trend, added "apple pie á la mode" to its menu, from which the recipe (and Cambridge's fame as its birthplace) spread worldwide.

However, fewer tourists came to town and the hotel's fortunes dwindled. The Cambridge Hotel closed in 1990, though its popular restaurant stayed open for another six years. It had a glorious past but seemed to have a dismal future. For three years the old landmark was totally silent, before a group of investors and history lovers bought it. They restored its elegance and planned a grand re-opening in July of 1999. Many local people booked rooms for the inaugural week. Excitement was high and nostalgia prevailed. Few expected what happened next.

The morning after the re-opening night, some guests complained about the noisy party on the third floor. Perplexed, the manager assured his guests that the third floor was unoccupied, not yet renovated. Incredulous, the guests countered that thumps on the floor above had kept many on the second floor awake all night! The manager showed them the third floor and its unfinished state. Inevitably, word spread - The Cambridge Hotel had ghosts!

These events suggested a good gimmick for promoting a Halloween Mystery Party that year, and The *Bennington Banner* carried a feature story on the hotel, supplemented with digital photos of restored second floor rooms. But the reporter's digital camera refused to work on the third floor. When brought downstairs, the camera worked. Upstairs—nothing. There is *something* about that top floor, and nobody has yet figured what it is.

Beth Waters, hotel restaurant manager at the time of the reopening, had heard that "in the old days," a murder/suicide had occurred in an upstairs front room, though she hadn't found any documentation. She noted that the chairs on the veranda are often seen rocking when the air is still. She also remembered bare footprints tracked through the dust in the center of a third floor room, with no prints leading to or away. Who made them, and how?

"In the two years since we reopened there have been over thirty ghost reports from guests," said Rowland Bryant, former manager. "Curiously, all but one have come from women. Perhaps it is female sensitivity that causes this disparity, or male reluctance to admit to such experiences."

Recently, a Chicago couple stayed at the hotel. The wife was combing her hair while the husband was out buying a newspaper. In less than a minute after he left, the door opened. She asked her husband why he'd returned so soon. Silence. Nobody was in the doorway or hallway outside when she looked. She closed the door, locked it, and resumed her grooming. Within a minute, the door opened again. The housekeeper? Who else would have a key? She moved to greet the woman. Again, no one there. She had never heard about the hotel's ghosts, and went to tell the manager, "The strangest thing just happened...."

In the spring of 2000, Jim and Kristen vacationed at the Hotel. "We didn't see any ghosts, or even hear them, but we had very vivid dreams at night," Kristen said. I didn't tell her that their front room was said to be the scene of that long-ago murder.

"Ghosts, are just another part of my job. They don't frighten me," said Bryant. " Not long ago, I took a dismantled bed up to the third floor. As I placed the pieces against the wall in an unfinished third floor room, I said (to nobody in particular) 'Now, don't knock this over!' All was quiet until after midnight, when a second floor guest heard a great crash on the third floor above him. He told me about the noise at breakfast. I went up, but found the bed parts just as I'd left them." Bryant didn't disclose what he said then to the unseen residents of the third floor, but it was likely courteous. Courtesy is a way of life at the Cambridge Hotel.

Perhaps an autumn weekend during "leaf peeper season" would be a good time to visit this wonderful old building, now finally listed as a National Historic Landmark. Be sure to request rooms 4,5,6,7 or 8 if they are available, as they may offer "something extra." And don't overlook the dining room's apple pie á la mode—now truly an American classic!

Olivia

Olivia Goodnow, nineteen, came to Hopkinton, NY, as a servant girl. She loyally worked in the Brush family's large house, but yearned for more. She thought she'd found life's "more" in John Griffiss from nearby Nicholville. Friends warned of his tainted past, but she believed he could save her from a humdrum life of cleaning, and that she could make him respectable.

As the Potsdam *Courier and Freeman* later reported, on the evening of March 25, 1901, the engaged couple played cards with Mr. and Mrs. Brush, who then went to bed, feeling sleepier than usual. The newspaper stated that Olivia had "submitted to a delicate operation about a week or ten days before—at the hands of some skillful person," suggesting a botched abortion. It was known that Griffiss obtained morphine from a physician that evening, allegedly to ease her post-operative pain. The paper also suggested that he drugged the snack peanuts he brought to the card game. What happened later is speculation from the coroner's inquest.

Charles Brush found Olivia's lifeless body sprawled on the couch the next morning. The position of the body and the carefully arranged clothing indicated she had not arrayed herself in that manner. The coroner's jury finding was death by foul play, and her lover was the prime suspect. "Girl Murdered—Lover Sought" trumpeted the *Courier*. But Griffiss left a cold trail near New York City, and was never seen again. Olivia's body was laid to rest in the local cemetery, but her spirit seems to remain, still tidying up for the current owners of the Brush house. In time, the house was purchased by retired sheriff's deputy William L'Esperance and his wife, Jackie, who converted the old farmhouse into a stately Victorian bed and breakfast.

146

On occasion, guests sometimes reported a presence opening their doors at night. They would hear the door open, footsteps, the spirit leaving and the door closing. Jackie and her daughter have sometimes heard footsteps on the upstairs wood floors when nobody was there. Jackie shared her suspicions of a ghost with Bill, who at first scoffed. But when *he* heard the footsteps he grabbed his pistol, and went hunting for a trespasser. Finding nobody, he scoffed no more, and accepted his house had a "somebody." The L'Esperances put up with lights that wouldn't stay on or off. When Jackie says, "Come on, Olive, I'm tired—stop playing games with me!" the mischief ceases. She remembered the previous owner had told her of hearing the front hall piano play by itself.

"One of the hardest things to contend with is Olivia's effect on our big copper bathtub. It tarnishes if you don't scrub and dry it after each use," said Jackie. "I've had times when I finished cleaning and drying the tub and went about my chores. When I returned later it was tarnished. The only way this could an happen would be if someone filled and emptied it without me either hearing or seeing it!" The L'Esperances shared these reports in 1994; since then Bill has died.

When I spoke with Jackie in 2001 she said things had been calm during the winter, except for strange noises and objects mysteriously moving about or disappearing. She had recently searched for family photos for six months, and couldn't find them. They had disappeared from their usual location.

"Bill is still here," she said. "After his funeral, when I was sorrowing and feeling the burden of running the house by myself, I complained out loud, 'Why'd you go, Bill? Now, I'm the only soul in this house!' I continued cleaning, then found the toilet cover raised—a habit of Bill's, not mine! I lowered it, continued cleaning, and later found it raised again.

"We got permission to bury Bill in the side yard, under a tree. He still takes part in running this place. Last summer I had trouble with the riding lawn mower—it was smoking. I'm definitely not mechanical, but took it to the barn, removed the cover, and finished the repair all by myself! Surely it was with Bill's guidance. I couldn't have done it by myself.

"Once, recently, our son stayed here overnight. In the morning he said he had heard loud stomping and doors slamming in one of the front rooms. I think that Olivia and Bill are fighting for that space. Olivia used to live in the servant room at the back of the house, but now she thinks she can be 'somebody' and live in the front room. I don't think Bill will allow that!"

Olivia and Bill may have other company. An intuitive Native American friend recently came to dinner at Jackie's. He knew little about the house's history. "At dinner I could see he was uncomfortable," said Jackie. "His attention kept wandering to something I couldn't see. Finally, he blurted out, 'Why is the judge touching my shoulder?' One of the former owners of this house was a Justice of the Peace. There was no way he could have known that!"

After all the escapades, Jackie L'Esperance knows she is not "the only soul" in her old house. She takes fewer bed and breakfast guests since Bill's passing, just friends and family now. She realizes she could have a ringside seat at an otherworldly tussle between her Bill and a former servant. She has delegated Bill to keep Olivia in her place, and reserves the right to call on The Judge to keep order, if needed. With her infectious sense of humor, right now she is enjoying life fully.

Nathaniel Porter Inn

Warren, RI's Water Street is quiet today. Here and there are run-down buildings, but more often restored ones. The Nathaniel Porter Inn incorporates part of an old cooper's shop built in 1750. Ship captain Samuel Martin ordered the new construction in 1795 as a home. The Martin family lived there throughout the 1800s, but the old house slipped gradually into disrepair. In the early 20th Century it was a tenement building, then abandoned to vandals and the elements for almost a dozen years. In the early 1980s the Lynch family recognized its potential, purchased it, and began a six-year restoration.

Upon entering the main dining room with its large fireplace, my family felt we had stepped back into history. Chairs and coat hooks are adorned with tricorn hats, colonial uniforms, and muskets, as if their owners had set them aside while in the dining room. After a delicious meal we adjourned to "The Twin Room" at the top of the stairs. My wife, Linda, joked with our daughter, Sarada, "Watch out or Martha will tuck you in tonight! If you see a woman with a lit candle, you know you'll be looked after." We all laughed and treated it as a joke, and Linda, thinking she'd made it up, gave no further thought to her levity. With the wind outside blowing the late spring sleet over the multi-paned crown glass windows, and feeling that we'd truly traveled back to early America, we went to sleep.

As we left The Twin Room in the morning, we peered into the unoccupied guest room across the hall. Linda saw a shadow spring from the wingback chair near the sunlit street window and into a nearby corner. Even though the inn was reputedly benignly haunted, it was hard for Linda to take this as a genuine paranormal experience.

Throughout our stay we heard stories from staff, travelers and diners, that suggest people of another time are still carrying on their lives as if *we* were the invisible ones. In the front dining room a few years ago a guest was startled to see a transparent ghost moving through the room and described his sighting to the waitress. Another waitress experienced an electric light snapping off and on in the dining room, though she could see the switch, and it wasn't moving.

The innkeeper, Claire, when alone in the building, twice heard a female voice crying out in distress. Although she never was able to locate the source, she felt the sound came from the front stairway.

Two chefs, both named Daniel, alone in the kitchen after closing, were once startled by a voice calling out "Dan!" They were the only ones in the inn.

In the Twin Room, where we'd lodged, a guest had once been awakened and routed by a light circling the room's wall.

We wanted to know not just the phenomena, but also about the unresolved spiritual issues in the hearts and minds of these souls. Upon our return home, we asked Paul, our intuitive friend, about the house. Whether he travels with us or analyzes the houses from a distance, we've found him reliable and spiritually attuned. As usual, Paul operated in light trance.

Linda asked if there was a presence in the Twin Room. Paul affirmed its reality, identifying Martha, a housekeeper. Linda was stunned at her perceptiveness, thinking that she had only jokingly made up the name. Paul saw Martha fluffing the covers and tucking people in bed in that room, even the guests of today, as she did in 1810-1823. "It was her job to bring the bed warmer," he added. I remembered the story of a guest who'd awakened to see a light traveling around the room's walls. Could that have been Martha with her night candle, checking the beds before retiring?

Paul identified the corner in the room where Linda had seen the shadow, as "her place—her refuge. This woman's name is Esther—cook (or Cook?). She is in denial about her child's death and her own. She keeps hoping to see her child playing once more. You startled her when you suddenly walked into the room. It seems to be about 1840, and the child was all she had; she can't let go. The child has gone on, so we can pray for her to let go also. She was a sister. Her husband was lost at sea, leaving her a widow with a son, Alexander. The boy died of consumption, tuberculosis.

"She, herself, fell downstairs and died in 1856 at age thirty-eight. She may have thought she saw Alexander on the stairs, and reached for him, but fell. Esther was the one calling out in pain and grief. She broke her shoulder and spine—it paralyzed her. As she lay dying at the foot of the stairs, she thought 'I can't leave—my son is coming back' so she returned in spirit to her room. She sits in a straight-back chair with a woven rush seat in that corner, in order to watch the street below." (An upholstered chair is there today.)

Paul saw a very busy Water Street, with horses, freight wagons, and ox teams. A sail maker's workshop was across the street. Esther loved to watch Alexander from her window, playing with a hoop on the then-cobblestone street.

Paul perceived a "common garden" at the rear of the house, where residents raised flowers and vegetables. Small bushes and stone slabs formed its borders. Esther loved to grow lavender and used flowers to overcome cooking smells.

"Another favorite was larkspur, thought to have medicinal power." Today that area is a blacktopped parking lot.

I had sensed a male ghost in the house attic, though we hadn't gone up there during our visit. Paul concurred, "Yes, he was a brother, a clerk who developed palsy in his hands and could no longer write in a steady hand. So he was turned out to pasture. His family kept him in a small room up there—out of obligation. He knew that, and they knew that. He felt too poor to buy a candle. It was 1868, and the man's last name sounds like Walters or Richards. He was cranky because he was so precise. He appears in dark clothes because of his mood or attitude. He says, 'I'll show them!' He wants to prove something to others, but those he wants to prove it to are gone now. He hopes to regain his health and be self-employed again. He is a rigid personality, and wants to control all aspects of his life, but can't control the shaking in his hands, and eventually his legs. It's a form of bitterness, resentment, and denial of death that has overtaken him. He has no formal moral or religious orientation. He was what we call 'a free thinker.' He didn't believe in Heaven—so he can't accept that The Light is available to him now."

Asked if this was his final condition, Paul said, "No, holy people may come into the house and pray for him." Paul's guidance said it was a great opportunity for spiritual people to help all these souls to move on.

When asked if the upstairs back meeting room was used for military meetings, Paul said it was more a meeting place for Whigs during the early 1800s. Many tankards of ale had been drunk and pipes smoked there.

He saw entire families living in a single room during the apartment house days of the early 1900s. Some men found temporary jobs in the neighborhood. (The inn's brochure indicates that over twenty-four people lived in the house during that tenement time.) Others later could move to small apartments nearby after finding steady work. Some of the tenement dwellers encountered the ghosts in the Porter Inn, Paul said. The "darkness" in the cellar stemmed from illegal activities during Prohibition. "Very selfish people," Paul commented. He urged us to pray for the ghosts' souls. "This isn't fashionable in America any more. The highest vibration of love is to pray for the dead," he added.

Seldom have I visited such a charming "haunted house." When Captain Martin named the building in 1795 he honored Nathaniel Porter, a twelve year-old lad from Warren who joined the minutemen at Lexington and Concord in 1775. Porter became a local hero, whose life eventually inspired the Lynch family to restore the old building to Porter's era. Today it offers delicious meals, an Early American atmosphere and an assortment of spirits—people not much different from folks that you know—struggling with the issues of life and death. Put this inn at the top of your list of places to stop, stay, dine and "listen."

Drilling

Eleanor Fielding liked the old Victorian house in Westport, Ontario, when she first saw it in 1990. The architecture hinted at the prosperity of the Canadian physician who built it in the 1870s. She bought the place and moved in by September. Her first night in the house she knew she was not alone. Each time she laid her head on the pillow she heard footsteps on the kitchen floor. She got up and checked a dozen times, but never found an intruder.

Dr. G.H. Berry's name was still etched into the front door's glass, though she discovered the next owner, Dr. W.D. Stevens, a dentist, had turned the glass pane upside down, reset it, and painted his own name. Both owners' names are visible today. She also discovered that a merchant owned the house after Dr. Stevens.

During her first year, Eleanor heard strange buzzing or rushing noises in the morning—like air vibrating in the water pipes. The noises continued for years, and were heard by many family members and visitors. The loudest sound was heard in her downstairs bathroom, a buzzing that she couldn't identify. She suspected a contractor was working somewhere in the neighborhood, but couldn't find any. A woman caring for Eleanor's ill mother heard it, too. In order to keep her equilibrium, Eleanor decided the noise must originate with power tools in her neighbor's garage. Another day she heard the strange noise when his garage door was closed and he was away—her theory was destroyed. Her son visited and together they determined that the noise was loudest in the bathroom, then realized the room had been Dr. Stevens' treatment room. They suspected they were hearing his long-vanished dental drill.

As Fielding House Bed and Breakfast Inn became more popular, Eleanor decided to offer a diversion—a Psychic Sunday. Several local psychics attended and, between readings, they investigated the house. Several sensed old Dr. Stevens was still around.

A carpenter, building a workbench for her in the cellar, noticed a section of the floor had been cut and resealed. "It had the appearance of a grave," she said. "I was apprehensive about it, but the workman told me it would be a good location for my pottery kilns if I first covered the spot with stone. I put the stone in when I was alone, and heard a sneeze in mid-air over that spot. It made me very nervous for a while! Compounding the eerie atmosphere, neighbors told me a previous owner had discovered bones while digging in the garden. Westport Police had labeled them 'human—very old,' but halted their investigation with that. Dr. Stevens' granddaughter brought her children one day, to show them the old family residence. She told me the dentist had also found bones under the barn, but the police decided they were just the physician's amputations.

"One night as I slept next to the porch window, I awoke after a half-hour. My puppy was barking. My night-light was not visible—either it was out or being blocked. I was so tired, though, that I went back to sleep. But I awoke three more times with the same sensation—someone or something was blocking the light. I wondered if a guest was in trouble, but a tour of their quarters revealed nothing. My mother was in a nursing home, and died the next night. I wondered if she'd been out-of-body the night I couldn't sleep, and that her spirit body had been blocking the light. I told my guests Mom had died and I had to close the house. I spent two weeks away at the funeral and its aftermath.

"When I reopened, a guest from the night Mom died returned to Fielding House and told me that she had been in bed that night and heard a knock at her door. Before she could respond, the door opened and an old lady walked in. She came to the guest's bed, looked at her, shook her head 'no,' and went to the other guest's bed in the room, shook her head once more, and left. Another of that night's guests awoke, saw the old woman, and ordered her out of the room. So the old woman left." Eleanor believes it was her mother, trying to tell her she was dying. A few weeks later another returned guest revealed having had the same nocturnal experience.

As the latter guest was recounting her experience, Eleanor's carpenter came downstairs from the attic and reported that the new window which he'd just installed had been scratched, as if with a diamond – a long, beautifully scripted letter "F," Eleanor's mother's initial. Eleanor recalled that her mother had loved and worn diamonds, and wondered.

Fielding House guests often relate out-of-the-ordinary experiences. "I've come to think it's old Dentist Stevens looking out for me and my guests," she said. "I've had no break-ins or disasters of any kind here. It's a happy house. Guests immediately feel its comfort. We've only had one event that troubled anybody. A gabby psychic visiting here once yelled, 'Ouch!' and reported being hit on the head during one of his pompous commentaries," Eleanor smiled. "Maybe the old dentist was trying to tell him, 'Shut your mouth.' That's a departure," she laughed, "he must have been so used to saying 'Open wide!' Dr. Stevens did a lot of drilling here, but his activities are never boring."

The Captain and the Angel

Early in the War of 1812, Canadian Militia Captain Colin Swayze was killed in the cellar of The Harmonious Coach House near Newark, Ontario, now Niagara-on-the-Lake. According to the legend, he'd gone to the log structure that May afternoon in 1813 hoping to "rescue" a keg of army-ration rum before advancing American forces overran the town. But the American Army swept through, and he was bayonetted. Apparently Capt. Swayze has remained, even though the Coach House was torched by retreating soldiers, and a new inn built in 1818.

Named "The Angel Inn" by John Ross, an early owner, the inn was once a Masonic lodge, a doctor's surgery, a dental surgery and a post office. Most of the time, however, it has provided room and board for travelers, many of whom were convinced it is haunted by Capt. Swayze.

"He was like family when we were kids because his antics were so frequently responsible for some mischief or another," long-time owner Florence LeDoux told reporters during the mid-1980s. "My parents owned the inn and I lived here as a child. My parents' ancestors claimed to have seen Capt. Swayze die in that battle." As a child she often heard dishes rattling in the cupboards when his ghost passed by. Her grandmother feared eating from dishes touched by a ghost, and made the children wash them after they rattled, so his passage meant extra work. Eventually, the youngsters learned to sing at the top of their lungs to cover the rattling sounds.

A visiting Englishwoman donated a painting of Swayze to the inn. During a New Year's celebration in the 1970s, some inebriated young men vandalized the portrait. Florence took it to be restored. The restoration artist, however, was unable to remove a small, thin, unidentifiable crystal-like object at the corner of the Captain's eye—it looked like a tear. He tried three times to paint over it, and three times it reemerged. She re-hung it, nevertheless, and one day a patron poked at it, knocking the "tear" off, and it has not, yet, reappeared.

Florence remembered that chairs used to fly across the dining room without apparent cause. Her innkeeper, Mr. Cartwright, at first scoffed at the idea of ghosts. One day an ale tankard was thrown at his head. "It is difficult to sustain an old attitude after you've had a tankard of ale fly at you in an empty room! His disbelief was also challenged as he witnessed a cupboard door opening, saucers inside it levitating, then flying around the room, past the fireplace, and landing on the bar, one after the other, like ducks," Florence said. "Then they slid off the edge and fell onto the floor, where they shattered."

In 1992 Florence sold the establishment to Englishmen Peter and Diane Ling. While awaiting the closing, Peter lived at the inn without incident until he nailed a horseshoe from England over the fireplace. One night he heard a loud crash downstairs and, finding nothing amiss, returned to bed. But in the morning, he found his heavy horseshoe near the front door, fifteen feet from the fireplace.

A waitress informed me that the ghosts are still active, but now more subtle. "Lights go off and on, and our electrician usually can't figure what causes it. Objects go missing, and never reappear. We don't know what The Captain is doing with them. A year ago, a family staying upstairs woke us in the middle of the night, and left without explanation. Something had bothered the wife and she 'refused to stay another minute.'"

The British flag flies proudly on a pole outside the inn. "It seems he's mollified by that sight," the waitress continued, "but if we forget to run it up some days, he gets agitated, comes out of the cellar, and the dishes start to rattle again. After the tragedy at the World Trade Center in 2001, we ran the American flag up the pole as a sign of solidarity with our American friends. The Captain seemed to tolerate that quite well. He probably understood that today Canada and the U.S. are all 'Americans.'"

10

Ghosts Afloat

Captain Proctor's House

"Capt. Proctor"

Captain Nelson Proctor was one of Maine's last real "sailing ship captains" to carry cargoes under sail. For almost sixty years he hauled lumber and grain up and down the East Coast of the United States. He died in 1973. His widow, Daisy, lived on for seven more years, enriching the small hamlet of Starboard with her memories. For a few years their white clapboard house overlooking the harbor and Ingalls Island sat vacant. Then retired businessman Mike Aschettino and his wife Paula bought it. Still deeply involved in careers elsewhere, they hoped the old house would be their seasonal vacation home. They rented it to vacationers during the rest of the year.

John McAlpin and his family found it an ideal vacation spot away from the hustle and bustle of Boston. They first came to Starboard in the summer of 1987, and were surprised when the Proctor's grandson dropped by to inquire, "Well, have you seen anything yet?"

"We thought that was funny. My wife and I weren't really believers in ghosts. Anyway the house is bright and cheerful—who could imagine a ghost there?" said John. "Soon after, however, Miles, our two-year-old began to puzzle us. When we'd put him in his chair at the dinner table, he'd look over at the kitchen door and say, 'Funny man! Funny man!' Of course we followed his gaze, but nothing was there. Miles wanted us to close the door for some reason, but he wasn't afraid.

"One year both sets of grandparents joined us. On previous visits they had visited as separate couples, so neither of them had shared their personal experiences of the house with the other couple. Now, with both grandparent couples, my wife and the children and I in the house, we could observe and share our experiences with one another. While seated on their bed, my wife's parents saw the hangers in their bedroom closet move—as if someone were sorting through the clothes. My father was upstairs sleeping on a mattress on the floor in a small pass-through room. He had his toiletries arrayed along the back of the couch seat cushion in the room. When he awoke, he saw a man with sideburns looking down on him. 'Am I imagining this? This poor guy is sitting on my toiletries!' The man faded out." John's parents went to visit the local historical society, and were mystified to see an early photo of Captain Nelson Proctor wearing sideburns.

"Once, when I was in the shower I felt a hand on my back, which was pretty hard to do, because there was a wall right behind me," said John. His family always enjoyed their stays in the old house between 1987 and 1992.

Herb Martin came to teach at the University of Maine in Machiasport in the autumn of 1992. Terri, his wife, was pregnant. When they found the Aschettino's home available, they were thrilled. They settled in and Herb went to work. Terri was excited about the arrival of their first child, and loved solitary walks along the shore. On one of these, she met a year-round resident, a woman who remembered Daisy Proctor, and who related what she knew of Starboard's early history. She told Terri the legend of buried pirate treasure in the area. The big white Proctor house sat nestled before a backdrop of huge spruce trees. It was enchanting when the autumn fog rolled in.

"From time to time things would turn up missing, but sooner or later they reappeared," Terri said. "Maybe the strangest thing that happened there took place in the rear upstairs bedroom. Whenever I tried to look out the bedroom window that winter, I couldn't do it. I felt the urge to look out, but my head just wouldn't turn that way. Sounds strange doesn't it? It was as if somebody or something didn't want me looking out. I could look out any other window in the house, not that one. All there was out there was a small back yard and the big spruce trees. So, I didn't look.

"Next spring our daughter was born, much to our delight. One day I took her out in the sunshine, leisurely strolling through the back yard. We decided to walk among the big trees. We had only gone about ten or fifteen feet, when I came upon a small tombstone. 'Emma Ida Kinghorn, died August 2, 1873, age 10 years, 4 months' it said, giving the dates of her short life and death. It was an awesome feeling, finding the gravestone of that little girl, a child who'd died at such a young age. She must have had parents who would have been devastated at their child's death. They had found such a beautiful protected resting place for a loved one that they couldn't protect from death. I could only say a prayer and hug my sweet baby close.

"Then it struck me. Maybe, if there was a ghost in Captain Proctor's house, he or she didn't *want* me to see the child's gravestone. Maybe they didn't want me to worry about infant mortality. If that's what it was, I'm thankful. Our daughter is such a joy to us."

I met the Proctor House owners, Mike and Paula Aschettino, when I visited Starboard. Their experiences while living there amounted to little more than creaky floors and small noises that anyone might hear in an old house. They have had no ghost encounters. "However, *everyone* we rent to has those," he smiled, and encouraged me to contact the McAlpins and Martins. Before I left, he invited me to visit them at Eastham, Massachusetts, where they have a year-round home. "It's an old ship captain's house, like this one. And it has a ghost too—one that *we* have experienced!"

Captain Smith's House

"We're only the second owners of this house," Mike Aschettino told me in Eastham, MA. "The Smith family owned it for almost three hundred years. Captain Smith built the house in the 1700s, and all his family were sailors along Cape Cod's shores. All but one of his sons were lost at sea. This section of The Cape is marked by many shipwrecks. Did you ever hear of the *Whydah*? It was an old slave ship from the 1700s, bought by Captain Sam Bellamy, a privateer who turned to pirating. Known as 'Black Sam Bellamy,' he had a short but profitable career before his ship was wrecked in 1717 off Marconi Beach. They found the wreck in 1985, just after we bought this house."

I noted that Mike's second "sea captain ghost house" looked so much like Captain Proctor's house in Starboard, ME; he seemed to have an affinity for finding such haunts. Strangely, both houses have a connection to "Black Sam Bellamy." Sam had gone into the pirate "business" in 1716, capturing a number of very rich cargoes in the Atlantic, then sailed north to the area that is called "The Point of Maine," which includes Starboard, as well as Bucks Harbor. He careened the *Whydah* on its shore, scraping barnacles and doing minor repairs. It is said that he buried a sizable amount of treasure there, though it has never been found. With a lighter ship he then sailed south, hoping for more treasure, but only found a watery grave off Cape Cod. Only three men walked out of the ocean after a hurricane destroyed *Whydah* and took the lives of Bellamy and his crew.

In 1985 underwater archaeologist Barry Clifford found the submerged *Whydah's* ribs protruding from the fast-shifting sand along Marconi Beach. Those waters are also strewn with marine wreckage of two world wars. Mike and Paula had just bought the Smith house as an eventual permanent home but, not yet retired, chose to rent it. Needing a base of operations for his underwater archaeology and salvage operation on Cape Cod, Clifford saw the Aschettino's rental ad, and moved his dive crews into the old house.

"There were enough hazards under the ocean, and Barry didn't need to contend with ghosts here," said Mike, "but apparently that's what they got at night. One member of Barry's crew, after one night in our house, encountered a ghost and refused to return. He lived out the dive season in a small tent in the back yard."

Bob Cembrola, archivist at the Naval War College in Newport, RI, told me about his experiences as a dive team member during one summer excavation headquartered in Eastham. "I spent a couple of nights in the old Capt. Smith House, and remember Barry and I, working on the next day's plans, saw an interior door slam by itself."

"It was Barry Clifford who first told us the house was haunted," said Mike. "Finally ready to make it our home, we moved in during October 1998. I went through the house looking for things needing repair. I checked and closed all the windows upstairs. After closing the dining room windows downstairs, I turned away. Suddenly, I heard one window raise itself, then crash down. I never understood how that could happen. That was our introduction to the ghost!"

Paula, when alone in the house, often catches movement out of the corner of her eye, but no one is ever there when she looks. "During the summer of 1999, Mike's mother visited here," Paula recounted. "She opened the window in her bedroom before going to bed. During the night she awoke and felt cold. 'It's freezing in here. I've got to get up and close that window,' she remembered thinking, but she couldn't wake up enough to do so. She was surprised to find the window closed when she awoke in the morning."

"One day I worked on my laptop computer downstairs," Mike added. "Overhead I heard a very loud thump, almost as if someone had fallen. I knew no one else was here, but I went up and looked anyway. Nothing was out of place, and nobody was there. Another day when I was here alone I heard the sound of our outdoor hose being unwound from its carrier. I thought Paula had come home, so I yelled out, 'That you, Paula?' There was no response. Her car wasn't in the driveway, but I was so sure of what I'd heard that I searched the entire house, even the buildings out back. She wasn't here and nobody else was visible. A few days later I heard that thump upstairs again, even felt a little vibration in the ceiling or walls but, as before, found nothing."

It may be the ghost of Black Sam Bellamy, upsetting the routines at the Smith House on Smith Lane. Or, it may simply be the spirit of the last Smith to leave the house, which she wasn't anxious to do when she sold in 1985. Isn't it curious, though, that Bellamy may have buried his treasure in the front yard of Mike and Paula's house in Maine before he died almost within sight of their yard on Cape Cod? The Aschettino's are so good natured and friendly that Black Sam probably would have been hard-pressed to change his evil ways to woodworking and painting, Mike and Paula's hobbies. They may yet have this influence on the old pirate, if indeed it is he, trying to fit into the role of landlubber homeowner.

Selkirk Light

"Selkirk Light"

"I always keep the light right on the bow, so it's just an easy swing to starboard when I enter the harbor," said Lou. "Late one afternoon in 1966 I was coming in early. I'd had a good day fishing, and wished my family was at the dock so I could brag. I looked at the Selkirk Light, as I always do, and saw a lady watching me from the rail outside. 'Well, at least *she'll* know,' I said to myself. I checked some of my gear and then turned my attention to the light again. She was gone. I remember she wore a full-length dress, and that was strange for August, but I wondered who she was. After I'd tied up, I saw the man we called 'harbormaster,' and asked him who the lookout was. He smiled and muttered something softly to himself. 'That's the ghost lady, Lou,' he said out loud. 'People have seen her for years, but she ain't real. Just a ghost.' And he moved away. I went home baffled. I had plenty of fish, but a big mystery too, and I never solved it."

Port Ontario is an old lake port, lying just northeast of Oswego, NY, at the mouth of the Salmon River. Its harbor entrance is guarded by The Selkirk Lighthouse, as it has been since 1838, when a Customs Office was also built there. For many years the port was also a Lifesaving Station for boat people in trouble on Lake Ontario. A center of marine business and trade, over twenty-five boats, mostly schooners, were built at Port Ontario between 1811 and 1887. In 1858 the lighthouse was officially deactivated in a period of government cost-cutting. Civil War veteran Lucius Cole lived there sporadically from 1852 until his death in 1890, keeping the light at his own expense when in residence. In 1893 a German immigrant from Syracuse, Leopold Job, bought the entire lighthouse reservation from the U.S. Government, turning it into a home. Two years later he constructed a small luxury hotel on the site. After his death in 1914, the Heckle family bought it and doubled the hotel's size.

Smugglers bringing booze from Canada during Prohibition frequented its wharves, warehouses, and dining rooms renowned for fine German food.

After years of neglect the lighthouse is now in automatic operation, and vacationers can rent the lighthouse and attached house from Jim Walker, current owner and member of the Lighthouse Historical Society, to experience the vibrations of two centuries.

If there is a ghost woman in the lighthouse, to which Lou attests, who is she? There are several legends that may explain the sightings. One tells that a young woman of the community spent many months or years on the walkway looking for her father's ship, which never returned. Dozens of ships were sunk or wrecked in storms on the lake over three hundred years. This squares most with Lou's observation.

Another story informs of a lighthouse keeper and daughter who lived alone at the light. Bringing her father's meal up to the lantern room one night, the girl stumbled at the stair top and tumbled downstairs, breaking her neck. Her spirit is said to remain in the building where she died.

In more recent times, a man and wife rented the structure and slept on the second floor. Both awoke to hear footsteps coming up the wooden stairs from below. Investigating, they found nobody on the stairs and nobody downstairs. The doors were locked.

A local psychic received the impression that a young Indian girl had died on that site in the fall of 1684, during a treaty signing between the French Governor-General of Canada, de la Barre, and Onondaga chief Garangula. Uncertain as to the specific manner of the girl's death, the psychic felt that the girl died violently, perhaps at the hands of a French soldier, and was surreptitiously buried on the site.

For history buffs, it is interesting that Selkirk Lighthouse is one of only four surviving "birdcage lanterns" in the U.S. Selkirk Light has the last remaining wooden lantern room deck in the country, along with the last wood spiral staircase. These are well worth seeing, even if one doesn't encounter the ghost girl. And the sunsets on Lake Ontario are breathtaking.

Southeast Light

"Southeast Light"

Lighthouses, by their nature, are often lonely places, remote and isolated on shores that are a hazard to shipping. The highest light in New England, 258 feet above sea level, is found on Block Island. Commissioned under President Grant, it began operation in 1875, flashing a green beacon, very unusual among New England lighthouses. Perhaps not so unusual for lighthouses, for part of its history it was haunted.

The brick structure was under U.S. Lighthouse Service jurisdiction until after World War II, when it was closed. Southeast Light reopened under U.S. Coast Guard control in the late 1940s, and remained a Coast Guard installation until the early 1960s, when its light was automated, no longer requiring a live-in maintenance staff. The Atlantic never ceases its destructive pounding of the land and it became evident that Mohegan Bluffs had eroded dangerously. In order to preserve Southeast Light, the government moved the structure inland in 1993. Today, it is a top tourist attraction for visitors to the island.

A lighthouse keeper in the early 1900s, according to local legend, is said to have become enraged at his wife. A struggle ensued, and she tumbled off the catwalk and died. Some say she was hanged from a cat-eye fixture on the lighthouse as she fell. Others claim she hit the ground sixty feet below. Each storyteller has a slightly different version, and hard facts are difficult to come by, but stories are generally the same: the ghost is an angry woman, and Block Islanders who tell the tale assume she is the wife of the light-keeper.

When we asked our intuitive friend, Paul, about this incident, he said that the lightkeeper and his wife were in the process of cleaning the lamp in 1921, when an argument ensued. In the midst of the fracas, she fell to her death. "For many years she was angry at her life being cut short after all the sacrifices she made to help her husband become a success. And she took out her anger, but she did pass." Paul noted that her husband (perhaps named Slocum) eventually retired, but blamed himself for his wife's death, feeling as guilty as if he'd murdered her. Likely his guilt mixed with her anger to create ghostly phenomena before "moving of the lighthouse broke the energy connection to that spot."

Almost all the phenomena created difficulties for men, while women visitors were left alone, which caused many to suspect the ghost was a vengeful woman. Coastguardsmen who served there were sometimes locked outside the building at night, or at least locked out of their quarters inside. Some reported having their beds lifted at night, then slammed to the floor. Others reported pots and food flying through the air in the galley. Cooks reported difficulty in controlling their stoves, as cooking flames suddenly turned to high heat. No one ever saw the stove knobs turning.

Even in the pre-World War II days of the Lighthouse Service there were stories of a constant mysterious re-arrangement of belongings and furniture. Locked doors were sometimes found open, and doors that had to be open were unaccountably found closed or even locked. Many who served there reported hearing and feeling a rapid "swoosh" of air, sometimes cold and sometimes not, as the ghost woman charged through the residence or up the circular stairway of the tower. There were the usual icy spots in otherwise warm rooms, which spots were felt by men and women visitors alike.

When the government moved the lighthouse the ghost apparently vanished. Often, when physical objects such as houses or possessions that the entity loved or hated in life are destroyed, their last hold on the physical world can dissolve. No longer is there a familiar vibration to cling to. When the ground she died on slipped into the timeless ocean, perhaps her soul was also ready to leave our time and move into the Everlasting Light.

Ghost Ship

In the early 1600s, English settlers at New Haven, CT, built a "great shippe" of 150 tons. They expected to load it with furs, hides, lumber, grain, and dried fish and sail directly up the Thames River to London. There was great expectation that those who invested in this enterprise would reap immense fortunes.

Captain Lamberton was hired to deliver the cargo, which included a few hardy passengers. The harbor waters froze on the departure day in January 1646, and when the matter was concluded, many saw in retrospect that it had been a bad omen. Saws were brought to laboriously cut a path through the ice to open water, and the ship could only be towed backward through the narrow opening to the ocean. Rev. John Davenport blessed the ship as it slipped its mooring, and the crew must have shuddered as they heard his valedictory: "Lord, if it be thy pleasure to bury these, our friends, in the bottom of the sea, take them; they are thine; save them." The ship, whose name is no longer remembered, sailed eastward and was soon lost to sight.

During the spring and early summer other boats returned from Europe, but not the "great shippe." The settlers grew anxious as autumn brought its usual storms, but no ship. Autumn turned to winter, and still the voyagers did not return. Families and friends, beginning to fear the worst, redoubled their prayers for the wellbeing of passengers and crew. Spring came, then early summer, and still no ship. Finally, harbor lookouts spotted the square-rigged ship, a misty cloud hovering overhead, approaching before an offshore breeze.

The joyful settlers hurried to the wharf, some with telescopes. The crew didn't shorten sail, and no deck gun fired a salute. No voices hailed the shore. But not one hand was seen on deck—only a lone figure stood in the bow, signaling with his sword toward the open sea.

167

All at once, the maintop snapped, its sails and rigging toppled, carrying other masts with it. The ship's hull maintained its course toward shore, though observers could see timbers and planks falling away. Then, like a New England right whale, the remainder of the ship slipped beneath the harbor's waters, leaving only a wake pushing shoreward. At the spot of the ship's disappearance only a hovering mysterious cloud could be seen. Not a lifeboat, spar, or barrel floated to the surface. The settlers stood dumbfounded, overwhelmed by myriad questions. How could such a thing happen? How could the ship simply vanish without a trace? Why was there no flotsam and why were there no survivors?

Reverend Davenport identified the event as a collective apparition, mercifully sent to show friends and families the fate of passengers, crew and investors' hopes. He gave the eulogy: "This was the very mould of our ship, and thus was her tragic end. God has condescended for the quieting of our afflicted spirits, this extraordinary account of His sovereign disposal of those for whom so many prayers were made continually." This is one of the first great mystery stories to emerge from the settlement of the New World—not just a single ghost, but an entire ship of departed souls! Drawn from historical records, the story has been printed several times in the *New Haven Register.*

Captain's Mom

Peter McDougal was captain of a sailing ship engaged in the China trade during the 1820s. One evening in the South Atlantic, as the ship was making for New York City, Capt. McDougal surveyed the deck, checked the stars, and noted the calm ocean surface. Then he went below for the night, donned his nightshirt and dropped into bed. He had hardly closed his eyes, however, when a sailor charged down the companionway and into his cabin.

"Captain, there's something very odd up top, you'd better come look!" the sailor exclaimed.

Pulling on a wool hat, McDougal climbed the stairway and beheld in the mainmast rigging a softly glowing woman. Nobody recognized her, but as the captain came on deck, she stretched forth her arms, as if to enfold him. Awestruck, McDougal and his crew stared, until, after five minutes, she gradually faded. This was not St. Elmo's Fire. They had never seen such a phenomenon before, and it was dutifully entered in the ship's log.

In another twenty days they made port and began to off-load their cargo. A man in black mourning dress hailed the deck, boarded and handed the captain a sealed black-bordered letter, a traditional funeral notification. Suspensefully, McDougal opened it and found his mother's death notice. Reading the date and time of death, he rushed below decks. Opening the ship's log, he found that she had died at the exact time he and his crew experienced the apparition in the ship's rigging.

I am indebted to Bobbi Carleton of Tamworth, NH, who shared this tale from her family's folklore. It was long ago inscribed in the family Bible.

Uncle Devolson

Devolson Bamford had lake water in his veins. Born not far from the St. Lawrence River in Jefferson County, NY, he was attracted to boats and water from a young age. When he was old enough, he married his sweetheart, Rachel, and formed a partnership with his brother, Wells, in owning the schooner *Reindeer*. The two men sailed many a profitable voyage from Wolfe Island, Ontario, carrying lumber, grain and assorted farm products, mostly to the western end of Lake Ontario, where cities and townships were multiplying. They traveled as far west as Chicago.

In early October of 1867, with the *Reindeer* laid up for repairs, Devolson hired on as a hand on another ship, just to provide for his wife and two children. After midnight on October 16th, Rachel awoke with a start. Something was terribly wrong. At the foot of her bed she saw Devolson standing in his oilskins, dripping wet. "Volty, what's wrong?" she asked. The figure simply said, "Goodbye," and looked so sad. In a moment she understood. Her beloved husband was dead out on Lake Ontario. He vanished as this realization came to her.

The next morning, the men in the harbor recognized the ship that Devolson had hired onto was overdue. Then they received a telegram that confirmed their worst fears—the ship wasn't coming back; it had sunk in a notorious White Squall. "Who's going to go up to Devolson's house and tell Rachel?" they worried. They drew straws and the unlucky man made the trek.

The door opened as soon as he knocked. Rachel greeted him dry-eyed. Before the unlucky man could utter a word she said, "It's all right. You go back to the dock. I know Volty is dead. He came to me in his wet oilskins last night. I know he won't be back." His body was never found, so a memorial stone was placed in the Bamford family plot in Sand Bay Cemetery, near Cape Vincent, NY. For years the people on Wolfe Island docks told and retold this sad event. It was a true ghost story, involving one of their own, and it helped others, when they lost a loved one on the lake, to know that love can transcend time and space.

11
School
& College
Ghosts

Spirits and the Rose

The College of St. Rose, in Albany, NY, is almost eighty years old. Its founders took pride in the loyal alumnae who often formed lifelong bonds with one another and to the college. Some may have returned to campus after death. On Morris Street is an old Catholic convent, converted into a dormitory in the 1960s. Since deciding to end daily mass there, the chapel was closed off to students. Now a permanent wall separates the old chapel from a student lounge, where those immersed in TV sometimes report seeing a priest in old vestments saying mass while intermixed with the wall. He stands with his back to those in the lounge, facing a no-longer-visible altar.

For forty years Morris Hall residents have also reported hearing sweet flute music echoing in the building, though no one has ever been able to locate its source. But, until recent years, spectral music existed elsewhere on campus, too. The now demolished music building, Cabrini Hall, on Madison Avenue, was replaced by The Hubbard Interfaith Sanctuary in the early 1990s. When Cabrini stood, many students and teachers heard piano music emanating from the locked building at night. Often, students there also complained of having "someone or something" brush against them when no one was visible. Most of them believed it was John, a former music professor, who, many years ago, had traveled to Chicago and hanged himself in a hotel there. Several of his colleagues feel John's duty-bound spirit returned to Albany to watch over his former students. Masses have been said at the campus chapel for the repose of John's soul.

Peggy, now principal of a Catholic elementary school in Ohio, was among a group of plucky students who convinced the security officer to let them stay in Cabrini on Halloween. Trying to catch John in a nocturnal concert, they stayed the night without result. Peggy admits the group was keyed up and found it hard to achieve the quiet that John likely needed from his concert audiences.

The Music Department used to keep costumes and props for college plays locked in Cabrini's attic. Sr. Dorothy Flood, retired Music Department Chairman, recalls finding the attic floor strewn with broken wooden swords where, an hour before, they had been neatly stacked and unbroken. Knowing she had the only key to the room in her pocket, she said a prayer, then hastily retreated. The attic also figured prominently during The Great Northeast Blackout in November 1965. No electric power flowed in the City of Albany. St. Rose coeds, however, stood in awe, staring at the attic window in Cabrini. The attic light was on, and nobody ever was able to explain why. Perhaps John was listening to "light opera?"

In the 1980s, when Sr. Dorothy was housemother in Carey Hall, she worked alone in the dorm the night before students returned from Christmas vacation. She observed a beach ball sized light glowing in an open lavatory. "The girls in Carey had been playing with Ouija boards for some months. I warned them they might bring something unpleasant into the building," she said. When the light began moving toward her, she hastened into her upstairs room, closed the door, and waited to see if the orb would come through. It didn't. "I wasn't really afraid," she told me, "I just didn't want to tangle with it."

Today's ghosts are an integral part of campus legend. Dennis McDonald, Student Affairs Director, mentions them at the annual autumn dorm orientations. "Just another dimension of campus life," he smiled, "nothing to get upset about. We tell the students where they can get assistance if they encounter those parts of St. Rose's history. We approach it all lightly and with good humor." St. Rose of Lima, who lived in Europe, and yet, was seen teaching Peruvian Indians, is likely amused by these activities at her namesake college.

The Maiden

"Jackson Gardens in 1906"

Fred and Judy sauntered hand in hand up Union Street in Schenectady, NY, on a summer evening in 1995. They were in love and the evening was balmy. They turned left through The Blue Gate into Union College, meandered across the green lawns, and found themselves in Jackson Gardens, off Nott Street. They sat at the base of a large tree, and affectionately kissed a few times while savoring the fragrance of flowers which drifted through the semi-dark glade. As they chatted, they could hear traffic moving on Nott Street, but were only attentive to each other's thoughts. Suddenly Judy smelled smoke, just a bit at first, but then stronger. "Freddy, what's that? Something's on fire!" Fred sniffed, couldn't smell anything, but then both clearly saw what Fred describes as a "bluish-white light," flitting across the path and disappearing to the east, in the direction of the Achilles Rink. It scared them enough to pick up immediately and leave. They had encountered Union's three hundred-year-old ghost.

The Stockade section of Schenectady, just west of Union College, has many old buildings and a ghost or two of equal vintage. First settled by Dutch traders in the early 1600s, Schenectady became a trading center for the wilderness to the west. One merchant who profited greatly was Jan Van der Veer, whose house and store once stood near today's railroad bridge in Rotterdam Junction. Though enriched by his business, he possessed little wealth in human kindness. His neighbors and customers feared his crankiness on good days and his violent temper on bad ones. Townsfolk couldn't understand how such an old crank could have fathered a most beautiful and gentle daughter, Alice.

Alice, renowned for her charm, should have been eagerly sought in marriage, but her father's ill temper and possessiveness kept most men away. One young grocer in the Stockade ignored Van der Veer's foul temper and, enthralled by his daughter's loveliness, covertly courted Alice. The pair found ways to meet under cover

of darkness along the shores of the Mohawk River. Van der Veer followed her one summer night and, near the present location of Lock 8 on the Barge Canal, he spied a young man emerging from the shadowy trees and linking arms with Alice. They strolled toward what is now Union Street.

Van der Veer, carrying a rifle, followed the pair to where they were seated beneath a tree, and shot the suitor through the heart. Despite Alice's screams and the outcry of neighbors, Van der Veer then dragged his daughter westward toward home. As they neared the riverbank, however, he heard an outraged mob in loud pursuit. He released Alice and fled into the Stockade, hoping to escape his pursuers' vengeance. They caught him near the old Yates House at 109 Union Street, bound him to a hitching post, and summarily burned him to death. Justice was emotional and swift.

Alice, when released by her father, attempted to return to her dying lover, and fled uphill to a grove of oak trees, which later became Jackson's Gardens. The furious mob, still incensed, came upon Alice prostrate and weeping there. Fired by anger, the throng believed she had been a party to the young man's death. They seized her, tied her to a nearby tree, and set her ablaze. She is said to have remained silent as the flames engulfed her beneath a full moon.

For many years, sightings of "The Maiden" were frequent in Schenectady. According to folklorist Helen Caekener, The Maiden was seen for three centuries, sometimes with a burned dress. When she does appear, it is often at 9 p.m. near Rotterdam Junction, where the Van der Veer's house once stood. Sometimes she is an evanescent light, other times a more substantial form. Those who have encountered her in Jackson's Gardens have reported the detectable smell of wood smoke. From time to time the old *Union Star* chronicled the tale when city residents came forward to recount their sightings. The phenomenon has dramatically lessened over the years, and local papers seldom print the grisly legend anymore.

The summer of 1672 is now long past, but there are still occasional personal experiences, such as Fred and Judy's, in which two lovers may have prompted the spirit of a long ago lover to reappear. Perhaps the filmy figure roaming the banks of the Mohawk or wandering through the Stockade and Union campus is finally readying to sever her connection to the physical plane. When the first full moon of summer rises this year, you may want to visit Union College and seek the apparition for yourself. And if you *do* see her flitting among the lilies, you may want to utter a prayer that Alice, once deprived of all she held dear, will find peace at last.

Elaine

The Kappa Delta Sigma (KDS) Sorority House at St. Lawrence University is a delightful haunted house. The Canton, NY, house was once the residence of a prominent family in the 1920s and has been impeccably maintained. In a chance encounter with a former student, Allison Corwin, I heard of this sorority's ghost. "You've got to come to Canton some time, and meet 'The Lady in White.'" Allison had been a hard-working high school student, and was about to be installed as her college sorority's president, so I knew she wasn't pulling my leg. I scheduled my "North Country expedition" to hunt for ghosts in the northern Adirondacks.

Arriving at the end of the school term I found myself in the midst of a social hour—intelligent sorority women chatting with their dates. Heather McKnight and Missy Troy escorted me into the lounge and related the building's history, including the background of The Lady in White. Missy's aunt also attended St. Lawrence in the early 1980s, and said The Lady's story had been circulating long before her time. It always helps to name ghosts. Personalizing makes one less likely to startle when suddenly confronted by an incorporeal form. This ghost was named "Elaine", daughter of the wealthy builders.

She had been betrothed to a rich young man with whom she had planned a lavish wedding. The young man personally betrayed Elaine and the wedding was cancelled. Humiliated, she went to her upstairs bedroom and hanged herself, perhaps in her wedding gown, in the closet. Elaine died and The Lady in White was born into the spirit world.

Years later, St. Lawrence University purchased the building and it became a sorority house. The sorority sisters began hearing strange noises upstairs and began finding items missing or moved. During the 1990s a number of strange events were recorded. As a spirit, Elaine has never been seen, only the evidence of her activity is experienced.

During a vacation, when no students were on campus, and after KDS residents had been instructed to disconnect all electrical appliances and had turned off all switches, security officers found the light on in "Elaine's closet." Once, during a blackout, with no power anywhere in Canton, campus residents were surprised to find Elaine's closet light on, again. At other times, even with power in the house, unseen hands constantly turned on the closet light, though residents just as doggedly turned it off.

About ten years ago five girls (with a lit candle, as in Hollywood thrillers, of course) went into the closet with a Ouija board. They began the session by asking personal questions, the answers to which not even their best friends knew. The respondent, apparently Elaine, gave answers of such detail that three girls, unable to handle the reality, immediately fled in panic.

Jamie Heimburg lived in Elaine's room for a year before gaining enough "house seniority" to find a less kinetic environment. Dressers would vibrate while other objects remained quiet. Jamie had a stuffed animal sitting atop her TV. She looked up just in time to see it sailing across the room, one of many objects that became airborne without anyone touching it. No one was ever able to explain any of this.

Jamie also had to struggle to understand how the answering machine in her room could suddenly turn on, even though her phone hadn't rung. Telephones randomly disconnected themselves in the house when there was tension among the girls. One sorority sister transferred to another residence after she had an unnerving experience. She had been in bed on the second floor and heard the telephone ring in the downstairs hall. Throwing on her robe, she shuffled downstairs, only to find the phone unplugged.

On occasion the TV screen in the living room slowly turned itself on one dot at a time. Several times when all the girls had been out, they often returned home to find old black-and-white films playing on the TV, unwatched.

One evening a sorority sister was wrestling with her boyfriend in the living room. He started tickling her so relentlessly that she screamed, "Stop!" Immediately, the fire alarm went off. There was no fire. On another evening, the fire door on the third floor opened by itself as several girls stood watching in the hallway. It was impossible to open from the outside, and no one was near it on the inside.

All these phenomena are attributed to Elaine. Perhaps it is time for the KDS sisters to initiate her into their sisterhood formally, helping her feel that her presence is known and accepted, and that she is loved, even if rejected by a suitor. In the spirit of oneness, the women of KDS would surely support a sister in distress. Until then, however, the frequency of The Lady in White's activity seems likely to keep KDS on their toes.

Old Main

"I'll tell you a weird story," Susan said. "When I was a student at the State University in Fredonia, NY, I spent time building sets and gathering props in the theater at the Old Main building. Our crew scattered for a brief bathroom and smoke break one night. I was relaxing alone atop a heavy old steamer trunk in the prop room. Suddenly I felt movement. The trunk started to rise off the floor. Now you know me, David. I'm not the lightest person in the world. That trunk rose almost half a foot in the air, *with me on it, and then it started to rotate slowly!*"

Jumping off as the trunk settled to the floor again, Susan sought out the other students and professors for an explanation. They assured her that this was not an isolated incident, and that "strange things" did happen in the theater, which had been built in the old Fredonia Normal School era.

"After the Fire"

One professor believed that Susan's experience was probably initiated by "the girls," long suspected of creating the theater's glitches. The Normal School had installed iron grids on the windows to keep interlopers from entering when the theater building was Old Main Dormitory. On December 14, 1900 a fire broke out in the building, and none could get to the fire escapes or enter the fiery hallways. The window grids became a death sentence for six women students and the custodian who tried to save them. The college and community were traumatized. Only little May Williams' body had been identified by her ring. She and the others, charred beyond recognition, were interred in a common grave in Forest Park Cemetery, where their resting site is marked by a monolith.

The modern Old Main was rebuilt on the original foundation. In December of 1974, on the 74th anniversary of the fire, sixteen students decided to seriously investigate the facts of the horrible story, seeking to document whatever ghosts were still present. They enlisted campus security officers to keep out pranksters while they

investigated the building during the night. Entering Old Main at 11 p.m., armed with infrared cameras and audiotape recorders, they began their search.

The group listened silently for long periods. "The most disturbing thing we experienced," said group member Miss Hewitt, "was the distinct sound of voices, though we couldn't quite make out what they were saying. For me, the most frightening, and yet, lovely experience was hearing a girl singing somewhere in the building. Even with our acoustic equipment we were never able to locate the music source." It was a mild winter, and even though the infrared photos taken there were not remarkable, the group experienced bitter cold spots that couldn't be explained in the building. Today Old Main has been restructured and sold, and is a senior citizens' home. It is no longer a part of the campus.

A few years ago the college television station planned a "Santa Call-In" to allow youngsters to speak with The Old Elf. Program Director Ron Warren spent countless hours on the preparations in the Communications Building. Just before Christmas he died of a sudden heart attack. The rest of the crew rallied, each taking over some of Ron's duties. The program was a success. As the final credits rolled on the screen, they stopped at Ron's name. The control crew tried to move the image. Nothing happened. None of the faders worked. They couldn't "go to black" to end the program, as they had done at the end of every program before, and have been able to do every night since. Had Ron Warren decided to tease his old companions and produce a memorial at the end of a program to which he had devoted long hours?

One might wonder who but Ron might be responsible for the never-before-experienced mischief in the Communications Building. Alterations to communications equipment take place after the studio is locked each night; little, but annoying adjustments. Objects are moved from where they stood at closing the previous night. Pre-set volume levels are found changed at sign-on. Other small objects disappear, though they usually reappear later. It is as if Ron is still producing his own nighttime show after hours. Stay tuned!

Fifth Floor

"We heard that somebody hanged himself up there, but nobody would ever tell us who," said Tom, a student. "Some say it was a young religious brother or monk; others swear it was a student. Today the dusty floors are littered with broken furniture. The administration won't let students live there, though you can see the old cubicles where the monks slept. The school tries to keep it locked, but we find ways to get in when we can muster our courage. Most kids come right back out again, pale and shaking." Tom referred to the Fifth Floor of Devereux Hall, one of the oldest buildings on the St. Bonaventure College Campus in Olean, NY.

Something more insidious than a "Casper" may live there. A group of students is alleged to have held a satanic mass during the middle 1960s. Some were expelled from

"Entrance to Devereux Hall"

this Catholic college for their decidedly unspiritual activity. One ecclesiastical source believes these students may have attracted an evil energy into Devereux that never *was* a part of the college's history. "It's also possible," he said, hinting at demonology, "that the being never even was a person!"

Students discovered that administrators once asked Fr. Alphonsus Trabold, advisor to the Hollywood film, *The Exorcist*, to rid them of the ghost or ghosts of Devereux Hall. Referring again to the college administration, Tom said, "They know about this stuff, but they don't say much to us. I lived on the Fourth Floor and sometimes you could hear footsteps on the floor above us. We knew that no student was up there."

One student suggested the good friar may not have brought along "all his good stuff" which he tried to clear Devereux of its spirits. Apparently, something malevolent is still there. Yet, thinking themselves invulnerable to forces that our materialistic society refuses to acknowledge, students still try to sneak upstairs. "You can get into that attic through the trap door in the Fourth Floor ceiling," another student said. "I didn't go, but one of my friends went with three others. She stayed for almost half an hour, but when she came down she had very fine scratches all over her body." Demonologists recognize this pattern as evidence of very unholy presences.

"The weird stuff isn't limited to the Devereux attic," said Kate, who lived downstairs during her freshman year. "One of my friends, Kara, woke up one night and saw a small boy in a baseball hat and sweatshirt sitting on the floor. Thinking she was dreaming, she forced herself to get out of bed and turn on the light. The boy quickly dissolved. She reported it to the Resident Assistant. Kara was astonished

181

to have her observation given credence, "Oh, yeah. I've seen him over in my room, too," said the R.A. Who was the child and how could he possibly be connected to a room and building that had always been used by grownups?

"I was one of three girls living there," Kate explained. "One night all three of us awoke at once, with shivers and prickling scalps, and our hearts racing. As none of us could return to sleep, we started talking and realized we'd all shared the same experience, although none of us could remember what had frightened us."

Meanwhile, college officials stress the quality of a "Bonnie education" and the fame of St. Bonaventure's sports teams. College years are a time for young adults to explore many worlds, and the unseen resident of Devereux Hall may be an impetus to the students' faith formation. Prayer is a blend of consciousness and energy, and those attending a religion-based college might do well to explore the power of prayer where results can be demonstrable. Have many students ever experienced the power of a single-focused prayer, with all who pray in one accord? I wonder what might happen if all the Devereux residents were mobilized to pray the unwelcome Fifth Floor visitor right out of Olean.

The TEΦ House

"TEΦ House, Clarkson College"

Many old mansions have been taken over by college fraternities or sororities. They usually offer plenty of spacious rooms for students, including dining and relaxation space. Many were private residences for wealthy families of bygone eras or served as religious meeting places. The old Sisson mansion in Potsdam, NY, evolved in this manner. The Sissons made their fortune developing, shipping and selling raw materials. Their twenty-room house, built in 1887, later became the property of the Tau Epsilon Phi Fraternity.

On a hot day, as the spring term concluded at Clarkson College, I knocked on the fraternity's door and was ushered in by Nili Gold, the fraternity president. He smiled when I informed him of my mission—to follow up rumors of a building filled with ghosts. "We certainly have our strange occurrences here," Nili said. "Let me take you first to 'The Salesman's Suite,' as we call it. This room at the top of the main staircase was set aside by the Sissons as a haven for any passerby who sought shelter for the night. It is a strange room because the windows and door lock both on the inside and the outside.

"An unsolved murder was committed in The Salesman's Suite long ago. One evening before 1900, a traveling salesman requested hospitality and the family graciously opened the room to him. In the morning, they knocked at his door because he had not come down to breakfast. He didn't immediately respond, so they decided to let him sleep awhile. By ten o'clock he still wouldn't respond to their knocking, so one family member went out onto the porch roof to get a look inside. The salesman appeared to be asleep but, again, gave no response to the banging on the windowpane. A few hours later, they broke down the locked bedroom door and found him dead of a gun shot to the head. They called the constable, who ruled it a homicide, though he found no weapon. Both windows and the door were locked on the inside even before the family forced entry. Though the window along the driveway had been locked, the only footprints found were in the soft soil below, as if someone had leaped from the second story window to the ground. No suspects were ever discovered and the crime was never solved. It is surmised that some ghostly activity in the house is related to this man's soul not yet finding rest."

Ushering me into a side bedroom, Nili roused one of his fraternity brothers and urged him to describe his experiences in "The White Lady Room," where he was rooming. Katherine Sisson reached marriage age around the turn of the century, but the family was distressed that her choice of husbands would bring an "outsider" into their empire. A "deal" was worked out for her to marry her uncle, but Katherine was outraged at what she considered an incestuous union. She threatened to run away, so the family locked her in her bedroom the night before the nuptials. In the morning she was found dead in her veil and wedding dress, having hanged herself.

"It's terrible," the young man told me. "You never know when you'll see her hanging there. When I'm sleeping I feel a sudden, bitter cold draft from the closet. And you can't block it. The guy who lived in this room before me tried to keep the door shut with a cement block, but it would be open every morning!" Some of the frat brothers' girlfriends have slept here. Some have left in the middle of the night because they are so uncomfortable in "The Lady's Room."

Tunnels beneath the house are alleged to have been used to conceal escaped slaves from the South while they awaited transportation to Canada before and during the Civil War. However, the Sisson house wasn't built until twenty-two years after the Civil War's end. Who might have constructed the tunnels isn't known. Nili suggested that the tunnels might have been used to store rum during Prohibition, as the Sissons owned the house until 1958.

The family's loyal Negro servant, Otis, was injured in a collapse of a section of tunnel beneath the house. A doctor gave the man only a few days to live, so the Sissons carried him to a rear upstairs room. Otis remained alive for a week, then realizing death was imminent, called the Sissons to his bedside, thanked them for their care and attention, and promised to remain with the family after death, as their protector. Otis' death room became known as "The Chancellor's Suite."

One of the fraternity brothers returned early from spring vacation one year and found a light turned on in The Chancellor's Suite. He entered and was about to turn it off, when he momentarily spotted a black man lying on a couch bleeding. He turned the light off, then thought, What did I just *see*? He flipped the light back on, but the figure had vanished.

Otis is the ghost blamed when the large front door is found open on bitter cold winter nights. The frat's television sometimes changes channels while its remote control sits untouched on a table. When the VCR ejects a videocassette, the tape is literally "spit" out of the machine several feet onto the floor. All this activity is attributed to Otis.

The fraternity used to have a pool table in the basement. The brothers would often hear the "Whack!" of the cue ball breaking a rack of balls on the table. If they rushed into the cellar they'd find the pool balls still moving, but no one there.

"Ghosts certainly provide a diversion for us when we're not in classes," Nili said. "I didn't believe in ghosts at first, but I have changed my mind. Some of the guys once brought in a Ouija board. Addressing our ghost, they asked, 'Who are you?' The board spelled out OTIS. I scoffed. I was sure they were moving the pointer. After all, we Clarkson men are supposed to be 'engineers.' So, I said, 'If you're *really* here, how do we *know*?' Instantly I got kicked in the back. That was enough for me. I urged them to knock it off. They put it away in its box and went to bed. The next morning we found the board out of its box and lying on the floor. We really didn't want to think about the engineering principles involved in *that*, so we haven't used it since.

"I know you've seen booze bottles and beer cans on the floor, and I can see you're skeptical," said Nili, "but though the brothers do drink, we're very sober about what we've seen and experienced. Wes Craven, the famous author, used to teach at Clarkson, and his book, *Children Under the Stairs,* contains many incidents based on Sisson House legends."

As I left the Sisson House I was perplexed. I had scrutinized the students' faces as they spoke. Several brothers were wide-eyed and nodding assent as others' experiences were narrated. It would be naïve to think they were strangers to inebriation. But alcohol and drugs can temporarily open the body's psychic centers to other worlds, though the user loses the capacity for good analysis. I am unable to discriminate between their hallucinations and real discarnate beings. But to the men of Tau Epsilon Phi, their "roommates" are all the latter. Finally, I wondered why Otis was labeled the main prankster. Isn't it possible that Katherine Sisson is undergoing a transformation in the spirit world and has opened to some new light? Perhaps she now enjoys tweaking *men*, who made her short life so miserable in the old house? But the brothers seemed content in assigning blame, so I kept that thought to myself.

Annie and Jane

"Ames Hall"

If you want to start a friendly fight at Green Mountain College in Poultney, VT, try *identifying* their ghosts. Most of the students and staff acknowledge that "old timers" haunt various campus buildings, but they don't agree on who's who or who haunts what.

"I've been around here for quite a few years," says Carl Stoddard, Chief of Security on campus. "And I've had the experience of sudden ice-cold drafts in buildings. It doesn't matter whether it's summer or winter. And I've heard doors open and close in corridors I *know* are unoccupied," he declared. "The students have heard and seen this too. I think old Mrs. Ames is still around, overseeing Ames Hall." Jane Williams Ames was a benefactor who came to the aid of the college when its oldest building burned around the turn of the last century.

"Not so fast," says Ruth Kniermen, Poultney author and college biographer, "if there is *anybody* haunting that campus (and personally I don't believe there is), then it's Annie Lucy Richardson."

Begun in 1834, the coed school was for many years under supervision of the Methodist Church. In the Twentieth Century it became its own institution, a private college that today pioneers in environmental liberal arts. There were difficulties in the old days, however, and greatest of these was the flash fire of April 1908 that consumed their oldest building. Jane Ames offered a munificent sum to the trustees in return for their promise to let her live in the building until her death. They consented, and then named the building Ames Hall in appreciation.

Both sides honored their agreement, but perhaps Mrs. Ames stayed longer than planned, attached to her building and job. She may be trying to cut the heating bills

186

by continually closing doors in Ames Hall. Maybe she looks in on the girls sleeping upstairs from time to time. Many will attest that *someone* does. The old building has a cellar that few students visit, but once it sported a bowling alley and theater. Carl Stoddard believes Mrs. Ames can be found there today, throwing strikes and spares and applauding dramas that are no longer visible. Mrs. Kniermen reminds us, however, that Annie Lucy Richardson was the building's preceptress between 1895 and 1930, watching the old building burn and being the first preceptress in the new Ames Hall. "Who lived there longest?" she asks rhetorically.

In late July 2001, I visited Green Mountain College for a third time and met a young woman registering for a Welsh Culture Conference at Ames Hall. She didn't know the building's history, and gave a strange smile when I mentioned that Ames Hall would appear in this book. "When I first entered my dorm room upstairs, I thought I ran into a spider web. I looked and couldn't see a thing," she said. "I could walk into it and feel sticky, then back out of it and feel nothing." After our chat she eagerly looked forward to returning upstairs, prepared to greet her *roommate* as "Jane."

"I think Carl is right," says Noka Garrapy, college staffer. "It makes sense to me that Mrs. Ames would stay on in a building that she invested her money and name in. *I* say it's Ames in Ames and Richardson in the building named for her. Each ghost has her own building. I worked in Richardson Hall across campus for two years in the early 1990s, and I believe old Annie Richardson still is taking care of her building. There are three floors in Richardson, but nobody ever uses the top one; there are only beds and cots stored up there. Once used for guests, it's all storage space today. When I worked there alone at night I was never 'alone.' Upstairs, you could hear the springs on those beds creak but, though I *knew* the rooms were empty, I ran up and checked each time. I don't know what I would have done if I'd come face to face with a ghost!"

"Richardson Hall"

"Yes, Richardson is an interesting building," Jan Edwards smiled. An Alumni Office official, she had also worked in the building for several years. I felt that there was more that she might have revealed if ghosts were more openly accepted.

"I'm the first one in each morning." Jan said, "I never feel alone here. Early morning is a good time to work, before the building gets busy. After I get engrossed in my paperwork I begin to hear people outside in the hall. It's as if others have come in early, but there is never anyone there. In the corner of my eye I catch the movement of people outside my open door. I hear them and catch snatches of conversation, though I can't make out the words. Some days it gets too much—the footsteps are just too real. I get up from the desk, go out and check the hall—of course nobody is there. At times I've even gone downstairs and outdoors, but there is nobody anywhere. And I don't even want to talk about the computers—there's someone or something here that seems to love making them malfunction. When I work here on weekends, getting ready for special events or projects, I bring my dog. From time to time he'll pick up his ears, rise and walk to the doorway and look out. He comes back in with a 'Funny, I thought I heard something' look on his face.

"Well, there's other stuff too. Do you want to hear that?" She made a wry face. I assured her that I did. Jan and I have college degrees. I must say, my sense of the preposterous just loves it when "degreed" people prepare to tell me a tale that their common sense and erudition tells them "just can't *be*."

"This building is devoted to alumni," she explained. "In the fall of 1999 we were putting together the College Bulletin. I placed a notice in that issue for the Classes of 1930-1955, trying to get alumnae to remember the name of a choir that performed back then. I was surprised a few weeks later when my notice yielded a letter from a woman who said she graduated in 1922, and who signed herself as A.L.R. At first I didn't pick up on the initials because I was interested in her old woman's cursive handwriting. I went back through our records and could find no graduate, or even non-matriculating student, with those initials. Her letter didn't answer my query about the choir and was rather general, which puzzled me. A day or so later it dawned on me that any graduate of 1922 would have to be almost 100 years old, and I (in my role in the alumni office) would surely know if we had a graduate that old. Whose initials were they? *I just didn't want to think* about it being Annie Lucy Richardson, because everyone knows she laid down her pen and died in 1946," Jan exclaimed.

So there you have it—two main spirit-ed contenders: Ames and Richardson. Both dearly loved Green Mountain College. Students come to Green Mountain College to pursue disciplines our world badly needs. There is, however, more in education than academic study. Buildings, themselves, can be wonderful archives, if one is sensitive enough to let them to speak. This beautiful, small campus afforded me a glimpse of a world that many academicians there do not even suspect.

Goddard Ghosts

Vermont's Goddard College often hosts education conferences and has pioneered in innovative education since the 1930s. Staff member Frances' job, as Conference Coordinator, was to ascertain that all was in readiness for the next day's program. One evening, as she and her two young daughters approached Martin Manor, the conference site, she was surprised to hear beautiful piano music wafting from inside. The door was locked each evening, so she assumed some talented staff member had gained entry with a passkey. Not wanting to interrupt, the three silently entered the conference room and saw a figure dressed all in black, including the veiled head, at the grand piano. Frances saw piano keys being depressed, *but the figure didn't move—and it seemed to have no hands!* Knowing that a female ghost had long been associated with The Manor, Frances ushered the daughters into another room. But the music immediately stopped, so the trio gingerly re-entered the room, only to find the piano bench empty. Whoever was playing would have had to exit past them. And nobody had. "Well, this is just another of *those stories* about The Manor," she mused. She knew other people had also heard the faint sound of chimes in The Manor, though there are no chimes in the building. She also knew several other ghost stories circulated among students and administration at the Plainfield campus.

Alumna Susan Green wrote in a college publication in 1996, of her years in Martin Manor, when the second floor served as student quarters. She recalled her friends playing with a Ouija board in the building's lounge on a lazy afternoon and receiving information from the ghost of a supposed alcoholic poet. There is no evidence as to the identity of that bard. No staff member at the college could connect him with a person from the college's past.

One student told of a series of slamming door incidents and footsteps echoing in the conference building, when nobody was inside. When no rational explanation for mysterious events presents itself, people are inclined to confabulate, even if it involves juggling facts or straining reason to the breaking point. In an attempt to rationalize mysterious events in Martin Manor, for instance, some students asserted that a Martin family butler hanged himself in the building years ago. Lucille Cerutti (former switchboard operator, who had lived on the grounds all her life) rejected this as a fabrication. Several students also insisted they had "seen things" while reading in the Garden House outside. Others said they had seen apparitions near the roof. In that regard, there might be a germ of fact behind those observations. Some of life's profound truths aren't easily or logically verbalized, and can only be assessed through experience.

Knowing the history of the Goddard campus and how its buildings came to be, we might apprehend how the garden area outside Martin Manor came to be associated with "things that go bump in the night." Willard S. Martin built an estate outside Plainfield in 1908, where his family had farmed for almost a hundred years. The Georgian Revival style of the manor house indicated his love of history. And it was this love which rankled him at the injustice done to one of his ancestors. Susannah Martin from Amesbury, MA had been hanged as a witch during the famous Salem witch trials of the 1600s. She was blunt and sarcastic in speech, willing to confront legal authorities, and ridicule the girls who accused her of witchcraft, making her a likely candidate for accusation. She steadfastly maintained her innocence, but was, nonetheless, executed on July 19, 1692. She was not allowed a Christian burial and her body was hurled into an unmarked grave. Due to legal oversights in the Massachusetts Legislature in 1957, she was not officially exonerated until 2001.

When Willard Martin built his formal garden in the 1920s, his Boston landscape designer made a remark that reconnected the two Martins. In idle conversation, he mentioned to Willard that the old Ipswich Court House, containing the "witch prison," in Massachusetts, was about to be demolished, but that its timbers were for sale. This was the building where Susannah Martin had been imprisoned, tried and sentenced to death. In 1921, Martin hired a truck and sped to the coast, where he purchased several of the timbers and incorporated them into his Plainfield Garden House. Susannah's spirit may have come to Vermont with the timbers. After Martin's death in 1938, the buildings and grounds and any residual ghosts, were sold to Goddard College.

After almost eighty years, Martin Manor and its grounds are undergoing a restoration. Students still sit reading and conversing along the garden walls and

pools, watched over by the carved relief face of a Celtic nature spirit. From time to time the roof timbers of the Garden House, and the stairway in the Manor creak unaccountably. Perhaps the executed women of Salem find solace in this academic atmosphere, where Women's' Studies are a popular concentration. They can forget their cruel deaths and regain hope for the future in this setting. And maybe their sadness is assuaged by the music of Satie or Ravel wafting from the untouched keyboard in the conference center.

When I was a student at Goddard in 1989-1990 I heard vague stories about ghosts, especially at The Manor, but my experiences there were overshadowed by

"The Garden House Spirit"

the intense work devoted to my graduate degree. A dozen years later, however, I had the opportunity to more thoroughly research the legends, and present them here. Willard Martin's garden is newly planted with flowers and shrubs, and is renamed The Helen Pitkin Memorial Garden, named after a very distant relative. Now I have occasion to be doubly grateful to Goddard for what I learned for my degree, and what I learned *about* in preparing this book.

Skidmore Stories

Lucy Skidmore Scribner started Skidmore College in 1920, using old mansions and school buildings in Saratoga Springs, NY, as classrooms and dormitories. Eventually, new structures were added and the college took on the appearance of a traditional campus. By its 50th birthday, however, the liberal arts college had outgrown its original structures. Purchasing the over six hundred acre Judge Hilton estate on North Broadway, and erecting state of the art residences and classrooms, Skidmore College pulled up stakes and left the old mansions and dorms. Before the coeds departed, several *good* ghost stories were reported.

At South Hall, on a June night in 1968, four coeds were studying for final exams. One noticed something strange on a wall of the room, and said to the others, "Girls, would you look around this room? I see something on a wall. If you do, too, point to that wall." The other three then pointed at the same wall, on which they saw a face. At about the same time they heard a baby's cry. All four jumped up, screaming, and ran down the hall. Claire Olds, the Dean of Women, was called. Solving "spectral problems" was not in her job description, so she called Tom Davis, the Protestant Chaplain. He interviewed the students but was puzzled. Then, Tom recalled that before Skidmore had purchased the building in the 1920s, it had been a convent, the Redemptorist Guest House. So, at 2:30 in the morning, he passed the buck to Father Jerry Tierney at St. Peter's Catholic High School on Broadway, figuring that these must be "Catholic ghosts."

Jovial Father Tierney came and blessed the room and counseled with the girls, and that seemed to have ended the matter for the students. An employee of the college, however, explored the vacated building two years later. She heard organ music in the cellar but, after researching South Hall's history, was unable to establish that an organ had ever been there. What energies did the nuns leave behind? What events might have created a phenomenon that still rippled over fifty years later.

* * *

In September 1982, after the new campus was well established, Marianne, a Skidmore student, rented a furnished room on Pine Alley in Saratoga Springs for the last semester of her senior year. The landlady lived upstairs with her seven-year old son. Marianne's room was attached to the side of the house, with its own entrance.

While asleep one night, she felt a blowing in her ear. At first she didn't want to wake up, but the blowing persisted. She finally roused, and saw a woman in a long dress or robe standing in darkness beside her. At first, Marianne thought this was a real woman and wasn't scared. Perhaps the landlady, she thought, maybe she needs some kind of help. Marianne waited for the woman to speak, but she didn't. Looking upward, Marianne saw no facial features, just a white blank where the face should have been. Also, the body seemed gradually to become lighter, turning a soft glowing white. Marianne reached out to touch the woman, but found only space. Then the woman disappeared.

She turned on the light. 3:30 in the morning. She sat awake the rest of the night, thinking someone had broken into the house. What other rationale could there be for what she'd just experienced? In morning she phoned her mother, who felt certain the woman must have been a ghost. The mother lived a short distance away and, after driving to the house, they debated whether Marianne should stay in the building. She did stay, but kept a light turned on each night. During the remainder of the semester she experienced anxiety over whether the ghost would return. It never returned, and today she is convinced she *did* see a ghost.

*　　*　　*

When I came to teach in Saratoga Springs in 1971, and let my new colleagues know of my interest in ghosts, one of them sniffed, "Well, if you're into *that sort of thing*, you'll want to get the story of 'The Hanged Skidmore Coed.'" When I asked who could tell it to me, he flippantly responded, "Just ask. *Everybody* knows it!" And that seemed correct; many Saratogians knew of it, but nobody knew any specifics: the girl's name, where she lived, the date of her death. I spent almost thirty years tracking down this "urban legend."

Responding to a query I'd placed in the Skidmore alumni newsletter in 1996, a North Carolina psychiatrist wrote, "I told my experiences to quite a few folks in Saratoga Springs before I left in 1970," she said, "so maybe this became your 'hanged coed' story."

As a freshman, she arrived at Skidmore in the autumn of 1966 and lived in West Hall dormitory at 75 Spring Street, across from the old Canfield Casino grounds. Returning to her dorm from dinner at the college dining hall one evening, she parted from dorm mate Kathy, who lived on the first floor in a single room. She had hardly settled in upstairs, when she heard pounding on her door. It was Kathy. "Laurie, Laurie, let me in! You won't believe what just happened!" When Laurie opened the door Kathy breathlessly told a strange tale. After leaving Laurie she had entered her room and snapped on the lights. Seated at her dressing table was a young woman with long brown hair, who abruptly stood and vanished.

"West Hall"

By the time Kathy had finished recounting her experience, Laurie's room had filled with other students, attracted by the excitement. Though Kathy had said the girl vanished, several of the onlookers dashed downstairs to see for themselves. Returning upstairs, they began good-naturedly ribbing her. "Sure, sure, Kathy. What were you smoking? What were you drinking?" a chiding which continued for weeks before gradually tapering off.

That probably would have been the end of it, except that one coed brought a Ouija board back to campus after spring break. Immediately, those girls who were curious dashed to Kathy's room to attempt communication with the "ghost girl." As soon as the coeds placed their hands on the planchette (pointer) it began spelling out a horrifying message that, in its entirety, read: *"I was killed in this room. He was waiting for me when I returned from work at the Casino. He strangled me and then pulled my body into the closet, where he bricked it up behind a wall."* Then the board fell silent. No amount of coaxing, pleading or threatening could make it reveal another letter. There was no further explanation. Gradually the girls drifted back to their rooms, and someone probably thought of getting hot pizza at D'Andrea's Restaurant to take the chill out of their hearts.

When the girls returned to campus the next autumn, many had forgotten the episode, and there really wasn't anything new on the story. For the next two years Kathy and Laurie and the others were swept up in academic and social pursuits, and the "ghost girl" was forgotten. However, in 1969, during Senior Year, students had to do a research report, and Laurie chose to do hers on a new New York State vagrancy law which the Legislature had recently passed. She chose to interview the Saratoga Springs' Chief of Police and made an appointment to learn how city government, especially in that resort city, would be affected by said legislation. The Chief was cordial and gave her a fact-filled interview. But, as they prepared to say goodbye at his office door, she spotted the Homicide Bureau next to the Chief's office. She was seized by an impulse.

"Chief, do you have many homicides here in Saratoga?" she asked.

"Yes, unfortunately, we do have our share."

"Well, do you have many *unsolved ones?*"

"Why yes, I'm sure we do. Every police department has some."

"Well, do you have any unsolved murders at *75 Spring Street?*"

"I don't know," he said. "That would be interesting. Come on in and we'll check it out." Leading her into the Homicide Bureau he picked up a carton of record cards and began thumbing through them. After a short period he exclaimed, "Yes, here we are! *Resident in rear apartment at 75 Spring Street reported her brick closet wall crumbling and bones were seen behind it. Patrolman dispatched and verified that the bones were indeed human,*" he read from the official document. Laurie recalls the document was dated early in the Twentieth Century, when the Canfield Casino in Congress Park, closed in 1906, no longer employed common people to serve elite American gamblers. Incredibly, this information seemed to validate the statements Laurie's friends received on the Ouija board almost sixty years after the crime had been discovered. The police file contained no record that anyone was ever arrested or prosecuted for the murder.

Who was the working girl whose disappearance seems to have gone unnoticed? Who was her murderer? How had the two met, and what led to his violence? Probably we'll never know, but one thing seems certain. The girl's spirit remained in the building after it was sold to Skidmore College in the 1920s, seeking someone such as Kathy, sensitive enough to hear how she died at the end of the Gilded Age in Saratoga Springs.

"There, that's the story," Laurie said in a telephone interview. "You know how people only half listen to you. Likely, people reassembled my narration into the story you heard about." By telling her tale once more to me, both of us seemed to feel a bit more unburdened by the telling: Laurie, because her profession usually distances itself from such phenomena; myself, because I had finally found the elusive "hanged coed" at Skidmore College.

The Roomie

They were roommates, sorority sisters and good friends. Barbara, Susan and Kate lived in an old Victorian house on Elm Street in Potsdam, NY. It was a quiet residence for the Phi Kappa Pi Sorority sisters, all students at the State University at Potsdam. Juniors expecting to graduate in a little more than a year, they had the first of their strange experiences in February 1990. Room 2 is at the front of the house. Susan and Kate slept in bunk beds at a right angle to Barbara's single bed. Incidentally, Kate and Susan were also blondes.

One night Barbara awoke suddenly. "I had the feeling that something had just changed or moved in the room, *and shouldn't have.* I glanced at the alarm clock and saw that it read 4 a.m. on the dot. There were shadows in the room, as the streetlight outside provided soft illumination. I looked in the direction of the big front window and first saw the blonde hair and then the white nightgown of a girl. She was slender, with long arms, and faced the window. My foggy brain tried to sort out whether it was Susan or Kate. I looked at my roommates' beds—they were both asleep! Then, I noticed *she* was transparent; I could see the bookcase right through her nightgown. Her left arm was lifted as if she were thumbing through a book." At that moment the figure at the window turned slowly in Barbara's direction and made eye contact with her. Startled, the wraith exclaimed, "Oh my God, you can *see* me!" and immediately vanished. Chilled with fright, Barbara sat wide-eyed, alone with her racing thoughts and pounding heart. She decided not to tell her roommates.

A week later she was chatting with Tom, a fellow Potsdam student, when he synchronistically confided, "You know, I've got this problem, I keep seeing this girl on campus. I don't know if she is a student or not, but I can see *through* her! What do you know about ghosts?" he inquired.

"Wow, I hadn't even mentioned the subject and here he was talking about my ghost. So I told him I had seen her too—in my sorority house. Then, he decided to level with me. He'd seen her more than once. He thought the specter's name was Angela, but didn't know why. We concluded that she liked my room at the sorority house. Obviously, the Room 2 ghost was the spirit of a young woman, perhaps a student, who had died. Who could she be, and from what period of history? Was she a former student at Potsdam, which had once been a teachers' college?"

That was the first of several incidents. Barbara recalled being in "the blue bathroom" one day when the lavatory faucet turned on by itself. Another time she heard someone heavy stumbling downstairs from the second floor, but nobody ever appeared at the bottom. The girls made jokes about a "traveling salesman" or "phantom fraternity guy." She heard a radio playing music in the room overhead, but the girls living there had no radio.

One morning in the kitchen several of the sorority sisters were discussing ghosts when the cook arrived. She listened more closely to the girls' conversation and turned white. "That's the same story some of the girls were telling ten years ago! You mean *they're* still around?" she cried. This ghost's identity was not easily explained. The sorority had purchased the house from a nearby church, and neighbors believed that clergymen once lived there. It wasn't likely the young woman ghost, as the sound was of heavier shoes. It is possible that the "heavy" footsteps descending the stairs are those of a clergyman's ghost that has not otherwise manifested in the house.

The young woman once may have lived in the village and, after death, discovered a house filled with educated women. She seems to seek knowledge of some sort in the sorority house bookshelves as long as she can do so surreptitiously. Perhaps this soul will find "learning" to be a metaphor for acceptance of her discarnate state. Then, as she comes to recognize her spiritual essence, she may choose to pass into The Light. In the recognition that she is a soul with work yet undone, she may come to understand why her life in Potsdam, NY, was necessarily brief.

The Old Medical School

With red lights blinking, the ambulance eased onto Bath Road in Brunswick, ME. No siren—it wasn't a life and death emergency, but the custodian at Adams Hall on the Bowdoin Campus had fallen downstairs and couldn't walk to Parkview Hospital. The EMTs wanted X-rays. As they strapped him to the gurney, which they slid into the vehicle, he'd chatted excitedly about being alone, then being pushed from behind by an invisible force. The EMTs eyed one another and considered suggesting a cranial CAT scan. Medics deal with bones, blood and people in shock—concrete facts; the janitor's story wasn't credible to them. But back in the Rhodes Hall security office, officers, too, eyed one another as they filed their report. It was another in a long list of unexplained "situations."

Adams Hall was built in the late 1800s as The Medical School of Maine. Later on it was sold to Bowdoin College. From the foyer you can look up the stairwell several stories to a ceiling where a great hook is embedded. The hook was used to hoist cadavers from the cellar to the dissection labs upstairs. A gruesome story, but is it possible that energies or personalities linger from those Medical School days?

Certainly, the security police believe so, and always warn "rookies" to be on their toes when working in Adams. In 1993 Officer Louann Dustin-Hunter and a partner informed the new man about custodians whose vacuum cleaners turn off in the middle of a job, and corridor lights suddenly extinguished when no one else was around. The pair left the rookie to patrol Adams Hall, moved across the campus green, and exchanged information alongside their patrol vehicle. "Very funny!" came the new man's voice over the radio. Looking back at Adams Hall they could see no lights. In a few minutes the new officer emerged from the building, approached the two officers, and angrily accused the two of dousing the lights to scare him on his first night. "Until the day he left the department, he couldn't believe we had nothing to do with the lights going off," said Louann.

Students, too, have had experiences. Tina Nadeau, Class of 2001, told the campus newspaper that her study group met nightly in a "sub-space" in the Adams Hall cellar during a summer program. Unknown to her, this was the old Medical School's morgue. As they worked one evening, a great thunderstorm swept Maine's Mid-Coast Region. One great flash of lightning cut the power. It was totally dark. The group at first giggled, made nervous jokes, then settled back awaiting the emergency power. "Suddenly, someone screamed: moving back and forth near the open doorway was a mass of bluish white light," Tina wrote. "It hovered about one foot above the ground, and moved back and forth across the doorway for about a minute." The group gasped and shuddered in the suddenly suffocating darkness. Finally, the lights came on. The entire group got up and left instantly. "We don't know what it was, but it wasn't a flashlight or anything like that. I think our visitor wanted to learn trigonometry too." she suggested. She was putting the best face on a scary experience. She probably didn't know that many thousands of people have seen this "bluish light" at haunted sites.

Louann Dustin-Hunter believes other campus buildings are also haunted. She calls Hubbard Hall "the freakiest building on campus" because of friends' experiences there. In the early 1990s a male officer entered Hubbard to make his post-midnight rounds. His duty was to secure all doors inside and outside, and extinguish all lights. Finishing, he moved toward the front door, only to hear a voice behind him call out, "Hello?" Surprised, he called back, "Hello?" No response. Working at Bowdoin was a good job, and he didn't want to lose it. He turned on all the lights again and made another sweep, opening locked rooms, lighting and then extinguishing all office lights and re-locking each room. Nobody was there. Satisfied, he reached for the front door a second time, while behind him in the deep recesses of Hubbard, again came that hollow voice, "Hello?" "He decided that he had checked *enough*," Louann said with a smile.

Founded in 1794, Bowdoin is one of the oldest colleges in America. That's old enough for lots of ghosts to take up residence. But exactly who these whispy characters are, nobody can say. Bowdoin is a beautiful campus and worth a visit. As you pass a security officer, give him or her a knowing wink—they'll know that *you* know their secret.

The Pit

"All the kids in town, anybody who's graduated from that school, knows it's haunted," Kathleen McGuire told me. She referred to Kennett High School in Conway, NH. The old building had been built in 1923 and expanded in 1938. "Ghosts have been there since I was a kid, and that was the late 1940s," she continued.

In 1992 Barbara Spofford, English teacher and advisor to the school's newspaper, *The Black and White*, suggested that the student staff write about Sam Fuller's ghost. Fuller had been a legendary athlete at the school in the 1930s, had become a teacher, and taught at Kennett around 1940. His father had been Conway's Superintendent of Schools for a number of years. Strong and intelligent, Sam was among the first men drafted into the army for World War II. A few years later townspeople were brokenhearted to hear of his death on a far-off battlefield. When his casket was returned to Conway, he lay in state in the old auditorium at Kennett. Not long after his burial strange events began.

Custodians heard voices or footsteps in hallways near "The Pit," the students' affectionate name for the old auditorium. These sounds also occurred near Sam's old classroom on the third floor. "Sam's Ghost" was known to prowl the school periodically, leading Mrs. Spofford to initiate the unique research/writing project.

"I worked the night shift for a few years," said custodian Rob Fuller. "I always brought Shammy, my golden retriever, for company because I worked alone. He'd constantly perk up his ears and go dashing off down the hall, chasing something I couldn't see. This was disconcerting because I knew the doors were locked and I was alone. Also, I heard voices, sometimes a group in conversation. They were always just around the corner. But nobody would ever be there when I looked. Eventually I just got tired of the interruptions—I had a job to do! I would always be on edge when I heard someone running, however, but there was never an intruder that I could see."

"The students at first took a lighthearted approach to the assignment," said Barbara Spofford. "My faculty collaborator was music teacher Mike Hathaway, who was also a certified hypnotist. His professional skills added another dimension to the students' research for the paper." Barbara and Mike designed a unique experiment that drew on students' listening and analytical abilities, as well as their writing talents. The student writers were to be divided into two groups. Each group would choose a volunteer member of their group to be hypnotized. Mike role would be to induce hypnosis, then give the suggestion that the volunteer would be able to contact whatever ghosts were in the school. The project would involve the group interviewing whatever ghost came through, then editing and assembling the interview into the final story. It was so different from traditional academics that most students, at first, thought it was a joke.

The sessions were to be observed and tape-recorded by adults from the community to assure objectivity. Following the "ghost interview" each group would compose their summation on a school computer. Would the two versions be similar or different? No contact would be allowed between the groups.

Today's Math and Guidance Rooms, where Mike conducted the hypnosis experiment, were the old location of The Pit, before the high school was renovated.

"I was one of the five community witnesses for one group, and brought my new tape recorder with me," said Kathleen McGuire. "Another person brought one of those little Playskool recorders. But almost as soon as one of the 'student mediums' began to speak, my recorder turned itself off and I was unable to restart it. The Playskool recorder, operating on batteries, picked up the entire session. The hypnotized student in my group reported the presence of three ghosts in the school. The first two were a mother and child who continually wandered through the building. They did not speak and did not identify themselves.

"The third one was a man who also did not identify himself. He was rather testy, demanding to know who the students were and what they were doing. He was uncooperative at first, but through conversation the student questioners opened him up a bit. He laughed and said he was an army veteran. He joked about the games he played on the janitors, especially leaving fresh footprints on the wet hallway floor they'd just mopped. It seemed likely that he was also responsible for the running sounds.

"When the two separate interviews ended, the student teams started writing. They edited and stored the stories on the computers. But those computers crashed and both stories were lost. These kids were computer-wise. They knew how not to lose a story, especially one they had worked so hard on. It was as if 'someone' did not want them written—at least in the humorous way the students intended."

Footsteps continue, mostly on the third floor near Sam Fuller's old classroom. The Pit has been absorbed into the reconfigured structure of the school. Sam may still be on "hall duty" outside his old classroom. Because the ghost never gave its name to the student journalists, we can't know if it was Sam. Perhaps he still exuberantly sprints through the Kennett hallways, urging today's athletes to not slacken their pace. Soldier Sam Fuller may, indeed, be the "veteran" who responded to the students, and who joked about the pranks he plays on the night custodian. Certainly, death has not prevented him from participating in the school activities that he enjoyed as a boy and a man.

Curiously, one custodian's daughter, waiting for him to complete his work, told him she often saw "murals" on the school's blank walls. She saw a man stepping down out of a picture as if to show them something. She got her father, who couldn't see the ghost, to accompany her as she followed the man to a certain wall. "My daughter said that the ghost man kept pointing at a wall, as if to indicate something inside," the custodian said. Unable to see the ghost or its gestures, the father couldn't make heads or tails of the episode. "Though I do believe my daughter saw *something*, I sure wasn't about to suggest that the school administration demolish the wall just on the word of a ghost! It sure makes you wonder what you'd find, though."

Spirit High

In 1977 Colchester High in Vermont staged *Charlie Brown*, the famous play with Charles Schulz's *Peanuts* characters. By all accounts the character Snoopy, played by Tracy Greene, was a favorite at the school. Within five days after the production she was killed in an automobile accident. In the play, Snoopy had sat in a special chair, which was later moved from the stage into the auditorium. Soon students swore they saw the chair glowing, and sought out John Coon, a friendly faculty advisor. Fortunately, the school had scheduled a lecture by Ed and Lorraine Warren, famous Connecticut ghost hunters and speakers on the paranormal. Their program had been planned long before Tracy's death to help raise funds for school programs.

Hearing the story of Tracy's death and Snoopy's chair, Lorraine went straight to the chair when she entered the auditorium. She felt no supernatural force or presence, however. This caused Mr. Coon to ponder who might be haunting the chair and creating a glow. He remembered two other students who had died violently: Jim, in a car crash, and Todd, by suicide. During a later play, Mr. Coon was called backstage to counsel David, who had missed an entrance cue because he'd seen a ghostly man backstage, in an area restricted to cast and crew. Mr. Coon found nobody. Auditorium fire doors are often found open when a drama is being staged. No prankster has ever been caught opening the doors, and thus violating state law. After all the years of unexplained events on and around the stage, at least one janitor will not enter the auditorium at night.

In 1999, the Warrens returned to Colchester and discussed the above incidents as part of their program. During the lecture Lorraine suddenly jumped from her chair, stared at something that nobody else in the audience could see, then resumed her seat. Later she explained, "I was concentrating on who was backstage." She had felt a bitter cold wind move past her chair and had leaped up. Mr. Coon was later questioned by the students, "Why did she bolt like that? At that same instant we also felt an icy breeze!" Twenty years after the first student deaths at Colchester High, it seems plausible that at least one deceased student still hovers near the stage, a place where he or she may have found happiness and meaningful activity during their brief high school years. The entire story was later written up in the *VT Cynic*, the University of Vermont's newspaper.

Not far from the high school is the "Counseling and Test House." The old structure serves the city school district day in and day out. One janitor, cleaning at night, recalled the lights clicking on and off while he worked there. Once, he saw his rubbish cart moving down the hall by itself. Then, at the end of the hall, a male form appeared, and disappeared. On another evening, a woman smelled cigar smoke in the computer lab, though smoking is prohibited there. Few other people were in the building.

Many homes and workplaces experience these enigmas, though most residents and workers don't automatically think "ghost" when they occur. However, more than likely, these phenomena can represent "energy memories" of someone's life, as-yet-unresolved routines, still being played and replayed in a setting from which a departed soul hasn't yet detached.

After the people and objects of the physical plane die or cease functioning, they slip into our "past," and one by one the threads of their meaning or importance disintegrate. If this were not so, we would fully understand past civilizations as well as the individual lives that comprised them. Not all of this information is unretrieveable, however, as intuitives often can recapture energized thought remnants of past human lives, though they are only disintegrating threads. Much as archaeologists recover artifacts and seek to assemble these into some greater meaning, intuitives and sensitives find themselves attempting to provide a greater understanding of ended lives by reconnecting fading threads of activity and emotion.

Jennifer, Jane and Jensen Hall

"Jensen Hall at Champlain College"

Christmas was coming, and the hills overlooking Lake Champlain were covered with snow. Jennifer anticipated a break in the drudgery of her classes at Champlain College in Burlington, VT. On the day before vacation, she tried to sleep in just a bit longer before resuming study, and attending her noontime class. Lazily, she rolled over in bed in Jensen Hall and stretched her arms above her head. *What??? Her arms from elbows to wrists were green!*

At first, she thought she was dreaming. But no, she pinched herself. She was awake. Now, she had to contend with discolored, if artistically pretty, arms. Could a fellow student have done this while she slept? Absurd! She had slept with her arms beneath her head. She went into the bathroom and began scrubbing. "It took me over two hours to get that stuff off," she said. "I figured it must have had something to do with our ghost lady, but nobody ever offered a satisfactory explanation," Jennifer explained.

Jensen Hall is a reminder of another era. A late Victorian house with a fashionable turret on the side, it is said to have been built in the late 1800s by a wealthy boat owner whose business interests kept him on the waters of nearby Lake Champlain, while his wife remained in her "castle" overlooking the lake. Feeling imprisoned by mores that kept her at home, and by a traditionalist husband who insisted on providing for the family by himself, she became melancholy. One day, she hanged herself in the turret. The story of her tragic death and unquiet spirit was passed along from owner to owner, with the house finally sold to Champlain College.

Jennifer told of a friend's experiences at Jensen. Visiting the classmate's room, she had chatted while the friend arranged her hair. The girl reached for hairspray on the dresser, only to have a hairbrush fly directly at her. "No, she didn't bump the dresser," Jennifer said, "I was sitting right there and watched this impossible thing. Then the two of us just stared at each other. 'The Lady' again, we mumbled."

One evening, several students were upstairs doing homework and chatting. "Everyone had left their rooms," she said. "and we were studying together while seated on the hall floor. There was a room at the end of the hall, and the girl residing there had closed her room's door when she joined us. She had left her bright light on—you could see it shining under the door. After awhile, one of the girls pointed at that space. A dark shadow moved through that light, as if someone was walking inside the room. The girl explained that nobody could be there. We just stared. It took us quite a while to get up the courage to look in, and there really was no one there!" she exclaimed.

Jensen Hall seems to be an "equal opportunity haunt" for students and parents. Jane, a mother from Connecticut, had heard complaints about Jensen Hall from her daughter all semester. Down-to-earth, Jane doesn't deny the possibility of psychic phenomena or ghosts, but she always assumed they happen to others. Her daughter first wrote about perfume smells in Jensen—a fragrance that "no coed would be caught dead wearing." Jane figured there must be a logical explanation. When her daughter wrote about hearing strange sounds in unoccupied rooms, Jane still tried to keep her objectivity, though worrying about her daughter's safety.

Her dispassion came to an end when she and her husband visited Burlington. They stood on the front step, enjoying the beautiful autumn colors along South Willard Street, and as Jane stepped down, she stumbled. As she regained her balance and looked toward the street, she was startled to see a wrought-iron fence at the front of the property. She remembers thinking it odd that she'd never noticed it before. Out on South Willard Street a Victorian carriage pulled by a sleek black horse was passing by. In the carriage sat a woman in a voluminous gown and broad-brimmed hat. A uniformed driver held the reins. Before she could blink, it all vanished. "That day I became a believer," she said. Maybe the The Lady wanted Jane to share her reality.

Jane is a self-made woman, an ideal that the hanged wife may have aspired to. Maybe the ghost lady wants to convey a deeper understanding of women's' limitations and the inequality in Victorian life. Perhaps she is also a bit jealous of the freedoms available to today's young women, who can enter college and advance to careers without family connections or political maneuvering. Busy with student life, few may take the time to appreciate the gulf of personal freedom between The Lady's time and theirs. Maybe the ghost lady stays on at Jensen Hall to remind them of their modern privileges, but also their need to escape from whatever "prison" *they* are in.

12
More Houses

Ethel's House

David, Frank and Brian sauntered down the abandoned road in the hill country overlooking North Blenheim, NY, toward the old farm homestead of Ethel Wood, a deceased schoolteacher. Forty years after her death David's family had bought it as a summer camp. Now the three headed there for a relaxing weekend.

"Ethel's House"

"You had to enter through the side door because the front door wouldn't open," explained Frank. "When we unlocked the door, something flew past my head. That spooked me and I ran outside. David laughed at me and said, 'That's nothing. Such stuff goes on all the time!' Eventually, I went back in and we sat at the table. Whoosh! Off went the tablecloth. I picked it up. A minute later, whoosh—the tablecloth flew off again. We decided to leave it off.

"That night at 9:30, as we sat at the kitchen table, all the cupboard doors opened at once. Someone said the word 'ghost' and we laughed, rationalizing it must have been a breeze. Then at 10 p.m. the dead-bolted kitchen door swung open—nobody was there. We'd had enough for one day! We went to bed.

"In the kitchen the next night, I looked toward the stairway where a single electric bulb hung on a cord. The light suddenly switched itself on. I went over and examined it. The switch was a red and black push-through type, and the black was in, indicating off. I pushed the red in, to the on position, then pushed black. Now, I *knew* the switch was off. A few minutes after I returned to my seat at the table it turned itself on again. Finally, we just unscrewed the bulb," Frank said.

The kitchen door opened and Brian came in from outside. "Hey, David," he called out, "who owns the cows?"

"Brian, there aren't any cows. This place hasn't been farmed for decades."

"Well, you'd better come look. There are a couple of Holsteins in the lower pasture," Brian said assuredly.

Brian and David went to the porch and looked into the lower pasture, where most of the open land had turned to scrub brush. Now, not a cow was in sight. Brian returned to the kitchen and sat in a chair shaking his head, sure that someone was playing tricks on him. None of the three have forgotten that weekend full of surprises.

Eventually, each man went his own way. David married and continued to bring his family to the old farmhouse for a few weeks each summer. His children all have special memories of the old house. His sons, Dan and David, once saw a greenish light shining under the bathroom door, though that room had been barred and unused for years. Nowadays, everyone uses the outhouse, which has led to some humorous experiences. When the youngsters brought a friend to spend the weekend, they neglected to warn about the ghost. On arrival, as the others went into the old farmhouse, the young friend dashed to the outhouse. In a few minutes he appeared with ashen face at the back door, his trousers around his ankles. "I went in and sat down. I'd latched the door, but suddenly it swung open. Maybe it's a breeze, I thought. I latched it again. Just a minute later the latch moved and it opened. Once more I latched it. But when it unlocked itself for the third time, I ran to the house as fast as I could," he said, while buckling his belt. Haunted outhouse stories seem to be rare.

"Rearview and Haunted Outhouse"

"We've never been scared in Ethel's House," said David's daughter Kim, "even though the dark front bedroom has a single shuttered window, I always felt love and warmth there." David's wife remembered the time her earrings disappeared from her bedroom dresser. They never were found. On another occasion she was making the bed, and saw the imprint of a body suddenly form on the sheets, as if someone had suddenly lay down. She left the bed unmade that day, and inspected it closely at bedtime.

Once, in 1983, when most of the family was shopping, teenagers David and Kim sat talking in the living room, in which the front windows are blocked. They heard men talking, and the conversation grew louder, as if a group was approaching. Unable to view directly the old farm road out front, they went to the living room's "uphill window" and looked out.

They saw a group of men in three-cornered hats approaching. Most had no real uniform, but all carried muskets slung from a strap or carried across the shoulder. Kim remembers seeing them stop and form a line facing the house. They saluted. Then the soldiers or hunters moved in front of the house, into their "blind spot." The two teens raced to the "downhill window" in time to see the troop move past the old barn and disappear. Both admitted they'd never been great history students in school, but to this day, they maintain they saw Revolutionary War soldiers, perhaps the Schoharie County Militia, still marching. This encounter gave them a new appreciation for the house and the land it stands on. They later found a stone in the cellar with "1820" carved into it, but wonder if the house doesn't date from the 1700s.

Every summer some family members still make it back to Ethel's House. Kitchen cabinets continue to pop open on schedule, and the kitchen door occasionally opens itself at the appointed hour. These seem to have been important times in Ethel's daily schedule, and they think she doesn't want something as simple as her death to deter her from her chores. They suspect that she not only serves as hostess to those who summer there, but keeps up her teaching duties, arranging with soldiers from the spirit world to help her provide history lessons to the young.

The Phantom Females

In Gagetown, New Brunswick, Canada, in 1810, British politician Hugh Johnson built a grand house near the St. John River. His high power and position, however, could not stay a series of tragedies among his family members. His eldest daughter died giving birth. In a freak accident, a boat carrying his son and fiancée overturned in the river and both drowned. Another engaged son broke his engagement and courted his ex-fiancée's younger sister. A few years after they married, the spurned sister came to visit but, overwhelmed with feelings of betrayal, hanged herself in a bedroom closet.

Eventually, the house passed out of Johnson family hands and, after 1900, young Peggy Lucas spent the night with the new owners. She was suddenly awakened by a lady in white moving slowly from the direction of the closet, past her bed, toward the window. The lady's hair hung below her shoulders. When Peggy challenged her, there was no response—the lady simply disappeared. As Peggy retold her experiences through the years, many believed it was the shade of the hanged Johnson sister.

Patricia Jenkins, a noted weaver began designing tartans during her residency in the house. She told many people that she felt a presence watching her as the wraith moved from room to room. The sensation of being watched was strongest in the upstairs bedroom where the betrayed sister had taken her life. Lights often turned off and on by themselves. Patricia's cat, Harry, seemed to watch intently as some invisible person passed through the downstairs rooms. Jenkins died in 1985, but others carry on her weaving and design work as the internationally famous Loomcrofters.

Enid Inch, a Loomcrofters employee in the old Johnson house, laughed when I queried her about the phenomena. "It's an old house, you know. What Patricia experienced still goes on. We think it is some member of the Johnson family. Not too long ago, our doorbell rang repeatedly, but no one was ever there. And our lights continue to turn on and off. Scoffers create problems for themselves. One found the door would lock itself whenever he went out, and he had to rap for us to reopen it. I think fear among the living stimulates the spirits, too. One night, a few years ago, a frightened guest, sleeping upstairs, felt a presence and kept her bed-side light on. In the morning, she found the fireplace irons in her bedroom had tipped over. I asked if she had tipped them, as they are quite heavy, you know. The guest was white as a sheet, because she and I were the only ones in the house. This particular mischief had never happened before.

"Well, I've got to go now," she smiled, "it's Halloween tonight. The children will soon be here for their treats. I have so much fun watching their faces when they learn this house really *is* haunted."

57 Gothic Street

"I knew there was trouble," Mary Ellen told me, "when my younger brother Charlie, wouldn't enter our family's new house after school until my brother Bob and I got home. Charlie would walk five blocks out of the way to Aunt Biddie's house and sit on her porch until Bob or I got home. Aunt Biddie gave him cook-ies and milk to bolster his courage. Charlie said he didn't want to go in the house because 'people are waiting for me in there.' Aunt Biddie said he had an overac-tive imagination."

This dismayed other family members because the house at 57 Gothic Street in Rochester, NY, was their first real home when they purchased it in 1963. For years Mary Ellen's mother had struggled with cancer, finally succumbing in 1958. Her dad's drinking problem had precluded them owning a home for a long time, and they had to live with her maternal grandmother. The family fortunes improved when her father began working regularly at the auto plant.

The father, his two sons and Mary Ellen fell in love with their new home's interior—real craftsmanship, hardwood floors, a great bay window with built-in cabinets on both sides of its window seat, all made of gumwood with leaded glass panels. A beautiful chandelier with over one-hundred crystals hung from the dining room ceiling. Their enthusiasm cooled when Charlie and Mary Ellen discovered the ghosts.

Charlie, returning home from school one day in 1966 was the first family member to attune to the former residents. Seeing strangers seated in the dining room, he immediately fled. Outside, he spotted Mary Ellen walking down the street from school. She remembered his pale face and big eyes. Inside, as she entered the dining room, she felt an abnormal chill but saw only the table and chairs. Charlie clung to his older sister the rest of the day.

Later, when he unlocked the front door, "the people" were waiting again, this time in the living room. Terrified once more, he took flight, and resolved not to be alone in the house, ever. On days when Aunt Biddie wasn't home, he sat on the front steps at 57 Gothic Street and looked backward to make sure "they" weren't coming out to get him.

His father reasoned that Charlie, who had grown up with a grandmother and others constantly present, had not yet adjusted well to being alone. So, he gave Charlie permission to stay at Biddie's after school each day, and the boy slowly began to relax.

One quiet summer day just before her 16th birthday, Mary Ellen sat in her bedroom writing. A creative girl, she treasured her "alone times." She loved to listen to the radio or record player, and write or paint. But, she always closed her door to avoid feeling "watched."

"One day I had really gotten into one of my projects when I heard knocking on my bedroom door. It startled me," she said, "and my heart raced. I almost tipped my chair over getting up. I stood by the door. I thought the boys were trying to scare me, but I heard nothing in the hall. I held the cool glass doorknob in my hand, with my ear to the door, and just as I was about to open it, the knocking started again, not lightly as before, but pounding this time, as if someone were beating the door with their fists!"

Mary Ellen was terrified at the ferocity of the impact, and couldn't believe a member of her family was the cause. She leaned against the door to keep it closed, and thought her racing heart might jump out of her chest. The pounding continued in a "horrifying rhythm," yet, strangely, it produced no vibration in the door. She couldn't feel the pounding, only heard it, and began to cry.

The pounding stopped as she slumped onto the floor, sitting against the door and crying. Her body was soaked with perspiration, and her head felt light. She was afraid she might pass out. Then, she heard footsteps move away and descend the stairs. For a long time she sat trembling and listening. Finally, she recognized her father's footsteps in the hallway. She opened the door. Her father and brothers were acting normally, as if nothing had happened. It was surreal, as if she had just awakened from a nightmare.

"I don't think I have ever been so terrified as I was that day," she wrote to me. "Whatever was pounding on the door was not of this earth or time."

The act of writing her account for this book caused Mary Ellen's traumatic memories to resurface. Nevertheless, almost forty years after the incidents, she prefers to remember the house fondly for its beauty and the security it gave after her mother's death. Her brother Bob, unperturbed by the invisible former residents when he lived there, was very active at school, and has forgotten the incidents. But not Charlie, who was uneasy in the house during the four years they lived there, and still holds the memories with trepidation. In 1967 they moved on.

The Cleaner

In 1992 "Maria," a businesswoman, bought the neat old house on Lake Avenue in Lake Luzerne, NY, in the foothills of the Adirondacks. Though the old German woman who had owned the house had been dead for several years, Maria found the house spotless when she moved in. She and her husband chose a bedroom on the ground floor, and their daughter Danielle slept upstairs.

"Every time I went away, something was sure to happen," Maria said. "One night, out of town on a business trip, I called home. My husband answered. He'd had a very bad day, he told me. The house was a mess, and he was going out to eat. About an hour and a half later, when he returned, he found the house neat as a pin. All litter had disappeared. Even the couch cushions were 'just-so.' Danielle was out and hadn't done it.

"We never figured out how this happened. I know Danielle wasn't responsible," Maria told me, "and my husband was too beat to do what was probably an hour's hard work. I sure wish I could find that cleaning person—I'd give her a full-time job!"

Danielle once felt an invisible person lie down on the bed alongside her, depressing the bed covers in the shape of a child or small adult, perhaps the size of the former owner.

"We had a rocking chair upstairs," Maria continued. "Once, I had a friend house-sit for us when we were away. She brought the chair downstairs, and put it near the laundry room, did her laundry, then popped the clothes into the dryer, rocking while she waited. All of a sudden the dryer began to smoke. My friend, fearing a fire, took down our CO_2 fire extinguisher and sprayed the dryer and most of the room. A fine white powder covered everything, including the rocking chair. 'That's just fine!' she snorted, and, exasperated, went for a walk outdoors. After a while she returned to sweep up the mess. As she entered the door, she saw the rocking chair abruptly stop rocking. She walked over to the chair and saw all the white powder gone from the place where some small person's bottom had sat on the seat." The little lady probably had not yet had time to clean the room, but she did "leave her mark."

Many readers, conditioned by Hollywood's horrific productions, think ghost stories are always scary. Not true. Ghosts remain on earth, attracted by ideas, emotions, unfinished work, and unfulfilled vows, to name just a few reasons. Some entities have obsessed so strongly on some aspect of their physical life that they are unable to detach after death. Most seem fixated on one thing, some aspect of their past life, and usually are *unaware of other ghosts in the house*, or their option to move on. In their labors to resolve some issue, they can also be oblivious to the living.

Sometimes, however, this compulsion can take the form of a humorous unintended help for the living. The Lake Avenue house was still *her* home, and the old woman's consciousness remained single-mindedly devoted to keeping it clean.

The Open Channel

Sonya was trying to adjust after the death of Ralph, her boyfriend, in Wolfeboro, NH, in the spring of 2000. She still missed him greatly, but was strengthened by memories of their discussions about eternal life. She knew he continued to evolve somewhere beyond this physical reality. Perhaps Ralph's death sensitized her more deeply to "the other world." She had experienced minor paranormal occurrences earlier in life, but Ralph's death seemed to initiate a heightened relationship with the spirit world. On the night after his funeral, while chatting with her friend, Annie, Sonya felt a gentle, repeated caressing of her hair, one of Ralph's loving habits. She mentioned it to Annie because, though she believed in the continuity of life, the reality of this physical sensation startled her.

Sonya often worked at her computer and watched television. One evening, watching the evening news from her favorite easy chair, she caught a sudden movement in the kitchen window's reflection behind the TV. An indistinct human form twitched back and forth, as if to catch her attention. When she recognized that the image was a reflection, she realized that someone was standing directly behind her chair. She whirled around, but nobody was there. The animated movement was reminiscent of Ralph's behavior.

Earlier in her life, she had felt constant surges of cold as she walked through the burial ground in Plymouth, MA. Sonya came to understand that the sudden chills that swept over her body at times were not air temperature changes, but spirit energy. And she realized that her growing sensitivity made her a "contact person" for the spirits of the deceased who wanted to reach out to others on earth. Sonya has also developed clairsentience, the ability to receive smells from the ghosts or spirits she encounters.

In the 1970s she and a former husband had lived in an A-frame house. One of his friends was staying with them. She awoke one morning, knowing that her husband and his friend had gone to work. As she descended the ladder from their bedroom loft, she saw the lights on in the living room and a man seated at a round table downstairs, reading the newspaper. She called down, "Good morning." But he didn't respond. Then, at the foot of the stairs, she suddenly realized the lights were off and that nobody was there. At that moment, an invisible energy shot past her, creating a breeze. When her husband returned, she told him of her experience. He said he'd seen their radio and bathroom light turning off and on simultaneously earlier that morning. Within a matter of days, they learned that the guest's close friend had died in a hit-and-run accident at the same time as these phenomena.

Sonya has several times been awakened from deep sleep by a male voice calling her name. She is not frightened by these experiences, but instead, uses her increasing sensitivity to study the wonders of the invisible world around her. Even as a child, she heard voices and realized that her extreme sensitivity to color, sound and light made her unique among her peers. She doesn't seek to "fit in," and has chosen to maximize the development of her special talents. Joining like-minded people in the Conway, NH, area, she studies parapsychology, and has dedicated her life to sharing her learning and experiences with others.

Still at Work

Assonet, MA, is a small town in a region that gave birth to some of America's first industries. Its mills employed generations of foreigners who poured into the United States in the 1800s. One of these was a bleachery that stood on Mill Street before burning to the ground in the 1950s, ending employment and causing many of the old homes near the plant to change hands. Not far from the bleachery is a house built in 1916. Karen and Tom, the current owners have lived there since 1987, and have pieced together its history.

"When we moved in," Karen explained, "there were two apartments in this old workers' house; we merged them into one. We hired local craftsmen to do the renovations. We had been out one night and found the inside lights on when we returned. The workmen swore they'd turned them out when they left."

During their first Christmas after moving in, Karen's family took special precautions with their Christmas tree, always turning off the lights when they went to bed. One morning, Karen came down and found the tree fully lit. Nobody could explain it. Later, they received a small electrical window candle as a gift, which they promptly placed on a front windowsill. It was turned off and on by twisting the bulb. When the holidays ended Karen unscrewed the bulb and left the candle on the sill. Then, almost a year later the family found the candle glowing brightly before Christmas decorating, though no one had re-tightened the light bulb.

A few months later, Karen awakened before dawn—something or someone was moving. Looking out her bedroom door she saw a man enter the room across the hall. For a moment she thought it was Tom, but she saw him still sleeping beside her. She breathlessly roused him with the news that they had a burglar. They searched the other room. Nobody. They searched the rest of the house. Nobody.

When she shared her experiences with a co-worker, the friend told of also having a ghost, and noted similar experiences. Karen learned that ghosts often meddle with electricity. Also, they often produce cold spots because their vibration is so slow, and occasionally produce audible sounds or voices. A long time passed, however, without Karen's family experiencing anything unusual. She began to doubt herself.

In their living room was an old Windsor chair. It wouldn't hold a person's weight but was decorative, so Karen filled it with teddy bears. One morning she came downstairs to find the chair and bears facing the corner.

On July 4, 1994 they took in a needy woman and her twenty-month-old baby. The next day, while Karen was away, the woman's cigarette ignited some dry papers and a fire engulfed the interior. No one was hurt, but the house had to be gutted before repairs began.

Tom became the general contractor, hiring carpenters, electricians and plumbers—all local men he respected for their craftsmanship and honesty. Within a few days, Mike, the electrician, asked Tom if there was a ghost. Tom answered in the affirmative and asked what prompted Mike's question.

"I was doing my work and felt someone watching me. I turned and saw a man about ten feet away. When he saw me looking, he vaporized into nothingness," Mike explained.

Shortly thereafter, carpenters and sheetrockers in the living room smelled a "garbage smell." They checked the garbage barrel but there was nothing rotting in it. They examined the new kitchen. Nothing. But the putrid smell continued. They even examined the yard for an animal carcass. Nothing. As Assonet's construction men shared experiences, many believed the house was, indeed, haunted. The work was finished in April 1995, and Karen and Tom were able to move back in.

In May, in-laws came to celebrate Tom and Karen's "new house." At breakfast a few mornings later, they reported shadows moving in the upstairs hall the previous night. "We had a nightlight there, which would have cast shadows if someone moved past it, but it wasn't Tom or myself," Karen said. "We have a private bath off our bedroom and would have had no reason to enter the hall. A few nights later our bedroom door opened slowly, but nobody was there."

The events have since ceased. I think an old factory worker may have remained in his apartment after death. When Tom and Karen moved in, the worker may have experienced strangers in *his* house, and found their activity interrupted his routine from a hundred years ago. The fire seems to have been the turning point in his consciousness, however. Watching the fire, demolition and renovation, perhaps he realized he was dead, and signaled that recognition with the smell of rotting flesh. Hopefully, he returned to a celestial bleachery where, sooner or later, all darkness is removed.

Still Dancing

To Jan Herder, Charlotte, VT, looked like a nice town. Attached to the rear of the Frost House was a small downstairs brick apartment for rent. The 1840s Frost House stood next to The Old Brick Store, famed for rich pastries. With a private entrance, the apartment seemed ideal. He paid the first month's rent and moved in. Not long after, he had his first encounter with a forgotten episode in village history.

In October 1983 he locked the outside door, as usual, and went to bed. Darkness came early and he was tired. In his rear apartment he couldn't hear traffic on Ferry Road, and quickly fell asleep.

He was suddenly jolted awake after what seemed like just a few minutes, though the clock indicated two hours had passed. The deadbolt lock on the door had clicked open and an icy breeze blew through the bedroom. This was followed by the wraith of a woman in white, sweeping past his bed and through the closed door that separated his apartment from the rest of the house. At that point, after her passage, the outside door slammed shut and he heard the deadbolt lock. He lay awake the rest of the night, anticipating more visitations, and realizing he'd witnessed an activity from another time.

Next morning, savoring a cup of coffee, a pastry and real people in the store, he asked other customers about the Frost House's history. "Yep, that's her," was the laconic reply from several old timers. They knew that a lady in white had often been seen throughout the years in various parts of the old Frost House. One man believed a suspiciously large number of automobile accidents at the nearby bridge could be attributed to the ghost. But nobody could tell Jan who she was, or what prompted her nocturnal passage. During the next months, the woman in white appeared several more times, sweeping past Jan's bed and through the door.

A few months later, friends from Montreal came to visit and Jan put them up in his bedroom. At breakfast the next morning the visibly tired wife said, "Jan,

you have a ghost in your house. She kept us up most of the night!" His guests suggested he put basil leaves on the threshold as a deterrent, which Jan readily agreed to do. The ghost never reappeared in his apartment after that. Jan, however, wanted to know the identity of the ghost woman and why she repeated her rapid passage through his bedroom. With the help of local historians, he gradually pieced the story together.

The adjacent Old Brick Store was a tavern during the 1860s, and its upstairs was a dance hall. At that time an iron bridge connected the dance hall to the second floor side of the Frost house. This allowed proper young women and their escorts

"Side view of Frost House showing rear apartment"

to cross from the ballroom to the upstairs of the Frost House for non-alcoholic punch and other refreshments between dances. According to legend, sometime after the Civil War, there was an accident on dance night. A young woman and her escort began to argue as they crossed the bridge, and one of them pushed the other. The girl, dressed in white, plummeted to the ground. She died of a broken neck. As her spirit still scurries from beneath a long-vanished bridge, through Jan's rear apartment door to the old upstairs dance hall, she may be trying not to miss another waltz.

The Glasier Mansion

The Glasier family came to New Brunswick, Canada, in the late 1700s, when the forests seemed to stretch endlessly. They built a thriving logging operation on the St. John River near Fredericton, with several lumber mills and shipping facilities. In 1819 Duncan Glasier was born, destined to become the driving force in the company fortunes. He grew to over six feet and over two-hundred pounds. Though he was gentle and generous, his physical stature awed most people. Eventually, he married Sarah, built a large mansion in Lincoln, and raised a family there. He was predeceased by Sarah, and was himself mourned by many when he died in 1884. One would have thought this kindly man would have gone speedily to Heaven, but apparently, *someone* stayed on.

As the Glasier Mansion passed to new owners, rumors spread that it was haunted. One family reported they'd carefully turned off all the lights before leaving home, but found them ablaze when they returned. Once, while the house was vacant, two young skeptics spent the night in sleeping bags daring the house's spirits to show themselves. Before dawn they fled the house, claiming to have felt the presence of someone watching them and having heard strange noises all night.

"I'd heard all these tales when we moved in," said Colleen Thompson. "In fact, they only enhanced the mansion's allure! I wasn't afraid of any of it. I even bragged to my friends with glee about the house's ghostly notoriety. My kids were sixteen, thirteen, and eight when we moved in, and from the start we felt a warm, welcoming atmosphere. Coming home at day's end, we felt the house's hearth had been kept warm and welcoming, awaiting our return. We were proud to live in a 'heritage house.'

"Natalie, my eight-year-old, decided the vacant back upstairs section of the house was her playground. We let her play make-believe games there for hours. Eventually, she prattled about someone named 'Black Peter.' I chided Natalie about it, not liking the term. 'But, Mommy, that's his name. He told me!' she asserted.

"Still, I put it down to childish imagination. One day Natalie said Black Peter had been there, upstairs, but had gone down the back stairway and hadn't returned yet. There was a locked door at the bottom of the staircase, so I didn't pay much attention. Imagination, I was sure!

"Sometimes I'd tell visiting friends about the ghost stories or the dining room's cold spot, located at the point where you'd enter the front hall. Some of them, also, felt an icy chill there. A visiting museum curator once ridiculed our observations. A few minutes later the man turned deathly pale. He told us the hair on his arms rose when he walked through the spot, and something ice cold touched him on the shoulder."

Researching the house's history, the Thompsons discovered that Duncan Glasier was popular with businessmen, politicians and travelers of his time. Many stopped in for meals when they passed his mansion. The generous Glasier even gave travelers a change of clothes if theirs were soiled or dusty.

A freed black man, employed as major domo in the house, opened doors for guests, served meals and cared for the children. He lived in a small house that Glasier built for him behind the mansion, and when he became terminally ill, Glasier hoisted him on his shoulder, carrying him to an upstairs room in the mansion's rear wing, where they cared for him until his death. The Thompsons discovered that Glasier was a bear of a man with a heart of gold.

"There were all kinds of things still in the attic when we moved in," Colleen continued. "The house had never been entirely emptied by former owners. I found a cubbyhole up there with an empty antique gin bottle, a signed temperance card, old York Sunbury County historical records, and ancient account books. In one book I discovered the name of Glasier's servant, *Black Peter*! Natalie had no interest in dusty old account books and would never have read Black Peter's name. We were amazed she knew this old servant's name long before we did.

"We'd brought an old sleigh chair down to the front hall, where Natalie also used to play. We never used the big front door there because the hardwood floor in front of it had warped. The door could only be opened with lots of tugging and squeaking. One August Saturday, working alone in the kitchen, I walked into the hall to get something. The old chair was rocking gently and the front door was wide open. I knew it was Black Peter, waiting for visitors from long ago and resting in his favorite chair. Our family always felt a warm presence. None of us minded the footsteps that creaked up the stairs at night, though we never heard them descending. Peter keeping watch was comforting, as if he was still trying to repay Glasier's love and generosity."

But Black Peter had company, it seems. Once, when the Thompsons were away on vacation, Colleen's sister-in-law volunteered to help with the housework. Scrubbing dishes in the kitchen sink, she turned to see an old man standing over the dining room table, peering at charts spread out before him. The woman thought he was a houseguest that Colleen hadn't mentioned. Wiping her hands on her apron, she went to greet him, but he disappeared. She described the man as short, with a round belly, a fringe of white hair, and a rough seaman's coat. His charts had appeared old and yellowed by time, though they, too, had disappeared.

When Colleen returned, she couldn't convince her sister-in-law that she'd seen a ghost. The woman "just *didn't* see things," and scoffed at the idea of ghosts, even though she could offer no rational explanation.

"About two weeks later, I brought a friend home. She sat in the dining room while I made coffee in the kitchen. I heard her talking to someone and peered in. She was staring in the direction of the hall door.

'Who are you talking to?' I asked."

"'I don't know. Is he your uncle...or someone?"

"'What did the man look like?'"

"'An old man with a potbelly, white hair—bald in the middle. He was just looking at me from the hall. When I said hello, he answered 'I'm looking for my wife.'"

"Neither my sister-in-law nor my friend had ever spoken to each other.

"On another occasion, a friend and her thirteen-year-old visited from San Francisco. We chatted until midnight, then went to bed. I slept like a log, but in the morning my friend was sitting at the kitchen table with dark circles under her eyes. 'My God, you're still here!' she said. When I asked what she meant, she replied that the noise had kept her awake all night. It was as if someone were packing things, hangers jangling in the closet, trunk lids slamming—noise that went on for hours. We'd never heard those sounds before. The next night, the whole family heard sounds of someone digging. I even took my flashlight and went into the yard. Nobody was there. As we reminisced about it in later years, we speculated that the presence of adolescents brought out these poltergeists." Many experts on the poltergeist phenomenon claim that almost all such phenomena are instigated by adolescents, especially youngsters who are troubled, or by pre-pubescent children's undisciplined psycho-sexual energy flaring out.

Colleen and her husband eventually sold the old house because of high maintenance costs. A retired military man who had restoration plans, bought the house, but soon after, received a lucrative job offer from the West Coast and sold out quickly. An antiques salesman bought the old mansion and filled it with "ugly bric-a-brac." It wasn't maintained, and a few months later, The Glasier Mansion burned to the ground. Only the massive living room fireplace and chimney remained.

"My family always felt the beautiful old house died of shame. Whether or not the ghosts left, I don't know, but I've heard that employees at the animal hospital that was built over the mansion's ashes have had some interesting experiences," Colleen Thompson said with a playful smile.

Fanny and Company

Roswell Terry built a snug farmhouse on a knoll outside Simsbury, CT, in 1840, from which he could view his fields and Terry's Plain Road. After he died, it became the residence of a spirited trio of women. The owner, Fanny Herring Young, was an English-born actress, who brought Ada Colby, her seamstress, and Pearl Lasalle, her housekeeper, to live with her in the Simsbury house. In 1925 the last of the trio, Pearl, died, and the old house changed hands once more.

In 1978, when Evan and Betty Woollacott bought the house, responding to its elegant and simple beauty, they did few renovations. One day their key disappeared when they prepared to lock the back door for the night. Resolving to do a search or have a new key made in the morning, they went to bed. The next morning they found a door key on the floor mat inside the back door. It fit perfectly, but wasn't the key they'd misplaced—it had an entirely different design! A few months later they found the original key near an upstairs chimney, which completely baffled the family. When I questioned the intuitive Paul about the incident, he said, "the spirits meant no harm, but it was a way of saying to the occupants, 'There is more you should know about the world you live in. You have an interest in history—learn more about us. We return your key, but not *your* key.' They returned an old key which had been on a shelf in the attic. So, it was a mild prank, but it also had the purpose of awakening the family to the presence of spirits."

While shopping one day, Betty met a former resident of her home, who believed the house was haunted. When she had owned Terry's house, she had stored many cartons of books in the attic. One day, after hearing a resounding crash and racing upstairs, she found many of her book cartons and their contents scattered in the second floor hallway. The door to the attic remained closed. Perplexed, she couldn't understand how the feat was accomplished, or what the ghost's activity implied.

The former owner once had a visitor who said he'd seen a girl bouncing a ball in the upstairs hall. He had thought the child was the owner's daughter, a plausible solution, but impossible, as her daughter was away at that time. A few years later her husband, who didn't believe in ghosts, came downstairs with the color drained from his face. "Three of them!" he blurted, but refused to elaborate on his experience.

Evan Woollacott, hearing these tales, began to rethink his own experiences there. During their second week in the house, he'd heard strange noises at night, but chalked them up to the house "settling." One night at 4:30 a.m. he felt someone sit on their bed, but saw no one. Later, after the Woollacotts had fully accepted their ghosts, Betty's mother confided that an invisible someone had also sat on her bed when she had visited. Whoever sleeps in their son's room, Betty said, usually feels someone sit on that bed, too, during the night.

We asked our intuitive advisor, Paul, to explain the energies in the house. He noted that the women "are a quiet presence in the house. At times, they interact with the residents. The old key had long ago been lost by the chimney upstairs, and they provided it for the new family. They still go about their quiet activities as if no family but themselves lives there. They are the ones that sit on the beds. It's not that they're not paying attention to the living person, they're still living in their time."

He further explained, "It is as if your attention was turned to a book you are reading. You would not be aware of someone walking down the street outside your house. They are focused on their lives as they remember it. They are often not aware of the Woollacott family."

Evan and Betty, dedicated members of the local historical society, enjoyed researching their house and land. They discovered a fire had flashed through the house around 1930, and killed the owner's dog in what became their son's room. The Woollacott's son and his wife have heard a dog bark when they have slept there. On another occasion, when their son returned from shopping with arms laden with groceries, the back screen door mysteriously opened for him to enter. Needing a helping hand, one was provided.

So, small vignettes of Simsbury's history are re-enacted from time to time. The *dramatis personae* appear to be Fanny Young and her supporting cast, who seem to approve of the drama in the Woollacotts' lives.

Mechanic Street

The Lanfear family sold the house at 105 Mechanic Street in Corinth, NY, to Rich Eggleston and his wife in 1967. Though she was just three when they moved in, Kim, Rich's daughter, has vivid memories of their years there. She remembers a rocking chair rocking by itself on an enclosed side porch. Before it rocked, its cushion would indent, as if someone had just sat on it, though clearly no one was visible. Even more incredible, a book was suspended in the air over the chair, its pages open for the invisible reader! She watched her father walk across the porch, oblivious to the "ghost reader," and at that instant Kim felt a cold chill pass her.

"When I was thirteen," said Kim, "I came home from school to find the telephone ringing. The call was for my dad, and I informed the caller he wasn't home yet. From upstairs, I heard a booming male voice, 'Yes I am!' I knew it wasn't Dad, but went up reluctantly to check—the upstairs was empty.

"We often heard footsteps climbing the stairs and walking back and forth in the hallway at night, as if someone was patrolling the house. When I was fifteen, I awoke to find two strangers standing at the foot of my bed. The man wore a top hat and tails, and the woman a fancy party dress, as if going to a New Year's Eve celebration. They seemed curious and concerned about me, so I struggled to speak, and said, 'I'm okay.' They vanished.

"Duke, our dog, absolutely hated thunderstorms. He'd run upstairs and hide under the bed, quivering. He died in 1984. Whenever there were thunderstorms after his death, we noticed the bed Duke hid under would shake.

"Once, my father's hunting knife disappeared and was later found beneath the mattress at the foot of his bed, a place he'd never put it. After I married and had children, sharp objects began to disappear whenever we came to visit Mom and Dad's house—knives, scissors, anything with a cutting edge. Sometimes, if we asked out loud, the object would be returned. Other times, not until after we left. We came to think that a ghostly presence was protecting the kids from harm.

"Among other things that disappeared were my brother's baby pictures. They never turned up again. We began to suspect the ghosts hovered over the house's children, keeping protective vigil by night, and preventing hurts by day."

When the Egglestons remodeled, they found few physical traces of the Lanfears. Behind the house stood an old garage that may once have been a stable. By 1985 the garage was so shaky it had to be torn down. After that, all ghostly activity ceased. Perhaps the garage held some remnant of earlier owners, and once it disappeared, so did the links to its spirits.

Release

Gary's wife, Barbara, died soon after her 40th birthday, leaving him to raise two teens. As the pain of Barbara's passing subsided, he joined a local singles group. At their monthly Friday night dance he met Carol Ann, a most attractive woman, began dating her, and soon introduced her to his children and showed her their home.

"As I stepped inside the house on Marlyn Drive in Burnt Hills, NY," Carol Ann told me, "I felt a strong presence, as if I was being watched! Over the next three years, we became engaged and Gary invited me and my daughter to join his family. Before long I began to have strange experiences. Whenever I went into the shower, but only when I reached the point where I had my hair all lathered with shampoo, the hot water would turn off. Every time! At first, I thought it was my husband, who is quite a prankster. Later, I realized it happened even when Gary wasn't home."

As a professional woman, Carol Ann treasured her home time, especially when she could cook a special meal. "New problems arose that I had never experienced before, or since," she said. "Every time I came near the stove I burned myself. I just couldn't avoid it, though I tried to be exceedingly careful. It happened so frequently that my husband and children began to comment on the burn marks on my hands and arms.

"At night my daughter and I began to sleep with a nightlight for the first time in our lives. And sometimes, when I worked nights she would call me to reassure herself, as there would be loud noises in the house that she couldn't explain. These noises were very unsettling to myself as well as to her. Many times I'd awake with a start, mystifying Gary who was oblivious to the strange noises and events. One evening, startled awake by something, I saw a mound-shaped dark shadow slowly move along one wall of our bedroom. I suggested to Gary that we might have a ghost, but he scoffed at the idea. Soon, however, he had to admit that in several rooms he *did* smell a perfume that I didn't use, but he knew who *had*—Barbara.

"Finally, one evening I found myself reeling down a flight of stairs for no apparent reason. Eventually, when I'd return home from work at night I'd just sit there in the car, not wanting to enter this house where so much seemed out of control—where I felt in danger. I decided it would be in my best interest to find another home. Our marriage seemed jeopardized by these events, but Gary and I worked out an agreement to rebuild our relationship in a new location. By that time, we both suspected that Barbara had not fully left what had been her house and children.

"At first, I was afraid we might be 'followed,'" Carol Ann said, "but when we moved out I felt as if a tremendous burden had lifted from me."

Gary and Carol Ann didn't discuss most of these events with their children. "I never actually discussed my suspicion about Barbara with my daughter because I worried it would make her afraid to stay in the house. When we had moved to our new home and were taking a walk one day, she turned to me and said, 'You know, Mom, I never felt alone in that house!'" Carol Ann sighed, knowing she had done the right thing.

The current owners of the house seem happy with their purchase and have no experiences to relate, so it seems that Barbara may have "seen the light," and decided to release herself into a Greater Love.

Kenwood Ghosts

The house at 65 Kenwood Avenue in Glenmont, NY, has been in the Kleinke family for two hundred years. When the grandmother died, it sat empty for over a year. In 1995, Wendy, a Kleinke descendant who'd just moved in, experienced cold spots. Hearing footsteps upstairs at night, and fearing a break-in, she called the police, who found nothing out of place. The phantom walker was more frightening than she could bear, and one night she ran to the security of her mother's nearby house in her nightgown. Two days later she moved out, leaving the old homestead to her sister, Ruth.

Ruth Van Denburg, enjoying the old house's aura of family tradition, eagerly completed her family's move in 1997. Soon, the unusual events began for Ruth and her family, as they had for Wendy. One day, in the cellar, she saw a white flash, as if someone had sped past her. In October 2000, she clearly saw a woman in white walk past a doorway, and described the woman to her father at Thanksgiving dinner. "That's your great-grandmother, and my grandmother. You described her perfectly. You saw her walking into your kids' playroom, but I remember when it was her bedroom," he said.

At Christmas, Ruth saw her standing at the foot of her bed. "I couldn't make out her face, but saw the nightgown in detail. Long hair fell down her back. It was as if she was inspecting me, sizing up another generation. Maybe she doesn't like my fiancé, Scott, living here. She regularly turns his radio on and off. Ironically, if we go to bed and leave the TV on, she turns it off for us; it never fails. Lights flicker frequently, though the electric utility company inspection revealed nothing mechanically wrong. Maybe Great-grandmother has a soft spot for Scott when he's vulnerable, though. In the winter of 2000 he broke his foot and was bed-ridden for a time. He saw her hovering in the air around his bed until he was able to get up and move around by himself. We know she watches us, probably just trying to fathom our modern way of life."

*   *   *

In the late 1940s, just down the road in Delmar, Galen Ritchie grew up near the old high school, in a rowhouse at 346 Kenwood, built about 1890. When he was fifteen and a newcomer to Delmar, he awoke one night to see a figure at the foot of his bed, watching. "Moonlight streamed in the window, and I could make out the man's old-fashioned black and white three-piece suit. Across the front of his vest dangled a gold watch and fobs. He just stood there. Finally, I could stand the suspense no longer, and asked, 'Who are you?' He smiled, then slowly faded. The experience lasted about five minutes. I jumped out of bed, turned on the lights, but he was gone. This experience happened only once, and I have often wondered if my visitor was the businessman who'd built the house.

"Since then, in the 1950s, the three-unit rowhouse was converted to a single-family residence. From time to time, I stroll past the house and wonder if the old man is still smiling at the residents."

Gina's House

"I lived in that house on 23 Eagle Street in Gloversville for quite a few years," Gina told me. "It always scared me. When I was seventeen I began to hear footsteps going upstairs about 5:30 a.m., then a loud swishing, and the footsteps would stop at the top of the stairs. All I could think of was old-fashioned crinolines beneath a woman's skirt, but, of course, no one in the house wore them in this day and age. When I told my mother, she admitted she'd heard the sounds, too, before I did. She didn't tell me because she hadn't wanted to alarm me.

"That house was for sale surprisingly cheap, which attracted my Mom to buy it. Customers at Mom's hairdressing shop warned her that women who'd lived there developed 'mental problems,' but Mom believed we were made of stronger stuff. She could also save money by moving her shop into the house once we moved in. When she began to lose weight and say the craziest things, however, I really began to worry.

"After a while, we noticed that each of us was missing some possession, which all reappeared later; odd things—Dad's work shirt and my ceramic pumpkin, for example. I became anxious because of this, and was afraid to come home too late at night for fear of what new mystery I'd encounter. My brother and sister felt the same way, but there was no rational explanation for our fears and apprehension. Once, my sister couldn't get her bedroom window to close. By then, we figured we had at least one ghost, so she flippantly asked for help, and immediately the window came crashing down—slam!

"Another night I awoke at 2:35 a.m. A slight movement had caught my eye—a man was standing at the corner of my bed! I pulled the covers over my head, too scared to look, and eventually fell back asleep. The next night I awoke at the same time. *He* was there again. This time I looked at him more closely. He was thin and had short white hair, and I thought he looked like a professor. I covered my head again, shaking with fright. Thankfully, he didn't come again after that.

"Mom said that each morning, after everyone went to school or work leaving her alone in the house, she'd hear the floor creaking as someone walked through the doorway of my bedroom. Our dog reacted by running back and forth, with his tail tucked between his legs."

Gina's parents argued more frequently, struggling with marital problems. Her mother began sleeping downstairs on the couch, and began hearing someone walk through the room, though she couldn't see anyone. One night she awoke, hearing the floor creak, rolled over in time to see a shadow, and screamed. As she did so, the shadow zoomed up the stairs. Shortly afterward she had a serious car accident, and believed it was somehow connected to the ghost.

"My sister and her boyfriend stood in the kitchen chatting. During their conversation, a movement in the pantry caught his attention. He saw the back of a short man, bald headed, fringed with long hair. He slowly turned toward them, and they described the man as 'troll-like.' Her boyfriend was very scared by the experience, and only told me about it years later. He noted that it's one thing to seek a good frightening horror film in a theater, but *something else* to have to cope with such characters right in one's house!

"I think I'm attracted to such entities," Gina mused. "Once when I was shopping at Nellick's Warehouse in Troy, I bumped into 'something' that would not let me pass. Upset, I turned and ran outside.

"That Eagle Street house was an eye-opener. It showed me another world right next to what most people call 'reality.' I've learned that this dimension can be experienced in old houses, but back then, I didn't anticipate those events or realize that former residents could still cling to our house. It caused me to seek more information about the world of ghosts and spirits."

Baker's Island

Offshore from Salem, MA, lies Baker's Island. In summer it bustles with vacationers who inhabit the small houses, but after Labor Day only a caretaker remains and, in the stillness, the energies of years past emerge. Buildings replay the sounds and emotions of those who've lived there in bygone days.

Bob Cahill of Salem, whose niece was once island caretaker, visited two old houses on Baker's Island in his research on strange New England phenomena. In the first house there were many 1930s furnishings, accompanied by the musty atmosphere often found in buildings whose time has passed. He walked alone through the structure, glancing out a window toward Halfway Rock in the harbor. As he looked, a great sorrow overwhelmed him. Usually an energetic and positive person, he startled at this overpowering emotion and backed away. The melancholy faded as quickly as he retreated. To confirm what had just transpired, he stepped again toward the window, and once more felt the despondency. Old timers on the mainland told him a young summer visitor with a fatal illness had died there many years before. Perhaps, he thought, she'd spent her last days looking out to sea and pondering the long voyage she was about to make.

Former island caretakers had told Bob of strange events in a second house that he dubbed "The Party House." A dozen years before his visit a woman caretaker on the island had clearly heard the sound of merrymaking from inside the apparently deserted building. Talk and outbursts of laughter were punctuated by the clinking of glasses. Through the window she saw only cobwebs and old stacked furniture in the dark interior. The first snowfall of the winter covered the ground, and there were no footprints entering or leaving the house but her own. Her ears and eyes were telling different stories, and she fled.

Bob later discovered that two other caretakers had also heard clinking glasses when the house was dark and deserted. Rather than the talk and laughter, they heard "whisperings." Circling the house they noticed dim, flickering lights within. Figuring college kids were enjoying a clandestine beer party, they dramatically flung the doors open, only to find a dark shroud of winter stillness within. On Bob's visit the partygoers were taking a respite. He noted that wherever strong emotions are expressed, a remnant of energy can linger long after the participants have left.

Dean Street

Steve is a repair technician living on Dean Street in Niskayuna, NY, just outside Schenectady. He's lived there most of his life, and knew the Howe family—their daughter, Karen, was his wife's best friend in high school. Mrs. H died in 1985, and her husband passed away in 1991. Following his wake, Steve and his wife, Evelyn, made an offer to buy the Howe house, which they'd always liked, and Karen accepted it. "We moved in after Christmas, and one of the first things I noticed is that my packs of cigarettes kept disappearing," said Steve, "oftentimes, entire unopened packs. On some level, I remembered the Howes were both smokers, though I didn't put these things together at first. Another night we sat watching TV in the living room, when suddenly pots and pans started crashing together in the kitchen. It was awfully loud, almost as if a cabinet and its contents had fallen off the wall. My wife and I bolted to the kitchen expecting to find a mess. Nothing was out of place! We looked at each other and scratched our heads. We were starting to get the message that the prior owners hadn't *moved out* yet.

"Things would disappear. They still do today," said Steve. "Then we began to hear footsteps in the attic over the living room. Most of the time now, we hear noise up there. We also hear unexplained sounds in the kitchen and basement. There is always a sense that someone else is in the house, though we don't feel threatened in any way. Whenever we hear unusual noises we take a headcount of people and pets. Almost always, it's evident that none of *us* is making the sounds.

"In December 1998 I received a small box of repair parts in the mail. I checked to make sure the order was correct and everything was there, then left the box open on the arm of a chair overnight. When I came downstairs in the morning I found the box tipped over on the floor, though when I repacked the box, I found a large piece was missing. I left the room to ask Evelyn if she'd taken it, but just a few minutes later I found the piece on the floor, where it *wasn't* when I repacked the box a few minutes earlier."

Karen often drops by when she visits the area, and thinks the mysterious events are humorous. Steve's children sleep in her old bedroom. The treasured remote control for their bedroom TV suddenly disappeared several years ago and the children protest they'd never have been irresponsible enough to lose it. Its loss means the children now have to change channels manually, which they find irritating. They blame it on the ghost, and grownups not understanding.

Karen has one suspicion as to why her parents may not be in a hurry to vacate. Mr. H bought the kitchen stove as a Christmas present for his wife, who used it only a month before she passed away. She'd wanted a new stove for years, and likely stays in the kitchen, rattling those pots and pans, to let others know she still appreciates the gift. Summing it up, Karen feels she has left the house in the possession of both family and friends.

The Old Ballard House

Moving into an old house can be a jarring experience for those who never consider that such dwellings often retain the vibrations of previous dwellers. Even minus a certified ghost, houses seem to act as recorders of strong emotion – love, fear or terror. East Poultney, VT, has one such dwelling, rented by Jack Gutches and his wife, Lynn, in the early 1980s.

"It was an old farmhouse that today has been converted to apartments," Jack told me. "It was cozy and we were happy to find it. Soon after moving in, however, our dog Gutch, a Siberian Husky/Wolf, normally not afraid of anything, began to whine. There were rooms he wouldn't enter, even when we coaxed. After a while we began to feel icy chills. Lynn maintained that she never felt alone there, even though I was away at work every day in Rutland. On occasion, she was so sure she heard me come home that she'd call out, and go into the room where she thought I was—only to find it empty and no car outside.

"We used the unfinished second floor for storage. I piled automotive catalogs there, but often found them relocated when I went up again. Also, we had a bookcase along one living room wall, in which the books kept changing places! We'd look at one another and ask, 'Did *you* move it?' We never figured out how all these objects kept moving themselves. It was as if some invisible person kept rearranging our stuff. Neither of us was scared until one night, after we'd gone to bed. I heard a noise near our bedroom closet, which had large bi-fold doors. When you opened them you exposed the whole interior. I got up and opened the doors. Our dog growled.

"I saw a large man in there. He was larger than myself, had a bare and muscular upper body and very slim waist. His face was almost animal-like, and I believe he wore a loincloth. In some ways he resembled an Indian, though I found myself wondering about Satan. I was stunned. Then, he suddenly dissolved. The dog kept growling and Lynn said she heard voices, though I heard nothing. Maybe it's a coincidence, but a few hours later a strong earthquake shook Vermont."

Despite this apparition, they were in no hurry to move. After two years of high heating bills, however, the Gutches moved. Jack has heard that, even today, from time to time, new tenants in the building relate similar stories.

"The Not Knot"

The Not Knot

In 1986 a young mother, "Mary," and her four year-old daughter rented a house from two older sisters on Brightman Road in Stillwater, NY. Soon after moving in, as she walked through the hallway toward the dining room, her cat streaked ahead. The animal suddenly skidded to a stop, hunched its back and hissed at the room's doorway, then scrambled upstairs and did not come down for the rest of the day. Across the dining room, at the doorway leading into the living room, Mary saw a dissolving apparition. Defensively, she scanned the room quickly and, looking back at the doorway, found the spirit gone. She was uneasy for some time, but rationalized it as too little sleep and too much imagination.

Mary was irritated when her golden necklace chain suddenly developed a knot, which she couldn't untangle, even with a needle. She took it to the fireplace mantle and laid the chain out to see it in a better light, but was interrupted. When she returned to the room the next morning the necklace had disappeared. The mantle top was too high for her daughter. She puzzled over the chain's baffling disappearance.

A few weeks later, the chain mysteriously reappeared on the mantle. The knot was gone and the necklace was wearable again. She never could understand what person or force had helped her. The cat, obviously, was no fan of ghosts, but Mary was eternally grateful for this "repair service."

Susan's House

Susan Slabe had just gotten her kids off to school that morning in April of 1993, and was working at the stove in her house on Vosburgh Street in Ilion, NY, when she heard a noise behind her. Moving a pan back off the hot front burner, she turned and saw a soda can rise from the kitchen table, then fall to the floor.

"While I was still trying to comprehend what I'd just seen, I turned back to the stove and saw my pan had moved itself back onto the burner and was cooking away! I got a tad nervous, to say the least. Then, my back door opened. I walked over and closed it and returned to my cooking, but when I glanced back, it was open again. After I finished, I turned the stove off and went over to my neighbor's to talk about it.

"She suggested that someone in the spirit world was trying to get in touch with me. 'O-kay,' I said to myself, and took a deep breath; I thought I understood. My grandmother had died in March, so I assumed it must be her. I remembered her death vividly. She'd died at Bassett Hospital in Cooperstown. When I visited her on the night she died, I'd fed her some strawberries, which she enjoyed. Then I returned home. Next morning at 6:31, I was awakened by Mom's call—telling me Grandmother had died. Somehow I knew, before I picked up the phone, that the call was about Grandmother dying. I had just had the sensation that she was standing beside me in my bedroom when I reached for the phone. I was grieving all day, so at 10 p.m. I turned off the lights and TV and went to bed. As I left the room, the TV came back on. I firmly believe that was Grandmother's way of contacting me.

"A day or so later I heard rustling in a bag used for storing Christmas wrappings. I brought the bag into the kitchen, expecting a mouse to scurry out. The bag sat there a minute, and then a cardboard tube fell out onto the floor. I picked it up, intending to toss it in the trash, when something inside the tube caught my eye—a rolled-up piece of paper.

"I took it out and unrolled it. It was the high school diploma of my great-grandmother, Esther Fenton, whom I'd never known. Probably getting that diploma had been the proudest day of her life, and I wondered if she was giving it to me. 'Give me a sign if this is true,' I said, and the TV remote fell off the chair. That was good enough for me, remembering the TV set turning itself on a few days before!"

Susan has since experienced other paranormal events and seems to be getting more sensitive to other realms. A few years ago she took photographs of her son's birthday party. Small balls of light appeared in the photos. Such orbs are sometimes considered a photographic manifestation of ghosts. She thinks they represent her grandmother's spirit energy, still taking an interest in family life.

Mason

Professor Mason Griff met Effie, another professor, in Israel. They fell in love, married and returned to academic jobs in the United States. When they retired a few years later, they built a house at 14 Lawrence Avenue on Westport Point overlooking the Westport River in Westport, MA. The retirement years were not to be long, however, as Mason was afflicted with a bad heart. His sudden death came as a shock to Effie. She was a cultured woman, however, and resumed a normal social life after a few years. Effie began dating again and eventually remarried. Following her marriage she sought tenants for the Westport Point house, and went to live with her new husband in Rhode Island.

The renters, also a professional couple, had a six month-old daughter, Jessie. Kim, the wife, immediately sensed a fourth presence in the house. Although their house had two wings, they lived only in the center part and one wing; the other half was locked securely. One late afternoon, while washing dishes at the sink with her back to the kitchen doorway, Kim felt pressure on the floor and heard someone entering. When she turned in greeting, no one was there. This occurred a dozen times or more in the next sixteen months. Invariably, she thought someone had come through the kitchen doorway, but no one was ever there.

Kim wondered if this might be Mason, whose death had been sudden. The Griffs' old telephone still graced their kitchen, and she often received calls from people who didn't know that Mason had died and Effie had moved. Kim couldn't understand her powerful urge to pry open the closed doors on the house's other wing, and discover its mysteries. Nevertheless, she restrained her curiosity.

"It felt like someone was still there," she told me. "When a woman friend from Florida entered the house, she said, 'Oh Kim, there is such a sad spirit here!' So I told her about the short marriage of Mason and Effie, and how I'd been feeling his presence for over a year by that time. From time to time, Effie returned to the house to visit and check on things. She always left in tears.

"After our second daughter was born," Kim related, "I think Mason didn't want us there any longer. I used to get at least one phone call each week where the line was dead when I picked up. After a time, we decided to move, and Effie returned to ready the house for rental. She opened their locked wing, and it was creepy inside—all of Mason's books and papers, untouched since the day he died. Bit by bit she cleaned everything out. I asked the new renters later, whether they'd met Mason. They said simply, 'No.' Without his books and papers, maybe Mason felt free to move on to even higher learning."

3 Fairview Street

Bill Varnum, age fourteen, and his mother sat by the bedside of his seriously ill younger brother. His father was still at work, so they were startled to hear a commotion downstairs—people raising a ruckus. Bill scampered halfway down the stairs, where he could see that the downstairs was dark—no people there.

"It was one of those things you just brush aside, because you can't understand it at the time," he said. "But my mom had been telling me there was something strange in our house ever since my folks came to South Glens Falls, NY, in 1965. My young friends said that the previous owner had gone insane there. Maybe that's why my folks bought it at a bargain price. One day when she was alone downstairs, Mom told us of hearing a group of people running upstairs. Back then, my brother and I gave her a hard time over her incredible story. But this new event had involved the three of us.

"Sometime later, when Mom and I were in the cellar, making Christmas wreaths to sell, we heard Dad's car horn beep twice in the driveway. He always did that to let us know he was home. We heard the kitchen doorknob turn. I ran upstairs to let him in, but the kitchen was empty and there was no car in the driveway. I had to file that incident away, too—'unable to understand.' My Dad died in 1979.

"In 1993 my brother died of a rare bone cancer. After the funeral we spent some time in Florida visiting relatives, and then returned home. That's when it started for real! Kitchen cabinet doors opened and slammed shut. Other noises occurred that we couldn't trace to a source. Our poor dog ran around with his hackles up, growling and looking at something on the kitchen ceiling that we couldn't see.

"One winter night in early 1994, I came home from work and parked my car in back. There was about three feet of snow. I was within fifty feet from the back door when Mom snapped on the back light for me. At that moment I heard someone trudging toward me in the snow—crunch, crunch. But there was nobody visible! Then I heard whoever it was veer off and plod back to the house. From the window, Mom could see that I'd stopped dead in my tracks. Then I bolted for the back door, and came inside to turn on the side porch light—sure that whoever it was must have gone alongside the house. There were no footprints in the snow except mine.

"I taped a lot of music from the radio, but began to get strange sounds—cards being shuffled, a barrel being dragged, coughs, doors opening and closing, people walking in, closing doors, then opening them and leaving.

"I invited our priest over so I could play the tapes for him. He brought his dog along. As the tape played, it set off both dogs, who ran and barked throughout the house. The priest blessed the house, especially the cellar, where he felt dark forces. Mom asked me not to go out that night, but I did. I visited a bar, then phoned home to check on Mom. She was crying and said I should never have had the house blessed. I dragged my girlfriend home with me. When we got there our dog was running around sniffing under the doors, especially in the kitchen. Mom said my cassette player, which I'd left in the kitchen to record the activity, had been turning on and off since I'd left. She felt the floors shaking, and heard dishes being pulled from the drainer over and over. The next day, I borrowed a friend's movie camera and got a shot of a pan moving by itself in the drainer. I believed something evil was in our house. When I called the priest the next day, he said, 'Sell. Get out.' So, we put it up for sale."

While waiting for the house to sell, about seven o'clock one morning, Bill saw a dark shape plunging out the kitchen window—legs and feet only. He believed he had caught the transparent entity off guard, and it was diving through the glass to escape his scrutiny. He looked back ruefully at the incident, a few years before, when he thought his mother was imagining it all.

"Another time, I returned home very tired after working a double shift. I slept until 6 p.m. When I opened my eyes I saw a steady two-foot-wide circle of light on the bedroom door. The two window shades were down and, being November, it was dark outside. When I looked back at the door, the light was gone. Maybe it's a coincidence, but Dad died a little over a month later."

On one fear-filled occasion, the family just took what they could carry and moved out for several months. But the phenomena were still there upon their return. They eventually sold the house in 1994 and moved into an apartment. Since that time, Bill has often wondered what caused these phenomena. His family never was able to discover much about the house's past, just the fact that it was built in 1891, and the names of some former owners.

Never much of a writer before, Bill felt impelled to write song lyrics describing the strange occurrences. He became interested in the paranormal and scientific explanations for hauntings. He has come to believe that ghost energies are composed of "tachyons," sub-atomic, charged particles that carry thoughts or energies from those who were once alive. He has sought to understand more about his

Fairview Street experiences, and has developed his own psychic sensitivities. To Bill, life is full of magic, and after he's passed over, expects to discover how all these events helped define who he is as a soul.

When I lectured on ghosts recently, and told this South Glens Falls story, a woman sitting nearby in the audience gasped audibly. "That's my house! I know those sounds!" the woman blurted out. She was incredulous that I was enumerating phenomena that occurred in her house, and, after hearing the address was Number 3 Fairview, identified herself to the others as the house's new owner. Her family had heard all the sounds, but they were never really bothered. "Yes, we hear the car driving in, but no one is ever there, so we ignore it. And we hear the other sounds too. And yes, the cupboards did open, but we replaced them with new ones." She was more amused than frightened, and fascinated that her house had a "history."

Ghost Boy

Frieda Saddlemire, octogenarian, lived on Zimmer Road in 1925, in the Town of Wright, in the northern part of New York State's Schoharie County. In a recent interview, Frieda reminisced about the old inn, which had sheltered stagecoach passengers since the mid-1850s. A regular visitor to their home was Mrs. Spateholts, a nice neighbor, who came for coffee and conversation with Frieda's mother. She often mentioned her son Otto, who had died suddenly of illness at age six, about five years before. "But he still comes to see me," Mrs. Spateholts had ventured, "I hear a knock at the door, open it, and there he is, standing there, asking for something to eat."

"'But how could he?' my mother asked. 'He died of pneumonia five years ago, you told me that!' But old Mrs. Spateholts always spoke as if she'd just finished talking with her son. To her, he was still somehow alive.

"Four years after that conversation, my father bought the old Spateholts farm and they moved away. Without a son to do chores, the Spateholts' hadn't been able to keep up the farm. Mrs. Spateholts' husband was overworked and depressed. Farm prices were dropping, and The Depression was starting—those were hard times for us all.

"I remember that our family moved into the new house on a cold winter's day, and we moved our belongings in a large sleigh. We piled all our belongings on it; it took us several trips. Our new house was large and white. Attached to the back was a rough structure called 'the woodshed,' with a crude upstairs room.

"When we finally got settled, mother allowed me to go into the front parlor. Immediately, I felt the boy's presence. Later, I learned that his wake had been held there. His small coffin was placed on sawhorses, while the neighbors paid their respects. But that first day, around dusk, I saw him all dressed in white, floating in the air, with his forefinger pointed forward. I was terrified and ran upstairs. When I got to my room I pushed a chair under the doorknob, so he couldn't get in. I was ten then.

"Another time, when I was playing in that room over the woodshed, I found a small wooden train, which must have been Otto's. Again, I could feel him, as if he was happy I could play with his train. That's the last time I remember feeling him *close*. For years afterward, as long as I lived there, we knew he was around—everyone could feel him. I guess he's still there."

The last time I talked with Frieda, she was still enjoying life. She volunteers at the Berne Library and serves as a living encyclopedia for those curious about early residents and life in the hill country of the Helderberg Mountains.

Theresa

In the early 1960s, when Theresa Ebert was old and ailing, she sold the house that she and her husband built at 147 Herbert Avenue in Elmont, NY, to Leonard and Delores Chudzikiewicz. Leonard and Delores eventually raised four sons there, the same number and sex of progeny that the Eberts had raised. Perhaps a year after selling the house, Theresa died. And then the "activity" started.

Delores can't remember what happened first, as so many unsettling events beset her family. The doorbell would ring but nobody was there. The house lights and the TV began to flicker on and off erratically. When the family was upstairs, the downstairs TV would switch on, and when they were downstairs the upstairs bedroom TV would click on. Then the VCR and the vacuum cleaner joined in. The toilet began flushing by itself.

"My worst experience was walking into something invisible that made me tingle all over, like electricity. I went to the doctor, thinking I was ill, and all he could talk about was me being 'crazy.' But I knew what was happening in my own house and body, and I *knew* I wasn't crazy. My home had become a madhouse! The rest of the family confirmed my sanity, as they heard much of this tumult, too.

"One day, cleaning upstairs, I heard the crashing of dishes downstairs. I thought someone had broken in. I rushed down and found our hard-to-open china cabinet open. Broken dishes from that cabinet littered the floor. Some of my neighbors suggested a ghost, but I didn't *believe* in them. Yet, the longer I was subjected to these experiences, I thought, who or what else could it be?

"These events continued all through the '60s. Theresa was the only woman we knew who'd lived there before us. Maybe, thinking that she'd survived death, she wished she hadn't sold the house to us. In 1969 we had a fire, and much of the interior was burned. We rebuilt and modernized at the same time. When we moved back in, the strange events ended. We had peace for almost twenty years. The boys grew up and moved away. Then in 1988 my husband, Leonard, died."

A few weeks after the funeral, while Delores was cleaning, the vacuum started itself again, then shut off. She immediately recalled Theresa's antics. Then all the lights began to flicker off and on. Wiser this second time, Delores began to suspect Leonard wanted her attention. It was hard to think of him as a ghost.

Because she had shared married life with him, she wasn't scared. Her son, Tom, returned home and she was glad to move him into the bedroom she and Leonard had shared. While cleaning his room one day, she picked up a recent newspaper to throw out. As she began to fold it, she saw Leonard's signature in large handwriting on the paper!

"I lived with him long enough to know his handwriting. And I knew Tom couldn't have done it. 'OK, Leonard,' I said, 'I know you're there. I know you made it to Heaven, and are still watching over us,' I said aloud. And I am sure it's true. He's still watching over the house, though it's quiet now.

"How Leonard managed to write his name on a newspaper that was printed after he died, I'll never know. That's the first thing I'm going to ask him when I get to Heaven!"

Reese's Peace

In 1841 Mr. and Mrs. Jim Brown bought a house facing Route 40 near West Granville, NY. Eventually, they took in a cousin's boy with the surname of Tyler, and a Tyler married a Chapin. Since that time the house has been owned by Chapins and their descendants. In 1994 Paul Barber, a Chapin descendant, and his bride, Reese, moved in and, in addition to their professional jobs, began to restore the house.

"During that first winter, just as Paul and I finished watching a video, I glanced up to see a man's face at the window on our big front porch. I could clearly see his chalky complexion. He had a long face and a mustache with twirled ends. I directed Paul's attention at the man who returned our gaze. We went out onto the porch to see who he was, but nobody was there. I thought, I know that face, but couldn't think who he was. Evelyn, my mother-in-law, had grown up in the house and had photographs of former family members in a book. In that book, we found him, an ancestor who'd once lived there!

"That old house had lots of family memorabilia. We found another old-fashioned man's portrait in a closet, and hung it in our kitchen. His eyes seemed to look at you from whatever angle you viewed him. One day the picture was missing—11 x 16 inches, and it simply disappeared!"

Shortly after that the Barbers began to hear knocks at the back door. Even the dogs heard it, and eagerly ran to the door to see who it was. But the doorstep was always empty.

In November 1998, while Reese was away, Paul's brother and other family members came to visit. Volunteering to cook supper, the brother inadvertently started a small grease fire on the stove. Corey, a visiting cousin, ducked out and ran into the living room. After the brothers extinguished the flames, Corey told them he'd just seen a man's face in the front window. This was the same window where the ancestor had appeared in 1994.

In the winter of 1997-1998, Reese moved a cabinet beneath the "face window," and half-seriously muttered to herself, "The ghost isn't going to like this!" When he returned from work, Paul liked the arrangement, but also wondered whether the ghost man would approve. At that moment the top section of the "face window" dropped with a crash. Simultaneously, there came a knock at the back door. Reese went to greet the visitor, but no one was there.

Near Christmastime, Paul's Grandma Mimi (who had once lived alone in the house and often sat near the "face window.") came to visit. She noted the rearranged furniture and Reese commented that she believed the ghost disapproved. One morning at breakfast Grandma Mimi confessed that she had seen a man's face in that window the previous night. Several years later, following Mimi's death, Paul's cousin remarked that Mimi had called her several times during the period when Mimi lived alone in the Chapin house. Each occasion was a snowy night and Mimi reported seeing a man's face peering in the window. When the cousin came to comfort Mimi, she'd always checked for footprints in the snow outside the house, but never found any. Most relatives were inclined to think Mimi had imagined the specter.

In 1998, when the Barbers replaced their refrigerator, they found the ancestor's missing portrait underneath, and put it back on the wall. "None of this mysterious activity ever scared me," said Reese. "We *all* had our experiences. In wintertime, Paul and I worked different hours. During that winter Paul woke me up to tell me he'd heard the ghost knock again at the back door. He'd gone to check, but, as usual, nobody was there. A few days later, when I was alone, the same thing happened to me. I called my sister, who advised me to talk with the ghost. I didn't, at that time, but the following winter, after another knocking, I said, 'I know you live here, and that it was your home, but I don't want you scaring us!'

And that marked the end. It seems he was just trying to let us know he was there. He hasn't been back since. The house is peaceful today."

Most ordinary earthbound spirits respond to the human voice, if you tell them they're bothering you. The majority of the people I've interviewed admit regularly chatting with the unseen when things "get out of hand." It usually works. As spirits apparently work out the details of completing their transition (and in this case "the mustachioed man" apparently needs plenty of time) they seem to require understanding from the living that the spirits are still struggling. If their presence is acknowledged, as Reese did in the above story, spirits will most likely comply with your wishes. Validating their presence confirms to them their continued existence.

In my interviews, I've found that some people who have ghosts enjoy the notoriety of "having a ghost," as if it's a pet kept around for amusement and ego-gratification. Many "host families," obviously unwilling to face the truth of The Golden Rule, have no intention of freeing the trapped spirit. Nevertheless, those who seek to live fully spiritual lives have the *obligation* to assist others, *living or dead*, to complete whatever journey they are on.

If you encounter a ghost, you may assist that spirit's journey by speaking to them of The Light that is available to all. Many, because of the life they've lived, don't even know of its existence. Others, not realizing they have died, have not yet been willing or able to see its brilliance. The living can also speak of the loved ones that are present in the spirit world to assist the soul's passage. A great percentage of the estimated thirty-one million near-death experiencers (NDEs) in the United States alone, attest to both The Light and the loved ones that they found awaiting them when their consciousness was out-of-body. Urge the spirit to look at and recognize these helpers and to follow them. The world into which their soul is passing is one of Total Love. Most NDEers testify to having felt unconditionally loved and totally accepted, no matter the quality of their earthly life, when surrounded by The Light.

Even among the living, there are so many to whom we have not yet given a loving touch or kind word. Perhaps for this reason, Confucius (when asked about the spirit world around five-hundred B.C.) responded that living people don't even understand the purpose of *physical* life, why then should they speculate about an afterworld? As did Ebeneezer Scrooge, any of us may yet avail ourselves of the opportunity to expand our lovingness.

The Lethal Prank

Howard Hayes died at eighty-two in Schuylerville, NY, in the year 2000. I spoke with him a few years before his death, and found he retained a sharp memory of strange tales that he heard and experienced as a youngster living near Brant Lake in the Adirondacks. He unselfishly shared the wisdom and folklore he'd accumulated in over eight decades. One tale, especially, has relevance for today's youngsters who are willing to do anything for a laugh.

A small schoolhouse once stood near the top of Graphite Mountain overlooking Brant Lake. A stranger purchased a small house near that school in the early 1900s. The man, who lived alone, always dressed in black and never mixed with his neighbors. He was only seen occasionally on area roads, driving his wagon and two white horses. Local boys, who couldn't understand his reclusive ways, were frightened by his "grim reaper" appearance.

One Halloween, in the early 1900s, three local lads spotted the stranger driving his team homeward along the dark road. Seeking to return the fear that he created in them, the three screaming miscreants leaped off an embankment alongside the horses' path. The team bolted, galloping blindly down the road. At a turn, the horses, wagon and driver careened over the mountainside and crashed onto the rocks below, killing the man and his horses.

The stranger's house was taken over by heirs, but within three years, was rented to newcomers. Upon the heirs' urging, the tenants agreed to live there for a year before purchasing the house. One uneventful year later they formalized the purchase. At 5 p.m. the day after the closing, the new owners heard a wagon and team approaching rapidly up the hill. They saw a ghostly team of white horses driven by a wild-eyed, black-suited man. They sold the property within a month, also urging the buyers to live in the house for a year before concluding the sale. The newest owners likewise complied, but after signing a binding contract, they too, encountered the phantom driver and his team. They abandoned the house, which then lay vacant from then on, and made no effort to re-sell it.

As a young man, Howard was shown the deserted "ghost house" by his father. It was overgrown with brush and large trees. As an older man in his 60s Howard returned while visiting family graves in Horicon. The old house had vanished. It looked as if no one had ever lived there. All the participants in that long-ago Halloween prank are now dead. Only Howard Hayes remained, for a time, to warn us of the reverberating effects of a Halloween joke turned deadly.

Much hard-won wisdom of earlier generations passes daily from society's memory as oldsters die unquestioned, and hopefully, move on. What fascinating accounts might the world lose unless you perpetuate the stories of the elders in *your* life?

The Popcorn House

"This house was pretty much a wreck when we moved in before Halloween in 1976," Penny Christopher said of her home on River Road in Melrose, near Troy, NY. "Before 1850, it had been a wonderful farmhouse for a well-to-do family, but had suffered abuse from later tenants. Neighbors remembered a fire here in the early 1900s, so some of its original structure is gone."

Within a year Penny had met her neighbors, including Penny Szell, whose family had owned the house until she was age eight. Penny Szell said her family used to move across the road each summer to a small camp on the bank of the Hudson River. They only returned to the big house for necessities throughout the summer. One of their mother's "necessities," involved piano practice, and, as a girl, she and

her sister hated the trek across River Road to practice. After a while they told their mother they wouldn't go any longer—the footsteps upstairs scared them. Their mother acknowledged hearing the noises, though they didn't frighten her.

The Christophers became accustomed to former residents that they didn't know dropping by and sharing memories. Sometimes they brought old photographs of the house. Bernice, a tenant during the early 1930s, introduced herself and shared photographs from her family's tenure. Bernice remembered her family wasn't allowed to use the entire house, and that one of the upstairs bedrooms remained locked. She and her sister believed someone was living in the room because of noises inside, but they never saw anyone. It scared them. One of the exterior photos she brought shows the shutters closed over that bedroom window.

"Popcorn House 1931 - note closed blinds over porch"

Penny Christopher discovered that the property was originally part of the old Colonial Knickerbocker Land Grant, and that a family named Webster originally owned the land in the early 1800s and, likely, built the house. At some point in its history, perhaps after the fire, a previous owner of the house acquired a staircase from a demolished church at Reynolds' Crossing, a hamlet east of the house. This stairway became a focus for ghostly activity.

Over coffee one day, the two Penny's swapped stories. Penny Christopher used to put her children in bed around 8 p.m., and herself around 9 p.m. For many years, soon after getting into bed for the night, she'd hear footsteps ascending the stairs and going to the door of her daughter's bedroom. The footfalls would stop, turn and descend the stairs. She believed it was her husband, Lou, a late-night television watcher, checking on their daughter.

"One night, I grew peeved as I listened to the footsteps coming and going; why did Lou feel the need to check on our daughter, didn't he trust me? So I marched myself downstairs and confronted him. He swore he never got out of his chair when he settled down to watch television, and he never came upstairs to check on anyone. He never even heard the footsteps and believed it was my imagination." Penny, however, now sensed the stair-climber was definitely a woman with heavy feet. In retrospect, she wonders if the woman was pregnant when these energies became ingrained in the house's vibrational memory.

"I discussed this experience with my grown-up son a few years ago. He was astounded, and breathed a huge sigh of relief, saying 'I always wondered why Dad was so protective of my sister. The footsteps always went to her door, but not mine. I felt inferior and wondered why he never checked on me. Now, I know it wasn't Dad, after all!'"

Neighbor Penny Szell recalled that when she was eight, her aunt and uncle had lived in *that* upstairs room. It was a small apartment for them, having a stove and sink. One day when they were out, she heard people moving and talking behind the closed door at the foot of the stairs. She was curious but, knowing her aunt and uncle were out, was too scared to open the door and look. At other times she smelled popcorn, though nobody in the house was popping any. Excited, Penny Christopher exclaimed that she, too, has smelled popcorn and had never figured out where the smell originated. In renovating the house, the Christophers opened up the stairway and removed the door.

"In the winter of 2000, I got up in the night to go to the bathroom, and looked out the window," Penny related. "Behind the fence, where the horses are, I saw a glowing form, a farmer, working and waving at me. I could see his jeans, checked shirt and a straw hat. I watched for a while, then went to the bathroom, thinking that, half asleep, I'd imagined it. On the way back I glanced out the window again—he was still there! Finally, I went to bed. In the morning I looked for footprints. None— not even from the horses!"

Lou listened to the interview, smiled and said, "Soon after we bought the house, my mother came for a visit. I took her through the house and showed her every room. Eight months later she returned for a birthday party. I offered the guests a tour of the house, and my mother asked if she could come also. 'But Mom, I took you all the way through just a short time ago,' I said. She is in pretty good health, but had no memory *at all* of seeing the upstairs before. We wondered if someone or something blocked her recall."

Penny Christopher raises prize-winning guinea pigs and shows them at the county fair. Lou goes to his engineering job each day. Life continues on River Road. If you ever travel River Road, drive with your window open. You, too, might smell the fresh popcorn.

Hale Street

Maybe because the street is named after a Puritan minister who railed against witches, or maybe because the house's residents were a contentious sort, but 181 Hale Street in Beverly Farms, MA, has its share of troubling ghosts.

Maureen roomed there in the late 1990s while attending college. The first night in her new apartment she saw flashes of light in the room, and felt a presence, though she could discover no physical cause. Within days, she saw her hairbrush fly across the room.

Her most striking experiences began shortly thereafter, when she awoke to a loud crash at 2:30 a.m. Quickly turning on the bedside light, she saw that the middle flowerpot, of the five on her counter top, had been pushed over the edge and the floor was covered with potting soil. She heard a buzzing and experienced a strange inability to move from the bed, almost a paralysis. Most frightening, she saw a man's head moving through the dark recesses of her room, followed by his body. Then, a young blonde-haired man, perhaps twenty-five years of age, wearing khaki slacks and a red shirt, stood beside her bed, saying, "Do it now!" As she struggled to sit up, she saw her cat staring at a vacant ceiling. All the bodies and faces were now gone. Exhausted, she fell back asleep, and when she awoke, everything seemed normal again.

For several days she kept this to herself, but finally asked another tenant in the apartment house about it. "Ghosts? Yes, but nobody has ever seen them," he said. "The woman who lived in your apartment before you also had ghost trouble. The ghosts seemed to be a father and son, who first appeared in her dreams, and always together. Three times she heard one say, 'I'm not George, but Thomas!' She went through quite a spell of doors opening and closing, and nobody ever being there. *They* always seem most active around October, when lots of stuff seems to fly around."

Before she gladly left the apartment at the end of the college term, Maureen received some perspective from Todd, a carpenter who lives in the building. He said, "I often hear what sounds like wrestling in the third floor apartment, and once, that rumpus caused my kitchen light to fall from the ceiling. Several times I've gone up to the supposedly vacant room and yelled, 'Knock it off!' That always ends the racket, but only for a while. Sometimes,I've come into the kitchen in the morning and found all my chairs turned backward."

Todd showed her the historic plaque on the front of the building, which states it was built in 1799 by Samuel Ober. Todd once invited a psychic to do a reading there. She told him a father and son were trapped in spirit in the house. The son had died tragically but hadn't left the earth plane, fearing his father would be lonely.

"Originally, after the Obers," Todd said, "a Dr. William Tyler bought the building as a residence in the 1830s. Eventually, his heirs donated it to a museum, which sold it to Joseph Foster in the early 1900s. It was always a single family home until the Fosters bought it and converted the house into apartments.

"A few months ago," Todd said, "I heard someone walk into my kitchen just before dawn, and then into my son's bedroom. He wasn't there, and I wondered who had come in. Then I heard footsteps coming out and hurried to the bedroom, just in time to see a dark figure exit. But I couldn't bring the being into focus; he was just a blur. I wonder if it was someone from the house's past.

"I don't feel threatened here, though. One of my kids was having a party the next day, and I bought a bag of balloons. I came home, tossed them on the kitchen table and went to bed. When I came into the kitchen in the morning, I found it filled with balloons. They'd been mysteriously inflated and double-knotted during the night. So, I think some of our ghosts are playful. Maybe they need more parties!"

While some experiences can be disturbing, most people find ways to co-exist with their ghosts. I have found few people who really want the spirits to leave. Structural changes to a building can sometimes free a spirit to let go and move on. Changes, including new people moving in, can also stimulate ghosts to become more active until the "two sides" get acquainted. Then things seem to quiet down. When I checked with Todd again in September 2001, he said things had been very quiet lately in Samuel Ober's house. He seemed disappointed. But then, October was coming.

Sweet Tooth

When Bertha and Ed Woodfin spotted the old farmhouse on the Troy Road in Marlborough, NH, they knew the house was just what they wanted. It had a large screened porch, a magnificent view of Mount Monadnock, and five acres of trees and overgrown gardens. As soon as they bought it, Bertha set about cleaning and organizing the old place, while Ed, her husband, worked at Northeast Airlines in Concord during the day.

There was an air of tragedy about the place, however. They gradually pieced together the house's history from neighbors' stories. David Farnum, heir to a shoe manufacturing fortune in Massachusetts, had lived there unhappily years before. He had become a recluse when his wife left him, and hadn't kept up the place. He fell into a depressive and apathetic lifestyle. After his death, heirs sold the old farmhouse.

On February 14, 1964, soon after their arrival there, Ed gave his wife a large Valentine box of heart-shaped chocolates. "Thank you dear," Bertha responded, "but you know I'm not much for sweets. Let's each take a chocolate, then we'll put the box here on the coffee table." They did, and Bertha removed the empty wrappers from the box.

A few days later they noticed the box tipped over and the candy spilled on the floor. Each thought the other had inadvertently upset it. They both picked up the candy and empty wrappers, and put them in the box. Noticing more missing pieces and empty wrappers, Ed said, "You must be enjoying them."

Bertha, somewhat offended, replied, "I haven't had one since Valentine's Day!"

"Well, you *know* it wasn't me," Ed responded, "I really don't eat chocolates."

They stared at one another for a moment, Bertha secretly not believing her husband. She now relished the prospect of catching him nibbling the chocolates.

A few days later she opened the box. Five more empty wrappers, five more chocolates gone! "Just wait until he gets home," she chuckled, removing the empty wrappers, "I've got him this time!"

But when Ed returned, he again denied being the candy crook.

"I'm sure you are," grinned Bertha, "and I'm going to catch you!" Marching to the kitchen she got a measuring cup of flour and sifted it onto the wooden floor all around the coffee table. "There!" she said, "When you snitch the next piece, you'll leave footprints." Still maintaining innocence, Ed went off to bed shaking his head, slept well, and left for work early the next morning.

The next week was busy, with Bertha occasionally glancing at the flour-sprinkled floor. No footprints yet. About to welcome Ed back into her good graces at the end of the week, she went to the coffee table, lifted the Valentine's cover, and found seven more empty wrappers! Ed hadn't eaten them she was sure now, and when she related her discovery to him, he was sincerely shocked.

Bertha became frightened—did this mean their house had a marauding candy ghost, maybe old David Farnum? Mindful that tossing out the gift chocolates without consulting Ed might be an insult, she, nevertheless, vented her frustration, "Either that candy box goes or I do!" Ed did the right thing.

Neighbors said that old David was depressed and fell into poor eating habits, mainly nibbling and snacking, before he died. Maybe the only thing that held him there in the 1960s were the images of a happy marriage (which the Woodfins had) and the opportunity to sneak an occasional sweet.

Ed and Bertha lived in the old farmhouse for many years until he was transferred. They never again had an object disappear or move from its accustomed place. During those years in the Marlborough house, they joked about being haunted by a chocolate ghost. Finally, it seemed, old David had moved on to "the big candy store in the sky."

The Houses on Halcyon Street

In 1997, when they moved into their new house on Halcyon Street in Scotia, NY, Tom found a gargoyle statue on the back porch, decided it wasn't his favorite décor, and disposed of it. A few days after they completed moving in, Tom came downstairs to ask his wife, Susan, the identity of the child watching him from the doorway of their son's bedroom. At first, he and Susan thought it was a neighborhood child visiting. However, after he felt a woman lay down on the bed, then disappear, and knowing it wasn't Susan, he knew the house had ghosts.

"Right away we were intrigued," said Susan, "my son often dreamed of being chased by dead people in a cemetery. His closet door would lock itself, and we couldn't open it without removing the latch. He'd awaken in the night to hear scratching on his bedroom walls, and his alarm clock would go off at all hours. In 1999 I heard a bang upstairs and ran up to my son's room. My son hadn't heard the noise, but said he'd just watched the bedroom doorknob turning itself.

"A few nights later, Tom came home from work and didn't recognize me in bed," said Susan. "He saw a sleeping woman with long hair instead of me, then she faded and I was there. After he went to sleep, I awoke to hear a woman's voice say, 'It's all right.' Then I saw her floating by the bed in a long dress. And all these incidents took place in just the first six months here!"

"One night in 1998, our son was camping out in the living room downstairs," said Tom. "When I went to the bathroom, I saw his bedroom door opening and closing rapidly. Walking to the door, I found it tightly closed. In the morning, I told Susan I also remembered seeing something like a heat wave in front of the door. Our garbage disposal turns itself off and on. We have a downstairs telephone that beeps when picked up, and several times when we're all in bed, we've heard that beep, as if someone just lifted the handphone. I know we have ghosts, but we don't know what they're up to or how to understand them. Are they trying to give us a message or show us something?"

One night, after reading *Saratoga County Ghosts* for awhile, Susan placed it on the bedside table, and picked up the Bible to read for twenty minutes before turning out the light. In a few minutes there was a bang, and, turning on her light, she found the ghost book had been tossed under the bed. Tom and Susan know the names of previous owners, but not their traumas. They want to ease the spirits' predicaments, if possible, and asked me to investigate the house.

My intuitive friends Paul and Sue W. accompanied me to the Halcyon Street neighborhood. Early in the 20th Century, many of the area's residents worked at the General Electric plant in Schenectady. The street contained working people's homes. We knew nothing about the house except its location.

Sue W. usually explores the house by herself first, because her receptivity is better in solitude. Paul and I accompanied her a second time. As we climbed the stairs Sue W. heard a child or young woman crying, and glass breaking. She saw a small blonde boy, about five years old, on the landing. Entering the small computer room at the stair top, all three of us felt discomfort in the neck or upper arm area of our bodies. I experienced a sharp pain below my left ear, which did not go away until we left the room. Paul experienced sharp stomach pains in the main bedroom.

Sue W. felt her arms wanted to rise, as though she might fly, as we headed for the son's bedroom. When we entered, we observed the wallpaper covered with fighter jet designs. Sue W. could see where the urge to fly had originated.

In the bathroom, she saw a blonde-haired woman in her twenties opposite the shower. At the same time she wondered aloud if a large piece of furniture had originally stood there. In the dining room she sensed a very different décor that preceded the new owners. In the living room, Paul perceived a man nervously reading a trolley schedule, while glancing out the window. As they entered the bright, modern and tidy kitchen Paul and Sue W. again heard breaking glass, though nothing was out of place.

In the cellar, Sue W. felt a strong negativity and saw a ghostly man who wanted to smash shelving and toys, and turn the family's stereo off and on. Paul saw a laborer in hat and overalls sprawled on the floor near a coal furnace that no longer exists, and drinking from a pint flask. In the attic, Sue W. heard the name, "Martha," and saw a little boy crying, "Daddy, Daddy!" At the attic's rear window, she saw the ghost child turn toward us and say, "I fell."

The owners walked through with us a third time. Susan and Tom informed us that previous owners had a tiled "mud shower" in the cellar, where Paul had seen the laborer. A prior owner, Tom said, a construction worker, showered there when he returned home. Whether he and the phantom drinker are the same, we couldn't tell. We felt the combination of alcohol and anger may cause the breaking glass sounds. The owners have no knowledge of a dead or injured child in the property's history, a matter that we agreed needed more investigation. The pains we experienced upstairs might have come from illnesses that led to the deaths of the still lingering former residents.

* * *

Next-door neighbor Lisa's house dates from the 1920s. Many nights, when her husband works late and her daughter is in bed, she hears footsteps on the stairs.

"Matt, is that you?" she'll call. "There's no response. As I drift back to sleep, I'll sometimes feel someone sit on the bed. It's emotionally difficult to feel a presence but see nothing. I know it's someone from the house's past. On another occasion, when I was pregnant again, I heard footsteps in the hall that turned into my bedroom. A minute later I felt a gentle hand placed on my stomach. I didn't know whether or not to be scared.

"One morning I folded my sleeping baby's blanket and placed it at the end of his bed. Re-entering a few minutes later, I found the blanket neatly and snugly tucked around the baby. Over the past two years I've seen a figure climbing the stairs, but only out of the corner of my eye. I can't tell if it's a man or woman, but I wouldn't be surprised at both. I think some long ago residents are still quietly going about the lives they once lived here, and they treasure children," she said.

The Harrison House

The architecture of the Harrison House in Danby, VT, suggests the mid-1800s. Nobody remembers who built it, so it has a variety of names. Danby businesswoman, Annie Rothman, is the latest owner and has lived in the house herself, calling it "The Harrison House," as the Harrisons are the earliest owners she is aware of. She has rented the house to many tenants, among whom is Linda Mastrobuono, who owns a local antique shop. Linda calls it "the old Sumner Place," after another long-ago owner. But most everybody else in town simply calls it "the old haunted house."

"I bought the house from people who bought from the Sumner estate," said Annie. "When we signed the papers, they joked about a ghost, but I didn't believe that stuff. I asked the previous owner, 'Jim, is this house really haunted?' He gave me a story about Igor, a white albino man, living in the cellar when Mrs. Sumner was here. I thought he was pulling my leg! But the next week, the local oil company sent me an advertisement: 'Welcome to the haunted house of Danby!' I figured they knew more than I'd been told!

"As my family moved in, we found the house all lit up, when I thought the power was still disconnected. I called an electrician and he found all the circuit breakers off. I never understood how that could happen. While inspecting the house, he'd heard a 'Hi' in the cellar, and absent-mindedly responded, 'Hi!' When he looked for the speaker nobody was there. Then he smelled a strong perfume. Nervously, he decided it was time to go.

"The former owner had spoken of hearing 'old peg-leg Obadiah' stomping around on the second floor, and reported many instances of doors opening and closing themselves. The previous owner called one day to inquire if I was having trouble with the attic door. I said, 'Yes, I often find the door open after I'm sure I locked it.' I wish he'd told me *everything* he knew, but I guessed the door with a mind of its own was a frustrating phenomenon he'd struggled with. He probably called to assure himself I could handle it.

"I decided to do some cleaning, now that the house was mine and, working at the foot of the stairs one day near Thanksgiving, I heard that stupid stomping in the attic and got mad. 'Come on out and let me take a look at you,' I yelled. No response. And that is all that happened while I lived there. Later, I rented the house to Michelle, and she told of hearing conversations upstairs, when no one else was there. 'Okay, I'll pick it up' came through the air once, though no one was there to say it. Michelle stayed only a short while."

Linda rented the house for a period after that. She learned that Mrs. Sumner had died on the porch. She believes there was an Igor, or another servant, because she often found deep foot impressions in her shag carpet near the cellar entrance—always coming out of that doorway, but never going back down. She often experienced cold spots at the top of the stairs on the second floor, and sometimes smelled perfume, too. Many times she and her family found objects moved from their accustomed places, when none of the family had shifted them. "Sometimes you'd feel a breeze, as if someone had just walked past, but there was no one."

A collector of antiques, Linda had a nice old grandmother clock that was broken. One day, she found it ticking away, even set to the right time. "I have a Mason Jar mug that I often took to bed filled with iced tea. I used to get it before bedtime, take it to the kitchen, fill it and take it upstairs. One night, I couldn't find it on the bed stand where I'd left it. Several days later, my husband found it in the front foyer, and I hadn't been there in days.

"My biggest surprise was when my heavy old wingback chair was moved from the guest room to the sitting room. Neither of us could move the chair alone, and we hadn't touched it!"

I questioned my intuitive friend, Paul, and he informed me that old Mrs. Sumner had died in her sleep, seated in a rocker on the front porch. "She doesn't know she is dead," he said. "She still roams the house, leaving a scent of perfume. She witnesses the flow of tenants and owners and doesn't understand who they are, but she tries to wait on them and help make them comfortable—hoping they'll go away soon. Igor was a man down on his luck who came to work for Mrs. Sumner and lived in the cellar. He was in love with her, but never told her. When he died, he found her still there, and continues doing his accustomed chores, helping her until she moves on."

Paul also saw "part of the spirit of an American Indian" in the back yard, an ancient hunter who came to drink at a spring, suffered a stroke, and died at that spot long before the coming of the Europeans. His body long ago vanished into the soil, and his spirit has mostly transitioned to the higher plane.

The old house is once more for sale, and when I pass by, and see its striking silhouette against the sky—the epitome of a haunted house—I ponder what it would be like to own the house.

Belmont House

Courtesy, Dr. and Mrs. John A. Findlay

Loyalist Daniel Bliss fled Concord, MA, as the American Revolution started, and emigrated to New Brunswick, Canada. He received a land grant on the St. John River, 13 miles below Fredericton, where he built a small house, *Bellemonte*. His preparation in law soon elevated him to the position of senior justice on the Court of Common Pleas. Following a distinguished career, he died at home in 1806. His son, Jonathan, Solicitor General, greatly expanded the house before 1820. Its seven bedrooms lodged many relatives and visiting members of the judiciary. Eventually it was purchased by the Wilmots, whose son Robert Duncan Wilmot, became a Father of Canadian Confederation, and later Senator and Lt. Governor of New Brunswick. During the Wilmot ownership, the house's vast cellars sheltered escaped slaves from the U.S. before the American Civil War. The Wilmots simply called it *Belmont House*. Robert Duncan Wilmot died in the house in 1891.

In between recent owners, when the house was unoccupied, and after a number of the house's former tenants reported ghostly events there, two journalists received permission to study the phenomenon by staying overnight. Arriving at 7:30 p.m., they did a cursory exploration of the house, then tightly locked and secured all the windows and doors. In order to detect any ghostly mischief, several layers of tape were placed over these closed doors and the locks were secured by twisted wires.

Settling down in front of the fireplace at 10 p.m., they went off to sleep without incident. However, around 1:30 a.m., they awoke to the sound of doors slamming throughout the house—they observed there was no wind outside. The lock binding wires were unbroken but removed and laying on the floors beneath the slamming doors. Then, they heard footsteps at the top of the main staircase. As they heard a presence descend, a series of photographs was taken. When developed, the first photo showed a misty, indefinable object or image on the stairs, then the next shot revealed a more coalesced image, almost as if a man in uniform were descending. *Eight* of the thirteen shots taken revealed some image on the stairs. The journalists later wrote a short article outlining their experience in the *Camp Gagetown Gazette*.

Journalist Jackie Webster lived at Belmont House with her daughters between 1972 and 1986. "Before we lived there, we heard plenty of stories about the old house. It had a reputation even when I was a child. We just loved it, though. One of my first experiences was the sound of slamming doors, followed by footsteps hurrying across the downstairs hall and running up the stairs. We never saw who was doing it. We'd all be accounted for around the dinner table when we'd hear it. We also had a sticking kitchen door with a jammed latch. One day emerging from my home office, I found it wide open. When I went to close it, I was engulfed in an icy draft. I was on deadline right then, and didn't have time to indulge the ghost, so I spoke out loud, 'I don't have much time to finish this article. Now, I want you to behave. Leave off opening my door!' And the presence, which I sensed was a woman, obliged me. We usually found if you spoke to her, she'd comply. Throughout it all, there was a nice feeling during those episodes.

"Many times when I worked in the kitchen, I'd hear footsteps in the next room, but when I went to investigate, nobody was there. We continued to hear someone climbing the stairs, but never found anyone on the staircase. One Christmas we put up our tree on December 15th and left off having a fire in the fireplace for safety's sake. As we gathered on Christmas Eve, the cold ashes in the fireplace suddenly ignited. We couldn't see any wood in there, but it gave a cozy warmth for over two hours. Our locked doors would sometimes open, and lights throughout the house went off and on as they pleased. There never was any fear on our part, only the sense of a pleasant nuisance living with us. Houseguests sometimes reported with certainty that someone had entered their bedroom and stood quietly beside their beds during the night, though they saw no one.

"A medium offered to do a séance for us. I was thrilled—at first. She received the image of a female ghost residing there. We tried to send the spirit on her way, but within a week or so, the disturbances *increased*. At night, we felt a new uneasiness. The disturbances increased in frequency and volume—thumps, bumps, rattles and bangs all over the house—and very cold spots. A parapsychologist later told us that séances are seldom a good idea, as they invite in other, more troublesome spirits."

After the Websters left Bå House in 1986 the building was divided into two apartments, and the new tenants have not reported any disturbances.

*   *   *

You began this book with a chapter of eighteen haunted house stories, and now have finished a chapter containing thirty more. These are dwellings in which the living and the not-quite-passed-over exist side by side. This might be a good time to reassess your personal beliefs on ghosts and hauntings. What do you believe about ghosts? How does one *become* a ghost? Are these stories mere entertainment, or do they have more profound implications for the manner in which you lead *your* life? Note that there are *so many* such stories, reported by people of all ages and backgrounds. Common threads run through these stories: the movement of objects, vibrations are set up in solid objects to create noise, a dashing through electrical circuits to create interruptions, the taking of objects, among other phenomena. In general, the purpose is to establish contact; recognition of their state. Most ghosts that you will encounter are not demons or depraved beings. They are, instead, ordinary people, who laughed and cried, ate and slept, worked and played just as you do. Their body life ended, but their consciousness did not. They began a journey to the Other Side, and it has not yet been completed. What would you do if you encountered a stranded live traveler? Would you lend a hand?

It would be wonderful if each person hearing, seeing, or perceiving a ghost would then talk to the beings, inform them of their passing, and urge them toward the Light and dissolution. Unfortunately, so many are fearful because they don't know what they believe about life and death. Many are troubled or startled by the ghost's first appearance, though almost all experiencers cohabiting a residence find some way to co-exist with the spirits, and some even feel bereft when the ghost finally leaves the house.

So many times, the ghost seems just to want to achieve or maintain contact with the living, to say, "I'm here," or "I'm still here." Ghosts are *sensed* much more often than seen, though there can be variations in experiencing a ghost. As with most experiences in life, if you have a ghost, the enduring question is: what are you going to do with, to, or for that unquiet spirit? Your response, whether it is abject fear or transpersonal love, likely shows how *you* will react to the after-death state when you reach there. Your beliefs will either lead you to wallow in self-absorption or to easily depart this life by walking straight out among the stars!

13
Restaurant Ghosts

Little Lost Girl

November 1, 1971 was his birthday—the Feast of All Saints in his church. Beyond the date, however, he really isn't sure what happened. He took his wife, mother-in-law, and kids to the McDonald's on Second Street in Troy, NY, to celebrate. The children, aged two and three, welcomed a night out at the restaurant. They went to an uncrowded rear section, where four heavyset laborers or truckers sat in a booth. A few seats past them, his wife, Elizabeth, slid their three-year-old into the booth first, and got a McHighChair for the two-year-old at the end of the table, leaving the entire opposite seat for his mother-in-law and himself. He took their food order and walked to the front service counter to get the burgers and fries.

Elizabeth sat for a few moments staring out the glass entrance doors at the front of the store. It was 6 p.m. and already dark outside. There was little activity in their half of the restaurant—just the children chattering to themselves, and her mother fussing with them. Lost in thought for the moment, she suddenly noticed a little girl near the front tables. The child made a beeline toward the seated men, and pleaded "Please, may I have something to drink?"

"She was six or seven, I'd estimate," said Liz, "with the most beautiful long blond hair, and a hounds-tooth fabric coat, which definitely suggested 'high class,' but not of our era. None of the men even looked at the child, to say nothing about offering her a drink. I wondered why such a classy little girl would be begging drinks at McDonald's.

"She then approached our table, 'May I please have something to drink?'

"As a mother, I was immediately concerned for the girl's safety—where was her mother? I asked her. Her response: 'She's dead.' My second question: 'Where is your father?' Again: 'He's dead. They're all dead, you know?' No, I didn't. My next question: 'Where do you come from?' Answer: 'Pleasantdale.' That's a hamlet about four miles north of Troy, and I wondered aloud how she got there. 'I walked.'"

Though concerned, Liz was unable to think of any other questions, and urged the child to go home. The girl turned and walked toward the front doors, around the corner, and out of sight. At that moment, Dad turned the same corner, loaded down with a tray of shakes, burgers and fries.

Liz couldn't believe her eyes. Surely the child and her husband had collided! Her husband proceeded at full speed with the food and set the tray on their table. Liz blurted out, "Didn't you see that little girl by the counter?" She expected him to say yes so she could fill him in on her strange conversation with the child.

"What little girl?" her husband asked quizzically. "I didn't see any little girl."

Elizabeth vaulted from her seat and rushed to the front of the store. No one there—not a customer. She asked the counter clerk. He had seen no child. Desperately, she approached the laborers or truckers and asked if they had seen her. "Mind you, she talked to *them* first," said Elizabeth. But the men denied seeing the child. Throughout this brief experience the front glass doors of the store neither opened nor closed. Still, she went out and scanned the length of Second Street—no child. When she returned to the table, her husband struggled to comprehend his wife's activity. None of it made sense. It was his birthday, after all. What kind of present was this?

Thirty years later, her husband still scratches his head, but Elizabeth remembers every detail of the experience. "My only regret is that I did not realize until it was over, that I literally saw and spoke to a ghost child!" She recalled later that the child more glided than walked, and that she only remembered details of the child's appearance above the waist. Also, upon questioning, she discovered that her mother didn't recall seeing the child or hearing Liz's conversation. Perhaps most telling— her two-year-old never seemed to notice the other child only a foot or two from her high chair.

Liz christened the girl "Sarah" in her mind, and had a mass said for her at their church. Today she firmly believes in ghosts and prays that she did her part in leading the spirit of a beautiful ghost child to eternal rest.

The Orleans Inn

THE ORLEANS INN 125TH ANNIVERSARY CELEBRATION 2000

Ed and Laurie Maas had owned the old Nauset Beach, MA, inn for just a short time in 1996, when local people dropped by and informed them the building was haunted. Ed had at first thought it needed demolition. Whatever decision they made, he knew it was a valuable commercial property and, one way or another, he'd launch a profitable venture there. However, once Laurie heard about the ghosts and the inn's colorful history, they gave up all thought of razing the building, and decided on preservation.

The old structure, dating from 1875, had originally been an inn on Aaron Snow's dock. Shipping grain, timber and whale oil enriched the Snow family, who expanded their commercial enterprise by adding a general store at the wharf. After the deaths of Aaron and his wife, Mary, in 1892, the old building sat empty for almost eight years.

In 1900 two women entrepreneurs opened a rooming house in the Snow's inn, though the activity "diversified" during the Roaring Twenties and Prohibition, when much illegal alcohol was shipped from the old Snow dock. About that time, several women roomers seem to have established their own "small business operation" out of their rooms. Two of these "ladies of the evening" were murdered; one was gunned down in the front parking lot. After World War II the building was sold and expanded, with new wings on either side of the original square structure. The Orleans Inn prospered for a while as a restaurant and inn for summer visitors. But after almost half a century, the old Victorian building was run down.

Ed and Laurie beautified the grounds and created a restaurant theme that blended fine dining and friendly hospitality with history. In the midst of their renovations the ghosts made themselves known. Ed recalls finding previously locked doors open. On one occasion he returned to the Inn around 3 a.m., found an entrance door unlocked, and entered, catching the sound of footsteps and creaking floorboards on the floor above. Hoping to trap a burglar, he called the police. They searched thoroughly and found nobody.

A mysterious janitor seems to remain at his post in the cellar, shoveling coal into a furnace that no longer exists. Ed sometimes hears the scrape of a coal shovel across the cellar floor, and learned that a coal furnace had once been the inn's heating source. Guests in the beautifully restored rooms have been startled by the sound of meowing. Laurie discovered that in the late 1800s a Snow family member had many pet cats.

Waitresses at the inn tell of closing a dining room at evening's end, only to return and find candles re-lit on the tables. The waitresses think of this spirit as one of the murdered "ladies of easy virtue," and call her "Hannah," after a member of the Snow family in the late 1800s. Besides candlelight, Hannah brings a chilling breeze whenever she passes.

He also met Peg, a previous manager of the former restaurant. One of her rituals at closing time had been to yell "Goodnight Fred!" to the empty building. Peg knew about Fred, a former bartender, who had hanged himself in the inn's ornate cupola years before. But one night Peg's exit routine changed when a hollow male voice responded to her goodnight from somewhere upstairs, "G'night!" Fred wasn't the only employee to kill himself there, as a later chef named Paul was found hanged in the cellar. The current chef occasionally spies a well-dressed transparent man in early 1900s garb walking down the cellar stairs. Ed is careful to pay his chefs well today, to head off a third tragedy. He doesn't want former chefs to "hang around," so to speak, feeling unvalued.

It is as if the old inn "remembers" its former employees and patrons, both the schemers and the dreamers, and "replays" the sounds of their lives and labors. I have not found a more beautiful setting in all New England for ghost hunting and excellent food, than the Orleans Inn. It's well worth a ghost-hunting trip to Nauset Beach. When you visit, trek upstairs and catch a view of the scenic harbor, and ask to see the cupola where Fred met his end. If you're brave enough, and take time to make a reservation, you can enjoy your meal in a small private dining room just below Fred's "hang-out." And when you leave, don't forget to wish him goodnight.

The Bear's Steakhouse

The young man angrily slammed the kitchen door, strode to his car, jammed the gearshift into low and "burned rubber" out the driveway onto Route 7, south of Duanesburg, NY. Wherever he was headed, he never arrived. A few hours later, a passerby discovered his smoking and smashed car wrapped around a tree just a few miles away. The boy was dead. His wake was held in the house's front room. Not long after the funeral, the grief-stricken family sold the house and moved away. New owners, after World War II, converted the old farmhouse into a tourist home.

In the late 1940s the old farmhouse became The Sportsman's Inn, and was later incarnated as Duane Manor, a cocktail lounge. In 1959, Bob and Pat Payne bought it and converted it to The Bear's Steakhouse, after Bob's nickname. Pat often heard strange noises in the upstairs living quarters but couldn't identify them or track them down. While tending bar downstairs, she also heard weird sounds but attributed these episodes to the house "settling."

One morning, as she sat reading upstairs, a large fig tree in a heavy pot suddenly launched itself in front of her. "That's just too heavy—no way it could hurl and dump itself," she marveled. Exasperated at the cleanup, she blurted out, "Now look what you did—I've got to clean all this up!" Then she caught herself—who was she talking to?

A few weeks after opening, their teenage son reported hearing music in his bedroom every night at 2 a.m. Sometimes he'd awaken to find his record player on and spinning, but other times, just the music. But from where? Fortunately, this happened once when friends slept over, so he had witnesses and confirmation. Pat, concluded the spirit must be that of the dead young driver, that he must have liked music, and this may even have been his bedroom. She took the matter to their priest, who advised saying the Rosary and praying for the young man's soul. They followed his advice and, for a while, the room was quiet. Sometime later, Bob and Pat's daughter inherited her brother's room, and the music resumed. She discovered that she'd hear the music until she stood—then it would cease.

One night the family was awakened by the strong smell of smoke. In the cellar Bob found his compressor engulfed in flame. Strangely, however, the objects near it weren't even singed. "How could that fire *not* spread?" he pondered. Had the ghost awakened them and suppressed the fire at the same time? That was very hard to believe, but strange events continued in the steakhouse over the years, and the family began fondly referring to the young man as "George," though they knew that hadn't been his name.

Bartender Toni, after closing one night, went home, then called Pat. "As I was leaving the parking lot I saw you waving to me in the upstairs window. How'd you get upstairs so fast?" Pat, who hadn't gone upstairs until after Toni had left, replied, "It wasn't me, Toni, maybe you saw our ghost!" Pat realized that they'd become so used to the ghost activity that an unrecognized person in a window now prompted a joke instead of a frantic search.

Pat believes that George is becoming a "lover" of sorts, toward the young women who work there. Whenever Toni passes a certain picture on the wall, it suddenly tilts. She thinks George wants to get Toni's attention. Also, whenever Toni is around, the kitchen cooler pops open. "She's very attractive," Pat told me.

During my kitchen interview, Bob continually checked the roasts cooking for dinner, and plied me with succulent cuts of rib eye beef. It was hard to concentrate on ghosts. He reminisced, "We had a customer once, who barged into the kitchen after her meal. She wanted to know if we knew about the ghost. We looked at one another poker-faced, and then burst out laughing! She'd felt a cold breeze in the front corner of the dining room, where many others have had the same sensation. I stopped my hilarity and told her about the dead young man, and that we'd learned his coffin was placed in that spot during the wake."

One night, while his son's friends were again staying overnight, Bob got up to go to the bathroom and found the light on. He blamed it on his son's friends, but, back in bed, he saw the light turn on again. When he arose and turned it off, it re-lit itself once more before finally staying off.

Pat told of another woman friend visiting overnight. She awoke to see a chair rocking itself. She's never returned. Another time, someone broke into their storeroom. They came downstairs to find the window open, but nobody there. Pat believes George frightened the intruder away, as nothing was missing. "Once in a while we still hear footsteps creaking down the upstairs hallway, though nobody is there. Corky, our harpist, often plays in the dining room during dinner. In mid-performance his harp will suddenly go out of tune. 'Pat, it just can't *do* that!' he tells me, but it does. We hear it go!

"Perhaps the young driver has now found a brighter and more leisurely path and has forgiven himself for his teenage tantrum. The restaurant has been pretty quiet lately. After fifty years we think he's pretty much at peace and doesn't have to show off as much anymore," Bob concluded.

In time the young man's spirit may also realize that he's closer to Heaven than he first thought, with The Bear's succulent steaks always available.

Ghosts of the Wayside

Hotels have operated in the structure on the corner in Elbridge, NY, since the early 1800s, when Squire Munro built a stagecoach stop for turnpike travelers. Over the years owners came and went, and fires partially destroyed the three-story building twice, but The Wayside Inn has continued to cater to thousands after each rebuilding. Over the years each visitor seeking food and shelter brought an array of energies in their spiritual, emotional, and hand-carried physical baggage.

It's strange, then, that ghosts didn't manifest until after 1967, when owner Fred Weber mounted his collection of over 130 coffin plaques on the bar. Coffin plaques were copies of metal ornaments affixed to coffins before burial in the 1800s; families kept duplicates as mementos. Or, maybe it was the tombstones Fred used for "decoration." Spirits of both kinds were already there, but Fred's humorous personality opened wide the door for an even greater variety of spirits traveling the turnpike from another world.

Fred called him "Harry," a mischievous spirit known for turning faucets and lights off and on, and always at the "wrong time." Fred threw an annual Halloween party on the second floor, where Harry's antics were frequently displayed. Lights flickered and voices murmured from obviously empty areas, but partygoers came prepared to blame Harry for everything.

Katie Ferris, the cook, one day saw a man enter the dining room and, pointing him out to the seated waitress, asked, "Aren't you going to serve that man?" When the waitress stood and turned, nobody was there. Was it Harry? The waitress shot Katie a strange look, but Katie described him in detail as "in his late forties, clean-shaven, with sandy hair, and wearing early 1900s garb." She believes she has seen this same man over ten times, but he always vanishes before he gets a menu.

The inn was remodeled in the early 1970s, but with Route 5 no longer the major east-west thoroughfare, it didn't pay to keep the guestrooms open. Gift and antique shops occupy the second floor now. Fred collected all the Gideon Bibles from the closed rooms and stacked them in one guestroom. In time they became covered with dust.

One morning, Fred's cleaning woman came scrambling down the main stairway clearly distressed, as her pallor indicated. In the "Bible Room" she'd seen a Bible on a bed, opened to the Book of Isaiah. Then, one page turned. Then, slowly, another. The window was not open and there was no breeze. Was Harry getting religion?

In the early 1970s, one of Fred's customers related how she'd found the second floor restroom locked. She politely knocked three times. No answer, but as she turned to leave, she heard two loud knocks from within. She waited ten minutes, then jiggled the handle. The door easily opened. Nobody was inside. There were no windows or doors for anyone to escape.

In 1997, Fred's wife, Joan, told of feeling a strong grip on her upper arm while she counted money in the office. Turning, she saw no one. She and Fred once hired some young boys to cut and fold cardboard boxes for recycling in the cellar. The boys concentrated and worked rapidly until the boxes began levitating from the cellar floor. They all quit. Immediately.

One day in the late 1970s Cathy, a waitress, suffered a ruptured appendix at work. She was rushed to the hospital and later recovered. But after closing that day, the Webers heard a man's voice calling from upstairs, "Cathy! Cathy!" Several staff members searched the second and third floors. Nothing.

In the fall of 1980 the Webers hired Fred Wortman as bartender. Unfortunately, they forgot to tell him about Harry. About a week after he began work, Wortman finished cleaning the bar, when he heard a blood-curdling scream from upstairs. Everyone else had left. He knew for a fact that he was alone. So, at age thirty-eight, Wortman became a believer, especially in Harry.

George Marshall, another bartender, often had difficulty leaving work at night. He'd shut off the lights and head for the door, only to have the lights click on again. Sometimes, he did this several times before Harry tired and left them off.

Who might Harry be? Many speculate. One person believes he's Harry, the husband of a hotel maid who once lived on the premises. He became seriously ill and died there in 1973. Ghosts began to appear in 1974. Others think he might be a Harry that was incinerated in the 1911 fire, though nobody by that name was registered. Many psychics have volunteered to help, though none have provided conclusive evidence.

Mrs. Weber heard that a young girl committed suicide in the building long ago, though details were sketchy. Kate Ferris, washing her hands in the lavatory, once noticed a dark-haired girl reflected in the mirror. When she turned, the girl was gone. She had enough else to contend with, however, because Harry regularly banged on pots and pans in her kitchen. When the Webers retired and sold the

Wayside Inn, most locals expected the restaurant would revert to peace and quiet. They were wrong.

Today, it's Smart's Wayside Inn. Mary Smart gave me a building tour in 2000. "When we bought the inn, my Dad repainted the liquor storage room. He set his paintbrush down, but a minute later found it standing straight up. That was *our* introduction to the ghosts. Sometime later, our bartender, heading through the lobby, glanced up the stairs and saw a woman sitting on the top step. We haven't had guests up there in years. He looked again and she was gone."

One waitress told me, "Years ago, at the waitress station outside the kitchen doors, three of us watched a glass coffeepot tumble off the warmer, hit the floor hard, and *not* break. We just picked up the coffeepot and mopped up the spilled coffee in silence. Nobody dared to comment."

Another waitress, Liz, used to hear a man's voice calling her name. But when she turned, no one was ever there. One of her compatriots told me that salt and pepper shakers constantly disappear from her tables. "I like to get in early and set up my tables, because we do a terrific lunch business. All the napkins and dinnerware are placed just so. A few minutes later, when I return from the kitchen, the knives and spoons are just as I left them, but the forks are all turned over, resting on the tine tips! There are over twelve tables just in this section, and nobody could turn them all over and get them to balance in that small amount of time!" she said.

Townspeople seem divided about Smart's ghosts. Some want to believe and others refuse. But I could find no one who'd ever worked there who *didn't* believe the old stagecoach stop was haunted.

Longfellow's

Before it was Longfellow's, (named after a famous racehorse, not the poet) the Saratoga Springs, NY, restaurant was called "The Canterbury." But long ago, in the early 1900s, it was a mammoth dairy barn, one of two at the site owned by the Farone family. When Prohibition started in 1919, old Doc Farone found rum more profitable than milk, and became a rum-running kingpin between Canada (where booze was legal), Albany, and New York City. The large barn became a storehouse for the alcohol before it was shipped elsewhere. Many bootleggers, bringing their product to Doc's barn, removed the rear seat from their big, powerful cars and replaced it with a 150-200 gallon tank for bulk transportation of booze. Everyone (Doc, the bootleggers, and crime figures who came to Saratoga) was obsessed with profit. Old timers remember that most bootleggers sought to profit from each other's hard work.

Those caught cheating "the organization" were invited to "walk back to Owl Pond," about one-quarter mile behind the barns on Route 9P, east of the city. None ever returned. Recently, the pond area was converted to an eighteen-hole golf course, but the disappeared have not yet "surfaced." At one time an old stable, later used for storage, stood on the south end of today's restaurant parking lot. Canterbury Restaurant employees of the 1960s and 1970s related sensing vague presences, "something moving," and feelings of malevolence in the old building. Were these energies a residue of greed and death that once stalked this old farm?

Just up the road was Newman's Lake House, a famous pre-World War II nightclub and gambling joint. Gamblers who didn't pay their debts, some suggest, often ended up paying with their lives, and disappearing into nearby Saratoga Lake. In the 1950s a human skull was found along a fence line two hundred yards from the old barns.

In the mid-1990s an elderly woman came to dinner at Longfellow's. She asked

Nick, a waiter, if there truly was a ghost in the restaurant. Nick said there was. Several of the employees had seen a man's head (that's all—no body) from time to time, hovering about nine feet over the bar. The head had dark hair and bushy side-whiskers, (something like a sea captain) so they called him "The Captain." When Nick described the man, the woman's face paled. She abruptly ceased her questioning and turned to the menu.

Later that summer she returned and showed him the photo of a man that was a dead-ringer (so to speak) for The Captain. "This was my father," she ventured. Motioning toward the road out front, she continued, "See that white house across Route 9P? That used to be our house. My father had a funeral home there for years in the early 1900s. When business got 'real good' (so to speak) and Dad ran out of storage space for his 'customers,' he used to bring them over to the ice house at the barn, and put them 'in cold storage' until a funeral could be held."

This left Nick and the others to ponder if some of those "old customers" might still be hanging around. Nick and a waitress had seen a filmy woman in white leaning over the second floor balcony, where a smoking room was once located, looking down into the dining room. Who could she be?

Several years ago a heavy life-sized plastic horse was set up in the main dining room during the Saratoga racing season. Clearly, the horse wasn't alive, but throughout that evening and for several days, the staff were unaccountably jostled by something large, strong, and invisible as they served customers. At times they swore they heard a galloping horse, but nobody could locate the sound's source. A plastic horse couldn't have a "spirit," could it? Donna and April, waitresses, also heard a whinny and stomp, and were brushed by something ponderous but invisible. Was this spirit energy left over from the dairy farm days? Or was it somehow related to the plastic horse? Horses and racing have been a part of Saratoga's summer season since the first stakes race in 1863.

Another waiter, after closing, saw the ceiling fans still spinning in the dining room's "loft" section, though he was sure he'd turned them off. The fans' speed increased until their central axles wobbled. He sprinted to the upstairs breaker box, but the switches were all off when he arrived. He noticed the fans were slowly stopping. On another evening after closing he saw something like heat waves moving in the center of the dining room. As he crossed the room, he approached a waitress with a stunned expression on her face, staring past him. "What's wrong?" he asked.

"You're not going to believe me," she sputtered, "but when I looked in your direction a minute ago, I saw something moving between us, like wavy air!"

Unbelievers would agree: ghosts are only air. But then, they haven't visited Longfellow's on a Saturday night in August when the horses are running and "the money is in town," and something in this great restaurant responds to this combination of energies.

The Chart House

"The Chart House"

Colonel Jonathan Pettibone built a tavern in Simsbury, CT in 1785, which burned within a few years, but was rebuilt and reopened in 1802 as the Pettibone Tavern. During its two centuries of existence the old landmark acquired a plethora of ghosts. The Chart House restaurant chain, which purchased it in 1973, has promoted the legend of Abigail Pettibone.

Traditionally, the legend claims that a young woman named Abigail married Colonel Pettibone, who is said to have returned home and discovered her in the arms of another man. The fable continues that the enraged husband killed both lovers with an axe, decapitating Abigail. According to the tradition, Abigail's ghost haunts Room 6 on the second floor, where the murders took place. Apparently the legend is untrue, as my research shows Abigail Pettibone was *born* a Pettibone, married Lt. David Phelps, and lived to age ninety-two. Nevertheless, the old tavern *is* haunted.

Jason Quick, restaurant sales manager, who lived in Room 6, the alleged site of Abigail's murder, in 1972, told of feeling an invisible presence in the room. One morning he found his silver cufflinks had become badly twisted and unusable during the night. He moved to another room quickly. Room 6 was converted to a ladies' room shortly thereafter. Whoever the mischief-maker was, it had a fondness for locking people in or out, and several women have found themselves locked in since that time. In 1992, waiter Kelly Lavigne's sister glanced into the restroom mirror while washing her hands, and saw the reflection of a woman in colonial dress, though no one stood behind her. She avoids *that* room now.

Objects disappearing, then showing up days later on top of his office desk, often troubled Bob Forsythe, tavern keeper from 1971 to 1973.

Rick Gamboa, Chart House manager in 1998, opened one morning and found that a large picture had fallen to the floor overnight. Secured to the wall with three-inch bolts, it had been ripped from its place, but none of the motion sensors had triggered the alarm.

One former manager, closing the restaurant by pushing all the chairs into their tables and turning out all the lights, looked back at the building from the parking lot to see a glowing candle on one table. Unlocking and re-entering, he went to the lit candle and found that table's chair pulled out.

Cooks, dishwashers and other employees often complain of a strange "burning smell" in the rear of the kitchen, but they can never locate its source. Workers sometimes smell wood burning in the fireplace of the "red room," though fires haven't been lit there for years.

Next-door neighbors, the Hazens, sometimes smell fresh coffee brewing in their house when the pot isn't on. Their house was once an outbuilding of the tavern.

John Callahan, current manager, relates hearing the restaurant's mood music abruptly stop. When he unlocked the upstairs office to check on the sound system amplifier, he found the amplifier turned off at the switch. Apparently the spirit wasn't in the mood for that style of music.

Many report unidentified noises after closing, when the restaurant is almost empty. At other times the staff has felt sudden cold spots or observed dinner plates jumping off tables or shelves. Once, as the restaurant managers met in the "red room," a candle sconce flew off the wall. It was quickly refastened, but was found hanging upside down the next morning.

Before the Chart House sign was hung, when the old tavern was stripped of furnishings for remodeling, Callahan and Chart House Corporation President, Ron Smith, inspected some paintings to be hung as décor. Placed on the dining room floor, leaning against the wall, they were left overnight. The two men slept at the Chart House, rising early to hang the paintings in the morning. Ron was awakened by a pounding on the downstairs back door in the morning, and went to investigate. Returning upstairs, he found the array of paintings scattered face down all over the dining room. The ghost seemed to be a critic of both music and art.

The only verifiable modern story of violence in the building involved a Chart House waitress, who'd gone to the dimly-lit attic for supplies. The waitress felt two hands placed upon her shoulders, then a shove, and she toppled down the stairway, suffering a broken arm and severe concussion. Staff rumors had her involved at that time in an illicit affair, much like the legendary Abigail. Had the ghost punished her?

In recent years, several Chart House employees report hearing their names called out when no one is there to do so. Once, a waitress heard a woman's voice call out, "Hello! Hello!" but couldn't locate her either. In 1998 the coat check woman heard muffled voices and a child giggling when she was alone in the coat checkroom.

"We often have important corporate groups meeting here," John Callahan told me. "Some executives from the Trump Corporation recently dined here, loved our facilities and meals, and hearing the 'Abigail legend.' After the meeting, everyone went to the foyer and posed in front of the 'Abigail Portrait,' while a waiter took a group photograph for a conferee. The camera owner returned to Texas and called Ron Smith at the Chart House offices a few weeks later. He apologized that the group pictures didn't come out. In passing, he also mentioned that he'd since loaned the camera to his pregnant sister in Arizona, who had named her newborn 'Abigail.' Abigail was not a family name, and the sister couldn't explain rationally why the name just came to her. Coincidence?"

In 1998, restaurant managers hosted the Connecticut Paranormal Research Society meeting, hoping that experts might offer some insights. Their dowsing pendulums swung wildly and compass needles spun in certain areas of the restaurant, indicating an electromagnetic force field. Unaccountable cold spots were measured and electronic equipment went haywire. They found no ghost named Abigail, but discovered several other discarnates, who they helped release into The Light.

Only in the Chart House parking lot, after we left John Callahan, did my wife, Linda, who accompanied me on this interview, offer her own insights. Looking back, as we pulled out of the parking lot, she saw a woman wearing a long, black gown with an austere white collar, standing at the upstairs dining room window, looking down at us. She sensed the woman's voice saying, "I'm trapped, I'm trapped!"

Returning from our investigation, we asked our intuitive consultant, Paul, for more information on the old Pettibone Tavern, now The Chart House. He noted that the Abigail legend has been written and rewritten because some think it more romantic than the facts bear out. Abigail is not there, he said, but there are a number of entities in the building from years gone by—a former owner, many alcoholics, and traveling salesmen. Travelers, workers and owners' spirits come and go in consciousness. Paul termed the building "a way station" for the scores of spirits who, when alive, frequented the building. Processing the motives and activities of their Connecticut sojourn, they come and go from the next plane of existence.

In regard to Linda's perception of the woman in black, Paul identified her as "Bridget," the daughter of an Edward Pettibone, owner of the Tavern around 1828. Asked why she remains, Paul responded, "She is bitter. Never married. Felt saddled with work. Bitter attitude. Took to drinking." Perhaps this bitter attitude is the energy most often encountered by those who enter the space of old Room 6.

The old tavern and restaurant has stood at Routes 10 and 185 for more than two centuries now, catering to wayfarers, both real and ethereal.

Grace

"The Merrill Magee House"

One cannot tour Warrensburg, NY, without being impressed by the early-American beauty of the Merrill-Magee House. Its Greek Revival architecture lends quiet testimony to the vision of America's middle-class entrepreneurs of 150 years ago. Its white porch columns rise amid century old trees that shade the beginning of Route 28 North. Grace Merrill, who married Mr. Magee, lived there for fifty years. Her husband predeceased her, so when she died, all the house furnishings were auctioned, and the home sat vacant for a decade.

When Florence Carrington came to town, she fell in love with the house and decided to convert it to a restaurant. Shopping area antique shops, she purchased appropriate period furniture, restoring a vintage "family" atmosphere to the downstairs. An Open House tour was held for townspeople, who came and shared their memories of Grace and her home. Several recalled seeing specific pieces of furniture exactly where Florence had positioned them, which made Florence smile. Had she somehow purchased duplicates of Grace's furnishings? Had Grace somehow guided her in her selections? She wondered.

Before the open house, Florence's daughter stayed in the house alone for several nights because she liked its friendly atmosphere. Gradually, the Carringtons established a residence upstairs. The rear downstairs room was transformed into a modern kitchen, staff was hired, dinnerware was purchased and placed in the antique dining room, and they opened for business.

One morning, while Florence worked alone in the kitchen, her son Dan arrived and parked in the rear lot. As he entered, he asked, "Who's here?" She told him she was alone.

"That can't be," he countered, "Just coming in the driveway, I saw somebody up in my room!" They went upstairs to inspect, but no one was there.

Over the years both family and staff have heard voices coming from Dan's room, but it was always empty when they searched it. Eventually, they turned it into a sitting room where the television could do the speaking, without causing houseguests to worry. A sensitive young waitress from Ireland once told the Carringtons of several ghostly entities she perceived with her "second sight," but, as nobody else has seen them, few seem troubled.

Spirits seem most active in the oldest front part of the house. As you enter the taproom from the south entrance, you'll often encounter Dan, who tends bar. He'll tell of being amused in the winter of 1998, when on several occasions an inner door moved by itself. "No outside doors were open at that time, so there couldn't have been a draft. The latch clicked up, the door swung open, then closed and the latch fell back. Nice and neat, as if someone had just come through. I've never *seen* anyone there, though," he smiled.

Enid Mastrianni, a former cook, said that she often heard people walking upstairs over the kitchen when she knew there was no one there but herself. "It's all very soft," she told me, "like old Grace is still roaming the house, seeing what we have done since her time." Surely Grace would have appreciated the wonderful aromas that wafted from Enid's kitchen.

Elizabeth

As you travel into Nashua, NH, on Route 101A you might sail past The Country Tavern, which looks like a modern house done in colonial style. If you don't stop for a meal, however, you might miss one of the most fascinating ghost stories in New England. Underneath the façade, the house dates from 1741, and was only transformed to a restaurant twenty years ago. Since that time it has become the setting for national television programs, *Hard Copy* and *Inside Edition*.

According to legend, Elizabeth Ford married a ship captain in the late 1700s. He spent too much time at sea for the good of his marriage, and Elizabeth conceived a child out of wedlock while he was away. When he returned after a year, he found her and a newborn child. He killed the baby and buried it in the backyard, then killed Elizabeth and dropped her body into the well.

Captain Ford's fate is unrecorded, but Elizabeth's spirit is reputed to have stayed on the property since then, perhaps concentrating on finding her dead child. In her own mind, however, she seems to be "working" as a colonial housewife in her own home. She finds it difficult to comprehend that her home is now The Country Tavern.

The Fox family, the last owners to use the building as a home, said that Elizabeth often interacted with their son. "She rolls the ball back to me when I roll it to her—she plays with me!" his mother quoted him. At first she thought this was childish imagination, but she watched the ball's movements as she worked in the living room. She saw the boy roll the ball, then it would reverse direction and roll back to him! Mrs. Fox often turned from her work to find the ball in new locations, though her child had finished playing with it.

In 1982 the family sold the house to Jay and Judy, who converted it into a restaurant. Bonnie Gamache has been an employee since The Country Tavern was established. "When we opened that September," she said, "Elizabeth tossed two nice lunches right off a dinner table onto the floor. The customer just got up and left. Around Christmastime in 1982, while I was selling gift certificates alone, I heard knocking at the large window in the foyer. I thought it was kids playing a prank, but could see no one. I called Jay and he investigated, but saw no footprints in the snow underneath the window. Nothing happened until after he left—then the knocking started again. I knew the legend of Elizabeth's murder, but I also didn't believe in ghosts. Then, one day, a single cup from a stack of fifty suddenly flew at my head. It crashed against the wall beside me. I became a believer in Elizabeth's existence right there!

"One day, as I waited on customers, a heavy glass water pitcher suddenly flew from my hand and landed underneath a customer's chair fifteen feet away. He was amused because he didn't get wet." Some years ago, a psychic held a séance here and contacted Elizabeth. She said she was agitated that so many people kept entering and leaving *her* house. The psychic told her that her house was now a restaurant, but she didn't comprehend that word. So, they explained, 'It's now a tavern,' and she understood. Bonnie feels that Elizabeth is now her friend and has become less fractious since the séance. Perhaps all that Elizabeth needed was a talking to.

During the past twenty years, lights have snapped off an on, and doors have opened and closed by themselves. One woman customer, brushing her hair in the ladies' room, saw the reflection of her long hair being lifted off her neck. She left hurriedly.

Amy, another waitress, also saw the ghost. Clearing a table one evening, she glanced toward the emergency exit and saw Elizabeth as she is always seen: standing in a white, flowing dress with a blue ribbon sash, and holding a candle.

Amy fainted. Seven people, including Amy, in the last twenty years have seen Elizabeth.

Jon, co-owner since 1995, said that the previous owner had no break-ins during his six-year tenure, but in 2000 and 2001 *he* had three. It used to be just numerous false alarms that brought the police. "They used to rush here, sit in the rear parking lot, and wait for me to show up to unlock the door for their investigation. One night they were really jumpy when I pulled up, having seen a curtain at a rear window moving, as if someone were watching as they pulled in. Needless to say, they were on edge as they explored the building, but they found it locked up tight and no intruder was ever found," he said.

After our travels in New Hampshire, my wife and I asked the intuitive, Paul, to comment on this case, as we sought additional spiritual understanding of Elizabeth's life after death. He said, "She wants to be called 'Annie' now, and still doesn't fully understand what happened. She is in denial of her death and ignores those experiences as 'a bad memory.' She condemned herself after death for not being a good housewife, mother. She determined to return to the house, find her child, and do the job right. She is aware of The Light and ignores it because she is too busy setting the table, still trying to turn down beds from her time.

"She simply focuses on 'keeping house,' and continues the old habits of her time. But the walls have changed; the rooms have changed. She tries to keep doing her work in a house that is shaped differently. She's attracted to those who work and visit today's house, and is only partially successful in offering the hospitality that she'd like. So she wrings her hands sometimes, feeling ineffective. She feels the need to do this work because she turned away from those tasks in the last life, and sought her own comfort and pleasure. She is atoning for it now, and opening her heart to others slowly. She finds it rewarding to do these things. She may be prayed for."

He continued, "It would be as if you were to put on spectacles in order to see more clearly what is around you. You may say she has developed tunnel vision, focused on her guilt, and her need to atone for her unfaithfulness. When you pray, you help open the consciousness of the dead one, put spectacles on her, and allow her to see the fullness of the Light that is available to her in that place. It is good to inquire about what is in the woman's heart. She would have you know that she is trying to do her job. 'I AM trying,' she says."

My wife asked Paul about Elizabeth's husband, and he responded, "He is still there. He sits sulking. He does not admit to himself what he has done. He is even more so in a place of darkness. It is as if he has imprisoned himself after death. He is not anxious to let in The Light. He also may be prayed for. He has put himself in a black box in the back lot outside the house, outside the rear door, to the left of the entrance." She asked if it was a coffin. "No, it's like a black cubicle, where he sits with his elbows on his knees and his hands under his chin. He looks away from the house. He will not turn to look at the house."

Most versions of the Elizabeth Ford story concentrate on her alone. Our search for understanding included all three members of the Ford household. We asked why the

child would have chosen such a brief and violent incarnation, and digressed to questions about all children who die suddenly, including cases of Sudden Infant Death Syndrome (SIDS). Paul responded that "Elizabeth's child was one month and two days old at the time of its death. Many souls who have taken life in previous incarnations *must* return and experience a shortened life—to experience in the heart a dashed hope. For some, it is also the grief of not being wanted. One need not experience a long life to know what it is to be unwanted or condemned; one may experience that in an instant. So many children, who are helpless, die in this manner. Child abuse deaths are a different death from illness or natural disaster. Before taking on life, such souls have agreed to experience first the joyful promise of life and its hope, then the desolation of having these snatched away and shattered. Most can return once more to the earth and truly *appreciate* the hope of a new life when it begins again."

When you visit The Country Tavern enjoy the wonderful meals and say a prayer for Elizabeth or "Annie." This can help her to see more clearly the need to finish her *spiritual* work, as opposed to housework, and move on, although she may see your visit as interfering with her housework. If Paul is right, "She doesn't want to be disturbed by those who would turn her from her job, yet, she may be prayed for to enlarge her consciousness to her true state, which has passed beyond the body and may now find rest and peace." Most importantly, remember she *is* trying.

273

The Yellow Rose Café

"Penfield's House, formerly The Yellow Rose Cafe"

In 1783 Daniel Penfield was mustered out of the Continental Army and struck out for the frontier of western New York. He purchased land near a major crossroads and became a leading merchant in the small settlement that today bears his name. Just east of Penfield itself, at what is now 1784 Penfield Road, he built a home, barn and store. His influence spread in Monroe County, where he held civic and commercial positions. Upon his death his extensive holdings were divided and passed into others' hands.

In the 1950s the old house became The Yellow Rose Café, noted for a sometimes-eccentric menu. In the evenings the steady bar crowd whispered about the antics of a resident ghost. Soon after Chuck came to work there, he'd set something down, only to find it gone when he turned to retrieve it. At first, he feared he was becoming absent-minded. In exasperation, he mentioned it to a "regular," who was a former waitress at the Café.

"Maybe it's the old soldier, putting you through your paces," she grinned. Then, seriously, she added, "Many nights when I'd come up here I'd see him sitting on a bar stool staring at me. He wore some kind of old blue uniform. I thought he might be a Civil War soldier ghost. Sometimes you could see him and other times not. But, when I'd feel a tug on my ponytail at the top of the stairs, as I came up from the basement kitchen, I *knew* it was him because of his intense interest in me!" Could she be mistaken as to which war's uniform he wore; might it be old Daniel Penfield himself?

274

"I never saw him," Chuck said, "so I didn't want to accept her stories, but many strange events started to make me a believer. At times the cash register would fly open and bills would sail out. There was never any satisfactory explanation for that, nor was there any way to understand what happened after hours. We always kept some change in the register overnight, because nobody wanted to count it at closing. But when we returned in the morning it would be all stacked on the counter—pennies in one pile, nickels, dimes and quarters all in their piles. Someone was precise. We often speculated that it was old Daniel Penfield, the Revolutionary War soldier, a man who earned and counted lots of money in that house."

In time The Yellow Rose Café closed its doors, and was readied for its next incarnation as a business. "In September 1997, when I first bought the building," said Gertrude, the next owner, "we had an auction of old restaurant equipment stored in the barn out back. As we were dismantling a big cooler the police showed up. They said an alarm had gone off at the police station, but we were no longer hooked up to their system! Then it was the construction men's turn. One day a workman installing dry wall announced he was going over to turn on the radio. He took only one step in that direction, and it turned on by itself.

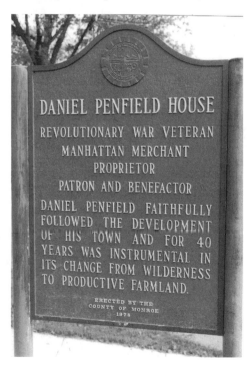

"Once we opened, a girl that worked here kept hearing the name 'Andrea' being called out in a man's voice, but we could never find him. She went into the bathroom one night and lit a candle on the back of the toilet. A few seconds later, the candle flew across the room and went out. Something kept starting our washing machine, too. We tried a séance once, but nothing happened." Gertrude sounded disappointed. She never solved those mysteries before her business closed.

Today the old house is a lighter shade of yellow and has become a hairstyling salon known as Salon Enza. The interior is bright and cheery, and there is no physical trace of Daniel Penfield's emporium, or even of the café.

Women in stylish hairdos emerge from Salon Enza unaware of the "spirited" role the old building has played in the town's history. Salon manager Laura Barbera has noted nothing stranger than the kaleidoscopic "retro" hair colors favored by many of today's youth. Here's hoping the ponytail-puller doesn't return.

275

The Farmhouse

Not far from Interstate 88, as it winds through the western Catskills, is the hamlet of Emmons, NY. People come from far and near to sample the fine cuisine at The Farmhouse Restaurant. The big building hasn't always served food, however, nor has it always stood in that spot. Carleton and Maria Emmons built it around 1865 as the centerpiece of a seven-hundred-acre farm. They took great pride in their holdings and the wealth that it generated. Carleton had a strong emotional attachment to the farm and, as he lay on his deathbed, is reputed to have told his heirs, "Don't sacrifice my farm!" His daughter's son-in-law, Kendrick Morgan, bought the Emmons' beloved house, moved and expanded it in 1901. The move brought the old house nearer to the main road. However, during that operation a young girl playing alongside the heavy equipment was crushed to death. Most of the farm's outbuildings were destroyed in a 1939 fire, though there was no known loss of life.

"Emmons Family gathering - early 1900s"

Cook, Gary Conrad, remembers seeing the shadow of a girl in the kitchen on several occasions. "When she passes, I know trouble is coming. Pots and pans hop off the shelf. We don't know what she looks like, as she usually appears as a shadow." There is a picture in the hallway of the Emmons family. The ghost girl may be among the several children in the picture. This hallway, near the salad bar, is the place where customers often feel they are being watched. Gary added, "Several have remarked at hearing vague whispers, as if some quiet presence is trying to get their attention, but they never can make out the words." While standing there, I, myself, thought I heard my first name called, though no one in the building knew it was David.

If you're touring haunted restaurants, this one bears investigation. At worst, you'll come away with a delightful meal. At best, an inveterate ghost seeker may glimpse a child's shadow or hear mischievous spirit whisperings and giggles from long ago.

Turned Tables

The Halfway House stood for almost a hundred years at the intersection of Routes 9 and 149, a point halfway between the City of Glens Falls and the Village of Lake George, NY. Three retired buddies, "Tom," "Dick," and "Harry," used to have coffee there each day. Tom, the spark-plug in the group, often irked Dick and Harry with his boasting. If you had caught a ten-inch trout, he'd tell of the time he'd caught a twelve-incher. If you had won five dollars on the Daily Double at Saratoga, he'd up you one and tell of the time he won a hundred. The two friends liked Tom, but he needed some "attitude adjustment."

In January 1949, after Tom had verbally outscored his companions for the umpteenth time, Dick and Harry decided it was time to teach him a lesson. They usually didn't get coffee together until about five o'clock, but the winter darkness abetted their scheme. Back in October, Dick remembered a spirited discussion about the plot of Washington Irving's *The Legend of Sleepy Hollow*, and The Headless Horseman, and had noted a glimmer of fear in Tom's eye. Now was the time to put that hunch to the test.

It took a few days, but Harry put together a pretty fearsome Headless Horseman costume. At their Friday get-together Harry excused himself from the table to go to his car, while Dick engaged Tom in his favorite topic—himself. The plan called for Harry to dress in the costume and knock on the dining room's back door. When the rap came, Dick was to sit still, so that Tom, always the over-achiever, would surely rise to help the waitress and answer it. Then Harry, in costume, would scare the daylights out of Tom. It sounded super.

And they apparently carried it off without a hitch. Harry exited, and a few minutes later there came a very loud banging on the rear door. Tom sprang to his feet, pushed the waitress aside, saying, "I'll get it for you!" Opening the door, he made an audible gasp, and fainted.

The waitress and several others rushed to his side to revive him. Dick stood smiling. He'd recover—Tom was strong as a horse, hadn't he always told them so? Soon, Tom stirred. As he did so, however, Harry re-entered the front door rubbing his head. Dick greeted him warmly, congratulating his friend on a super performance. But Harry, grabbing Dick's sleeve to get his attention, whispered, "There's something you don't understand, Dick. When I got out front, I slipped on the ice and fell down. I was knocked out for a minute and my head still hurts. I can't go through with our gag."

Perplexed, Dick stared at the revived Tom, who now babbled to the others about a gigantic black fire-breathing horse, ridden by a man in black with no head. It was the biggest event in his life, and he continued to tell about it for the rest of his days. Harry and Dick often scratched their heads too, trying to guess who or what had been at the back door. They never figured it out.

The Bull's Head Inn

George Ferster came to New York State's Schoharie Valley in 1752 and built a home near the Cobleskill Creek. His house was open to both white settlers and local Indians, but two of the latter became embroiled in an argument, and one stabbed the other to death in the Ferster house. Marauding Indians twice burned the building during the Revolution, and twice Ferster rebuilt it with his own hands. The last time, however, he made it into a tavern, and later sold it to German immigrant, Lambert Lawyer, who turned it back into a home.

During Lawyer's tenancy the building burned again. Around 1802 Seth Wakeman rebuilt and enlarged the house, and then reopened it as "The Bull's Head Inn." The Inn was also used as a town hall, a courthouse, and a public meeting place before 1839. The Dutch and German farmers were too frugal to spend much time or money in taverns, so Wakeman converted the building back into a home again, which it remained until the 1960s. Then, Monty Allen opened it again as The Bull's Head Inn, hoping to serve the steady influx of tourists who were rediscovering Schoharie County's old forts and museums, and the farms of America's patriot founders. Some of those founders may still be there.

John Stacy, whose home it was after 1920, had been was a heavy drinker, prompting his wife to join the local chapter of the Women's Christian Temperance Union (WCTU). Apparitions started in 1964, when Allen created a dining room and bar in Mrs. Stacy's old bedroom. Waitresses and bartenders sometimes saw a woman in a long white filmy gown, perhaps a nightgown, walking *through* the tables, chairs and walls of the room. From time to time, salt and pepper shakers disappeared, and pieces of silverware rose from the tables and flew at the bar. Then, as today, the ghost's likely identity is Mrs. Stacy.

One night around 1981, Jeff Patterson, the bartender, sat sipping a nightcap after he closed the bar. "Suddenly, I saw lights on the wall, as though venetian blinds were opening and closing several times. Then, I saw what seemed to be a figure sitting in the corner of the dining room. It appeared to be a woman in a white nightgown." Mrs. Stacy showed her displeasure many times after that.

Napkins and plates sometimes became airborne, and strange unlocatable sounds were heard. Lavatory faucets suddenly turned themselves on. Swivel chairs mysteriously revolved by themselves. Kathy Vedder, manager of the restaurant in the early 1990s, recalled a terrified customer who saw his table's butter dish levitate. She also told of seeing a woman's reflection behind her in a rest room mirror, but when she turned to identify the woman, nobody was there.

At various times, after closing, bartenders and staff in the recently built cellar pub have heard footsteps upstairs, but have never found anyone. On a recent Super Bowl Sunday, while the staff relaxed in front of the pub's television, they heard loud footsteps upstairs. Several went up to look, but a thorough search revealed nobody.

A former hostess named Nancy was speechless when an old hand-cranked telephone on the wall began ringing. No one was near it to turn the crank. It wasn't hooked up to any outside line—it was just a decoration! Maybe Mrs. Stacy was calling with a temperance message for the bar patrons.

Rose, a morning cleaner, said, "When I'm cleaning in the pub I often feel someone or something pass by—just a little breeze, but there are no windows open downstairs. I also feel I'm being watched continuously while I'm there, as if someone is standing right behind me. But I've never seen who it is."

The current owner, Bob Youngs, told me, "I soft-pedaled the ghost stories for the first dozen years I owned the place. I didn't want my restaurant to get an unsavory reputation, but events continue and the word spread. Then, I had my own experiences. One night, working in the pub, I moved to the corner of the room. I felt a heavy hand grip my shoulder, but I couldn't see it. I wasn't frightened, but that was proof enough for me that an unseen presence is here. The bar today sits below the spot where we think the Indian was stabbed over two hundred years ago. When a previous owner did some renovation in the first floor's north dining room, he discovered a series of cupboards hidden within the wall, and in them he found an old hatchet or tomahawk, swords, and things like that! This place is full of history.

"One night we had a wine tasting party. A man I know brought his wife, and about midway through the party, she left to go to the women's room. She returned with a smile, saying 'Gee, Bob, you sure encourage people to think about history. How did you get the idea of putting a costumed woman as an attendant in the restroom?' I just smiled. We had no woman in historic dress, but if I'd told her that, I'd have lost another customer.

"Today guests and staff talk openly about the strange events. A few years ago, some people came to shoot a video along the street outside. They videotaped not only The Bull's Head Inn, but also the other old buildings on this block. I haven't seen the finished product yet, but they phoned and told me the videotape showed ghostlike figures in front of just about every building along the street," Bob said.

The story of Mrs. Stacy now appears in books and on hauntings web sites. Students from the State University at Cobleskill make the Inn a regular "haunt" almost as soon as they arrive in town. And many others from outside Schoharie County go there seeking a good meal and some "unscheduled entertainment," if the spirits are so inclined.

14
Animal Ghosts

Chunk

In December 1998, in Gansevoort, NY, just north of Saratoga Springs, Shelley lived with her family and a cat named "Chunk." She had never loved any animal as much she did Chunk, and felt he was a family member. One evening, a neighbor came to her door and reported a dead cat in the road. Shelley's heart fell and she asked her husband, Tom, to go out and see if it was Chunk. It was. He placed the cat in a box and brought it inside the back door so they could bury him in the morning. Their young daughters were distraught. One of them awoke at 3 a.m., crying. The child had overheard her mom crying Chunk's name in her sleep. And when she felt a frigid breeze pass through her bedroom, the girl scurried to Shelley's bedroom and related her experience and heartbreak. As she did so, Shelly heard a meow, but couldn't locate its source. Finally the child returned to bed and went to sleep, but Shelley was wide-awake!

Then she heard a meow on the bed beside her, and could *feel* the cat's presence. She became frightened. Next morning, after Chunk's burial, Shelley told Tom of her fear of a ghost. He asked if she had ever been frightened of Chunk when he was alive.

"No, of course not."

"Then you have no need to be afraid of him now," he said.

She has made that her slogan whenever Chunk returns. From time to time she still feels Chunk's presence on her bed, but now responds to the cat's devotion with love and warmth.

Also Ran

At The Oklahoma Track in Saratoga Springs, NY, an old groundskeeper, working at the final turn, near the Eighth Pole, heard a horse galloping toward him on a cold autumn afternoon in the 1960s. The racing season had ended in August, and most thoroughbreds had left for warmer tracks in the South. Alone on the huge track, he was repairing the track rail. The neighborhood on East Avenue was quiet and the man's repetitive work had lulled him into a hypnotic state. But, as the hoof beats grew louder he looked around. No horse was visible. No horses are training here today; there isn't even one being walked, he thought. But it sounded as if he was about to be run down by a galloping invisible horse! His jaw dropped and his wrenches slipped from his hand. Just as the pounding hooves seemed ready to overrun him, there was a horse's shrill scream of pain, then an eerie silence. East Avenue was quiet except for the distant sound of boys playing football. He looked down at his tools and knew he could not share this with anybody—he needed his job, and people would think he was screwy.

In time, however, he did share his experience with another old timer, a blacksmith who came around in the track's off-season. The blacksmith was sympathetic, and told him of a racehorse, whose name he no longer remembered, that had been working out on the Oklahoma Track in the 1940s. "Maybe you weren't around then," the blacksmith said, "but I remember it like yesterday. That horse had just turned for home, about where you were working, when he stumbled, fell, and broke his leg.

They destroyed him on the spot." The two men silently looked at one another, slowly comprehending the implications of the horse's death and the worker's mysterious experience.

The old blacksmith thought he'd heard it all, but now he and the maintenance man had just one solution to ponder—a ghost horse is still running at Saratoga.

Tammy

When they moved into it in 1994, Mike and Shawn immediately loved the house in Randolph, MA. Each boy was thrilled to have his own bedroom. Kathy, their mother, was happy, also. But Mike, age two, who normally liked bedtime, soon began to complain that something in his room bothered him. "It's a dog, Mom, right over there!" he whimpered. "He's always right over there!"

Kathy couldn't see a dog, and it strained her ingenuity to get Mike off to dreamland each night. Mike could even see the dog during the day, though no other family member could.

"Go over to him, Mike, he won't hurt you," Kathy said, walking to the spot Mike indicated.

"He was just there, but he's gone now, Mom!" Mike answered.

One day Kathy asked her new neighbor what she knew about the old house. The neighbor said an old woman had lived there for many years and had recently died. "She was all alone, had never married and had no family. She doted on her little dog, and even gave it a bedroom," which Kathy learned was Mike's.

A week later Kathy met another neighbor, who was clairvoyant, at Shawn's Little League baseball game. The woman told Kathy that Mike was psychically sensitive and might develop that ability further, but was currently afraid of seeing things no one else saw. "He doesn't yet know what to do with that talent," the woman said, without knowing of little Mike's experiences with the invisible dog.

Kathy became more interested in ESP, and once hosted a party for sensitives in her home. Without revealing any of its history, she urged them to tour the house and seek intuitive impressions. In Mike's bedroom, one man saw a small dog sitting on its corner bed right where Mike often saw *his* ghost dog. "He's a small and golden-brown dog, and he never leaves the room," the man said. His never leaving was hardly encouraging to Mike.

A few weeks later Kathy met another neighbor who'd known the spinster. When Kathy asked about a dog in the house, the neighbor smiled. "Oh, you know about Tammy! He was a honey-colored poodle, and was her constant companion. They grew old and died together."

A few months later, Kathy met some of the old woman's relatives, who, she discovered, lived only a few streets away. They confirmed that Tammy had had his own bedroom, and it was Mike's present room.

Eventually, Mike accepted the invisible pooch and spoke no more about him. When Kathy asked Mike about Tammy in 2000, as Mike is growing more and more into "big kid consciousness," the boy said he now sees the dog only about once a week. Apparently Tammy's spirit may be preparing to leave the earth plane for good, and move on to whatever heaven awaits faithful companions. However, it is just as likely that Mike, although naturally psychic, as many youngsters are, is being more strongly shaped by social conformity, which dictates what can be seen and what cannot.

Austin

In the 1970s, when Art and Linda attended Utica College in upstate NY, Art had a snazzy Austin-Healey sportscar. They also had a huge furry cat, "Austin," often joking that he was almost the same size as the car. Austin didn't do a lot, as he slept most of the day. However, he had a special "trick" when his owners went to bed.

At the foot of their bed was a large blanket chest, whose lid never quite fit. Pushing down on it created a "clunk." Next to the chest was a television with a short circuit—bumping it just right would turn the TV on.

"Each night when we went to bed," Linda told me, "we turned out the lights and waited for Austin to do his act. He'd jump onto the chest—CLUNK! Then onto the television—CLICK! and we'd end up watching *The Tonight Show* whether we wanted to or not. He only did it once each night, so it became our 'settling routine.'

"After about a year, Austin became really ill. We took him to the vet, who gave him antibiotics. We left him overnight for observation. 'Call me in the morning and I'll tell you how he's doing,' said the doctor."

They left Austin in the strange vet hospital and went home dejectedly, already missing their companion. Just after 11:30 p.m., however, the bedroom began to reek with the powerful smell of overused cat litter. Then CLUNK went the chest, and CLICK went the television, and there was Johnny Carson!

Art looked at Linda and Linda looked at Art. "We didn't say anything," she said, "we just turned off the TV and went to sleep. In the morning the phone rang.

'Linda, this is the Vet. I'm sorry to tell you this, but Austin was more seriously ill than I knew. He died around 11:30 last night.'"

Linda hesitated a minute and then said, "Oh no, he didn't!"

Rufus

Clarence Batchelor, a Pulitzer Prize-winning political cartoonist, bought a house. He loved the quiet countryside and named the old house, "Far Twittering" for the area's abundant bird life. Away from his job at the *New York Daily News*, he was able to maintain a sharp perspective on American social and political affairs in the 1930s. "Batch," as nearly everyone in Deep River, CT, called him, loved animals and had several dogs. Each was given a personal tombstone, lovingly inscribed by Batch, when it died. After his death the Ballsiepers bought Far Twittering and moved in.

"It was in rough condition, especially the kitchen, and we had to tear that room down when we moved in," said Lorraine Ballsieper. "We wanted authenticity, and bought an old wreck house down in Killingworth and tore it down, just to get the antique parts this house needed. I scraped over fourteen layers of paint from the living room walls in Batch's old house! Bill, my husband, became the master carpenter, restoring everything as closely as possible to the 1700's look we sought. We wanted to be able to cook in the large fireplace, which I now do, even cooking the Thanksgiving turkey there. The house dated from 1734, when Nehemiah Pratt built it on Kelsey Hill Road, farming twenty acres and operating a small mill on the site.

"About six months after we began renovation, we still had no electric power. We slept in one bedroom while renovating the other. Rufus, our Great Pyrenees dog, was our companion and guard. He's an exceptional pet and almost never gets upset.

"One night Rufus became quite agitated, and took off downstairs, barking. I followed, suspecting a break-in. It was really dark, but as I passed through the dining room I saw a bright glow in the kitchen. What could that be? I wondered. Is someone in there with a flashlight? Entering the kitchen, I was utterly astonished to see a brightly glowing man suspended in mid-air, with a shock of dark hair. After calming from the scare, I recognized Batch, whom I'd met when he was still alive. Rufus sat expectantly at his feet, staring and wagging his tail. After about ten seconds Batch disappeared.

"Later," Lorraine said, "I figured Batch, the dog lover, had come to visit his old house and discovered our renovations, then found a new faithful dog on sentry duty—Rufus. Batch must have stopped to scratch him behind the ears then, knowing his old house was in good hands, departed. Rufus recognized the friendly hand of a dog lover when he felt one, and Batch left a new and admiring canine friend in Deep River."

Perhaps Clarence Batchelor now sits at The Great Drawing Board in the Sky, sketching a new subject—Rufus, the guard dog, one of a long list of admirers.

Servitude

Another New York ghost story in which animals figured prominently comes from Greene County, NY. Just north of the small hamlet of Leeds, on the road to Coxsackie, a girl died a violent death in the 1700s. For many years, ghostly phenomena at that spot caused travelers' blood to run cold.

In Colonial times, before the American Revolution, Ralph Sutherland farmed a vast tract of land in the Catskills with indentured servants, workers whose passage from Europe he had paid. They agreed to labor for him for a specified period, usually seven years, in return for their freedom. Jeanne, a proud Scottish lass in her early twenties, signed an indenture with Sutherland, but soon chaffed at her burdensome duties. Wanting to join her lover some miles to the north, she ran away, but was pursued and caught a few miles north of Leeds. Sutherland bound her hands tightly and tied her to his horse's tail. Mounting, he spurred his horse into a canter. Jeanne stumbled continuously and finally fell, but Sutherland did not stop. Her head slammed into a large rock, and she was killed. Her death wasn't discovered until Sutherland reined in north of the village. His neighbors, appalled at his cruelty, seized him and took him to the British colonial magistrate.

His trial ended in a guilty verdict, but the judge, mindful of the Sutherland wealth and influence, gave Ralph a delayed sentence. He ordered Sutherland to wear a rope around his neck as a sign of guilt, and to present himself to the court for hanging on his ninety-ninth birthday. Few believed he would live that long, but the condemned lived many years with the rope "already in place," just awaiting a final jolt. Over the years, he was shunned by townsfolk and withdrew into the company of his inner demons.

The scene of Jeanne's death horrified the good citizens of Greene County, who spurred their horses through that section of road in daylight, and avoided it completely by night. Legends grew of a huge white horse with fiery eyes galloping along the Coxsackie Road north of the village, snorting smoke and dragging a shrieking, bloody corpse. Nocturnal travelers described a moaning skeleton pulled by a galloping horse. Some told of seeing a woman seated on a large overhanging rock, with a lighted candle on each finger, singing in a distraught voice. Each year the tales became more fantastic.

Sutherland became a recluse in his farmhouse. Few came to visit or do business with him. Neighborhood children avoided his house, whispering and pointing with wide eyes from a distance. He grew deeply remorseful, having lost both his fortune and his zest for life. But he did not die.

Old timers claimed a large, shaggy white dog, like Jeanne's, howled nightly, facing Sutherland's house. The dog always vanished whenever anyone approached. Others reported that Jeanne's favorite cow refused to give milk and lay moaning in the rocky pasture. Sutherland, still wearing his noose, did not go mad or die, but outlived his bizarre sentence. No United States court would carry out the British colonial sentence when Sutherland turned ninety-nine, and he died at age 101 on February 2, 1800. Many neighbors believed he held out in order to die on his own terms.

For many years thereafter, those who remembered the story and those who feared the specters of the night avoided the legendary haunted road after dark. The tale was written down in 1940 under a federal program to preserve folklore. Eventually, however, the old dirt road from Leeds to Coxsackie was widened, paved and designated Route 23B. Today, automobiles and trucks rush past the spot, with their drivers distracted by less grizzly, modern concerns. Few are mindful of local history anymore, especially the gruesome details of this long expanse of highway. And the concept of selflessly serving others has today become even more loathsome for young Americans than Jeanne could ever have imagined.

Debbie's Dog

Debbie and her husband loved the old farmhouse in East Poultney, VT, at first sight, and began to restore it in 1984. There are two apartments, and other tenants, past and present, have recounted a variety of experiences in the house. "One tenant saw a wraith on her front porch one night, and then a few hours later, something swished through her apartment. She asked a clergyman to bless the apartment and, since then, her half of the house has been quiet. That experience, however, may have simply relocated those energies to my part," said Debbie.

In November 1999, she was alone in the house and noticed "inkblots" dancing around her. If she looked directly at them, they disappeared. "When children were visiting, I often caught movements out of the corner of my eye. A friend suggested they might be spirits. Maybe they are responsible for my bathroom light refusing to come on every so often," Debbie jokes.

There is a lot of energy there and it sometimes assumes a visible form. "Soon after we moved in, we took a boarder—a student teacher working at the high school. She once reached for a door and had it snatched from her hand by an invisible force on the opposite side. She looked, but no one was there. Amazed, she went upstairs to shower in the bathroom. When she came out, a man in formal dress, complete with top hat, stood in the hallway, as if waiting for her. He vanished and she stood there stunned—they didn't teach her about discarnates in old houses at teachers' college! We have no idea who he was, what historical period he came from, or why he was in the house. That's the only time he's ever been seen," Debbie said.

"One night, after my dog died, I sat reading in bed. I missed him, and hoped reading would take my mind off him. My eyes tired and I turned off the light. Suddenly, I felt an animal bound onto my bed, and it shook me from my light sleep. I was startled fully awake, but I also *knew* what and who it was! It was my dog, I was sure—he'd landed like that a hundred times before and this time was just like the last. He meandered across the blankets, stopping to sniff everything, and I felt him shift his weight as each paw pushed the blanket down. It was so real, even though I *knew* he was dead, that I was about to call out to him. Then, just as suddenly, he was gone! I'm sure it was my dog, but would never be able to prove that to someone else."

East Poultney is a quiet and picturesque hamlet. Green Mountain traditions linger long there: Holsteins in the pasture, maple sap tap lines on the trees, firewood stacked on porches, and overfilled church dinners and town meetings. Debbie and her husband have sometimes been surprised, but never frightened, at the scenes and pets from the past that emerge in their old farmhouse. Her good sense of humor undoubtedly sustains them in whatever revelations her house provides.

Dad's Cat

Nick and Judy built the house in 1990 at #3 Adirondack Court, a new housing development in South Corinth, NY. They moved in with two cats and a dog. Their happiness was diminished by news that Nick's father in New Jersey had suffered a stroke. "Why don't you come up and live with us?" they asked him. So Dad came to South Corinth and, though in pain, was happy to be part of an active household.

When he first entered the house, he went to an easy chair to rest from his journey. Smokey, their beautiful young jet-black cat, jumped into his lap, curled up, and went to sleep purring. Dad smiled—kitty's vibrating warmth against his stomach eased his pain. Developing a special rapport, the two companions sat day after day, each giving comfort to the other. On November 4, 1993, Dad died and was buried soon after. On the day of his funeral Smokey disappeared.

Eventually, Nick and Judy resumed a normal life, comforted that Dad was in The Land Beyond, no longer suffering. Then came the first anniversary of Dad's death,

November 4, 1994, a day of remembrance. As Nick went about his duties in the kitchen that day, he glanced out the back door, and there was Smokey! He opened the door to greet his long-lost pet, but in that moment Smokey simply vanished.

Neither Nick nor Judy saw him again, until November 4, 1995. That bright autumn afternoon Nick looked out the door with his camera ready, remembering his experience on the previous November 4. Suddenly, Smokey was there, sipping out of a milk saucer they'd placed on the floor. This time Nick got a picture before Smokey vanished. Neither Nick nor Judy saw him again until November 4, 1996.

Smokey appeared briefly that day, and was gone again before they could even say hello. He made his final appearance on November 4, 1997, and then was never seen alive again.

On Palm Sunday in 1999, Judy took a flower arrangement to place on Dad's grave in the Corinth Rural Cemetery, where her father was also buried. Near Dad's stone, she was surprised to see a small animal skull with black fur clinging to it. She recognized it as a cat's skull, and couldn't help but wonder if Smokey had finally found Dad.

Nick and Judy know there is more to this story, and wish they knew it all. All they have is Smokey's photo. Did he get a dispensation from Cat Heaven to revisit South Corinth on the anniversary of Dad's death—for four years in a row? And why did that conclude in 1997? Somewhere in Cat Heaven there is a purring cat, with a halo and Cheshire grin, who loved Dad and has the answers.

Lee's Pack

Lee's photo showed a camera's flash reflected in a picture window with a few feet of snow outside also illuminated. I couldn't recognize much else. The upper right half of the image was a mass of curly lines and shapes. I was about to hand it back to her when she said, "No, take another look."

I've heard it said that the human brain always tries to bring order out of chaos, and this time, looking closer, I saw a German Shepherd's face, then, to the right, a Chihuahua's head, then, to the right of that, a wolf's. I stared at Lee. She explained, "One winter night it was sleeting—almost horizontally. It was so dramatic and I wanted to capture it in a picture! I got my Instamatic, went to the window in the kitchen, and this is what came out!

"Turn the picture on its side, or upside down. It doesn't matter—there are dog faces everywhere."

I found a mutt, a Terrier, and a Cocker Spaniel. Then, upside down I was certain, one cat in the upper left corner. As I continued turning the photo, I saw more dogs. This photograph was eerie!

"Lee, what's in your back yard outside the window? What would I see out there in daylight?" I asked.

"Not much," she replied, "just the little hill where I've buried all my dogs, and I've owned the breeds you just mentioned as you studied the photo. I think they all liked this farm so much that they decided to stay. Even though they don't run with the horses anymore, they have each other for companionship."

I sat in her farmhouse in Greenfield Center, NY, looking at what I considered an uncanny photograph. Lee raises horses, not dogs, though she loves them. She is not a computer expert, and swears the photo is genuine. I share this photo with you, the reader. What do you see?

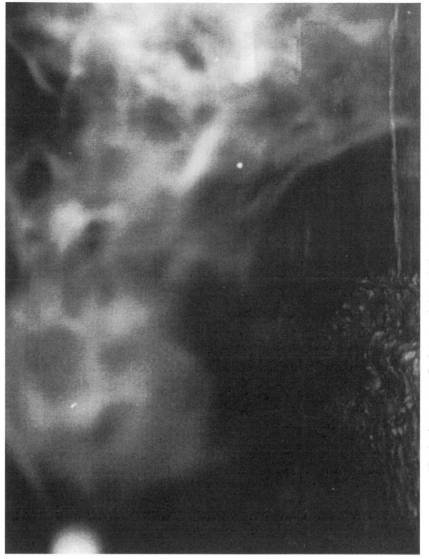

"Lee's photo - note flash (upper left) and illuminated snow at center left bottom"

15

Ghosts And Religion

I See You

In 1998, as I signed copies of my first book at Craven's Bookstore on Broadway in Saratoga Springs, NY, a small girl clutching my book, and accompanied by her mother, said, "Please sign my book." As I happily did so, she whispered, "I saw a ghost—last month." For a moment I doubted, but Mom nodded vigorously, and encouraged Arianna to explain.

She had just completed summer enrichment classes at Immaculate Conception School in Schenectady and would enter Fourth Grade in September. During a lunch break one day in July, she and her friend Kathleen walked around the block, from the school's location on Bradt Street. On Hegeman Street, behind the school, they stood in front of a former convent, a building now used for after-school arts-and-crafts. Beside the building is a small playground with swings and a seesaw. They noticed, in the dirt, three pairs of a child's footprints, which started and ended abruptly. "We couldn't understand how anyone could start walking, then just stop. Where did they come from, and where did they go?" asked Arianna. "We discussed it while we walked back to classes."

The next day they made a beeline for the playground, and found no footprints at all—as if none had ever been there. Then, Kathleen saw three small stones on the seesaw board. Upon closer inspection, she saw that someone had drawn pictures on the stones in still-wet black ink. The first one showed a sketch of an eye, the second, a stick figure circle of a girl's head with long ringlets, and the third, the letter U.

I asked Arianna what she thought it meant. "Well, it's obvious," she replied, "I—see—*you!*" Agreeing that was possible, I asked what happened next. The girls had left the stones there, puzzling as to who had decorated them and why. They knew of no art classes going on in the old convent in the summertime.

On the next school day, Arianna returned to the playground alone. It was a very hot day, and she knew that inside the arts-and-crafts building's side door, there was a water fountain. She was sipping water from the fountain when she noticed a girl standing nearby. The other girl wore an ankle-length maroon dress and a large maroon bow in the back of her hair. Her hair fell in ringlets. Her dress and hairstyle implied family wealth.

"I could see through her," said Arianna, "and I was scared for a minute. The little girl smiled at me and then faded. I got angry and yelled, 'When did you live here and when did you die?' But she didn't answer or return. I brought Kathleen to the playground the next day. All of a sudden, the seesaw moved up and down twice. It's a heavy board and we wondered who did it and how. Then, we saw something shiny on the board. I went over and picked up a 1912 dime." As we talked, she showed the coin to me—a 1912 Barber dime with some scuffing on the Liberty head, but the date was easily read.

Arianna remembered that later that day, after she'd picked up the coin, she walked on the sidewalk near the building. Suddenly, she saw the shadow of a little girl on the pavement. But no one was there to make the second shadow—it wasn't hers.

The next day, she and Kathleen visited the dusty playground again. They felt sad about the little dead girl, and proposed planting a garden for her in the dirt. They picked some dried seedpods from a nearby plant and "planted them." On the following day, the girls found a rainbow-shaped array of flowers blooming at that spot. From left to right they were red, orange, yellow, green, blue, purple and pink.

"I think it's sad," she told me. "The little girl died there and I think she gave us this dime, but I don't know what it means."

"How old was she?" I inquired.

"I'd say she was six or seven."

I told her that, if 1912 was the girl's birth year, and she was six or seven, that she would have died in 1918 or 1919. The great influenza epidemic caused many children's deaths then. Arianna was quiet for a moment. "I think it's so sad. She only got to live six or seven years, and now, her ghost is stuck in Schenectady."

"Maybe not. You go to a Catholic school, right?"

"Yes."

"You know, the Church urges members to pray for the dead—so that they can go directly to Heaven. Maybe you could go over to the playground and say a prayer for her."

Arianna was thoughtful for a moment more, then said, "Yes, I think that's what I'll do." And she and her mother left the store.

About eight months later, I called her to check on some details in my notes, and to see if there was anything else to add to her experience of the ghost child. "How's the little girl?" I asked.

"Well, she's not there."

"Where did she go?"

"Kathleen and I went over and said a prayer. We lit a candle and sang a song, and told the little girl that she didn't have to stay in Schenectady anymore. We said she could go to Heaven. Now, when we go back there, nothing out of the ordinary is going on. She's gone on."

That is the happiest, most beautiful ending to a ghost story that I've experienced in the many years I've collected them—children of this world helping those of the next.

Keeping Pace

In Glendale, on Cape Breton, Nova Scotia, Father John Angus Rankin went out for an evening stroll. It was pleasant weather and he took the longer route. It was quite dark as he turned homeward, and only a few lights shone on the road. As he moved through the night, he heard footsteps behind him, keeping pace. When he slowed, the footsteps slowed. When he sped up, the footsteps did also. He began to worry—what were the intentions of his pursuer?

At last there was a break in the clouds and the full moon shone through. Fr. John wheeled, and his heart stopped. He recognized his father who was long dead. He'd said the funeral mass and buried the man years before. There was no mistaking his father's features. And there was no mistaking the voice. "Now, pay attention." his father told him, "Go to the general store, find the billing clerk, and pay my overdue bill of $9. I owe it." Then the apparition departed.

The next day, still shaken, Fr. John arose, said morning mass, then walked to the store. The owner assured him that there was no overdue bill. "Your father always paid his bills promptly. Whenever he put something 'on the book,' he made it a point to pay it by the first of the next month. You have nothing to worry about."

Fr. John couldn't accept that. He didn't care to meet his father again, or be censured for failing to follow instructions. "I know there is $9 outstanding. Will you please go back over your books, and let me know when you find it," he requested. There was parish business to take care of, and he left.

Two days later, the storeowner met him on the main street. "Father John, I don't know how you knew. I was so intrigued by your earnestness that I did a search. Mind you, I had to go back nineteen years, but I found a charge of *exactly $9* that your father had never paid!"

The priest paid the amount and asked for a receipt, in case his father returned to check up on his effort. Thankfully, he never did.

Following Through

David Lloyd Sampson's mother, Rosella, remembered that in the early 1920s in D'Escousse, Nova Scotia, the priest hired a new housekeeper who was not from that village. She therefore didn't know many local people. One evening, while the priest was out, she heard a knock at the door. Opening it, the housekeeper was confronted by a pale woman in a grey gown, peering intently from sunken eye sockets. "Is the priest in?" came the hollow voice.

The housekeeper told her the priest was out for the evening, so the mysterious woman muttered a "good night" and left. The next evening, the woman returned. The housekeeper again told her the priest was out; he had gone for a drive. The spectral woman fidgeted and wrung her hands, and looked nervously into the house to see if the priest really was gone. Only grudgingly would she depart. The housekeeper promised to tell the priest she had come, though the pale woman gave no name.

When the housekeeper told the pastor of the strange woman, he decided to stay home on the third night, in case she reappeared. Sure enough, not long after 6:30 the next evening, there was a knock on the door. Opening it, the priest saw the same ashen woman and inquired, "What do you wish, my daughter?" She swept past him and entered the house. Moving into the priest's office, she went directly to his desk and placed her hand on some money piled on the desk shelf. "Do you see this money? Do you know what it's *for*?" she demanded. Abashed with a sudden recognition of both the woman and her purpose, the priest responded contritely, mumbling, "Yes, I had forgotten." The woman then moved swiftly from the room and left by the still open front door. Spellbound, the housekeeper stared at the departing woman until she disappeared across the street.

"Father, who *was* that woman?" the housekeeper asked breathlessly. "She went over into the cemetery." The clergyman answered, "Well, she is already dead. Just before she died, she gave me money to say a Mass for her, and I had forgotten about it until she reminded me just now." The next morning he fulfilled his long-overdue part of the bargain.

Backordered

Pat McAndrew felt old and tired. It was 1930 and he was only forty-five, but each night's work drained him of energy. He had finished his laborer's job at 2 a.m. and now shuffled westward on Warren Street in Glens Falls, NY. He'd seen only one automobile since he'd left work, and the street was quiet and dark. Ahead on his left, he saw the windows of St. Mary's Catholic Church brightly lit. It was too early for morning mass, and too late for Midnight Mass. What was going on?

He couldn't enter the church in his grimy work overalls and disheveled shirt. He decided to peek in the side window, though. There was a large wooden box in the street alongside the church. He pulled it beneath a window, stood on it, and looked through a clear pane in the stained glass window. What he saw took his breath away. Candles were lit. The priest stood at the foot of the altar, saying mass, and almost fifty people knelt in the pews. He couldn't understand it—he was a member of the congregation, but hadn't heard a Sunday announcement about a special mass. Something else was strange. Where was the organ music? Where were the voices of the choir? It was quiet as a tomb inside that church.

The priest turned and faced the congregation. Pat remembered him and tried to recall his name. He'd been pastor some years ago. Then it came to him. "But he died!"

He scanned the faces in the congregation. "I remember him—that's Joe. I thought he died in 1929!" He recognized Jimmy, then Agnes and Mary. They had died too. He recognized almost everyone there, though they were all dead!

What was this? A dream? A nightmare? Though the priest's lips were moving, Pat could hear nothing. "I gotta be dreaming," he concluded, and stepped unsteadily down, and sat on the box. "I'll just dream I'm walking to my house, then dream I'm lying on my bed, and then I'll wake up. Yes, that's what I'll do."

He rose and shuffled toward the intersection and home. He remembered lying down, but nothing more until he awoke next morning.

"Somebody's gotta help me understand that dream," he thought. "I know. Louie goes to St. Mary's. I'll go over and ask him."

Without even his customary cup of coffee, Pat walked over to Glen Street and turned into his friend Louie's barbershop. No one else was there to eavesdrop or ridicule him, so Pat began, "Louie, I'll put it to you straight. You know what I saw in St. Mary's Church when I was walking home last night?"

"Tell me about it, Pat," said the barber.

Pat related the experience. Instead of his usual good-natured ribbing, Louie looked thoughtful. "Gee, Pat, I think it all makes sense. You know, that old priest was forgetful and awfully slow in saying memorial masses. And people made offerings for him to say those masses. After he died, they found a whole bunch of mass cards stashed in a book—masses he never got around to saying. I'll bet he got all those souls together, and did one big mass for them all. Now he's caught up, and maybe they *all* can rest in peace."

Nellie

Ghosts have appeared in all eras of recorded history. Dogmatic clergy often ascribe these phenomena to trickery or a satanic force, and fail to inspire their followers to help another suffering, though discarnate, soul.

Two hundred years ago, Machiasport, ME, was a snug seacoast town filled with merchants and shippers, with many outlying small farms. On August 9, 1799, as the family of Abner Blaisdel went about their daily chores, they heard knocking inside the walls of their house. Puzzled, they looked for a cause, but found nothing. After a few days, the knocking ceased.

Then, on January 2, 1800, the Blaisdels heard a woman's voice echoing in the cellar, and identifying itself as Nellie Hooper, the deceased wife of Captain George Butler. Blaisdel sent a runner six miles to the Hooper house, knowing the young woman's father to be alive, and hoping he could identify Nellie's voice. A skeptical David Hooper soon appeared and, with Blaisdel, went into the cellar where they listened together. Hooper asked questions of the presence, and both men were amazed at the spirit's forthrightness and accuracy. "She gave clear and unresistable tokens of her being the spirit of my own daughter, as gave me no less satisfaction than admiration and delight," said the now-believing father.

In September, Blaisdel's son, Paul, saw Nellie's ghost floating over their farm fields but, being alone at the time, he kept silent and hurried to his harvesting chores. Within days, Nellie's voice was heard again in Blaisdel's cellar, this time chastising Paul for not greeting her when they "met." The harvest was in and the fishing fleet had returned to port. With not much activity in the village, rumors of the spectral phenomenon began to circulate in Machiasport. Shortly thereafter, a group of twenty inquisitive townspeople visited Blaisdel's to ascertain the truth of these claims. They entered the cellar, heard the girl's voice, and some of them saw a light in the cellar's gloom. Others saw a woman in a shining garment. Over the next few months, several hundred area residents visited Blaisdel's cellar and heard or saw the spirit.

When asked why she only appeared in the cellar, Nellie said she was afraid of scaring the children. Though this story is taken from an historical account, it's difficult today to imagine children not knowing something extraordinary was taking place, as throngs of people traipsed in and around the house for almost a year.

Reverend Cummings, the village minister, did not believe in ghosts. To him, all such talk was either nonsense or evil. On a crusade to expose trickery, Cummings pounded on Blaisdel's door, demanding permission to enter. Once admitted, he avoided entering the cellar, but instead accused Blaisdel of using ventriloquism to create the voice, and left. However, on the dark and lonely trek home, he later told close friends, he encountered a light that increased in size until it reached the proportions of a full-grown woman. Rev. Cummings never returned to the Blaisdel house again, and made no further public comments about the spectacle.

Near the end of 1800, Nellie Hooper made her final appearance. Capt. George Butler, her former husband, had remarried, despite his deathbed pledge to Nellie that he'd never do so. Asleep in his marital bed late one night, Butler awoke to see a stern-looking Nellie standing alongside. She looked and sounded angry and reminded him of his failure to honor his pledge. Then, she vanished. The phenomena ended.

For years to come, the worthy inhabitants of Machiasport retold the story of the man who failed to keep his promise, and they nervously huddled just a bit closer to one another and their fires on cold winter nights.

Dinnertime

Bishop John Medley arrived in Fredericton, New Brunswick on June 19, 1845, newly remarried after the death of his first wife. He and Margaret, his new wife, had been charged with building a grand Anglican cathedral at Church and Brunswick Streets, replacing the smaller original church. Four months later, Lt. Gov. Sir William Colebrooke laid the cornerstone and work commenced. The official opening took place on August 11, 1853. Today, Christ Church Cathedral is the oldest Anglican cathedral in Canada.

"Christ Church Cathedral"

Bishop Medley worked assiduously at his job, on many occasions long into the night. It became the custom for Margaret to bring his dinner each evening from the manse at Church and King Streets. He became one of the longest tenured bishops to serve the church, dying at age eighty-eight in 1892. He is buried in the cathedral vault. Margaret, however, who died in 1905, was buried in the church cemetery outside. Not long after her burial, however, cathedral neighbors attested to seeing Margaret continuing her nightly journey, carrying her husband's dinner. She has also been seen walking down Church Street and entering the cathedral's west door. Some think she visits her husband's grave, perturbed that they are now separated in death though they worked so closely in life.

On occasion, the heavy velour curtains that screen the choir stalls have been seen to blow in a wind that's possible only when the door is open. However, when cathedral staffers look, the door is always closed. In the 1990s, after an evening communion service, a parish member saw a spectral woman in long dress pass through the Sacristy room, on her way to the door, which opened and closed behind her. At times, parishioners report the scent of food in rooms flanking the altar, usually a signal that Margaret is near. However, she doesn't always show herself at such times.

Samantha, a former choir member, reported that when she was fourteen, she and two friends often visited the cathedral, hoping to glimpse Margaret's ghost. On a Saturday afternoon in November, 1989, she and one friend saw a grey-white shape descend from overhead in the sanctuary, rush between the two girls, then turn toward the altar and disappear. The cathedral clock overhead read 1:10. She and her friend fled outside before pausing to catch their breath and discuss their experience. Just then, the cathedral bells tolled 12, deepening the mystery.

When I discussed the story with a cathedral guide, I gained some understanding of the cathedral staff's technique for working with Margaret. "Yes, I believe in ghosts, and that life does go on. But, nevertheless," he grinned, "when it gets to be 10 p.m. I finish up my work and *leave* before I catch the smell of food!"

The Energy

Underneath the façade of a modernized two-family house at 214 Englewood Avenue in Buffalo, NY is an old church. "My husband and I were probably the second tenants after its conversion," Pam said. "We came there in 1981 and could see that the downstairs had been a Greek Orthodox Church, with an apartment for the priest upstairs. The congregation had dwindled and the church was sold. It was strange to find religious vestments and chalices in our attic and cellar. One day, my husband was rummaging in the attic and found a metal tabernacle. Curious, he opened the door of the sacred receptacle, and felt an icy wind blow out of the opening. He shuddered and put it down. In the cellar we found a large, life-sized wooden cross. Through friends, we found the congregation's retired priest, but he was old and had no use for the sacred objects, so we donated them to another church.

"Some kind of energy seemed to have remained in the attic. Whenever I went up there, I found dead blackbirds inside. One had crashed into the attic window glass, where it stuck fast, and died with its wings outstretched—that's how I found him. We reached our attic by opening a door in the kitchen and climbing a set of stairs. But it was hardly ever necessary to open that door, as it kept opening itself. I was pretty sure we had a ghost there, but since it had been a church once, I was never afraid. We met the previous tenants, however they'd had no extraordinary experiences during their eight years there.

"Once, when my husband and I were arguing in the kitchen, we heard two thumps in the dining room. When we went in, we saw that two framed caricatures of my husband and myself had fallen from the wall. To do that, they would have had to rise over the curved hooks that held them. We figured the energy 'helped them.' It also made us think about disruptions caused by our tendency to argue.

"One day we were packing for a trip and our lavatory faucet suddenly turned on full force. Neither of us was in there at the time. On another occasion, about 3 a.m. I woke up in the dark bedroom and looked across into the bathroom, where I saw a filmy shape solidifying into human form. It then rose to the ceiling and disappeared.

"Other times we could find no cause for the banging we heard on the walls and in the attic. I think it was all connected to the building having been a church, but I don't understand how it all related."

Pam gave birth to her baby in 1983, and the couple planned a move to Albany. Family and friends came to help them.

"On the last night in the apartment most things were packed and on the truck. Dad, my husband and a friend slept on the floor. Dad often joked about our ghost stories, but that night he heard for himself. The guys had all gone off to sleep when they awoke to hear someone walking in the hall. The sound was loud and echoed in the empty rooms. Dad roused himself and yelled out, 'COME ON, YOU GHOSTS, YOU!' They saw nothing, but all felt an icy breeze blow past them."

Pam and her family relocated to Albany, but often wonder about the new tenants in their old apartment. "What energy remains in a religious structure when its use stops?" she asked me. I had to admit I didn't know.

The Good Book

Rap! Rap! Rap! The sound came from the front hallway door. Strange, Esther thought, anyone who knows us, knows we don't use the hallway or door during the winter—who could be trying to get in?

It was 1973. Esther and Azro Fisk were living in the upper house of the old Earl Gilmore farm outside Tinmouth, VT. Esther opened the inner door and peered into the hall toward the door. "There was this cobwebby-looking thing. It didn't have feet—I mean, they were funny looking. I could make out it was supposed to be a woman. A voice summoned, 'Help me, help me!' She went back around and floated up the front stairs and I followed.

"She went around the upstairs banister and into a front room that we never used, then disappeared into its closed off chimney. That's that, I figured, and returned to the kitchen, peeling potatoes for dinner.

"When I told Azro about this, after he returned for lunch, he was surprised that I hadn't been scared by the ghost. 'Cobwebs can't hurt you,' I told him. So, we talked about her, just as we'd discuss any other stranger. We concluded that a woman must have died in the house, perhaps tragically and suddenly, unable to fulfill some intention or wish. And we figured she had come to us for help.

"That night before we went to bed, Azro wondered why I didn't take my Bible up and put it in that room. I did so, and placed the book on a small dresser. Azro suggested I place a pencil under the Bible, and I did that too. The next morning when we returned to the bedroom we found the Bible had been moved. Later, we returned to the room and this time found an underlined passage in the Book of Mark, from Jesus' agony in the Garden of Gesthemane: *My soul is very sorrowful, even unto death. Remain here and watch.* But I said to Azro, 'That can't be all. That's not going to help her move on—there's got to be another verse. So I took it downstairs, searched and searched, and stumbled onto the verse from Luke 23:46, *I commit my spirit into thy hands.* That ought to do it! I left the book open to that page when I returned the Bible to her room."

For a while there was no further communication, but one night before they were to move away, the Fisks placed the closed Bible on the small dresser in that bedroom. The next morning, the book was gone. Neither had removed it. After a search, they finally found it at the top of the seldom-used front stairway. Puzzling over how and why the book had moved, Esther concluded the ghost woman may have been unprepared to die, and the cause of death may have been sudden or mysterious. The Fisks speculated that the stairs had played a role in the woman's passing.

This was Esther's only experience with a ghost while in Tinmouth. "That experience stayed with me for weeks afterward," she told her daughter Connie. Esther had tried to use her "Good Book," her precious possession, to offer solace and direction to a lost soul. Azro and she had made contact, but she felt they had been ineffective in helping the ghost woman. A few days later, the Fisks left the house for good and moved to Rutland.

Connie's husband, Ed, had once told the spirit to leave his in-laws' house, but that, also, appeared to be ineffective. New tenants eventually rented the house, and most used the upstairs room. All of them claimed to feel a presence there, and several also directed the spirit to leave. In the 1980s, workmen were hired to repair the chimney's brickwork in the upstairs bedroom. They reported that when they removed some bricks, they heard moaning from deep inside the chimney. Perhaps the removal of bricks somehow allowed the trapped soul to depart, as the present tenants report no strange events in the house.

This Vermont story was told by Faye Moulton, Esther and Azro's niece, and published in the *Tinmouth Tales Newsletter.*

Ferry Beach

Quillen House, Ferry Beach Park, ME

"Quillen House, Ferry Beach Park, ME"

In the late 1890s the Unitarian and Universalist Churches bought a large beachfront property near Saco, Maine. It became a conference center for combining learning and joyful summer activities. Then, as today, Ferry Beach encouraged study of the deeper meanings in life. Several large frame buildings were constructed and named for outstanding individuals who founded "The Ferry Beach Association." Young and old still spend summer vacations there, seeking to enrich the community experience and expand their individual spiritual lives. The founders' dedication seems to have permeated the buildings, and those who have worked or summered at Ferry Beach have sometimes encountered remnants of energy from those zealous early days.

The scattered wood-frame dormitory style buildings haven't changed in appearance in a hundred years. They provide shelter and meeting space for week-long summer study of inspiring topics, from ecology to personal development. The maintenance crew, used to the busy schedule of moving equipment and teaching aids, store unused furniture in the attic of Underwood Hall. Unless someone is using the large attic space, the door is kept locked. A few years ago, a worker brought an extra table into the attic and had to move an old chair to the side. He noted carefully the chair's new location, with its back against the wall closest to the beach. He went out and locked the door. Two days later, he had to retrieve a folding easel and went up again. The chair clearly had been moved. It now stood in front of the window, facing the ocean, as if some "old timer" had wanted to continue admiring the gorgeous sunrises through the window. He is certain that no one else had used the key.

In 1993 a conference called "Empowerment Through Reiki," one of four

workshops offered during that early July week, was underway, drawing many who came to learn the Japanese healing technique. Quillen Hall, a main dormitory building, was filled to capacity with conferees from the workshops. One night Stephen got up to go to the bathroom at the end of the third floor hallway. Without his eyeglasses, he carefully felt his way out of Room 33 and down the hall. Looking left, he passed a tall woman standing at the open fire door, her waist-long white hair and nightgown blowing in the refreshing ocean breeze. The night was hot and the woman looked serenely out to the moonlit ocean beach below. On his return from the bathroom, she was still there, gazing out to sea. "You're not sleeping well either?" he inquired. No answer, though he blearily saw her smile as he passed within two feet of her to re-enter his room. He was soon asleep again.Next morning at breakfast he cheerfully greeted Penelope, the tall woman who had been taking in last night's breeze. He asked how long she had stood in the doorway and if she'd finally been able to go back to bed. "Couldn't you sleep?" he questioned.

Penelope responded quizzically, "Stephen, I don't know what you're talking about. I slept like a log all night and didn't get up once."

Penelope was a tall woman with long, flowing grey hair. If it wasn't her, then whom had he spoken to? Nobody else at the convocation resembled this imposing and unique woman. Stephen sat stunned. It was a powerful experience and he immediately understood that the encounter was a gift for his soul. In retrospect, Stephen came to believe he'd encountered a loving ghost or angel, and called her "The Spirit of Quillen." Hearing this story, I researched Quillen Hall's past, and discovered that it was older than surrounding buildings, originally built as a rest and relaxation summer camp for employees of the Boston & Maine Railroad. In 1901 it was purchased by the Ferry Beach Association. Was the spectral being from this earlier era?

A number of weekly summer programs at Ferry Beach are devoted to expansive education and recreation for teens. Campfire storytelling is always an enjoyable part of each camper's experience. Ruby McKay, for many years manager of the Ferry Beach camping area, "The Grove," was told the following story when she first came there as a young woman in the 1940s. When Ferry Beach became a Unitarian-Universalist camp, the auditorium/crafts building was named after Mr. Rowland, a founder of the Association. The tale involves the haunting of Room 3 in Rowland Hall. Crafts projects left overnight, are often found moved in the morning. Some personal belongings that disappear are never found again. Muted voices are frequently heard, causing residents and workers to feel they're never alone, or have somehow stepped back in time. Those who seek the source of such whisperings, always find the sound coming from "some other part of the building."

The strange goings-on are attributed to an incident involving Jonathan Petrie. In the late 1800s, before the creation of the summer camp, an outcast named Jonathan Petrie lived on Eagle Island, located a mile offshore from Ferry Beach. The mulatto child of an American Indian mother and a white father, he was ostracized by most "proper" folks in the Saco area, and kept to himself. Once or twice a week he rowed his boat to shore, cultivating a garden in the rich soil behind Ferry Beach, where The Grove is now located. To reach the field he had to cross the narrow gauge railroad tracks, where a train carried tourists north and south along the coast, from Old Orchard Beach to Ocean Park Beach to Ferry Beach, and then on to Camp Ellis.

One day the train didn't come. Searchers came upon the locomotive stalled on the tracks near Camp Ellis, its firebox cold and the engineer dead at the throttle. An axe with the carved initials J.P. was found buried in the base of his skull. Local folk immediately suspected Jonathan Petrie, and a mob marched to his fields. They found him calmly hoeing his corn. Without a trial, and despite his protestations of innocence, he was lynched on July 21st from a pine tree near his field. According to the legend, the corpse was left dangling for months, before some good soul took it to an unmarked grave.

Each summer, around bonfires in The Grove, where Petrie died, counselors recount the legend to teens. Ruby McKay notes that most of the youngsters, wide-eyed and shivering, return to their lodging, hoping not to encounter Jonathan Petrie. "But Ferry Beach isn't really about ghosts," Ruby states, "It's about a growth in consciousness for young adults. If 'old timers' are still here in spirit, they'd agree Ferry Beach is about expanding dimensions of thinking. We've done it for over a hundred years now. Jonathan Petrie's story just focuses their attention as they study the natural world of ecology in this undeveloped growth of oceanside woods," she concluded with a smile.

Trinity

"We only lived there for a year, but what an interesting year that was!" Anna told me. "We came to Croton-on-Hudson, NY, in 1942 and looked for a house to rent. My husband found an economics professor from Brooklyn College named 'Mac,' who had a nice house to rent. We met him on the porch, he showed us around, and we told him we liked it. He handed me the key and said, 'I hope you don't mind, but there's a friendly ghost here.' We three smiled. My husband and I weren't worried about ghosts, and were happy to have a new home."

The Kellerhouses had their furniture moved into the house and retired to bed. "Sometime during the night, I heard footsteps walking up the stairs and down, up the stairs and down. For a moment, I thought it was my husband, but no, he was right beside me. As I was very tired, I just chalked it up to imagination. However, another night I was suddenly startled awake by three sharp raps on the headboard of our bed. I leaned over and asked my husband what he wanted. He was sound asleep, but woke up when I spoke, said he didn't want anything, and went back to sleep. A few nights later he woke *me* up. 'Did you just knock on the headboard?' I told him 'No.' He checked the hallway. No one being there, we both went back to sleep. But I had begun to suspect someone was trying to get our attention.

"About a month later, we sat reading in the living room. Gradually, we became aware that our cuckoo clock was slowing down. The time between the 'tick' and the 'tock' increased to two seconds, then ten, and finally to what seemed like two minutes. Then, it simply resumed its normal operation. So this phenomenon couldn't have been electrical in nature, because it was a mechanical clock."

After some time and many incidents, they concluded that Mac was right about the ghost. The next time they paid the rent, they asked him about the house's history. "When I bought this house about ten years ago," he said, "I met the lady owner. As I stood in the doorway introducing myself, I saw a filmy image of a man over her head. I didn't say anything about it, as I didn't want to scare her or myself. She invited me in and we talked about a sale. She was the widow of a Methodist minister, who had worked very hard for his congregation. She pointed to the portrait over the fireplace. 'That's my husband,' she smiled. I recognized him as the individual hovering over her head, but still said nothing. We agreed on a sale and I left.

"After I moved in, I heard noises but, because I'd seen the minister's spirit, I figured it was just him, carrying on what he used to do. I didn't let it bother me. We have a big bay window on the front of the house, as you see. Entertaining a friend once, we heard three very loud raps on that window, and went out to see who it was. Nobody was outside. We came back in and resumed our conversation. Then came three more loud raps. Again, we all went outside, and again, nobody was there. Our friend said, 'What the hell's wrong with this house?' He was unnerved and left."

The Kellerhouses lived there until the summer of 1943, then transferred to another town. "It certainly was an intriguing place," said Anna. So many things happened in threes, that the number must figure in understanding this phenomenon. Perhaps the minister wanted them to understand the *threefold* nature of all life—physical, mental and spiritual. No longer having a pulpit or a congregation, he may have used his connection with the house on Franklin Avenue to educate whoever came near.

Father Knows Best

Those who attempt to force open the doors between this world and the next often invite consequences beyond their imagination, and sometimes, their capacity to cope. This was the theme of a story told by Father Alex McClellan in the small coastal village of St. Peter's, Nova Scotia. In his parish a new family moved into an old house. They had not been there long when the mother complained of furniture being moved when nobody was home. Then, for a period, there was a foul odor with no detectable source. Sudden temperature swings, from very hot to very cold, made the family apprehensive, as none of this had an obvious cause.

They knew nothing about the house's former residents, so called Fr. McClellan to perform a house blessing, a minor exorcism. His efforts were unsuccessful, however, and the phenomena continued. It looked as if more drastic action might be needed, so the priest consulted his bishop about a possible full exorcism.

The parents discovered their teenage daughter playing with a friend's Ouija board in her upstairs bedroom. She thought it harmless to invoke the spirits of any and all kinds, and invite them into the home. The priest urged her to destroy the board, take up the challenges of her life, and be done with spirits. He warned that Ouija boards often lead to more trouble than amusement, and warned her that she had no experience keeping troubling ghosts or spirits at bay. At first, the girl wouldn't cease contacting her "new friends," but as the phenomena became even more troubling, the parents seized the board and burned it. After one more house blessing, the doorway to the netherworld closed, and the home returned to normal.

Many young people, knowing little about their personal physical or emotional susceptibilities, and nothing about the spirit world and its operation, believe it is harmless fun to invoke dark spirits or the dead, as if such entities hover only to provide amusement. Many times the ticket price to subsequent inner peace is higher than they reckoned.

Ghosts
In
Historic
Sites

The Erie House

In 1917 New York State closed the old Erie Canal, remodeling, re-routing and renaming it the Barge Canal. This spelled disaster for Peter and Adelina Van Detto's canalside store, The Erie House, at Lock 52 in Port Byron, NY. For forty-four years, The Erie House had been a landmark for passing "canawlers," who moved their cargoes across The Empire State. Approaching the lock, boatmen often sent a runner ahead to order groceries or drink as the boat "locked through." The Van Dettos delivered their order before the boat cleared the lock. Many times the boats pulled aside and tied up, as crews entered the store's bar for a drink, or stayed overnight in the small rooms upstairs. Now, near the close of World War I, the canal activity ceased, and the old store simply became the Van Detto's home for the next seventy years.

Peter and Adelina died in the 1920s, leaving the house to their schoolteacher daughters, Marie and Theresa. By the early 1990s, those daughters also died, and the old building was auctioned off. Few original Erie Canal stores remain, and a non-profit group was formed to purchase The Erie House, and begin its preservation and eventual transformation into a museum. Work crews spent many volunteer hours cleaning and restoring the building and, as they worked there, some opted to stay overnight.

"That's when the fun started—if you can call it that," said Tom. "Because of what we experienced there, we feel that the vibrations from raucous nights in the saloon mixed with the quiet domestic life of the Van Dettos. Or, the building's phenomena may reach even farther back before the Van Detto's ownership, to 1873, when the building was constructed.

"I half-opened my eyes and saw a toothless old woman in a shawl, sitting there grinning at me."

"During one of my volunteer periods, which lasted almost five months, my wife and I lived in the upstairs of The Erie House," Tom said. "It started almost as soon as we moved in. The two bedrooms' doors somehow locked themselves from the inside, and remained that way for a week, after which they easily opened and closed. The bathroom door then locked itself in the same way for a week. At night we heard banging on the walls, and footsteps running, or children skipping through the hall. We slept on the living room floor until 'they' let us use the bedrooms upstairs."

One day, Tom took a fistful of stick matches to light his way in the cellar. Several fell from the box onto the kitchen floor, and he resolved to pick them up when he returned from downstairs. Returning upstairs after working in the cellar, he found someone had placed the dropped matches in a straight line, end to end, on the floor. Tom was alone in the building.

Once, as she returned from the bathroom, his wife smelled the scent of a particular old-fashioned heavy perfume in the hall. She told Tom that *somebody* was just outside their bedroom door in the hall. In bed, after turning out the lights, they heard footsteps approaching and entering their bedroom, and stopping beside their bed. Tom's wife's nerves had worn thin, and she moved out the next day. He remained for another week, and continued to hear "popping sounds," along with banging sounds at night, though he could never determine what they were or where they originated.

"The real treat for me was hearing the bedroom rocking chair creaking. One night, I half-opened my eyes and saw a toothless old woman in a shawl, sitting there grinning at me. I ducked under the covers, and when I looked again, she had gone.

"A few weeks after my work ended, a volunteer from the local historical society came by with some photos of the Van Detto family and their dog, Maud. There, amid the old photos, was the same woman that had grinned at me a few weeks before! We later found out that Adeline had lost all her teeth and had a spectacular set of gold dentures to wear. I suppose she was happy in her home, and was in no hurry to pass over. She probably was as startled to find us there as we were to 'see' her. She's just appearing to show she's happy there and wants to stay. Maybe we can hire *her* as the official greeter when we open."

Hyde Hall

The black coach rolled to a stop and Philip Hooker, architect from Albany, NY, peered out into the cold drizzle of the 1817 springtime. Storm-shrouded Otsego Lake to his left was beautiful, but otherwise the grim, rainy weather made its shores a most unappealing site for a gentleman's house. George Clarke was ready to commission Hooker to oversee the design and building of an estate worthy of the English countryside, where Clarke's ancestors originated. However, for the moment the architect could not even envision where to position the grand mansion. Then, the storm abated, the clouds scudded eastward, and a ray of light fell on the northwest bluff. In a moment, Hooker visualized the entire building, completed and illuminated, as on a summer's day.

The mansion he built still stands, now the property of New York State. Perhaps the largest domestic structure in the United States prior to the Civil War, Hyde Hall was praised by famed American architect Sanford White as "one of the most beautiful in America." The fifty-room mansion remained in the hands of Clarke's progeny until 1963, by which time the building badly needed repair. New York State coveted Clarke's six-hundred acres and two dairy farms for its new Glimmerglass State Park, and finally agreed to purchase the deteriorated house and outbuildings in 1963. Planning the restoration of Hyde Hall, state authorities never reckoned that Clarke family members and guests from 185 years of history remained in the house to supervise the entire project, staying on to enliven visitors' experiences.

George Clarke owned lands in New York State and Vermont, and held interests in sugar mills in Jamaica. His wife and family remained in England, declining to relocate to America with him. Clarke named Hyde Hall after English forebears.

Prior to 1813, he divorced his English wife. Ann Carey Cooper, widow of James Fenimore Cooper's brother, became his second wife, a marriage lasting until Clarke's death in 1835.

Their son, also named George Clarke, left a legacy of enlightened agricultural planning and animal husbandry experiments that improved his herds of milk cows and cattle. Despite a life plagued with debts and near escapes from creditors, the younger Clarke added internal and exterior improvements to Hyde Hall. It was the Clarke family home throughout the 1800s and into the 1900s, but Clarke fortunes declined, and so did the estate's upkeep. At the end, in the early 1960s, the Clarkes stayed one step ahead of the building's decay, moving to unoccupied second floor rooms as rain-soaked ceilings fell in bedrooms behind them.

After its sale, Hyde Hall was boarded up and posted against trespassing in 1968. Within a few years, the not-for-profit, Friends of Hyde Hall was created to oversee the rehabilitation effort and its funding. In the early 1900s, American writer James Fenimore Cooper's son, James, a friend of the Clarkes, first described the old structure as haunted. I visited the site in 1968, but was unable to see the mansion's interior until I was guided through in 2001 by Douglas Kent. This veteran historian has extensive knowledge about every Hyde, Clarke and Cooper that ever came near Hyde Hall.

Accompanied by my intuitive friend Paul, I asked Kent to take us from room to room without any introduction. This allowed us to absorb the atmosphere of each room and enable us to make our psychic observations. After that, Kent agreed to share pertinent information as we left each room. We crossed from a back door, through two first-floor servant workrooms and into the first large room. There, Paul visualized a large Christmas tree in one corner, and a fiddler in the front corner, near a punch bowl—an invisible long-past Yuletide revelry. Women in inexpensive empire dresses seemed to stand in conversation while the fiddler's lively music prompted others to dance. Kent verified that Clarke's tenants were usually feted at Christmas parties in that room.

We then moved into the vestibule or main hallway, where Paul noted the placement of furniture during Clarke's residence (although none of it remains today). Walking through the partially restored dining room, and into adjacent rooms of the rear wing, we encountered no real ghosts, but an abundance of "house memories," such as political discussions in the Library and linen storage in closets no longer there, all verified by Kent.

Our travels eventually brought us to a rear stairway, where Paul "picked up" an ominous feeling. Kent noted that the last two Clarke family members told him about their Alsatian watchdog, which had "once stopped dead in its tracks at the top of that stairs, bared its teeth and growled at something down in that stairwell. The dog refused to descend the stairs. They heard footsteps coming up, with no person in sight. They had beat a hasty retreat to another less 'busy' stairway to the ground floor," Kent smiled.

As we entered the second floor center front room, Paul exclaimed, "party room!" Kent acknowledged that the room had been used as a billiard room early in this century. As the last two Clarkes prepared to leave the house in 1964, Kent related, they had also heard someone coming up the main staircase just outside the billiard room door. Their dog bristled and growled again, but nobody appeared at the stairtop. Another ghostly resident?

Then we moved along to "the blue room," and a palpable change was evident in the atmosphere. One could enter, back out the door and then re-enter and feel the slightly ominous force meeting him. "Someone died in here," said Paul. "He died coughing—gasping for breath. That small bed, on the right of the door, doesn't go with the room; there was a larger bed that stood to the left of the door when he died."

Kent confirmed the old bed's location. We could still see the outline of the servants' bell pull rope on the ceiling molding. "And you are right about the death," he said. "A friend of the Clarke family in the 1800s, Arthur Sherwood, George Hyde Clarke's Columbia College classmate, died of a heart seizure in this room. Sherwood had always been sickly, so it isn't certain whether he ever got to practice law," Kent added.

In another bedroom, Paul saw an eighteen year-old young woman standing beside the bed. "She is not a member of the Clarke family, but a friend or visitor. She is concerned about some boy in the Army; she's worried he won't return." Kent confirmed that a young woman friend of the Clarkes lived there in the 1860s, and that two young men in the family had, indeed, died in the Civil War.

Down a long hallway, we entered a spot where Paul sensed "something unsettling." Kent said that a restoration workman saw what he thought was a cloud of dust there in 2000. The cloud had suddenly gathered into a form that flew up the hallway and into the blue bedroom. We had no sense of this energy's identity, but perhaps Sherwood remains in that room and corridor, still settling his personal affairs.

Kent related a story about young James Cooper, a family friend who occasionally slept at Hyde Hall. One night, after a party, he was given the blue room. In the pitch-dark chamber he awoke with a start. Unable to see anything he, nevertheless, knew someone or something was in the room with him. He heard the footfall of someone slowly approaching his bed, and felt the blankets being slowly pulled off. Cooper leapt up and, lighting a candle, seemed to bring the ghostly activity to an end. He found himself alone, and the room's doors were still securely closed. Later, he shared the story with his hostess who said the Clarkes seldom used the room, and reserved it for trusted friends, not strangers. The woman told Cooper of a family nurse and her daughter who had seen an old man in yellow, red and green clothing pass down that corridor and enter the blue room. They had known that George Clarke had worn such an outfit, and that it was at that moment packed away in an attic trunk.

Kent noted that, in his 1921 book, *Legends of a Northern County,* young James Cooper asserted that Ann Cooper Clarke was evicted from Hyde Hall by ungrateful children in the middle 1800s, when she was an old woman. According to his information, she paused at the roadside, looked back and shouted, "You may drive me out now, but I shall return and haunt it forever!" Cooper wrote that some witnesses also thought they heard her say, "May no woman ever be happy in it again!"

So, who is it that remains in builder George Clarke's country estate? One of the George Clarkes? Or is it the dispossessed widow Ann, keeping her vengeful promise? Could the presences include one of the dozens of servants who were charged with maintaining the house, one who hasn't relinquished her duties? Arthur Sherwood's energy or consciousness apparently remains. Political and domestic concerns of a young nation still seem to hang in the air on the bluff overlooking Otsego Lake, James Fenimore Cooper's "Glimmerglass," of the *Leatherstocking Tales*.

When you visit this beautiful site, ask to see the Clarkes' portraits. On my own tour, I felt uneasy gazing into Ann's stern and unsmiling face. Decide for yourself who still roams the still-unrestored corridors and rooms of Hyde Hall, as it nears its 200th year. Most of the back wing and courtyard still await restoration. If you can, leave a donation to help return this wonderful estate to its early-American magnificence.

The Chapman

The Chapman Museum, a house built by the DeLong family in 1865 in Glens Falls, NY, is a showpiece of Victorian architecture. Exhibiting the DeLong's furnishings and their collection of art objects from the last thousand years, The Chapman apparently houses at least one stealthy ghost.

A former director of The Chapman doesn't believe in ghosts, but admits being puzzled by his experiences. "Around 2 p.m. on a sunny spring day, the museum was closed and I was working there with a volunteer. Having had many discussions, I knew she was an atheist and didn't believe in an afterlife. She and I were busy installing artifacts in a showcase in the old Breakfast Room, when suddenly, there was a powerful shriek from upstairs! Because we knew we were the only people in the building, I immediately made an inspection. Nobody was there. Now, remember that I'd lived in that building for a while and knew all the regular noises, including the normal outdoor noises from Bay Street. This was definitely something else! The volunteer was visibly shaken because atheists don't believe in a netherworld from which such unearthly sounds might emanate."

Joan, who has served as both photographer and custodian in the building, has also encountered unseen residents. One day, as she worked past nightfall in a rear room, she heard the nearby door being unlocked. Someone entered, shut the door, and ascended the stairs to the third floor, which had been closed off by the Fire Department several years before. "Joe, that you?" she inquired, thinking it might be the director. No response, but Joe did enter that same door about a half-hour later, and they had much to ponder.

Kathy LaPan used to work as guide for visitors on the second floor. One day, as she stood at the top of the stairway, she noticed a movement in a second floor room. Though certain that nobody had passed her, she searched each room. Nobody was there.

On another occasion the museum had hired a secretary. The former director said, "We each let ourselves into the museum through the back door, arriving pretty much at the same time each morning. Each of us would smell a wonderful breakfast—bacon and eggs and maybe toast—but assumed it was a breakfast that the other had brought in. One day I mentioned that her breakfast smelled especially good. She looked at me puzzled and said, 'I didn't bring any breakfast with me; I never do. I thought the smell was from *your* breakfast.' Of course, I hadn't brought any food with me either."

There were no nearby restaurants to waft their aromas into the museum. But members of the DeLong family, still living in their reality, might have been commencing *their* day, as they had done happily for so many years in those rooms.

Edward & Mary

Two ghosts from the 1800s roam the rooms of the Historical Society at 55 Cayuga St. in Seneca Falls, NY. Originally a frame house, it was resurfaced in brick in 1855 by Edward Mynderse. Its Italian Renaissance style showed the prosperity of the businesses begun in 1795 by Edward's father, Wilhelmus. In the 1880s owner Ellen Partridge added a third story to the house, changing the style to Victorian. The Becker family lived there from 1891 to 1961, when the Historical Society took over.

Ghosts began to appear during the Becker tenure. Edward Mynderse, the "bad boy" of his family, squandered the family fortune bankrupting businesses, but when he had money, he was very generous to any and all who solicited him. Edward was a restless man, and some say he returned to the house after he died in 1896. Historical Society staffers surmise that he didn't like Ellen Partridge's innovations while he lived, and made this known to the Beckers by moving their paintings after he died. Because Edward was temperamental, he was also thought to be responsible for opening and closing the Beckers' doors, and starting and stopping their house clocks. Sometimes the smaller timepieces were turned toward the wall. They believed he sometimes moved their furniture and puzzled them with many strange sounds.

The Beckers hired the stout Mary Merrigan as a combination maid and nanny. Mary often conducted "dress-ups," outfitting the Becker children in costumes and acting out dramas. A hard worker, she lived on the third-floor.

"Mary became the family cook when the children got older. Her health began to fail after many years' service," said Frances Barbieri, Education Director of the

"She appeared stark naked in Cora Becker's room."

Historical Society. "Maybe it was her advanced age, or maybe she was just worn out. One night in 1957 she appeared stark naked in Cora Becker's room. On the family doctor's advice, they committed her to Willard State Hospital. But a month later, while Cora and her adult daughter Carol sat at home, at 8:25 p.m., Mary Merrigan suddenly appeared in their living room in a freshly pressed uniform." Had she escaped from the hospital?

"Shall we call Willard?" Carol asked her mother.

"No dear, we'll wait until morning," Cora said. "Tell her go up to bed."

The next morning they got up and dressed, ready to take Mary back to Willard. They went to her room but she wasn't there. Nothing in the room had been used or moved. They began a search of the house, but she was nowhere to be found. Then the telephone rang. The doctor at Willard told them that Mary Merrigan had died at 8:15 the previous night.

"That was her first appearance as a ghost, and I suspect she's still here," Frances continued. "Researcher Kathryn Hadley and I still hear noises and find objects moved when I visit the third floor."

The Historical Society installed a new furnace in 1994. At the end of the job, the boss said, "I'm sure glad we're done. My men are spooked. That woman in a gray uniform kept coming around, staring at us. Some days she brought a kid in costume with her!"

A few days later, returning for his check, he came to Frances' office on the second floor. She was readying photographs for a display to show the house's history, and many pictures were spread on her desk. "Hey, that's the lady!" the workman said, picking up a snapshot of Mary Merrigan.

"Whether it's Edward or Mary, it's often hard to say," Frances continued. "In our office we have a closet door that has no key—we've never had one. But there are days when that door is shut tight and *locked*. We can't budge it. Yet, on other days, if you just touch the knob, it glides open. We don't put important things in there because we never know when we'll have access," she grinned.

"Most of the time they leave us alone, but one day two years ago I tried to open the outside screen door when I came to work. I had left the building by that door the previous night, so I knew it should have been open, but I couldn't open it. I had to get help to break into our own kitchen! When we checked, we found the hook had been put in the eye, holding it shut tight. So, maybe Edward or Mary is now on night security," she laughed.

On my last visit to the old house I saw a lawn party, with real children in early 1900s dresses, rolling hoops on the front lawn. Frances was showing them how Victorian children played over a century ago. Every child looked perfectly at home in front of the stately old house. Perhaps Mary Merrigan stood alongside Frances, offering quiet tips on child management. And perhaps Edward stood sulking inside the door, wondering why he wasn't invited to the party.

Heritage

William Wentworth Brown turned his Berlin, NH, lumber mill on the Androscoggin River to making sulfite paper in the early 1890s. His foresight led the Brown Company to acquire over 600,000 acres of forestlands in Maine, New Hampshire and northern Vermont. The old company boarding house, constructed in 1853, faces the mill and stands at 961 Main Street. Used as son W.R. Brown's home for just one winter, it also has served as company offices. Today, the large building houses the Northern Forest Heritage Park offices and museum, which teaches Berliners about their lumbering and papermaking heritage. The guides, bright offices, and display rooms are modern, but other, less conspicuous employees from the past, seem impelled to tell their own stories.

Recently, a six year-old girl and her mother were viewing the large portrait of William W. Brown (W.W. to his friends) in the old dining room.

"That's the man who lives here," said the child.

"Lives?" asked the mother.

"Yes, he's the man in the front hall when we just came in!" the little girl said. The mother was speechless—she knew the hallway had been empty.

When I came to study the house, I tried to get a photograph of W.W.s portrait, which hangs in the old dining room. My camera refused to work in that room. I tried every trick I could think of to get it working, but to no avail. Outside, it worked fine. I wonder if old W.W., the papermaker, disapproved of *my* "business."

Beginning my interviews with the friendly staff, I discovered that the Heritage House's spirits become most active after dark. I met Jean Marie Boutin, who once stepped out the side entrance door, then found it deadbolt locked from inside when she tried to re-enter. No one else was then in the building. Another time, after hanging some pictures on her office wall, she turned back and noticed they were crooked. She straightened them and resumed work at her desk. Hearing a faint scraping sound behind her, she turned and saw them moving askew again. Straightening them one more time, she called out, "Okay, it's late and I have work to do! Stop!" And the prankster did.

"I often work alone here at night," she told me, "and always lock myself in. I've come to think of this ghost as a protector, watching out for me while I work, but sometimes, like a child, he's inclined to pester.

"We have a beeper under the rug to let us know someone has entered the building. The one at the back door has beeped on numerous occasions, when I know the doors are locked, and I'm the only one here. The other night it beeped and I got up to see who was there. It stopped. I sat down and it beeped again, then beeped continually *until* I left. I was upset until I surmised that the spirit may not want me to work all night and may be trying to shoo me out.

"Another time, my aunt was ill in the hospital. I was rushing to finish work so I could get to her during visiting hours. My jacket, hanging near the desk, moved; the sleeve shot up and my gloves inside flew out and across the room. I considered it a 'time to go' signal. My aunt was failing when I got to the hospital, and she died a few hours later. I'm so glad I left when I did.

"Another night, working late, the bulb in my lamp went out. I tried to work in the dim light, but the finial on top of the lampshade began unscrewing itself, then the lampshade flew up to the ceiling! People I've told this to look at me like I'm crazy, but I know what I've experienced. These experiences defy any logic. I think they're definitely a phenomenon from some realm outside our own."

Winding up another night's work, Jean was startled when a "music box program" suddenly began playing on a computer. Simultaneously, all the upstairs lights went on. As she walked through each room turning the lights off, all the lights downstairs turned on. Exasperated, Jean shouted, "Enough!" to the prankster, this time with less effect than in her previous experience. After turning out the downstairs lights and climbing the stairs to her office again, all the upstairs lights, *plus* radios in the offices, suddenly turned on!

Once, a co-worker came through the hall, heading for Jean's office, and saw a moving woman's shadow on the back hallway wall, as if someone in a rear room was passing in front of the office light. Investigating, the employee found the room's door ajar, but no light on, and no woman.

Joan Chamberlain, Executive Director, reports that the rug in front of her desk once suddenly bunched up, as if someone's feet had just pushed it. Phones in her upstairs front office once were mysteriously unplugged, though she had used them minutes before. "One night working alone, I smelled pipe smoke behind me. It scared me and I went home. When I came to this job, people told me the house was haunted, but I thought they were trying to scare me," she said.

Shelly, the Heritage Education Director, also smelled tobacco smoke during her first week. She and others believe that former company caretakers and housekeepers are still at work, and may reside in the third floor attic, which was used as dormitory space for immigrants a hundred years ago.

In June 2000, Yves Raymond, Operations Manager, saw a woman in a black dress cross the upstairs hallway, enter the attic stairway and slam the door behind her. He thought it might be Joan Chamberlain, as he'd seen her in a black dress that morning but, just then, Joan emerged from her office to ask about the bang. Several employees went into the attic, but found it empty.

Another time, Yves' wife, Carol, came to the house as a volunteer. Yves had told her that a dowser once claimed there were eight spirits inside the house, and five more *outside*. Soon after, Carol observed a transparent cat in the hallway, adding to the spirit tally.

Yves' teen daughter and her friend, volunteering as cleaners on another evening, were playing 'Spirit in the Sky,' on their CD player, when the lights began flicking on and off. The girls screamed. Then, their CD and the vacuum cleaner wouldn't work. The girls immediately called it quits and left, not even looking over their shoulders.

A Native American friend of Yves' came to visit the house one evening and did a "walk through" upstairs to see what he could sense. He opened the door to the attic, slammed it, and jumped back. The friend explained to Yves that he'd seen another man with his ear to the door, as if eavesdropping, sitting on the bottom step of the stairs inside. Apparently, his friend and the ghost startled one another.

Another friend offered to do a "spiritual cleansing" at the house, and things quieted, but only for a few months.

Yves remembered an incident involving the barn. "We tried to get in but the main door was locked and we couldn't find the key. We thought we'd have to break in, but then one of the guys found the rear door ajar. When he tried to push the door open further, it pushed him back out of the doorway as the door shut tight and locked itself. No matter what we did after that, it wouldn't budge. We were certain someone was hiding in there, but when we did get in, nobody was there. Inside, we found that back door held shut by a pipe wedged against its bottom. There's no way a *pipe* could push the door closed!"

Several workers in the house have felt a presence at the top of the main stairway, and some have experienced a chilling breeze there. One employee said he avoided the top of the stairs because he felt he was being invisibly "scrutinized."

When I returned home from Berlin, I asked Paul, my clairvoyant friend, for comments. He said W.W. Brown still takes an occasional interest in the building, passing through from time to time, though he doesn't stay long. "He's about finished reviewing his life and its purposes; like he's on a field trip. He has pretty well reached an understanding of that life, what needed to be done, what he did and what he's left undone. He's kindly, and that's why the little girl saw him so easily."

Paul said the ghost of Charlie, a "little tyrant" company official who worked with time clocks, and who used to push underling employees around, is one of the spirits interrupting Joan's night work. "It was the only important job he held in that life, so he's still trying to be 'somebody' by pushing Joan around. He still wants to be in charge of *something* and returned to the house after death—trying to show he's still in charge. He hates to let go of it."

There is another old employee, Emile, still on the job sweeping and cleaning after hours, Paul explained. "He wasn't very smart, but had a good heart. And he would always say to the people in the offices, 'It's late, you should go home to your families.' People depended on him, and that responsibility gave meaning to his life. Everybody knew him. But also, they talked down to him—made fun of him. He had no hair. They used to rub his bald head for good luck, which humiliated him. He stays to show himself useful. He likes the new people. They treat him much better than the old ones. He likes the women, especially, as they're so jovial."

Though the Brown Company had many housekeepers, Paul singled out one named Regine, who apparently was employed around 1893. "She travels through the house many times a day, still doing what the company paid her to do. She was like a housemother. She was the first person up each morning and the last person to bed at night. So she was more of a taskmaster, and not well liked. She worked for the company, and not for the people in the house. She was severe in her behavior and in her dress.

"She used to stand guard at the front stair top each morning, as the laborers from the third floor dormitory filed past her to the back stairs, which she forced them to use. She believed the front stairs, which was the most direct way to the street and mill, should be used only by the higher-ups. As a result, the back stairway became an accumulator of the resentments of the cooks, servants, and hired help in the house, whose negative feelings combined with the workers' resentments. Many can sense that even today. As a trusted employee, Regine really didn't care how the laborers felt about her severity." It was interesting for me to hear from the current employees in the Brown House, that most avoid that back stairway as much as possible.

Paul also attributed the "bad feelings" that current employees feel in the attic to a residue of anger, bitterness and resentments among some of the low-paid workers. "There were fights among the men. A man named Tessier was once stabbed with a knife and later died. Saturday nights were bad nights; close quarters, men were tired and frustrated, some drank. They missed their families and often played cards and gambled. They didn't have many rights and didn't have any status."

So it's a busy place. Old-timers who don't know or care that they're dead, continue to work at century-old jobs. The Brown House has many lessons to teach—ones not envisioned in the Heritage Park's charter. Modern educators aim to interpret the hard-working past of Berlin's major employer, and the forest industries in general. Wouldn't it be wonderful if there was a communication system that permitted visitors to interview the spirits about what they've learned about life since they departed?

Jacob's House

Just outside Lexington, MA, stands the restored late 1600s house of Jacob Whittemore. The house witnessed major Revolutionary War events that occurred between Lexington and Concord on April 18 and 19, 1775, when British forces marched on Concord to seize the rebels' weapons and gunpowder. It saw the rebels pour a withering fire on the British troops as they marched back to Boston on the 19th, leaving hundreds dead or wounded, including one soldier in the road out front. The war then spread to the coast, and the century-old house reverted to a quiet home.

After countless tenants in the two centuries following The Revolution, the colonial residence was incorporated into The Minuteman Historic Site, restored and became a residence for National Park Service rangers. Jim, a new ranger, whose family lived there in 1985, told me, "We lived there for a little over a year, and it was a year of activity. From the very first night, I knew we weren't alone. My wife and I just heard strange noises at first, but rationalized that every house has its noises. It was a beautiful and bright house, but after a week we began to share impressions of the little movements we'd catch out of the corner of our eyes, similar ones, and in the same places. Then, we instantly would comment to one another, 'Did you see *that*?'

"Our son was six and our little girl was one and one-half then. One day our daughter complained to her mother, 'the little boy is taking my toys.' My wife asked what little boy. 'The one wearing the dress,' my daughter replied. How could she have known that little boys in olden times were often put in dresses?

"A day or so later our daughter saw a strange man standing behind a chair, playing with her stuffed giraffe. She wasn't scared, but was irritated at his rudeness in not asking permission. Then she described a 'fuzzy woman' dressed in black and white, who had no feet. At first we didn't connect her visions with the noises, and instead chalked it up to childhood fantasy.

"One night I finished my work late and collapsed on the couch to watch TV. Everyone else was in bed. I heard a loud noise out back of the house and got up to investigate. It was dark in the back yard, but I distinctly heard people walking and talking, jumbled voices all around me, though I couldn't make out what they were saying.

"I mentioned it to my co-workers at the Interpretation Center the next day. They burst out laughing, saying they wondered when I'd be telling such stories, because the house was famous for its ghosts!

"Several recalled that Michelle, a former ranger, had heard footsteps coming up the cellar stairs. She ran over to look down, but found nobody. She turned on the light and went down, but still found nobody. And the outside cellar door was locked from inside, so nobody could have come in there.

"They also told me about an historian who'd lived there for twenty years. His coping technique was to challenge the spirits verbally whenever something occurred and, that way, he wasn't afraid when strange events occurred."

Jim continued, "Our life then settled into routine while we waited for the birth of our third child. We often heard footsteps upstairs, and doorknobs rattling, and we'd also hear footsteps on the stairs though all our family members were in the same room. When we checked, nobody was ever on the stairs.

"On the night Colin was born, Bonnie, a ranger friend, agreed to watch the other two children while my wife and I went to the hospital. The birth went well, and I arrived home late. Every light in the house was on. My daughter was crying, but my son was asleep. Bonnie was red-faced and upset. 'Don't ever ask me to stay here again!' she said, and left abruptly. A few days later, after she calmed down, she told me of having heard strange noises upstairs, on the stairs, and in the kitchen. She couldn't see anybody and was terrified."

In 1986 Jim changed job locations, leaving behind a dwelling where dimensions in time intermingle; where early Americans still go about their daily routines unimpressed with Lexington's status as a major American tourist site. Jim, thinking he would finally get an uninterrupted night's sleep, transferred to the Saratoga National Historic Park. His new residence is calm. But ghosts are plentiful there, too—out on the battlefield.

Major Rogers

Underwater archaeology group, Bateaux Below, concluded its meeting on Lake George shipwrecks in the old Warren County Courthouse in Lake George, NY. Marilyn Mazzeo went upstairs to turn out the lights. "Tweee-twee-tweet!" came the shrill sound from somewhere on the second floor. "Did I lock someone in?" she wondered. She reopened the door, turned on the lights and closely examined the room. Nobody there. She closed the door and started back downstairs, only to hear it again, "Tweee-twee-tweet!" She retraced her steps, unlocked the door, turned on the lights and checked once more. Again, nothing. Nobody. She re-locked the door and left without further incident. But next morning she told museum co-worker Grace MacDonald about the incident. "I've heard that before," Grace said, "but thought the sound was out on Canada Street."

"No, it came from somewhere on the second floor, I know that," said Marilyn. Then, for several weeks, they heard no noises out of the ordinary. One day an intuitive named Sue visited the Lake George Historical Association's museum in the Courthouse, where Grace and Marilyn worked. Sue took her children to an upstairs exhibit, then came down suddenly. They'd seen a man in buckskins, who suddenly vanished into thin air, and they wanted to report it to the staff.

"I thought about those happenings for a long time," said Grace. "Then one day I sat reading a book on Lake George history, and came to the part about Major Robert Rogers, famed leader of Rogers' Rangers in the French and Indian War (1755-1763). He and his men often launched raids on French garrisons at Ft. Carillon (Ticonderoga) and Ft. St. Frederic (Crown Point) from nearby Ft. William

Henry. I found a paragraph about the signaling system he and his men used in the woods—like shrill birdcalls, to recognize one another, and so the Indians or French couldn't be sure they were being spied on."

A few months later, Sue returned. Intrigued by the apparition she'd seen in the Courthouse, she had "opened up" her psychic ability to all of Canada Street. In her mind's eye she saw, in a ravine next to the High School, a man in a canoe, who suddenly stood and grabbed his chest before vanishing. She wondered if he'd been shot. Then, closer by, she was approached by a ghost who was mute, and who telepathically told her he had died not far from the present courthouse, but didn't want to leave the area because all his friends had died there. She couldn't make out what country's uniform he wore, but told Grace and Marilyn about it. The two women, very knowledgeable in Lake George regional history, recalled that the courthouse stands on ground occupied by French General Montcalm's artillery when they assaulted nearby Ft. William Henry in August 1757. Might Sue have seen a French soldier?

A few months later, as another evening meeting wound down, Marilyn's husband arrived at the museum to drive her home. As he waited in the bookshop, he wandered along the row of bookshelves. Responding to a sharp whistle behind him in the corner, he whirled around. He saw nobody, became nervous, and walked outside for a cigarette. Directly behind him, the sound came again, "Tweee-twee-tweet!" He went to the car and sat until his wife was ready to leave, chain-smoking several more cigarettes. A year later the Lake George Historical Association held an evening meeting, which was crowded, because a recently excavated mortar bomb fragment was on display. While members were examining it, the familiar three whistles sounded again, very loud and very shrill.

Whoever makes these sounds, whether it is the ghost of Major Rogers or one of his men, the French & Indian War still vibrates in the Village of Lake George.

A reconstructed Ft. William Henry hosts thousands of visitors each summer, and the Courthouse Museum has many special exhibits. A few years ago the Daniel Day Lewis film of James Fenimore Cooper's 1826 novel, *The Last of the Mohicans*, realistically recreated the struggle of almost 250 years ago. Bateaux Below has located and marked Rogers' sunken invasion fleet of bateaux. "The Land Tortoise," a British gunboat from that war was located in the lake in 1994 and, along with the sunken bateaux, has become New York State's first underwater historic site, The Submerged Heritage Preserves. In this village the past and the present continue to blend in very strange ways.

Skene Manor

Whitehall, NY, is the birthplace of the U.S. Navy, and also the location for preposterous legends about Skene Manor, a grand house built on the mountainside outskirts of the village. Many agree the building, home to the historical society, has ghosts. But who they are and how they got there is debatable.

Col. Philip Skene was Royal Judge for Charlotte County and Military Governor of Ft. Ticonderoga, and lent his name to a small community at the southern end of Lake Champlain: Skenesborough. He married Katherine, a shrewd woman who feared the corruption of the grave. Her will granted an annuity to the Colonel "as long as my body lies above ground." She died first, and he is said to have had her corpse soaked in vinegar, placed in a lead casket, and stored in the British garrison at the foot of Skenesborough's large hill. When Americans defeated Burgoyne in 1777, and the countryside became unsafe for the British, Skene left his wife's casket in the garrison and fled to Canada, promising her spirit that he'd return. He never did.

His name was taken from the village, and it was renamed "Whitehall." Some say Katherine's casket was taken from the garrison to a small house on top of the cliff overlooking the small village, and later shifted to its cellar. Others say American troops found the coffin, removed her bones, reburied them, and made ammunition out of the lead casket. In any case, strange events are said to have begun about this time because, wherever Katherine's bones ended up, she was now below ground level, and probably upset.

In 1872 State Supreme Court Justice, Joseph Potter, leveled the small house, leaving Katherine's coffin, if indeed it still existed, where it was. Potter built a magnificent Victorian stone house known today as Skene Manor. It still looks out over the southern tip of Lake Champlain and the village of Whitehall. Potter was well-to-do and always kept the house in the latest fashionable styles. In 1947 Clay Schere turned the old house into a restaurant. He found Katharine Skene's story intriguing and capitalized on it in his advertising. He also had a mechanical hand installed behind a curtain in the bar. On occasion, he'd tug an attached string and the skeletal hand reached through the curtain. Schere frightened many diners with the trick.

Then, in 1960, after the house became a home again, a member of the new family is said to have committed suicide in Judge Potter's old bedroom. Many who have visited that room feel ominous sensations and believe it hosts an unquiet spirit.

Mrs. Potter's bedroom has been essentially unchanged for a hundred years, regardless of ownership. Around 1980, when Skene Manor was home to another family, a man sleeping in Mrs. Potter's old room thought he heard someone walking in the hall. Fearfully, he pushed his bed against the door. He awoke in the morning to find the bed, with himself in it, pushed away from the door.

On another occasion, a woman from Middlebury, VT, crossing the Whitehall bridge on Route 4, looked up at Skene Manor, and noticed a woman in an upstairs window. Surprised that it was still occupied, she drove to the house via the access road. To the best of her knowledge, it was unoccupied. Knocking on the door, she was greeted by a workman. Laughing, he said there was no woman in the house, and she'd probably seen Katherine Skene. The Vermonter fled.

The workman, apprehensive about Katherine's ghost, and seeing the visitor's face suddenly turn pale, decided to call it quits for the day. When he returned the next day, he found the ceiling over his work site had collapsed. "Whew!" he said, "that might have fallen on me!"

Those who have encountered a female ghost in the house, say she originates in the Victorian era. She is usually described as wearing white garments in the height of late 1800s fashion.

Exploring the site myself, I decided that it looks "haunted." Maybe that's why many are inclined to embellish its history. I've heard an outrageous story that Katherine Skene's body is still hidden in a garnet coffin. Other fable makers allege that a mad woman-in-white runs screaming through the house. I could find no historical basis for either story. Nevertheless, the true facts of Skene Manor's apparitions, supplied to me by members of the Historical Society, still are pretty good ones, don't you agree?

A Grave Matter

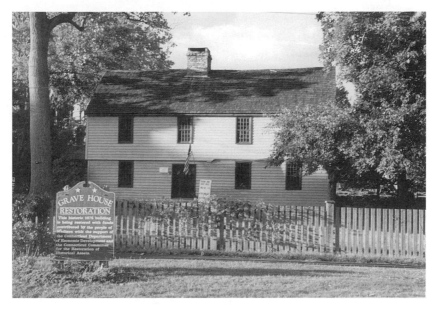

Deacon John Grave and Rev. Whitfield came from England and established a Congregational church in the small settlement of East Gilford, now Madison, CT, in 1639. Though Grave bought acreage, it remained for his son, John, to build the first house on it, a two-room dwelling for his wife and ten children. A self-sufficient farmer, John also operated a tavern in the house. Grave's descendants expanded it to a large New England saltbox over the next three hundred years. A family journal chronicled the house's use as a school, wartime infirmary, weapons depot, inn, tavern and courtroom over the years. Today, this record is on display at the Madison Historical Society.

John's third child, Ann, was seventeen when British forces commandeered the house as an infirmary during Queen Anne's War (1702-1713). Beautiful Ann fell in love with a British soldier who promised to return to her after France was defeated. For years she sat pining away in the upstairs window, daily watching the Boston Post Road. He never came, and she died heartbroken. Soon after her death, before 1800, the Graves began to notice strange events in the house. From time to time, over the next hundred or so years, the Grave journal records eerie sounds or objects moved or disappeared.

The Lage family, between 1930 and 1978, was the last of the Grave family line to live in the house. Lage heirs rented it to a family whose daughter slept in the West Chamber. She awoke in the night to find the rocking chair rocking. She refused to sleep in the room again.

New renters arrived, and their son continually found his carefully folded clothes rumpled on the bed. Objects from his bedside table were found knocked to the floor. On two occasions women fainted when a ghost woman appeared late at night. Another woman tenant heard footsteps on the stairs when no one else was in the house.

In 1982 the Historical Society bought the house and set about its restoration, removing non-traditional architectural features from recent times. Two workmen saw a female specter with an ashen face and fearful expression walk between the main parlor and taproom. Initially, they thought she was alive and searched the building to discover where the woman had gone. Only after their search revealed no one, did they realize *she* was probably a ghost.

When I visited the historic house at the end of visiting hours in September 2001, I knew I was alone, and that the house was reputed to have a ghost, that's all. I asked the guide not to give other details. As I climbed the stairs to the second floor, I entered a large, bright room that contained an old loom. Just for a second I thought I saw a movement between the window and loom. But no one was visible on second glance. I mentioned it to the guide, who smiled, "Yes, this East Chamber is the room where many visitors feel a presence when they enter."

Perhaps I glimpsed Ann just for the moment. To me, it was a bright and happy room that reflected the autumn colors, and it's hard to see how a ghost could be unhappy there, but I was just an American writer, and not the British soldier that Ann still hopes will return.

17

Apartment Ghosts

Bonnie's Place

When they first moved in at 211 Russell Street in Syracuse, NY, in the 1980s, she was thrilled. It appeared to be a comfortable upstairs apartment in a quiet neighborhood. Bonnie and her husband especially enjoyed having a large bedroom. Soon after they settled in, the partying started. Her husband was often on the road for a week at a time. One night, alone in bed, she felt she was in the center of a group of celebrating people. Noise, conversation and music seemed to reverberate from the walls. But the bedroom was dark and nobody else was there.

She asked the people in the downstairs apartment if perhaps they had had a party—maybe sound does funny things. "No," they responded soberly, "we don't have parties." They made it plain that they didn't welcome her questions. Then, for several subsequent nights she heard clinking glasses when she turned her lights out. A dinner party? A cocktail party? These events only happened when she was there alone. The owners were elderly and it certainly wasn't *them* doing the partying!

"It was one of the biggest mysteries in my life," she exclaimed. "A few years later we moved on. I wish I knew what events prompted those noises. The previous people must have loved to entertain. Too bad, we arrived too late for the party!"

Shared Apartment

He was suddenly there on her living room floor, playing with wooden toys she'd never seen before. With his blonde hair and blue eyes, he took in her quizzical look, then he explained, "I live here."

"Well, I do, too!" she retorted. She thought she was alone in the apartment when she lay down.

He was silent for a minute, pondering this reality. Then he responded, "That's okay," and resumed his playing. A strange light seemed to permeate the room. Then she woke up—or did she? The boy was gone, but the golden light radiated in the room. *Had* it all been a dream? If so, it was the strangest one she'd ever had!

Jamie Lynaugh went into the kitchen for a cup of coffee. She wondered if her meeting with the boy was only dream imagery, or if he was really there in spirit. She only shared the experience with friends later that month at a party. There, a psychic friend received the impression of the boy's name—David, and his appearance—in a brownish vest over a white shirt, and wearing brown pants, which corresponded with Jamie's vision. The friend thought she heard the boy say to Jamie, "I've fooled you a few times!" Then some prior experiences made sense. In the months before her dream she had felt touched three times on the back or shoulder, though no one was there. The ghost boy, who appeared about eleven years old, seemed to have a childlike sense of playfulness.

Jamie liked the apartment on Green Street in Schenectady, NY, as soon as she moved in. She believes her building once was a servant quarters at the rear of a big estate, perhaps belonging to the Ellis family. John Ellis formed one of Schenectady's major employers, The American Locomotive Company, in the late 1800s, and his sons Edward and Charles had adjoining mansions in the Stockade section of the city, putting them near Jamie's residence. The boy might have been a servant's child, she thought. "I began to be aware and hear him walking in the hall at night. Several times I got up, but could see no one. Once, as my husband and I lay in bed, I didn't hear anyone approaching the bed, but suddenly I was touched on a sore spot on my spine. I rolled over, expecting it to be my husband, but it wasn't—he was turned the other way. A feeling of benevolence spread over me when my spine was invisibly touched. I wondered how long it would last, and checking my alarm clock, I saw it was two minutes. I didn't hear the boy leave, as I fell asleep," she said. A few months later she felt a young hand touching her head.

"He takes things from time to time, but if I ask him, he always returns them," she continued. "My first experience with this behavior astounded me. I have a sterling silver cross, made in the Southwest, and I keep it in a small box on top of my jewelry. One day the cross was missing and I was frantic at its loss. I looked all over the apartment for three weeks with no result. Then I thought of the boy. 'If you took my cross, please put it back,' I said. A few days later, there it was, back on top of my jewelry. Now, whenever I can't find something, I ask *him* first!"

Jamie thinks the boy sometimes leaves her apartment to visit the old Ellis Mansion. She once knew a man that lived in the mansion, and a ghost child haunted his residence. Comparing notes, they found the physical description of the boy matched. The man said he'd had to instruct the boy to leave his house, as his constant activity, puttering and playing, bothered him. Jamie notes that she and her husband often hear the boy come in the house and ascend their stairs. "He has a penchant for mischief at times," she said. "I have a small candelabra on top of my TV, and once, while we sat watching a program, I saw a green candle wiggle itself up out of the holder and fly across the room, hitting the wall. Most of the time he responds when I speak to him, so maybe he needs human contact and just does these things to get my attention, if he feels I'm ignoring him."

Jamie and her husband seem content to share their apartment with the boy. Schenectady is over three hundred years old, and for years called itself "The City That Lights The World," because it is the home to the General Electric Company. Perhaps the boy enjoys the old days of big industry and hustle and bustle, and thus delights in bringing a little light of his own to an old apartment building.

And perhaps one day soon, Jamie and her husband can direct this young soul to The Brightest of Lights, where he can find playmates among the Beings of Light who can enrich his afterlife knowledge.

The Rapper

Donna Kennelly is a professional nurse in Portland, ME. Patient care in the Emergency Room at Mercy Hospital depends on her analysis of scientific facts. However, in the early 1980s, when she was attending nursing school in Portland, she had some experiences that are not covered in textbooks. She shared an apartment with a fellow nursing student in an old house on the first block of lower State Street. The rent was right and it seemed a quiet place to hit the books.

One night, when her roommate was away, she turned in early to catch up on some long-overdue sleep. She had just turned off the lights and stretched out when she heard a series of sharp raps cross the entire wall behind the headboard of her bed. It was as if some excited person was frolicking in the room next door. She hadn't met the other roomers in the house, so in the morning she questioned the landlady about her neighbor. "Why, dear, the room is not rented, and I haven't rented it for years," she said.

This made it difficult for Donna, immersed in logical and intellectual study, to fathom the noises that continually interrupted her throughout the rest of her sojourn there. Some nights there were bumping noises, as if someone had stumbled into a piece of furniture. On other occasions she heard windows or doors opening, then slamming. Once, in the hallway, she saw lights flickering on and off in the space underneath the door. Her roommate never seemed to hear the outbursts.

The next semester she found another room, this time in a house that not only appeared quiet, but also was fully occupied by people she could *see*.

Teasing the Tenants

Donna Cirone used to own a nice old house in Milbridge, ME. It was about one hundred years old and had a history of rapid turnovers on the real estate market when she bought it in 1967. Her two teenage daughters created a study area in the attic, and furnished it with old chairs, a sofa and desk. When they returned to do homework the next day, they found all the furniture moved. Each looked suspiciously at the other, but neither said anything. Soon after, however, the family began to hear scraping and walking sounds overhead after they went to bed. Investigations always showed nobody there.

About a week later, the commotion became more animated when the girls went to bed in their second floor bedroom. A half-hour after lights-out, their father followed. Donna remained seated in the first floor living room. Within a minute after her husband went upstairs, she heard footsteps climbing the stairs. Before she could ask who it was, she heard her husband yell out from the second floor, "Donna, did you just come up behind me?" When she answered in the negative, he responded, "*Somebody* did!" She not only had to answer in the negative, but also fathom who the invisible stair-climber was. Her husband, suspecting it was one of the girls, went into their bedroom, but found the pair sound asleep. They searched the house, but the parents and daughters were the only visible ones there.

For the next three nights Donna slept on the downstairs couch, intimidated and unwilling to go upstairs. On the fourth night she did go upstairs, but took the family dog with her. Aside from some suspicious flickering of second floor lights, the next few weeks were uneventful. When Donna's brother, Galen, visited the house he was surprised to see a door open itself several times, letting the family cat in and out.

Donna had bought the house from an old woman named Vera so, rather than deal with a nameless ghost, she began to address the presence with that name. "Vera, shut the door!" "Vera, open the door!" And the entity usually complied with the command. One day, Vera's daughter-in-law came by to ask Donna if she was experiencing many strange events there. During the discussion, the woman said that her family had many strange experiences in the attic room used by the girls for study. She related that one of Vera's relatives had hanged himself in an upper room after returning from World War II, so perhaps the unquiet spirit can finally be identified as a soldier.

Donna's first husband died in 1972. Most family members who came to the house after his death felt very uncomfortable. Many of them had the sensation of a small breeze, as if someone invisible walking past them. Within two months after their father's death, the two daughters went to college, and her son inherited the upstairs room. The noises continued.

Two years later Donna remarried. Once, a friend brought her three-week old baby to Donna's house. Donna was watching the infant while preparing a meal in the kitchen, when suddenly she felt someone's hand touching her arm. She ran out the door and was three hundred feet away before she realized she'd left the baby back in the house. She told her new husband about the incident, and how difficult it was to surmount her fears and run the house normally. He said, "I think we'd better find another place." So, in 1975 they sold the house.

The new owner converted the building into a duplex. He lives downstairs and rents the upstairs, and has experienced many of the same phenomena that Donna and her family described. His tenants sometime accuse him of coming in while they are away, and moving their possessions or furniture, but he hasn't done so. Likely, he's just waiting for the "right time" to pass on the stories that Donna shared with him!

Martin's Mischief

Clinton Avenue in Albany, NY, has been in transition for over forty years. Old derelict buildings are sometimes demolished, but in places, entrepreneurs have renovated them and brought new life to a moribund neighborhood. One such visionary in 1985 was an Irishman named Ed. On the lower end of Clinton Avenue he purchased a four-unit building, hoping to fully rehabilitate it as a rental property. He chose to live on the third floor and opened a sandwich shop on the ground level. As the renovations were completed, he readied the first and second floor apartments for new tenants. Getting to that rental stage was difficult and puzzling, however.

During the construction phase, the workmen often found their tools missing. Most often these same tools would reappear in the space between the old ceiling and a suspended ceiling. Who could the prankster be? The mischief continued with the doors too. At the end of each workday the carpenters and drywall installers would walk through the work areas, closing all doors, including those of the closets. In the morning, however, they were astonished (for the first few weeks, anyway) to find all doors standing open, as if somebody was inspecting the premises. The building had been secured throughout the night, and with Ed's store downstairs and his apartment upstairs—surely he would have heard any intruders.

The owner had his own troubles to contend with in that building. One night, about 3 a.m., Ed suddenly awoke to find dark shadows—four of them by his count—

standing at the foot of his bed. They began to rock the very heavy and completely filled waterbed. He shouted at them and they vanished.

It was the last straw for the would-be landlord. He invited famed Albany psychic Ann Fisher, who came to his building and walked throughout the structure with him. She assured him that his vision was not imagination—several spirits were afoot in the building. Fisher felt a man haunted the building's first floor, and that Ed had a ghostly woman tenant on the second floor, too. Fisher saw a lady with white hair who spent the better part of her day and night in a rocking chair, peering out the window onto Clinton Avenue, watching for the trolley cars (which have not run in the past half-century). "It's a funny thing," Ed recalls, "I was never able to rent 'her apartment' very successfully to anyone but single females. I guess she liked their company."

Over the years Ed did some historical research and found that a tenant named Martin Soule had lived and died there. "He took a liking to me. I'd hear him follow me all over the house, from my apartment on the third floor, down to the ground floor shop where I had my washer and dryer installed. Boy, did I feel creepy doing my laundry there alone at night!" he exclaimed. Ed acknowledges his sensitivity to spectral phenomena, and so chooses not to operate old apartment buildings any more. "The only scarier thing in Albany, besides these ghosts, is the politics!" he said.

Justine

"I had quite some experiences with ghosts for about seven months in 1995-1996 in Schuylerville, NY," she wrote to me. As a single working woman, Michelle had found a large old apartment building at 42A Burgoyne Street in that village. The downstairs apartment on the corner of Chestnut Street was available at a fair monthly rent, offering her room to move around, as well as peace and quiet. She had been told the apartment upstairs on the other side of the central hallway was occupied but she never heard or saw those tenants. "From the time I came there in September I felt a gentle presence, though I didn't see anything specific, so I felt whoever it was meant me no harm," she said. Then in October her experiences became more troubling. "The presence or presences became stronger and even overbearing at times," she continued.

One of her friends, who believes himself to be gifted psychically, visited her one day to see her new lodging. As he walked about the apartment he developed a powerful headache which, as he walked, got worse. The man left abruptly, saying that there was an evil presence. He refused to return to the apartment again.

A window in an extension of the house faced her back porch and this vantage point gave her a glimpse of the empty room inside. One evening, after returning from work, she saw a smiling elderly woman peering out. "Every night she stood at the window and smiled at me. As I walked through my apartment at night I could feel and sometimes hear her walking along her side of the wall, accompanying me. I mentally 'saw' her dressed in white and illuminated from behind by what seemed to be candles. I felt she was happy to have me come home each night," Michelle related. The seeming glow of candlelight distorted the specific details of the elder's face.

Whoever she was, the woman appeared inside Michelle's apartment only once. Michelle had a heated argument over the phone with her boyfriend, Matt, one evening.

When the conversation ended, Michelle lit a small candle and broke down crying. As she sobbed with head in hands, she felt warm and firm hands upon her shoulders. She was both surprised and comforted by the experience, and felt she would see her room filled with light if only she could get the courage to open her eyes. In a short time she was able to look around, but the room was empty, though she could still feel the warmth and pressure of those hands on her shoulders. She knew it must be the ghostly lady from next door that had visited her—an act of friendship and compassion. Michelle decided to call the elderly woman "Justine." With a friend to confide in, she often spoke aloud to the stranger as she struggled with issues in her relationship with her boyfriend, Matt.

Soon afterward she began to hear footsteps in the apartment above her, which had been unoccupied. The heavy footfalls indicated the unseen resident was male. Finally, Michelle and Matt patched up their differences and he moved in. "And that seemed to provoke the ghost man upstairs. Whenever we left the apartment," she noted, "we'd find something moved when we returned. On one occasion I found a favorite glass bowl shattered on the floor when I returned home. It had been stored in a high cupboard whose door was locked—too high for my cats to have reached. Within days, the cats became nervous and raced through the apartment wide-eyed, as if trying to escape an invisible interloper."

Finally, she saw the man she believed to be the heavy walker. Outside the building's basement door she spied a man with a dark beard and menacing dark eyes. "He wore a uniform or work suit of some kind," she said, "but disappeared when I walked outdoors to see more clearly." On the occasions when Matt had to be alone in the apartment, he became very nervous, though he couldn't explain to Michelle the reasons for it. He said he felt unsafe. He returned to his home during the daytime and only came to Michelle's at night, when she was there.

In December they began to have furnace troubles. The heat would sometimes be off for an entire day, then turn itself on again. When the landlord sent a repairman, he found no cause for the disruption. "Everything is working fine," he said. After he went away the heat stayed off permanently until the repairman returned to attend to the problem. As his service truck pulled up in front of the house, Michelle heard the heat turn itself on again. In time, three different heating service technicians examined the house's heating system, including her thermostat, and could find nothing wrong.

On New Year's Eve that year, Matt had to be out of town and Michelle spent her first night alone. Sleeping fitfully, she awoke around midnight to see a male figure standing at the foot of her bed. He looked like the man she'd seen in the back yard. Michelle felt anger emanating from him, though he said nothing. Unable to handle the fear and tension, Michelle cried out in terror, "Who are you and what do you want?" The entity simply disappeared without responding. Though she never saw him again, her heating problems continued.

Unwilling to endure the discomfort, she gave her notice to the landlord, who refused to believe her stories about the irregular heat. On her last day in the building, sad at having to leave Justine's comforting presence, Michelle went to the back porch to "call" Justine to her window. But the woman would not appear, even to say goodbye. Michelle locked her front door. An acquaintance from across the street saw her maneuvering boxes into her car, came across the street to help, and inquired which apartment had been hers.

When she indicated the downstairs apartment, the young man was stunned. "I thought you lived upstairs on the other side. I've seen dim figures at the window up there," he said, pointing. "The window shades are continually being raised or lowered." When she went to the landlord to turn in her key, she asked him about that apartment's tenant. "Nobody lives there because it's unsafe," he replied, "it needs lots of work and even I haven't been in that apartment in months!"

The Emerson

The Emerson Apartment Building at 284 Orange St., in New Haven, CT, was built in 1875. Some say it once housed clergymen. Others claim it once housed members of a secret fraternal lodge. Still others assert that the warren of tunnels under the cellar was used by both the Underground Railway (not likely) and bootleggers during Prohibition (more likely). The five current and former tenants I've interviewed all love The Emerson's "old time Victorian ambience." From the wonderful wrought-iron grille that flanks the front entrance to the beautiful interior woodwork, the five-story brick building is classic.

K. and M., tenants for two and one-half years, found their apartment peaceful for the first two years. On an evening that K. was having difficulty falling asleep, he stayed up watching television at 2 a.m. Knowing he was alone in the room, he was startled as a dried flower arrangement rustled in a decorator vase near the entrance door. Walking over, he expected to see a mouse jump out, but was puzzled as there were only flowers in the vase. As he stood pondering, he felt a sudden chill sweep over him. He backed away and went to bed.

On another night, K. was glued to the television set. "I was wide awake and suddenly heard someone walking through the hall. I got up, went to the doorway and saw an indistinct moving shape. We have good locks. I couldn't imagine who could have come in. Was it M.? I called out to her. No answer. I stood and walked toward the silhouetted figure. I couldn't tell if it was male or female. It retreated into the kitchen. I pursued, but found nobody there. I went to check on M. but she was still sleeping."

K. knew he was sensitive to spirits. While growing up in Norwalk, CT, on his way to the school bus, he had seen an old woman's ghost in a deserted house. Another time, in his family's house, he had heard a woman's voice calling from the attic. His family's religion treated all such experiences as demonic, and he found no one in his life that condoned his emerging e.s.p. This dichotomy between his personal experiences and his family's dogmatism created much inner tension.

As a seventeen-year-old he became a drug addict. In a hallucinatory state, he once saw his face take on a demonic appearance in a mirror, an experience that sobered him, and he no longer takes drugs. Today, his world is no longer circumscribed by family narrow-mindedness. He believes ghosts are real and are simply souls that have not yet completed their journey to The Beyond.

A. and S., former residents, left their Emerson apartment in 2000. "We never were really terrified there, but I'm a student and need the little sleep I get," said A. "Soon after we moved in, I awoke in the middle of the night. Something was going on. My eyes were open but I couldn't move. Male and female figures were slowly moving about the room. I couldn't talk to them or see much detail. You can always call these things dreams," A. said, "but I was also troubled by another phenomenon. After studying, I'd drop off to sleep with the lights on and the window open, and awake to find the window closed and the lights off. It made me nervous that someone alive or dead was wandering through my apartment!"

The absolute last straw, according to A. was when she and S. entertained friends at a small party. A guest asked her when she'd gotten a pet. "I told her I didn't have any. She said she'd just seen a grey cat walking through the other room. We investigated, but found no animal."

Later, she chatted with J., another tenant and reluctant psychic. Deeply spiritual, J. has asked clergy for hints on coping with these energies from the past. Her name was placed on a long list of those seeking help. When J. moved in in October 2000, her apartment doors would open and close themselves, as if an invisible dweller shared her space. Her roommate witnessed these movements. They always checked for open windows and stray breezes, but never found any. Once, a picture hanging in her bedroom flew off its hook and hit the wall across the room. This was followed by a putrid smell, which abated in a few hours. One night she awoke and, though seeing no one, found the apartment bathed in a strange red light and heard whispering.

"I've had electrical problems," J. told me, "appliances or switches that don't work. I'd call the electrician, but he'd never find anything wrong. I've seen a transparent male janitor walk into my apartment right *through* the door. I've maintained my composure enough to study his appearance. He has blue eyes and a medium build, and is still going about his work. He never pays attention to me, and seems totally focused on his tasks. A former resident told her that in the 1970s a custodian had hanged himself in the cellar. Two girls who lived next door once saw him sweeping in the basement, and thought he was real. They talked to him, and wondered why he didn't respond to them. Thinking he needed cheering up at Christmas time, they made cookies for him, but found nobody and no trace of anyone living there when they delivered their gift to the cellar."

Another resident heard a rumor that a woman had suffocated on the fifth floor in the late 1970s or early 1980s, though nobody at the Emerson can confirm this today. Another resident, hearing of the others' experiences, believes them, but as yet has no personal experiences to relate. Whatever the building's past, not all of it has peacefully passed. And the antics of the discarnate residents who remain are not being experienced as a "present."

18

Ghosts
In Business

The Back Room

Ruth, a bank accountant, felt the burden of responsibility when she became chairperson of a group of women bankers during the 1960s. Often, there weren't enough hours in a week for her group work and her regular job at the Ballston Spa, NY, National Bank. This meant she had to work Sundays. "It wasn't that bad, however," she said, "I liked to work alone in the Bookkeeping Department. One sunny Sunday afternoon I let myself in and got down to work at the big table in the back room. I had opened the vault and its door stood ajar. As I worked at my ledgers I began to hear soft voices and the clinking of coins out in the Counting Room. I was all alone, I thought. Who could have come in without me seeing or hearing the door open? I got up to check. Nobody was there. The entire room was unlit. I returned to my books.

"But I kept hearing those voices talking to one another quietly. I figured it was the air conditioner, or some other machine, and decided to ignore it. Behind my worktable was a rear door, with an old-fashioned wooden Venetian blind. WHACK! I turned and saw that blind, lifting itself away and slamming against the door all by itself! I dropped my pen, left the ledger open, left the vault open, grabbed my purse, and scrammed, locking the back door behind me!

"The next morning I was edgy when I entered the bank. I immediately got some coffee and was sipping it when Neil Hodsoll, the manager, came in. 'Neil,' I said, 'I don't know how to say this. I was here alone yesterday, and I think the bank is haunted.'"

Neil looked at her, grinned, and said, "Ruth, I'm surprised it's taken you *this long* to find out!" Several employees laughed knowingly. Ruth discovered another individual who, like herself, was uneasy in the old building. "We had a man named Jeff on the staff," she said. "He said he'd do anything to avoid going into the attic. It made him nervous, as if someone invisible was watching him. After hearing that, I didn't feel alone in my fright, and I laughed, too!

"I worked for the bank for thirty-four years, and ended up writing a book on its history. Originally, Hugh Hawkins, a building contractor in the village during the early 1800s, lived here. The house was sold to the Ballston Spa National Bank in 1838 as a 'counting house.' At the corner of Front and Science Streets, the bank has been a landmark for years."

The old building still looks much like the home Hawkins built, though it now has drive-through tellers and a great chime clock at the curb. Much of the money that developed the village of Ballston Spa in its early years was likely loaned from there. Apparently, a spectral staff still keeps track and counts after hours.

1310 King's Highway

The building at 1310 King's Highway, Barnstable, MA, has had many names throughout its long history: Captain Grey's, The 1716 House, The Old Jail House, The Andrea Doria Inn, The Sign of the Blue Lantern, and most recently, The Barnstable House. Before 1728 it was a country inn. Now it sits on Cape Cod's most heavily traveled road, no longer a tavern but an office building. It is perhaps the best known haunted building on the Cape.

The volunteer fire department received an emergency fire call there in December 1975. Fireman Charlie Matthews, one of the first to arrive, saw smoke pouring from the roof, but no fire. With Robert Klun he got a ladder up to the roof and found smoke pouring out an unlatched skylight. He knew, from the house's history, however, that the entire third floor of the house had been sealed for years. Who unlatched the skylight? The firemen entered the house, and seeing no flames, ventilated the house and let the smoke clear. Still no flames. Closing the skylight, they returned to the ground, and stood in the cold air, awaiting further developments, while work lights and truck beacons seemed to turn the night into day. They never found anything burned.

Though no one saw her approach, a strange woman suddenly stood in their midst, asking if they'd seen her Dalmatian. Dazed at her sudden arrival and bizarre appearance, they could only say, "No." After asking several more outlandish questions, she simply vanished, though none of the crew could remember which direction she'd gone. Later, at the fire station, the four firefighters who saw her compared notes. They agreed she was about thirty, had long brown hair and (they were stunned to recall) was wearing a high-necked, white wedding gown! Even more puzzling, the other six men on the squad hadn't seen her, and gave the four suspicious looks as they related their experience. None of the ten, all local residents, remembered ever seeing a woman of that description before. As with so many ghost sightings, it can be very difficult to fit such apparitions into one's understandings of everyday life.

In the 1980s, when Rick Linstead bought the building to use as an inn, he dismissed tales of its alleged ghostly cast of characters: Mingo, the Indian, and Martha, a strange woman seen there for over two hundred years. Yet, one day, while he worked in his office with his golden retriever sleeping at his feet, he felt a subtle indefinable change in the room. The dog jumped to her feet, hackles raised and teeth bared, snarling at something in the doorway that Rick couldn't see. She then backed away, whined and hid in the corner.

Another time, one of his lodgers came to the front desk in a fright. "Did you see that lady in the other room? She's got no feet!" Trying to make sense of it, Rick's mind raced, then he remembered that, a few years before, he'd raised that floor four inches. Isn't it possible that the ghost was walking on the lower, original floor?

Janet Johnson, a former owner, didn't believe in ghosts either when she bought the place after Rick. One night she was in her bedroom while a spirited high school group rented the guestrooms. Their noise drifted to her bedroom. They're just excited, she thought, drifting off to sleep. Suddenly, something changed. The kids became louder, and her bedroom nightlight flared to a new brilliance. Then she noticed a fire in her bedroom fireplace, which hadn't been there when she went to bed. She sat up, undecided which to attend to first, the noisy kids or the fire. For fifteen minutes she enjoyed the fire's warmth and listened to the kids. Gradually, she noticed the noise subsiding, and the fire dwindling at the same time, despite plenty of unburned wood. A short time later, the youngsters' noise stopped and the fire went out. Maybe not ghosts, she thought, but how will I ever explain this to anyone? A few months later she snuffed out the candles on the inn's main chandelier four times before the candle flames stayed out.

Most Barnstable residents have heard these stories. Few will venture a guess as to how many ghosts prowl the building. Some say they congregate in the attic, others think the cellar. And some have told me about their dining room ghost encounters.

In 1974, before it closed as a restaurant, Mr. and Mrs. Mike Welch, newlyweds, at a table just outside the bar area, saw a man in colonial garb walking toward them. Scruffily dressed, he carried a stained bar rag over his arm and a silver tray of empty tankards. He walked past their table and entered the bar. Mike, a lover of American history, got up and complimented the owner on his waiter's period dress. The owner looked blank. "Mister, we don't have time or money to dress up our waiters. What are you talking about?"

Allen, a local postal employee, remembers the night he and his wife waited for a table in the Barnstable House's foyer. "It was a hot night, and I was perspiring," he said. "As I stood there, I looked up into the dark stairway. I wondered if there really were ghosts. I took a few steps up the stairs, right into an ice-cold spot, maybe 25 to 30 degrees colder. The Barnstable House didn't have air conditioning then, and I came back down fast. That was enough for me. Give me the heat!"

Today the old building is repainted, and looks new. Passersby would never guess it is almost three hundred years old. Since its conversion to office space in the 1990s, it looks just like many other buildings that house small offices. Most of the ghosts' appearances seem to have been at night, when the building was relatively quiet, so daytime office workers may not notice their energies as much. But the ghosts are still there, and its office workers can be expected to come forth with their own stories in time.

The Spring

Since 1872 discriminating customers have relished a delicious sparkling mineral water from an old spring on Geyser Road in Saratoga Springs, NY. The carbonated beverage flows naturally from the depths of the earth, and has intrigued visiting kings and queens, presidents and industrial barons. Its lightness was deemed an aid to digestion. Queen Victoria of England used to order cases of the water sent directly to Buckingham Palace. Export boxes were stenciled "Que.Vic." for her name, and soon the source became known as the Quevic Spring, or the Vichy Spring, after its famous counterpart in France. Today, it's called the "Saratoga Water Company."

Mineral waters have flowed beneath the bottling plant for a series of owners for 130 years, but somewhere along the way the bottling plant acquired a ghost or two. In January 1990 John started working in the downstairs storage room. "At first my work was simple—loading empty glass bottle cases from a conveyor belt in the basement. At the end of the first workday my supervisor instructed me to sweep up. The other workers ended their shift and went upstairs, so I was surprised to spot another man wearing a grey uniform at the end of the bottling machine. I hollered out, 'Hey, Buddy, how are you?' But he just turned without answering, and disappeared behind the machine. I started sweeping in his direction, figuring he hadn't heard me. But when I got to the end of the machine, I found myself staring into a blind corner. Nobody was there, and there was no place to hide!"

A month later, John and Mark were working about fifteen feet opposite one another, and moving bottle cases from one spot to another near the old boiler room. Suddenly they saw a man walk through the cellar wall, pass between them, then walk through a concrete support pillar, and out through the opposite wall, into the parking lot. Mark was excited by the ghost, and took off upstairs like a shot. "I thought to myself, it's snowing outside and Mark is going to see if the ghost left footprints in the parking lot. Boy, was I naive! Mark wasn't interested in snow or footprints—he was on his way to Timbucktoo! I wasn't as scared, and was more curious, so I went upstairs and looked into the parking lot. There were no footprints. I found Mark and demanded that he return downstairs and help me finish the cleaning, but he did so only reluctantly."

Mike, the former plant manager, used to come to work at 4 a.m. "It was always dark then. I'd come in the front door, and walk toward the office, passing a stairway down to the production floor on my left. It was still dark downstairs, but every morning I'd hear voices from below. Nevertheless, I never wanted to know who or what it was, and I never went to investigate!"

Ernie, a thirty-year employee also encountered a ghost. John's experiences had come in the cellar of the old 1870s building, but Ernie's were more difficult to explain—they occurred in a newer facility on the building's western side. A forklift operator, he moved his tractor quickly and skillfully, even with a half-ton crate of bottles on his fork. "One day I was moving along pretty fast and, suddenly this guy was standing right in front of me, waving his arms and hands! I couldn't stop. I knew I killed him. But, I didn't feel any impact. I thought maybe I'd gone into shock and hadn't felt the machine hit him. Slowly I backed my forklift, waiting for bloody arms or legs to appear from under the contraption. I backed and backed, maybe fifteen or twenty feet. No blood, no body! I got off and looked underneath—there was just nobody! But I *knew* I had seen and hit him. Who was he? Why was he waving his arms? Was he trying to warn me about something? And where did he go?" Two months later Ernie retired.

Were Ernie's "dead man" and John's mystery workman the same ghost? We may never know. It might make sense to sight a ghost in the 130 year-old section of the factory, but where could a ghost come from in the newer building? No workers had ever died, or even been injured in that part of the plant. Ghosts are as independent as the rest of us humans it seems, and apparently operate by their own set of rules and logic.

As mineral waters continue to bubble from deep under the earth along Geyser Road, something else bubbles from a world unseen also. If the spirit of Queen Victoria were ever to return to earth and visit this favorite spring, she'd likely reiterate her famous statement, "We are not amused."

A Pinch of Salt?

Parke S. Avery had a sizeable interest in the salt production around the natural saline wells of Syracuse, NY, and his business grew prosperous. In 1853, he built a brick Italian style villa on Park Street, on a lot from which a cemetery had been removed in 1829. He had plenty of years to enjoy it, but one day in 1898, he leaned too far out an upstairs window, and fell to his death. In 1952, Harold Avery, the last male in the Avery family line, fell to his death on a stairway inside the house. Neighbors speculated about an invisible fatal force that might push Avery men to their death. The old mansion sat vacant for almost thirty years after Harold's death. Perhaps the graves should better have been left in peace.

In 1982 the Preservation Association of Central New York (PACNY) purchased the home as an office and museum, and began its restoration. Staff members and volunteers soon reported strange happenings in the house. Although the second floor was carpeted, they often heard heavy footsteps walking on the upstairs wooden floor.

Elaine became a guide there in the mid-1980s and enjoyed describing the lifestyle of a "Salt Baron" family. Staff members firmly believed that there was a ghost and, at that time, referred to him as "Edmond." One day a visiting family of Averys, unrelated to Parke Avery, heard Elaine mention Edmond, and thought it would be wonderful if she would ask him to appear. As Elaine answered that ghosts don't often appear on demand, everyone heard three loud thumps echo from the unoccupied second floor! She humorously took the credit.

In the early 1980s other volunteers had researched the house's history, discovering the lot's former use as a cemetery. They realized that all bodies or body parts may not have been unearthed, and invited a local psychic to do a reading. The seer felt the heavy walker was the lover of an Avery daughter, still distraught over her death from influenza, and still seeking her in the house. He identified himself to the psychic as a Syracuse brass band musician, still pining for his lost love. Thankfully, he parks his tuba elsewhere in the spirit world when he appears.

Another discarnate visitor may be a former Syracuse mortician, still angry at losing the lucrative contract for an Avery family funeral that he'd been promised. Elaine, who developed psychic ability, believed she often heard the entity saying, "Pay me, Pay me!" His ghost explained to her that he'd done much preparation for said funeral, and was never paid for his expenses and labor.

On one occasion, as the PACNY director and his assistant worked in the downstairs front office, they were distracted by a pair of trousers (nothing more) traipsing up the front sidewalk. Suddenly, papers flew all over the office, and the chair was pulled from under the director. Elaine told them of her theory regarding the angry funeral director. "I went out and placed a token payment of a penny on the front sidewalk. Then the three of us went inside, watched and waited. Nothing happened, but when we went out again to check, the penny was gone," Elaine insisted.

Perhaps, by that gesture, one ghost was appeased, and may have left the premises. However, others seem to remain, waiting to enliven the experience of those who next buy the house, now that PACNY has moved on to a new building.

There is one bit of "ghost lore" that I've learned that many help future owners. Many old timers sprinkled salt throughout a haunted house, to keep its spirits from being troubling. Ghosts, supposedly disturbed by scattered salt, must spend the entire day or night picking it up, and thus have no time to haunt. As the Parke S. Avery House is the haunt (so to speak) of an old Salt Baron, it's surprising that no one has ever tried it there. Just a pinch of salt, *please*!

The Dead and Dyeing

Derrick Sutherland transferred to a new job in Gloversville, NY, from Rhode Island, where he'd worked in the textile lamination business. His new textile managerial job with The Lee Dyeing Company placed him in several buildings, among them the old H.S. Schotwell Company on South Main Street in Gloversville. He applied himself earnestly, learning new regulations and techniques, often working until ten or eleven o'clock at night. "I really didn't know what the old rundown building had been used for before. I hadn't heard any stories from the Schotwell times and was intent on the demands of my new job," he said.

One autumn evening in 1986, at about 10 p.m., Derrick took the old elevator to the second floor, which company records called a storage area. The elevator had no lights and creaked its way upward in darkness. When it stopped, he slid the door open and was taken aback. In the gloom, there appeared a dozen workers busy with machines he didn't recognize. From time to time, they'd take large pieces of material and affix them to hooks hanging from the ceiling. Nobody noticed him. A woman worker walked his way, looking straight at, or through, him. Derrick waited for her to speak, but she didn't, turning to his right and disappearing. What were they doing? Nobody had told him of a second-floor work force. They all seemed surrounded in fog or mist, and were dressed in black and white or gray colors. Tired and amazed, he rubbed his eyes.

When Derrick looked again, nobody was there. All that was visible in the dim window light was fabric bales and packing crates—stuff that was supposed to be there. Everything was covered with dust, and there were no workers. Recognizing that he was tired, he went downstairs, finished his work and went home.

A few months later Derrick met and talked with Tom, a former maintenance man, who had worked in the Schotwell tannery years before. Derrick asked Tom the purpose of the upstairs ceiling hooks, and Tom was surprised. "There are no hooks in the ceiling now, but there used to be when I worked up there a dozen years ago. They used to hang hides and skins up there when this was a leather company. The hooks were all removed when Schotwell sold out, how did *you* know about them? That building was vacant from 1975-1986." Derrick told Tom about his vision of the workers and the machines. Tom didn't laugh, but instead became quiet—thinking.

Over the next ten years, Derrick noted that various employees resisted going up to the second floor. Some seemed scared, and wouldn't talk about the issue. "It only happened once to me," said Derrick, "but I wonder if other guys have seen something, too. How else can you explain their hesitation to go up to a storage area?"

Old timers described the building as "the rebel plant," and note that Lee Dyeing has stopped production there, expecting to tear it down in 2002. I dropped by the plant and found one employee still there. Robert Pitcavage is the inventory clerk who spends most of the day alone in the old buildings. "So, Derek experienced that?" he asked thoughtfully. "Well, I don't doubt it. Many times I *hear* people coming downstairs from the second floor. Even though I know nobody has come in, I go out and check each time. But nobody is ever there.

"Come and look at this old ramp," he invited me. "This is an old dock plate that we've moved to the foot of the ramp to make moving things easier. Several times a week I'll hear it clunk, as if someone or something heavy has just pressed it down. I jump up to look, but the building is quiet and nobody is in sight. There sure is something left over from the old days here, though it doesn't scare me. I laugh and yell at whoever it is—'quiet down out there!' But there's never any answer."

Gloversville is an old industrial city whose prosperous time seems to have come and gone. Many old leather and glove factories in Fulton County have closed in recent decades. But in one old mill, on certain nights and for certain people, the hustle and bustle of the good old days may all come alive again. The idea of returning to full employment and huge leather industry payrolls at the old mills, I think, would be enough to gladden the hearts of Gloversville's city fathers.

Split Rock

"I did a lot of biking in those days," said Tim Zorn, "and I remember a strange night in April, 1980. I was pedaling east from Auburn, more or less following Route 5, just west of Syracuse, NY. I took what looked like a shortcut through farm country. The sun had just about set, so I pulled off for the night to the side of an embankment, unrolled my sleeping bag, munched on some snacks and dozed off. It was pretty chilly, and I awoke in the night very uncomfortable, as if something invisible was going on around me. I stood up out of my sleeping bag and crawled to the top of the bank. Balls of fluorescent green light were bouncing around on a hillside back in a rock quarry that I hadn't noticed in daylight. If I didn't know better, I'd have thought the lights were alive. I watched this for ten or fifteen minutes, then figured maybe it was the Northern Lights or something like that, and went back to sleep. Next morning I rode into Syracuse and mentioned the whole experience to a man in a diner. 'Boy, you were at The Rock,' he said. 'Lots of bad stuff happened there a long time ago. Those were all ghosts!'"

Tim prefaced his experience with, "for what it's worth," when he related it to me. It seemed incredible, but I confirmed what Tim had been told when I searched the files at the Onondaga County Library in Syracuse a few years later.

On April 2, 1918, during the First World War, there was a great disaster in Split Rock, just southwest of Syracuse. Semet-Solvay, a chemical manufacturing company, was mining and processing ore in the hamlet's old Solvay Process Co. rock quarry. The mineral ingredients were used to make picric acid, a bitter, toxic, yellow crystal used in TNT. Semet-Solvay stood to make large profits from TNT sales to the Allies. A huge order from Russia in early 1917 had caused the company to begin round-the-clock operations—three shifts a day.

The great explosion occurred about 9:30 p.m., when an overheated gear in a grinding machine caused a fire that spread rapidly, leading to the explosion of over a ton of toluel, which rained down rock, acid and steel shards on almost eight-hundred night shift workers. When the mayhem was over, fifty men were dead and one-hundred were injured. Fifteen unidentified corpses and many body parts were buried in a mass grave in Morningside Cemetery. The only consolation was that the four-hundred tons of TNT didn't also explode! Because of the war urgency, the company went back into operation the next day, permitting little time for grief or remembrance.

In the summer of 1980 the Syracuse *Post-Standard* printed an article about then-current, strange events in Split Rock. The article noted that much of the old excavation had since been converted into a State Department of Transportation site. A Syracuse psychic's experiences with a deaf man, who complained of "hearing screaming" when he drove past that location, was also mentioned. The psychic brought other clairvoyants, who observed about thirteen greenish-yellow images along the ledges of the old quarry. Later research showed that picric acid turned clothing yellow and green, and pockmarked skin! Evidently, they saw the same "fluorescent green" that Tim had seen a few months earlier.

During the 1980s another Syracuse psychic and her friend saw figures that just stood, glowing, at the explosion site. Some were seen to hold greenish-yellow lanterns. 1918 newspaper articles describing the tragedy tell of the quarry lights going out just before the explosion, thus it is likely that some workers carried lit lanterns to their death. In the psychic's visits to the old quarry, several wraiths were said to have stepped forward and answered her questions.

Accidental explosions during World War I also took lives in Halifax, Nova Scotia and Eddystone, Pennsylvania. Many books are available detailing the numbers of ordinary people throughout the U.S. and Europe who had dreams or premonitions of screaming or drowning people prior to the sinking of The Titanic. There are also records of people who heard far-away screams or names shouted from "somewhere," that were later revealed to be Titanic drowning victims. Wherever there is great tragedy one can expect to find spirits confused by their body's sudden death. Not realizing they have died, they need compassion and assistance from those who can penetrate their in-between world.

Journal Ghosts

R.J. Humphrey came to Poultney, VT from Wales in the late 1800s and purchased the old weekly *Northern Spectator*, where Horace Greeley had begun his newspaperman's trade in the mid-1800s. Humphrey renamed it the *Poultney Journal*, and in 1908, moved his new business to a fashionable building block at 1 Depot Street. At various times, the cavernous three-story structure has also housed a bowling alley, pool hall, post office, barbershop, and dance hall. Today, the building houses the Journal Press, a pharmacy and an antique shop. Journal Press no longer puts out a weekly, but is a state-of-the art printing business, employing a most open-hearted staff. "We know what we've experienced here," one man told me, "and we're not afraid to share it."

Most employees were on morning coffee break when I visited. None have actually seen the spirits, but most have felt their mischief. In most cases, phenomena are experienced by employees working alone, when it is quieter. Most have sensed a presence behind them when they work. A darkroom employee always leaves her door open just a crack, believing the ghost can't trouble her if there is ventilation in the room. The dim light doesn't hurt her work, and allows her to see any other person when she's alone. So far, she hasn't seen anyone, but knows *they* are there.

One woman, a manager, working alone in the building at night, heard the knob on the hallway door behind her rattle. She spun around and opened the door. No one was there. She returned to work, and a few minutes later, the same thing happened. Finding nobody in the hall a second time gave her goose bumps, and she decided to go home at that point. On other occasions, when working alone at night, she has heard footsteps upstairs. She knows nobody is there, so finishes work quickly and heads home!

Others, also working alone at night, have reported footsteps prowling the second and third floors, though nobody could enter without a key. Another woman, alone in the main office, one night felt a hand on her arm. Turning, she saw nobody. She intuitively believes the ghost enters by the old post office mailbag chute, now closed by a trap door, though she's never seen it move.

A man working in an office created in the old third floor bowling alley often feels a chill, which makes the hair on his arms prickle, despite the heat of huge cast-iron radiators. He showed me names carved or written on the bowling alley's walls long ago: "J. Lyman, 1913," "FF & BP," "Mike W.," "April 5, 1943," "Liz & Rich 1942," "R. Jones, Poultney, April 1943." He is sure that one unseen presence is a male with a sense of humor. "It's as if the old bowlers or pool hall customers are still here, watching us work," he said. "Once, I wore a new pair of shoes to work. They hurt my feet, so I took them off. In just a few minutes they disappeared, and I didn't find them until a month later—in a freezer on the second floor!"

A woman worker on the third floor often complains when the radiator in her office is shut off on cold days. After the mechanic went through the effort of turning it on with a wrench, he pocketed the on/off valve handle to prevent tampering. It makes little difference to the ghost, however, who always turns the radiator off at night. Both she and the mechanic scratch their heads over such mischief.

Another woman working on third floor thinks the spirits are young men whose idea of heaven was "hanging out" in the pool hall. "They haven't gone very far since *they* died," she smiled.

A pressman in the basement, when asked who the culprit might be, suggested Louie Humphrey, the inebriated brother of a former owner, who plummeted down the elevator shaft and died during the 1920s.

Chuck Colvin, the present owner, admits to no strange experiences, but acknowledges those of his workers. He, likewise, is puzzled. A man working on the second floor often uses a layout ruler. He explained that there are only two such rulers in the building, but one or the other of them is always missing. He summed up the workers' frustrations, when he told me, "We have things disappearing from time to time, and the ghost seems to enjoy toying with us. Whoever it is, however, he never does our work for us!"

19
Ghosts
On the
Move

Eerie Canal

Henry J. Dornbos, a wealthy Michigan businessman, loaned his name to the steel-hulled fishing boat when her keel was laid in 1901. In addition to bringing in catches of sturgeon and bass, the Dornbos also took part in U.S. Life Saving Service rescues of imperiled sailors on the Great Lakes. In 1922 New York State bought the boat, renamed her "Urger," and put her into service on the Barge Canal. She was retired in 1986 and became a floating school for the State's school children. In summers she plies the canal, moving from town to town, offering exhibits and on-board experiences, helping youngsters learn the history of the Empire State's canals.

In a hundred years, a boat acquires what one crewmember called "little ghosts." Gerry, "Urger's" engineer has trouble finding his vise-grip pliers, which are needed to make minor adjustments on the boat's equipment, but they often disappear for days at a time. He always puts them in the top tray of his tool box, but like as not, when he really needs them, they're gone. After an appropriate absence, however, they always return to the toolbox. "Now there's only so much space on this boat," he said, "but you can search it from stem to stern and you don't get them back until the ghost is ready."

"You think he's got problems," the cook said, "my spaghetti strainer keeps disappearing! We've got to eat when we travel the canal, and a strainer is much bigger than his pliers are, but I simply cannot find it at times. I'll have the strainer ready on the counter in the galley, and be boiling up some pasta, but when I'm ready to put the pasta in, it's just gone."

Those who live with very scary ghosts would laugh *at these* predicaments. These good-natured teachers suspect their unseen crewmember is an old time "canawler" who enjoyed "locking through" so much, he just isn't ready to retire. And that can create problems for those who have to work alongside him.

Barging In

Not far from the famed House of Seven Gables in Salem, MA, is Hawthorne's Cove Marina. It stands in the old Miller's Wharf area of the waterfront, and has had ghosts in one of its buildings for over a hundred years. Local historian Bob Cahill heard about the house from a friend, who hoped to incorporate the old building in his new restaurant. He told Bob that *something* upstairs scared him. Cahill, well known for his interest in Massachusetts' ghosts, visited the old building. He found the downstairs of the old summerhouse was as ordinary and quiet as his own home, but when he climbed the stairs he walked into a sudden chill. "Get out of here!" a hollow voice commanded. A quick visual inspection of the room turned up nobody.

"At first I thought I'd imagined it. But when it happened even louder a second time, that was enough for me, and I left rapidly, not wanting to tangle with such a grumpy ghost," said Bob.

Bob loves puzzles and set about researching the old house's history. He found that the second story was not part of the original house, but was an old barge that had been lifted onto the single story in the early 1900s. Then he uncovered more gruesome facts.

In 1911 a tugboat and barge set out from New York to Boston. Somewhere in mid-passage, for whatever reason, a crewman hacked the captain to death with a hatchet. When the vessels reached port, the crewman was arrested and tried for murder. The tugboat and barge were impounded as evidence. After the guilty verdict, legal hassles ensued. The captain's property, the cargo and the tugboat were all sold at auction. The old barge was thought un-seaworthy, and sat unused on the shore for years. Then a neighbor, impressed by the strength of its timbers, bought the hulk as a second floor to his house. But he also bought its ghostly presence.

Bob learned that there was a long history of phenomena at the house after the second floor was installed. Over the years, onlookers reported seeing lights moving across the roof at night. From time to time, neighbors observed a man on the porch while the owner was away. A surveyor who lived nearby once heard a shout and saw the specter on the porch, waving frantically. When he went to investigate, nobody was there and the house was locked tight. Was it the murdered captain? Or was it the murderer? Now here was a mystery!

Long after the culmination of trials and executions, and long after trial transcripts are filed away in dusty archives, the crimes that people commit reverberate throughout time, and into soul memory. Sometimes they produce ghosts such as this one, which enliven American folklore. Ghosts are not docile pets. All of them are desperately driven by desires and motives that few lay people can apprehend. Only trained experts, who are spiritually armored enough to navigate the oceans of the spirit world, possess the thorough understanding of the energies behind malevolent ghosts or spirits. People troubled with such entities should seek professional spiritual specialists to evict them.

The Tunnel

In the northern Berkshires outside North Adams, MA, a five mile-long railroad tunnel, built 150 years ago, is still a vital east-west link for Conrail. An engineering triumph in its time, it permitted direct rail commerce between Boston and Troy, NY. But its construction required a high price in both money and life, and when it was finished in 1875, it had earned the name, "The Bloody Pit." *True Magazine* once labled it "The Tunnel from Hell."

The first of many disasters there took place on the cold afternoon of March 20, 1865. Billy Nash, Ned Brinkman and Ringo Kelly, explosive experts, were preparing a relatively new explosive substance, nitroglycerine. Black powder was considered more dependable and stable than "nitro," but they hoped the new explosive would yield faster excavation results. After placing the explosive in the rock face, Brinkman and Nash moved toward shelter behind a huge timber bulkhead. Kelly seized the electric detonator, hollered "Ready!" and then something happened. The entire cavern convulsed in a great explosion. Nash and Brinkman were blown to smithereens. Miraculously, Kelly escaped with his life, but only to face a hearing on the disaster. After testifying, he disappeared from Berkshire County. Exactly a year later, when the day shift entered the tunnel, they found Ringo Kelly's corpse, strangled, at the explosion site.

The sheriff was unable to solve the crime, as all the laborers professed ignorance. Some began mumbling about the ghosts of Nash and Brinkman returning to settle accounts with Kelly. After Kelly's death strange things began to occur inside the mountain.

In 1863 engineers had decided to sink a shaft from the mountain top down to a point where the tunnel's center would be, thus allowing miners to begin blasting toward both east and west. The Central Shaft would provide ventilation and access to the tunnel's center in the future. However, as it was being drilled in 1873, the Central Shaft was rocked by a gigantic explosive blast that entombed 13 laborers under tons of stone. Rubble had to be excavated, the mangled bodies had to be located, then lifted out before excavation could resume. Then came winter and the snow! The gruesome task of mining for corpses attracted spectators from North Adams and Clarksville. Many of the area's reputable citizens told bizarre tales of seeing ghostly crews marching to the pit in the snow, carrying picks and shovels, but leaving no footprints. At night, some reported muffled cries and groans emanating from the Central Shaft. All the morbid activity ceased at the Central Shaft when 13th body was exhumed. Not within the western and eastern portals, however.

In September 1868 engineer Paul Travers reported hearing the groans of a man in pain when he and Dr. Clifford, from Michigan, ventured two miles into the tunnel from the Western Portal. Dr. Clifford told of seeing "a light coming along the tunnel from the westerly direction. At first I thought it was a workman with a lantern, yet as it drew closer it took on a strange blue color and took on the shape of a human being without a head. It paused, as if it was inspecting us, then vanished easterly into thin air."

Similarly, another worker encountered the ghost of a headless man near the same spot. A local hunter, Frank Webster, once disappeared in the steep hills around North Adams while out hunting. Three days later a search party found him walking in a daze by the Deerfield River. He mumbled about having heard voices in the Hoosac Tunnel and, upon entering, was "knocked out" by an unseen presence. These are stories from another time, and today's skeptic might attempt to dismiss them. However, few modern theorists know the essential honesty that characterized the miner's life. And the skeptic must still contend with the reports of phantasms lurking within the mountain today.

In 1974 a railroad maintenance worker made his way westward in the tunnel. About one and one-half miles inside the Western Portal he noticed a lantern light and two people approaching. Nothing unusual—once or twice a week he'd meet kids or other trespassers, whom he'd shepherd to the tunnel's entrance ahead.

However, in this case the figures turned by themselves. Again, no problem—it was common for interlopers to retreat when confronted by railroad workers. But, as he exited the tunnel and headed for his parked car one hundred yards ahead, the trespassers were nowhere in sight. The eastern portal exits into a long narrow defile which cannot be climbed out of. They would have had to walk along the railroad tracks, but there were no footprints in the fresh snow.

Most Conrail workers, who maintain the Boston & Maine tracks through the Hoosac Tunnel, do not believe in ghosts, but the maintenance man said earnestly,

"I *know* I saw a light, and I know I saw backlit human shapes when the light changed directions. But, who it was, and where they went, I truly don't know," he told North Adams' *Transcript* reporter Gillian Jones. Nevertheless, as phantoms are still reported within the five mile tunnel, one would suspect Conrail workers speed up their pace as they check the track for safety in the tunnel. And probably "whistle a happy tune" at the same time!

Amateur ghost chasers would be wise to leave this site to Conrail. The property is posted. In the dark it is easy to misjudge distances, and it is a perilously long run to safety when accosted by locomotives, drifters, wild animals or specters from another time.

Tug Hill Annie

The June night in 1958 was warm when Anna and Johnny decided to drive to Barnes Corners for a jug of wine. He was pushing the old pickup truck over the speed limit when he came to the sharp bend near Sears Pond. He took it on two wheels, the passenger door flew open, and Anna was thrown into the night. Johnny brought the truck under control, screeching to a stop. Grabbing his flashlight, he retraced his erratic route. After a brief search he saw her legs protruding from beneath a tree. He knew she was dead. Without touching the body, he ran to a nearby house and called the sheriff.

The black 1958 Ford arrived quickly, its red beacon flashing as black on the green trees. The deputy took a look, then got on his radio and called the funeral home in Lowville, NY. When the coroner arrived and pronounced her dead, they draped the body and loaded it into the hearse. But there was a problem—the body was missing its head! More searching was necessary before the head was located, underneath another tree, where it had rolled after being severed. The deputy took a report, the hearse drove off, Anna's family was notified, and the funeral was held three days later in Lowville Rural Cemetery.

That should have been the end of it, but within months, drivers told of seeing a headless woman walking along Route 177 on Tug Hill. Some thought she was hitchhiking. "Tug Hill Annie" became part of the local folklore. Carloads of teenagers drove along the road seeking the thrill of a ghost sighting, and adding embellishments to the story. One woman told of driving along the road and seeing a ghostly woman (*with* a head) carrying a birthday cake with lit candles. When she backed up for a closer look, no one was there. Some speculated that "Annie" was looking for a child who died in the crash, but the funeral director contradicted that embellishment.

For a few years the mania to spot "Tug Hill Annie" swirled around Lowville and Montague, then abated when several teens were found to have hoaxed the Watertown newspaper with a fanciful tale. Nevertheless, a snowplow crew, in the winter of 1962, believed they had hit a woman pedestrian with the wing plow, though they found no body after thoroughly checking the embankment. And a school bus driver concluded his nighttime run, sure he'd seen Annie walking toward Adams Center.

Mary, a Lowville nurse, driving to the Lowville Library with a companion one night in the 1980s, spotted a woman dressed in black and white walking downhill on route 177. Mary slowed to ask if the woman wanted a ride. But, as they came abreast, Mary suddenly accelerated and didn't slow down until she parked at the library.

"Did you see that woman?" she asked her passenger.

"Yes—you could see right *through* her!" was the companion's breathless reply.

Another night they saw her again in the same place. "She had no color, and was dressed in black and white, like some Puritan," said Mary. "She looked at us and gave a strange smile, but I felt she wasn't physically all there. I didn't stop that time either!

"My friend and I talked about the incident for quite a while. Near that spot was a fallen-down old house. An old woman had lived in that house years ago. She used to tell people that she was afraid to go upstairs. She claimed to hear fiddling and people talking up there, and lived out her life on the first floor." Mary thinks that spot north of Lowville has a ghost of its own, whether or not it's Annie.

Was it Annie's ghost walking into town? Was it some itinerant person who has never been spotted since then? The mystery remains. All sightings of single women walking along area roads are added to the "Tug Hill Annie" legend. If you're riding Route 177 at night, look carefully at any hitchhiking woman—be sure you can see *all* of her before you offer her a ride.

20

Forest
And
Mountain
Ghosts

Breaking a Habit

Old Matthew lived in the desolate farm country north of Lowville, NY, in the late 1800s. An amiable man, he got along well with family and neighbors. He only had one shortcoming. He loved to "turn the cards" with his friends, though, on occasion, this hobby depleted his family's budget when he lost at Poker. To him card-playing for money was recreation; unfortunately it was his entire social life. Maggie, his wife, didn't see his obsession in quite that way. She considered herself the mainstay and moral presence of the family, and she determined to break his "sinful habit."

Harold Sammons, in his book, *The Other Side of the Hill*, quotes Maggie as saying, "I'm going to break you of your sinful gambling if it's the *last* thing I ever do." The statement was truer than she guessed. Her rigid demeanor may have predisposed her to a blood clot, which killed her one day. Old Matthew stood at her grave with mixed emotions. He missed his mate, but not her nagging. He missed a companion, but realized that he was now free to play poker—all the time! In the Tug Hill country, south of Watertown, winters are long, and people didn't often travel far in the deep snow. In those days, hardy farmers worked their wood lots, sugar bush and stony fields, often alone. Matthew believed he had found a good reason for the rural folk (the men, anyway) to congregate. He converted his residence into a gambling den—a place where you could lose your entire harvest bankroll if you weren't careful. For almost a month Matthew gathered his "house percentage" of the Blackjack, Poker and Pinochle stakes. "This is going to be really good," he told himself, "better than tilling my stony fields!"

Then, as if Providence silently threw a switch, his fortune changed. One by one his "regulars" began to offer excuses. "Maybe next week, Matt, gotta do a chore for the missus." One would say. Another begged off with, "See you next time!" Attendance and revenues fell to almost nothing. What had gone wrong? Separately, he asked them what he could do differently. Only old Joe Jackson, after studying Matt's anguished countenance for a long time, ventured a response. He confided that, on leaving Matt's house one night, a luminous Maggie had appeared on his path near the swamp. "That lady could talk an ear off a mule!" he said. Matt nodded, remembering his deceased partner. "She told me how the fires of Hell would incinerate a gambler. She said how it was contrary to God's Own Word for a man to descend into such a lifestyle, and how I'd suffer for it on the other side. Gee, Matthew, I recognized her as a ghost, but she seemed *alive*! And I get enough sass from *my* old woman, that I don't need *that* every Card Night. I'm not coming back because I know Maggie will be waiting for me," he vowed.

Matthew lost his old gambling cronies one by one. Circumstances forced him into spring planting and keeping up his small farm again in order to make ends meet. He realized he'd never have another friend, and never have another visitor until Maggie abandoned her "pulpit."

He gave up card playing. Some of the old timers say he became a regular at the little church, where he sang a pretty good baritone in the choir. And Maggie must have finally found peace, as she was never seen again.

Reverend Bull

There is a rustic old camp near the Blue Mountain Lake Museum in the Adirondacks. In 1980 it was available for rent when Bill's family needed a getaway, and they made a reservation. The strange events began the day they arrived. Throughout the night, they heard a man coughing. Bill knew it wasn't him, and his son, Joe, was still too young to muster such a deep sound. The deep coughing, whose source they could never find, continued throughout their two-week stay. Even more disturbing was what they called "the heart bed," a large double bed that emitted the sound of a beating heart all night. Whoever tried to sleep in it did so only fitfully.

After a few days they packed up their laundry, closed the windows, locked the door, turned off the lights in the cabin, and went to a nearby laundromat. When they returned they found the door unlocked and all the lights on. Bill's daughter, Laurie, mentioned the strange events to neighbor children. They scolded, "Didn't you know that old place is haunted? It's the ghost of old Reverend Bull, the man who'd built the camp in 1900. Everybody knows that!"

They had brought Ruby, their dog, with them, and she had a terrible time during their "relaxing vacation." She would not enter one specific room in the cabin voluntarily. When the family had to leave and do laundry, they locked Ruby in that room. Upon their return, Ruby greeted them happily in the kitchen. She had gnawed an escape hole through the room's soft pine door, rather than stay in that room. Why was she afraid?

During cool weather one day, they built a fire in the wood stove. After a while, Laurie, who was reading, called out in fright to her father.

"What's wrong?" he yelled from the other room.

There was a pause, then she replied "Oh, never mind, the stove's door handle turned and it opened. But it just closed, so, it's okay."

A rainy day provided time to fully explore the old cabin. An upstairs closet door was so warped that they could never close it tightly. Laurie's twin, Linda, pushed it open, went into the closet and started climbing the ladder to the attic. However, as she put her foot on the ladder, she heard the closet door suddenly bang tightly shut behind her and lock itself. Unable to push it open, she called her other sister, Carol, for help, scolding her for being mean. Carol denied the mischief, but was unable to open the door, and went to fetch their father. She'd taken only a few steps, when the door suddenly clicked open. Doors that opened and closed themselves, along with the nightly coughing, were the most common nagging problems.

Bill told me, "We had a hot spell one night, and I went to bed before my wife. I stripped, flopped down, and covered myself with a sheet, leaving only my feet outside. When my wife came to bed she was amazed, seeing several blankets over me, as if I was freezing! I partially awoke when she lay down and mentioned the blankets. Then, as I drifted back asleep, she said out loud, 'Must be Ruby.'

"Oh, never mind, the stove's door handle turned and it opened. But it just closed, so, it's okay."

"'What do you mean?' I asked, struggling to wake up."

"Bill, can't you feel her under the bed?"

"And I could. It seemed like Ruby was under our bed, moving from one side to the other.

"At the foot of our bed was a pass-through closet into the stove room. Suddenly, I heard the closet door open, and something rustled through the plastic bags on the closet floor, followed by a noise near the stove. Then Ruby, who had been sleeping on the floor *beside* our bed, yawned. I realized that whatever was under the bed, it wasn't her. Then my wife sleepily joked, 'Must be that ghost that the kids are talking about.' She went to sleep, but I lay there wondering the rest of the night. In those long hours before daybreak, I ran out of alternative explanations for what had occurred, and became a believer in ghosts," Bill admitted.

The next day Bill's wife told Betsy, an employee at the nearby museum, about their adventures in Reverend Bull's cabin.

"Oh, I see you've met 'ghostie'," Betsy smiled, encouraging her to visit the local historian. The historian told them old Reverend Bull had tuberculosis, and died in the hospital. After the funeral, his ashes were put into Blue Mountain Lake.

A few years later Bill gave an Adirondack folklore lecture in town and told this story. A man in the audience identified himself as a scuba diver. He told Bill that he'd found such a cremation urn in the lake a few years before, but had left it there.

"That cabin was about as rustic as *I* wanted to get," Bill said. "Next year, we found a different vacation spot!"

Abigail

The family watched the storm over Hogsback Mountain to the west for almost an hour that August afternoon in 1811. It was ominous, and soon became apparent that this was to be a downpour. Abigail West rushed to get her washing off the clothesline at her home on Traver Flats, a fertile farming area on the side of West Mountain, west of Glens Falls, NY. As she neared the end of her frantic task, lightning struck, but she didn't hear it. Abigail was killed instantly. Two days later, she was buried in a small burial plot off Butler Pond Road.

Abigail's spirit apparently has never left the mountainside. Hunters in the vicinity during the late 1800s sometimes told of meeting a woman in the forest when deer hunting, and several noticed that she wore a pale blue dress. Old timers mentioned "strange wailing sounds" that echoed in the forest, especially in August, and often during storms. Abigail was soon blamed for otherwise unexplainable neighborhood events. A sewing machine nearby often turned itself on. Doors in neighboring houses slammed, untouched by wind or human hands. A local college professor reported an eerie scream in the woods near his house.

In the early 1970s, WWSC-AM sent a sound crew to West Mountain to see if anything ghostly could be recorded for Bob Jennings' "Freak Week," when programs were devoted to strange phenomena. It was raining when the crew arrived. They sat waiting, sheltered from the downpour in a van, for two hours until they heard and recorded a faint scream in the woods behind the West Cemetery. Jennings played it for his midnight audience. Some believed it was Abigail. What hoaxer, *not* knowing that Jennings' crew was coming to record there, would have been hiding in those rainy woods?

A group of investigators from Parapsychology Study and Investigations (PSI), a former Saratoga Springs parapsychology group, investigated the stories in the early 1970s. The group leader saw a "gauzy light moving around" on the gravestones. One of the group's photographers found his camera inoperative within the boundaries of the West Cemetery. The camera worked fine in his car at roadside, but not in the vicinity of Abigail's grave.

When these events occurred, Abigail's gravestone was no longer there. Vandals had stolen her marker for a number of years, though it was later recovered. The West family placed her marker in another Glens Falls cemetery, though Abigail's body remains on West Mountain. Young people are often seen on the mountain road, hoping to sight her ghost. They don't understand that West Mountain folks, fearful of desecration, have become more protective of Abigail's resting-place. Today her grave lies invisible amid leaves and brush. Legends die hard and the "stories" continue.

George Stec, retired forest ranger, has a home not far away from the West Cemetery. He believes the "screams" are foxes barking, or perhaps a bobcat shrieking. "But there *are* things I just can't account for," he said. "In the fall we used to smell a strong perfume in the area of the old West farm. It went on for several years. It might not have been Abigail, but as a forest professional, I'm at a loss to otherwise explain it."

Thelma Nestle, another resident of the area, recently went for an evening walk along local roads with her husband, Ralph. They turned for home as dusk approached. "As we walked, I said to Ralph, 'Look, there's somebody swinging a lantern! Let's go investigate,'" said Thelma. "No!" Ralph balked, preferring a comfortable distance to a close encounter with Abigail, the farm wife felled by lightning years ago.

The Indian Princess

Kim worked hard for years to earn the money to build a home in the Town of Queensbury, NY, about three miles from the old West Cemetery. She cleared the land, built the house and began landscaping. A beautiful walkway was essential, she thought. She worked long hours to set each of the patio stones level, a difficulty with the early summer mud. One morning, using pebbles to level one block, she noticed an Indian arrowhead. It was the first artifact she had ever found, and it was on *her* land!

Though the land had been in her family 140 years, she knew nothing about the property's history. She did know that around Clendon Brook, just to the north, pottery, beads and arrowheads had been found. Kim eventually intuited that at least one Indian had been buried on her land. She is sure it is an Indian woman, and dubbed her ghost "The Indian Princess."

As soon as her house was ready, she moved in. So, apparently, did the Princess. "I sat one night on my back deck and was disturbed by what sounded like kitchen pots and pans hitting together," she wrote. Following the sound, she found it came not from the kitchen, but from her bedroom. There, she beheld the brass handles on her dresser rising and falling loudly, but not hard enough to make such a racket. It stopped as she watched. In retrospect, she believed the tapping sounded like someone urgently rapping on her front door. Next, her living room light began to flicker. She checked the bulb and it was tight. She plugged the lamp into another outlet, but it flickered there too, as it did in every outlet in that room. She tried a new lamp in the sockets and it flickered also. When she took the lamps to an adjoining room, the flickering stopped. This time, upon bringing them back into the living room, the flickering ended. She suspected that someone or something was trying to get her attention.

"I heated the house with a basement woodstove at that time, and used to throw wood in through the cellar window, then stack it against the north wall. One evening before I went to bed, I went downstairs to fill the stove for the night. The wood that I'd previously stacked into a pile had now moved. Part of it was laid end to end from the north to the south walls! I immediately called my Dad and asked his opinion about what the heck was going on. Until he came over and saw for himself—he had begun to think I was crazy," Kim smiled. Kim's son was only two and one-half years old at the time "and he could never have managed the steep cellar stairs on his own. Even in the best of times, he had difficulty with them. And he certainly wasn't strong enough to move heavy chunks of wood across the cellar," she recalls.

She believes her unseen visitor eventually took note of her newly planted trees, shrubs and flowers. "She must have recognized that I wasn't there to destroy the land, and so she wanted to play!" But then Kim fell in love and Steve came to live with her. From that point on, the Princess was in their bedroom. "From time to time I'd wake up in the night gasping, like I was being smothered. One night, I felt her at the foot of the bed. I knew if I looked down I'd see her, but didn't do so. I lay there wondering what to do and when this was going to stop. I thought Steve was asleep, but he spoke quietly 'Are you still awake?' Then, after a minute he declared, 'She's here, isn't she?' I answered 'Yes, she sure *is*!'"

Steve sat bolt-upright and said, "Leave us alone. We are your friends and we are not going to hurt you. Please, leave us alone." He reminded her that they were beautifying what had once been her sacred forest. "That did it, we never heard from her again," Kim said.

The neighborhood along Lilac Lane is quiet today. Kim and Steve married and moved to London, England, and the house's new residents live in peace. If, indeed, the presence that made their lives so exciting was an Indian Princess, and if she had been jealous that Kim had found a love that she couldn't share, all seems forgiven today.

Hadley Mountain

"This was the strangest thing that ever happened to me," said Jeff Baker, " and maybe it belongs in a ghost book. I don't know where else you'd tell it." He had just finished reading my first book, *Saratoga County Ghosts*, and was fascinated by the story "Stuck!" which took place in the deep woods in the northern part of the Town of Corinth, NY. The story detailed the efforts of a group of young men to free a stranded jeep from a mud hole. The jeep had taken on a life of its own, moving despite the driver's best efforts to prevent it. I had speculated that a ghost or nature spirit had impelled the action.

Now a resident of Hendersonville, NC, Jeff remembered, "In 1987 I worked at logging a large tract off Tower Road near Hadley Mountain, not too far from the site of the "Stuck!" story. There were about six-hundred acres of forest to cut there. Our job took two years," he recalls. Jeff liked the hard physical labor and was usually the first person on site each morning. "I enjoyed the early morning peace and became used to seeing wild animals and often heard coyotes until we started up our equipment. Then we couldn't hear them any longer."

They dragged the trees out of the woods and cut them into lengths on platforms called "headers" spaced along their logging roads. "At the foot of the mountain, way in back, there was a header that was *different*. I'd sit there in the early morning, waiting for the other loggers, and one day heard the scariest sound I've ever heard. It was not a bobcat, bear, coyote, coydog, or anything else I knew. I also felt it in my soul. It was a moaning or wailing, and *nearby*! The loud animal-like wail continued for a couple of months. I became very cautious back there on that header."

One day, working with his buddy, the two took the "skidder" up the mountain and picked up a "hitch" of wood. The pair then moved downhill, but Jeff saw another small stand that he could cut quickly. Motioning his friend downhill, he cut the trees, "limbed them out," then sat on a stump to catch his breath. He could hear the skidder's engine running far down the mountainside. Above and behind him there came a sudden CRACK! He spun around in time to see a huge live tree falling directly at him. He jumped sideways just in time! The tree crashed onto his chainsaw, flipping it end over end. Before he could recover, he heard the awful moaning sound again. "I spun around but saw nothing. All around me I could feel this presence. I was wondering which tree would fall on me next. And *what* was making that awful sound?

"I don't know how much time passed; I just stood there waiting and watching. Then, I heard the skidder coming back. When my buddy got there he took one look and knew something was really wrong. Then *he* heard the moan, too! It was as if it was in us and around us...we were both so scared! I remember standing guard with his running chain saw while he hooked up the hitch of wood. Then, we headed downhill fast! I've never heard such a sound before or since. It was unearthly, and that was one sound you could hear over the sound of the running equipment.

"I've never gone back to that place, but I'll never forget it. I have no explanation for that experience. My buddy was just as flummoxed as I was. He'd never heard such a sound, either." Safe in North Carolina, Jeff still wonders about his experience. "I'm *still* not sure there's enough distance between us—me and that ghost, or being, or spirit, or monster, or whatever it was or is, but I'll take my chances here," he said with a grin.

AFTERWORD

Though ghosts are not commonly discussed in public or religious education, there has been a gradual increase in people giving credence to their existence. An October 2001 Gallup Poll disclosed that, since 1978, the percentage of Americans acknowledging a belief in ghosts has risen from 11% to 31%. Among 18-29 year-olds the percentage was said to approach 44%, with less dramatic increases among older groups. Even among those 65 or older, the percentage has increased 2% since the initial 1978 poll. Perhaps this is because of the increased availability of books and TV programs devoted to ghosts and the afterlife.

When I wrote *Saratoga County Ghosts* in 1998, I had the limited goal of sharing some "neat tales" with readers. The goal hasn't remained that simple, however. During my lectures on the supernatural and in talk radio interviews, I've observed a hunger among all ages for a deeper assurance that life goes on after the body dies. This is clearly evident in the questions I get. Traditional religious answers no longer satisfy younger generations. Questioners expect me to explain why and how ghosts manifest and, in an attempt to provide answers, I, myself, have been drawn more deeply into study and research. Many of my newly acquired insights are in this book. My wife and I have sought help from trusted intuitives and sensitives to expand our understanding as we've investigated haunted sites throughout North America.

It is as if the western world passed through an initiation ceremony on September 11, 2001. Since then, disbelievers seem increasingly willing to listen to ghost stories or near-death experiences, as those that are non-sensationally told seem to excite some part of the spiritual imagination.

"Maybe, just maybe, there is something here that *does* promise that my consciousness and all I've been able to learn, will survive," said Robert A. Wentorf, a GE scientist and former skeptic. He worked many years in GE's Research and Development Labs, and had just become interested in spirituality as he neared retirement. His expertise was in hard science, and in early adulthood he didn't pay much attention to the spiritual realm. When he read Thomas Sugrue's biography of Edgar Cayce, *There Is A River*, however, he was stunned by intellectual connections that hadn't occurred to him before. Reading voraciously, he became a student of Cayce's work and assiduously studied and practiced the principles found in *A Course in Miracles*. After all those years in agnostic, theoretical science, finding so much of life's importance in spiritual matters, he became a meditator and a Quaker, filling a lifelong *void* before his death.

When life's crises become too great, many others also seek comfort and understanding in fields they previously spurned. The attacks on the World Trade Center and Pentagon likewise have prodded many Americans to deal with more profound issues. These are the themes that intrigued scholars of old: *Who am I, Why am I here, Where am I going?* Ultimately, each person must answer these questions for him or herself, and usually, that eventually involves questioning one's basic assumptions about life.

In a speech to the Society for Psychical Research in London in 1916, Dr. Carl G. Jung offered a motto that all of us entering a new century might heed:

"I shall not commit the fashionable stupidity of regarding everything I cannot explain as a fraud."

Because we cannot fully explain or understand ghosts and hauntings does not mean that one day a combination of science and spiritual study will not shed a brighter light on these millennial mysteries. In Peter O'Toole's film, *The Creator*, the professor and his student contemplate the star-filled heavens. The professor ruminates:

"It's said, Boris, that when science finally peers over the crest of the mountain, it will find that religion has been sitting there all along."

DP

Acknowledgements

This book would not have been possible without the cooperation and assistance of these fine people:

Curt Abbott
Jeannette Ackner
David Adams
Bonnie Albright
Aldrich family
Carol Ann Alesio
Bernice Arbour
Mike & Paula Aschettino
Dale Atherton-Ely
Warren Broderick
Bill & Judy Baker
Jeff Baker
Laura Barbera
Barbara Barbieri
Frances Barbieri
Sharon Barnes
Reese Barter
Tom Beauregard
Bruce Bedford
Mary Bellinger
Dan Berggren
Ruth Berrus
Steve Borgos
Jean Marie Boutin
Virginia Bowers
Jim Boyle
Richard Brouse
Brooklyn Public Library
Rowland Bryant
Ken & Mary Buckland
Debby Bunnell
Estelle Butler
Helen Caekener
Bob Cahill
Ted Caldwell
John Callahan
Lisa Canham
Cayllan Carey
Pat Carmichael
Florence Carrington
Robert Cembrola
Joan Chamberlain
Nancy Chamberlain
Mike Cicchinelli
Sonya Child
Joe & Helen Childs
Lou & Penny Christopher
Donna Cirone
Bruce Cole
Lynn Collins
Chuck Colvin

Chris Comeau
Jim Condon
Mark Conley
John Coon
David Cooper family
Barbara Corrice
Allison Corwin
Virginia Crossman
Connie Cummings
Peg Curtin
Karen Cusano
Tom Cwiakala
Laurie Daley
Mike Daley
Richard Dantz
Kristen Darbyshire
Helen Davies
Edmond Day
Michelle De Garmo
Pam Deitz
James DelRatez, Sr.
Karen Desjardins
Susan DeSorbo
Frank DiBiase
John Dingman
Bill & Nan Dixon
Tom Doin
John Dousmanis
Kate Dudley
Brenda Duggan
Sue Dygert
Chuck Eblacker
Michael Edson
Jan Edwards
Elmont Public Library
Rick Eno
Jack T. Ericson
Rich Erwin
Mona Ferguson
Eleanor Fielding
Annemarie Finamore
Mary Ann Flanders
Sr. Dorothy Flood
Audrey Forbes
Marielle Fortier
Linda French
Carl Fribolin
Mary Ellen Frisch
Rob Fuller
Squire Galbraith
Arianna Galluzzo

Bonnie Gamache
Victoria Garlanda
Noka Garrapy
Maghi Geary
Bill & Suzanne Getz
Pat Giaminelli
Mary Lou Gibson
Peter Gifford
Marianne Gillespie
Connie Gilmore
Nili Gold
Jim Gorman
Mildred Goutermout
Patrick Grace
Betty Grant
Kate Grey
Paul Grondahl
Dr. Steve Grove
Jack & Lynn Gutches
Kathryn Hadley
Laurie Hamilton
Randy Hammond
Nancy Harrington
Michael Harris
Deborah Haskell
Jane Haskell
Lisa Haskins
Mike Hathaway
Martha Havens
Howard Hayes
Jan Herder
Drake Hewitt family
Denise Hladik
Joe Holmes
Jack Horner
Frank Huckabone
Peggy Hunsberger
Kim Hupp
Evelyn Hutwohl
Joan Hyde
Enid Inch
Julie Jaus
Jennifer Jenkins
Jeannie Justice
Debby Keezer
Anna Kellerhouse
Galen & Norma Kelley
Julie Kennedy
Donna Kennelly
Douglas Kent
Ken Kincor
Ruth Kniermen
Art & Linda Kranick
Cynthia Krohn
Catherine LaBier

Mike Laflin
Kathy La Pan
Capt. John Larison
Paul Lear
Mary Lighthall
Walter Lipka
Vince & Kathy Lombardi
Jamie Lynaugh
Ed & Laurie Maas
Grace MacDonald
Frances Malgeri
Karen Mancini
Irene Manzer
Marblehead (MA) Library
Ethel Marino
Kathy Marshall
Herb Martin
Hervena Martin
Martinsburg (NY) Library
Todd Martyn
Enid Mastrianni
Linda Mastrobuono
Joan Matson
Paul Mattfeld
Ken Matthes
Stacey Mayette
Marilyn Mazzeo
Vin McAloon
John McAlpin
Dennis McDonald
Shirley McFerson
Kathleen McGuire
Heather McKnight
Melissa McNeil
Ernie Menard
Dick Mersereau
Grant Meyers
Dr. John Miller
Sheila Milot
Maureen Mooney
Moo Morrill
Rodney Mosher
Thelma Moye
Kate Musso
Ralph & Thelma Nestle
New Haven Public Library
Irene Noble
Mike Novik
Kevin O'Connor
Susan O'Dea
Peter Olsen
Kathy O'Neill
John Orlyk
Steve Ostrander
John Parker

Nina Pattison
Bob & Pat Payne
Peabody (MA)Library
Tim Perez
Mark & Sharon Perfetti
Claire Perretta
Judy Pihl
Linda Pike
Marjorie S. Pinkham
Bob Pitcavage
Lisa Pitkin
Gina Plumadore
Kim Preston
Susan Priest
Tom Prindle
Yves Raymond
Mary Reed
Arlene Rhodes
Galen Ritchie
Ruth Roerig
Annie Rothman
Mitchell Rozansky
John Ryan
Frieda Saddlemire
Salem (MA) Library
David Sampson
Sheila Satterlee
Nick & Judy Schkrioba
Eric Schnitzer
Kevin Schoonover
Bill Schwarting
Jeanne Schwartz
Allie Sedawie
Michele Sendgraff
Kristopher Setchfield
Sarada Setchfield
Glenn and June Sherman
John Shirley
Edgar & Mary Shopmeyer
Jeannette Simon
Susan Slabe
Mary Smart
Bill & Sal Smith
Barbara Spofford
Dallas Squyres
Carl Stoddard
George Strum

Sturgis Library
Derrick Sutherland
Penny Szell
Dorothy Taber
Dorothy Tabor
Don & Margie Tabor
Colleen Thompson
Frank Thompson
Linda Tremblay
Missy Troy
Chuck Turley
US National Park Service
Janet Van Cina
Heather Van Dyke
Bill Varnum
Ruth Van Denburg
Russ Vickers
Lawson Virkler
Jim Walker
Charlie Ward
Beth Waters
Watertown Daily Times
John Wawzyniak
Jackie Webster
Don & Sue Weeks
Vivian Weiss
Mike Welch
Terri Wheeler
Kim White
Ellen Wiley
Hank Williams
Jim Williams
Brad & Susan Wilson
Tauno Wirkki
Evan & Betty Wollocott
Bertha Woodfin
Doug Woods
Chris & Therese Wright
Elaine Yanow
Joan Youngken
Bob Youngs
Joe Zarzynski
Tim Zorn

Many thanks to my friend and editor, Graham L. McGill, an old newspaper man who is helping me learn to write well.

And finally, loving thanks to my wife, and second editor, Linda, who also provided the art work in this book, and whose inspiration sustained me through countless interviews and long journeys.

383

Index

Blue Door B & B Inn - 136, 137
Blue Gate - 173
Blue Mt. Lake Museum - 371
Blue Mt. Lake, NY - 371
Bob's Hill - 40
Boice, Chet - 50
Bolton Landing, NY - 2, 4
Bolton, Town of - 90
Book of Isaiah - 262
Boston, MA - 42, 108, 158, 190, 327, 363, 364
Boston & Maine R.R. - 307, 365
Boston Post Road - 333
Boutin, Jean Marie - 323
Bowdoin College - 197
Bradford St. Hill - 126
Bradt Street - 294
Brant Lake, NY - 240
Breymann, Lt. Col - 45
Brightman Road - 231
Brinkman, Ned - 364, 365
Broadway - 23, 65, 67, 69, 73, 191, 294
Brooklyn College - 308
Brooklyn, NY - 46, 54, 55, 87
Brouse, Richard - 130
Brown Company - 323, 326
Brown, Jim - 237
Brown, Dr. Seth - 124
Brown, W.R. - 323
Brown, William W. - 323, 325
Brunswick, ME - 197
Brunswick Street - 300
Brush Family - 146
Bryant, Rowland - 145
Buckingham, Gov. William - 85, 86
Buckingham Palace - 350
Buffalo, NY - 302
Bull, Rev. - 371, 372
Bulls Head Inn - 278, 279
Burgoyne, Gen. John - 44, 45, 331
Burgoyne Road - 116
Burgoyne Street - 341
Burlington, VT - 202, 203
Burnt Hills, NY - 224
Butler, Capt. George - 298, 279
Butler, Estelle - 19
Butler, Mr. - 137
Butler Pond Road - 374

C

Cabrini Hall - 172
Caekener, Helen - 175
Cahill, Bob - 227, 363
Caldwell Library - 48
Callahan, John - 267, 268
Cambridge Hotel - 144, 145
Cambridge, MA - 44
Cambridge, NY - 144
Camillus - 120
Camp Ellis, ME - 309
Camp Gagetown Gazette - 253
Campbell, Dougal - 32, 33
Campbell, Maj. Duncan - 41, 42, 43
Canada - 19, 20, 36, 39, 123, 127, 130, 132, 155, 163, 164, 184, 209, 218, 252, 264, 300, 331
Canada Street - 48, 329, 330
Canterbury, The - 264
Canton, NY - 176, 178
Cape Breton - 296
Cape Cod - 161, 162
Cape Cod Ghost Map - 22
Cape Vincent, NY - 169
Capt. Grey's - 347
Capt. Proctor House - 158
Carey Hall - 172
Carillon - 41, 42, 43, 44
Carleton, Bobbi - 166
Carrington, Dan - 270
Carrington, Florence - 269, 270
Carson, Johnny - 18
Cartwright, Mr. - 154
Casino, The - 192, 193, 194
Catskills - 276, 286
Cayce, Edgar - 379
Cayuga Street - 320
Cembrola, Bob - 162
Central Bridge, NY - 9
Cerutti, Lucille - 189
Central Shaft - 365
Chamberlain, Joan - 324. 325
Chambers, Marilyn - 54
Champlain Canal - 127
Champlain College - 202
Champlain Valley - 44
Chapin Family - 237, 238
Chapman Museum - 318
Charlie Brown - 200

ORDER FORM

Check the books you wish to order, indicating the number of each desired:

	Title	Price	No.# of Books
Currently out of print	Saratoga County Ghosts (SCG)	$13.95	
	Spiritual Numerology: Caring for Number One (SN)	$14.95	
	Ghosts of the Northeast (GNE)	$18.95	
Totals			

In NY State please enclose 7% sales tax on the total order

Please make checks and money orders payable to AURORA PUBLICATIONS

Please enclose $2.50 shipping and handling on each book.

Special Offer: Buy one of each and shipping/handling is free.

Total Purchase amount: _____

Total Sales Tax: _____

Total Shipping/Handling:_____

Total amount enclosed:_____

MAIL YOUR ORDER TO:
AURORA PUBLICATIONS
18 E. BROADWAY
SALEM, NY 12865

ORDER FORM

Check the books you wish to order, indicating the number of each desired:

	Title	Price	No.# of Books
Currently out of print	Saratoga County Ghosts (SCG)	$13.95	
	Spiritual Numerology: Caring for Number One (SN)	$14.95	
	Ghosts of the Northeast (GNE)	$18.95	
Totals			

In NY State please enclose 7% sales tax on the total order

Please make checks and money orders payable to AURORA PUBLICATIONS

Please enclose $2.50 shipping and handling on each book.

Special Offer: Buy one of each and shipping/handling is free.

Total Purchase amount: _____

Total Sales Tax: _____

Total Shipping/Handling:_____

Total amount enclosed:_____

MAIL YOUR ORDER TO:
AURORA PUBLICATIONS
18 E. BROADWAY
SALEM, NY 12865